Wealth After Work

Wealth After Work

INNOVATIVE REFORMS TO EXPAND RETIREMENT SECURITY

Edited by
William G. Gale
J. Mark Iwry
David C. John

BROOKINGS INSTITUTION PRESS
Washington, D.C.

THE BROOKINGS INSTITUTION
1775 Massachusetts Avenue, N.W.
Washington, D.C. 20036
www.brookings.edu

The Brookings Institution is a private nonprofit organization devoted to research, education, and publication on important issues of domestic and foreign policy. Its principal purpose is to bring the highest quality independent research and analysis to bear on current and emerging policy problems. Interpretations or conclusions in Brookings publications should be understood to be solely those of the authors.

Library of Congress Control Number: 2021937238

ISBN 9780815739340 (pbk)
ISBN 9780815739357

9 8 7 6 5 4 3 2 1

Typeset in Karmina Sans and Minion Pro

Composition by Westchester Publishing Services

CONTENTS

PREFACE

The American retirement system has accomplished a great deal. It has helped tens of millions of working households build financial security while amassing a vast pool of long-term investment capital that helps fuel the US economy. But the system also suffers from major weaknesses. Millions of other workers lack benefits or savings sufficient to sustain their standard of living once they retire. They have neither pensions nor access to the workplace retirement saving vehicles that have proven to be the most effective way for most people to save. Unbiased and unconflicted financial information that is affordable to most households is often difficult to find. Wealth management in retirement, especially converting retirement assets into income, creates significant challenges that current financial instruments and practices do not adequately address.

The chapters in this volume expand on these topics and propose ways to address the problems. The first set of chapters examines broad patterns of wealth accumulation and retirement adequacy across time and generations and by gender. The second set focuses on the wealth accumulation process in an increasingly complex retirement system. The discussions of policies and proposals here aim to ensure that people can understand the choices they face and have access to saving vehicles that help them build retirement wealth. The final set of chapters looks at ways to help people manage their wealth in retirement and use it to provide income without either running out of funds too early or holding on to their funds too long.

This is the third volume of research produced by the Retirement Security Project (RSP) at Brookings Institution. RSP was created in 2005 to focus on common-sense solutions that would make the retirement system work better for the vast majority of Americans.

In a 2006 volume entitled *Aging Gracefully*, RSP focused on making retirement saving easier and more rewarding for low- and middle-income households. Many of the chapters addressed the value of automatic features in 401(k) plans, including enrollment, escalation of contributions, allocation of contributions, and rollovers. Several of these policies were included in the Pension Protection Act of 2006. Notably, RSP's 2006 volume presented the case for the creation of Automatic IRAs, which continues to be the most prominent proposal to close the coverage gap in the United States and which is now receiving proof of concept in several state-facilitated retirement savings programs. In addition to proposing strategies to make it easier for working people to save, the RSP authors advocated making saving more remunerative through structural reform and expansion of the Saver's Credit targeted at lower- and middle-income working households.

In a 2009 volume entitled *Automatic: Changing How America Saves*, RSP addressed a variety of related topics, including lessons from other countries' retirement systems; the creation of automatic annuitization of retirement benefits; and retirement saving policies tailored to meet the specific needs of women, Hispanics, and Blacks.

We gratefully acknowledge that much of the work in this volume was made possible by several generous grants from Arnold Ventures and, earlier, the Laura and John Arnold Foundation. The Peter G. Peterson Foundation provided additional support, as did the Arjay and Frances Fearing Miller Chair in Federal Economic Policy at the Brookings Institution. In addition, we are grateful for the extensive support RSP received at its inception and in subsequent years from the Pew Charitable Trusts and the Rockefeller Foundation. The views expressed in each chapter are those of the authors of that chapter alone and should not be attributed to the authors of the other chapters or to any other individual or organization.

Wealth After Work

Introduction

William G. Gale, Claire Haldeman, David C. John, and J. Mark Iwry

The US retirement system is continuously changing. While each reform and product innovation ideally resolves some problem, it also frequently creates new challenges as well. Most prominently, society is still absorbing the impact of a long-term shift from defined benefit (DB) pension plans to retirement saving accounts such as 401(k)s and individual retirement accounts (IRAs). This book addresses many of the problems that arise in a system that is increasingly dominated by retirement saving accounts.

From World War II through the 1970s, most workers with retirement benefits had DB plans, which provided regular retirement income payments—annuities; the amount was based on an employee's years of service and often on the employee's final or highest years of wages. These plans had several advantages; in particular, they were funded entirely or primarily by the plan sponsors and were invested professionally and collectively, rather than by individual employees, and in accordance with fiduciary standards. In addition, the DB plans protected workers from most of the relevant financial risks (failure to participate; inadequate contributions; poor investment choices; leakage risk; investment risk; sequence-of-returns risk; longevity risk; death, disability, and sometimes inflation risk), and relieved participants of the need to take initiative or make many decisions in preparing for retirement. Choices regarding enrollment, contribution levels, investment, rebalancing, and withdrawals were almost always predetermined. Generally, the only real decision necessary was when to retire and start claiming benefits; the age- or service-based incentives in such plans were typically very strong and made the right choice clear. But the plans had drawbacks as well: They were not available to those without the stable, often-unionized jobs that offered retirement benefits; they provided lesser benefits to employees whose careers had been interrupted or who changed jobs frequently; they tended to provide the largest benefits to those who stayed with the plan sponsor until retirement age; they left participants exposed to some degree of underfunding risk (though mitigated by pension benefit insurance); and employers often complained that the DB plan funding requirements could be volatile and hard to predict.

Beginning in the 1980s, 401(k) plans emerged as a significant alternative vehicle to provide retirement benefits. These plans required that employees make active choices about participation, contributions, investments, and withdrawals. When 401(k)s came into existence, they mainly served as supplemental plans for higher-income workers already covered by a DB plan and Social Security. The burdens they placed on those workers were not a primary concern.

However, as 401(k)s expanded to become the primary retirement plan for wide swaths of the population, most of whom did not have DB plans, the burdens these plans placed on workers to "do it yourself" by taking initiative and making informed decisions led to a host of new problems. The diffusion of automatic features regarding enrollment, escalating contributions, investments, and others in 401(k) plans has helped address some of these problems, but many issues remain.

Today the American retirement system works very well for many people. Those with stable, well-paying jobs can accumulate substantial wealth in employer-sponsored 401(k)s or in their DB plans by taking advantage of tax subsidies and employer matches. These benefits—especially when combined with other private saving and Social Security—make it relatively easy for those who are well paid in their working lives to remain prosperous thereafter.

For many Americans, however, the retirement system is inadequate. About half of all workers either are not offered or do not participate in employer-sponsored plans, a figure that has remained persistently low for several decades.[1] Many employers have decided not to offer any type of retirement benefit to their workers, either because of the cost and administrative burden of these plans or because they have a largely transitory workforce. And many who are offered a plan cash out when they change jobs or use their savings for other purposes. As a result, almost one-third of the elderly depend on Social Security for at least 90 percent of their income; about two-thirds depend on Social Security for half of their income.[2] While it is possible to attribute some of the lack of participation in private pensions to the existence of Social Security, there is no doubt that many people are not accumulating enough for retirement and that more private retirement saving could help.[3]

And even for those who have accounts, it can be difficult to obtain unbiased financial information that helps make retirement saving choices easier to comprehend. Free advice, while plentiful, can be complicated or contradictory, and in any case is often not tailored to a saver's specific circumstances. Many paid financial planners receive commissions for selling specific investment products, sometimes making their advice both expensive and suspect. This problem is complicated further by the low level of financial literacy in the population. In a Federal Reserve study, only 35 percent of people surveyed could correctly answer three *very* basic financial literacy questions.[4]

Even when families accumulate wealth, there is little guidance about how best to manage and draw down those assets while in retirement. Households thus face twin concerns: if they consume too much too soon, they risk running out of savings, but if they consume too little in retirement, they risk having a lower retirement living standard.

How society addresses these issues has important implications for who can have and maintain prosperity after their working years are over. This is particularly important because people often spend a significant amount of time in retirement: the average life expectancy at age 65 is about age 83 for men and age 86 for women. Broadening access to retirement saving and retirement income strategies will make the United States a more prosperous and equitable society but will require substantive changes. This book explores many of these problems and offers analysis and solutions, relying on three essential underlying principles.

First, retirement security should not be the province solely of the privileged. The retirement system should enable people from all backgrounds to participate and save enough to maintain their preretirement standard of living after their working years. The current system often excludes or disadvantages minorities, contingent workers, and women. If the work experience of particular groups differs from the norm—for example, because of the unique circumstances facing contingent workers or because of the family responsibilities that many women take on—the retirement system should accommodate such differences rather than the current one-size-fits-all approach that penalizes these groups.

Second, the retirement system should be easy to navigate, especially for nonexperts. People do not need to understand how internal combustion engines work in order to drive cars. They should not have to become financial experts in order to productively engage with the retirement system. This concern is increasingly important as 401(k)-type plans and IRAs have come to dominate retirement saving for middle-income workers.

Third, in a retirement system that relies heavily on the 401(k) plan, people need effective and secure ways to manage the drawdown of their wealth in retirement. While most professional and public attention on retirement programs focuses on the accumulation of wealth, how and when the funds are withdrawn define people's ability to fund an adequate retirement.

With these framing ideas in mind, our goal is to promote sound, concrete, and evidence-based ideas that improve the retirement system. The proposals in this book largely aim to work within the existing retirement saving system. They would not dismantle the system wholesale and replace it with something else. Instead, we propose reforms that would improve outcomes. This was a deliberate choice, and it reflects our varied experiences, informed by government service, private sector work, and research.

The book is divided into three sections. The first section provides information on wealth accumulation patterns across age, race, and gender. It is intended to provide context for the later discussions of retirement policy changes. The second section proposes a series of reforms designed to help people access and navigate the retirement system as they accumulate wealth during their working years. The third section examines ways to help people manage their assets and use their savings in retirement.

Chapter 1 explores the question "How Will Retirement Saving Change by 2050?" Though millennials will have several advantages in wealth accumulation over previous generations, such as more education and longer working lives, they also face several disadvantages, including weak prospects for economic growth and delays in home purchase and marriage. In addition, the proportion of millennials who are nonwhite is substantially greater than in previous generations. The chapter shows that minority households have tended to accumulate less wealth than white households in the past, even after controlling for other observable characteristics, and that the difference between Black households and white households appears to be growing over time.

Chapter 2, "Changing Wealth Accumulation Patterns," examines household wealth over time across birth cohorts using data from the Survey of Consumer Finances. The chapter shows that although the Great Recession reduced wealth in every age group, longer-term trends indicate that the wealth of older age groups has increased while the wealth of younger age groups has declined. A substantial share of these changes, in both directions, can be explained by changes in household demographic and economic characteristics.

Differential retirement wealth across gender lines is the focus of chapter 3, "How Does Gender Equality Affect Women in Retirement?" Over the past few decades women have made substantial gains—both in absolute terms and relative to men—in educational attainment, employment, and earnings but their status in retirement has not improved proportionally. This is due in large part to continued disparities between men and women in important determinants of retirement security: labor market earnings, retirement saving derived from those earnings, marital status, life expectancy, risk aversion, and financial acumen. For a variety of reasons, women earn less on average over the course of a lifetime than men do. Lower lifetime earnings make it harder for women to save for retirement. Exacerbating these differences in retirement saving adequacy, women are on average longer-lived, more risk averse, less financially literate, and more likely to have greater caregiving responsibilities than men. Public policies that aim to boost women's status in retirement should focus on the ways women participate in the labor market and in wealth accumulation programs as well as on specific retirement programs and benefits.

Chapter 4, "A Retirement Dashboard for the United States," initiates the examination of access and information issues. Following the example of several other countries, the chapter advocates the creation of individual, online retirement dashboards to help savers better manage their retirement preparations. The dashboard would include an online registry that makes it far easier for workers to track their current and past retirement accounts and benefits. The dashboard could also offer services such as recovering and consolidating lost accounts, projecting future income, and perhaps even providing or referring users to unbiased financial advice. While a retirement dashboard could improve the retirement prospects for millions of American workers, the process of establishment and implementation would confront significant challenges.

But a dashboard would not provide retirement savings vehicles to those who do not have access to them. Chapter 5, "Retirement Plans for Contingent Workers," acknowledges the unconventional job market status of independent—or contingent—workers and the need for special retirement accounts to accommodate them. Contingent workers are not covered by employer-sponsored retirement plans, and they often do not benefit from payroll deductions, employer matching contributions, automatic enrollment, or other provisions that encourage retirement saving. Better use of financial technology, judicious changes to tax policy, and in particular the widespread adoption of Automatic IRAs, would help independent workers save for retirement. This chapter also proposes the creation of retirement saving accounts that attach to individual workers and move with them from job to job as a supplement to, and possible replacement for, the current system of employer-sponsored accounts.

Another issue affecting contingent as well as traditional workers is the widespread tendency to choose to begin taking Social Security benefits at the earliest possible opportunity—age 62—without carefully considering that beginning early reduces the amount of all future monthly Social Security payments well below the monthly benefit amount people would receive if they chose to begin benefits at a later age. Chapter 6, "Supplemental Transition Accounts for Retirement," proposes the creation of Supplemental Transition Accounts for Retirement (STARTs) that each worker would be required to exhaust before receiving Social Security benefits. Employees, employers, and in the case of low-income workers, the federal government, would make contributions to the STARTs. An independent board would serve as the fiduciary for the program and set the investment guidelines for its pooled assets. Beneficiaries could begin to receive monthly START benefits at their earliest Social Security eligibility age but would not be required to do so. Federal contributions would be fully financed over time by taxes on START withdrawals. The plans would ease the transition into retirement and induce most people to claim Social Security benefits later than they currently do.

States, the common thread in the next several chapters, can play an important role in promoting retirement saving for their citizens, in addition to providing pensions for their employees. Chapter 7, "State-Sponsored Retirement Saving Plans," addresses state-based proposals for people whose employers do not offer any type of retirement plan, including the expanding state-based Automatic IRA programs. The Auto IRA, an idea developed at the Retirement Security Project by Mark Iwry and David John, has enormous potential to increase the number of Americans who are saving.[5] Auto IRA programs feature two crucial characteristics: requiring firms to offer retirement saving arrangements and automatically enrolling eligible workers. Under current legal and regulatory conditions, the Automatic IRA programs now operating in Oregon, Illinois, and California and under development in several other states are the only model that requires employers to help employees save, in contrast to state-based Multiple Employer Plans (MEPs) and online marketplace websites where employer participation is optional and therefore will be far more limited.

Chapter 8, "Structuring State Retirement Saving Plans" provides additional analysis of the structure of state-facilitated retirement programs. As discussed earlier, too many American workers do not have access to employer-sponsored payroll deduction plans for retirement saving, making it especially difficult for these groups—including members of minority groups, women, those with low to moderate incomes, and small-business employees—to build retirement wealth. Although workers without an employer-based plan can take the initiative to contribute to IRAs, only a small fraction does so. With these considerations in mind, we have long advocated, as have many other experts and policymakers, for more widespread retirement plan coverage using vehicles that are simple, low-cost, and accessible to those left out by the current market. A nationwide approach would be desirable, but because Congress has not yet enacted our proposed Auto IRA, states have been encouraged to, in effect, pilot the idea, and a growing number of states have enacted it for in-state private-sector employees.

Although in many policy-related situations the states can be useful laboratories for determining the most appropriate federal actions, many state and local governments currently face difficulties financing future defined benefit pension obligations for their workers—an area where the federal government faced similar problems in the 1980s and implemented a successful reform. Chapter 9, "Public Pensions in Flux," describes how the federal government retained the old Civil Service Retirement System (CSRS) for existing employees and created a new Federal Employees' Retirement System (FERS) for new employees. FERS combined a less generous defined benefit plan than CSRS, mandatory enrollment in Social Security, and a new defined contribution plan with substantial employer matching. Although a "one size fits all" solution would not apply to the diverse situations that different states face, the authors of chapter 9 believe that durable, effective, and just reforms for state pension plans should and will likely include the major elements of the federal reforms.

Some proposals have called for guaranteed returns as a central element in state-based or federal retirement reforms. Chapter 10, "You Get What You Pay For," invokes the classic economics dictum that it is impossible to get something for nothing. Guaranteed returns would protect savers from losses and ensure that they receive at least a minimum return on their investments. But in practice, they raise a variety of complex issues and are more costly than meets the eye. First, someone—the saver, the plan sponsor, or the taxpayers—has to pay for the guarantee. When the government pays the costs, budget documents tend to severely underreport the actual economic costs associated with the guarantees. When private insurers offer guarantees, the costs are often quite high. Second, the net benefits may not be as obvious as they seem, since markets often respond quickly, making poor investment performance and the harms it causes temporary; and for most people Social Security, Medicare, and housing are the source of the vast bulk of their retirement resources, meaning that even sustained investment losses do not often result in financial ruin. Ultimately, the value associated with a guarantee and its economic costs depend on how high a rate of return is being guaranteed and what time period is covered.

The third section of the book turns to issues related to converting retirement savings into retirement income. Chapter 11, "From Saving to Spending," proposes a default decumulation solution. The proposal centers on pooled investment accounts known as managed payout funds, which deliver a monthly income that may vary in amount and is likely, though not guaranteed, to last a lifetime. Coupled with longevity annuities that begin to make payments when the owner reaches an advanced age (such as 85) and a separate fund for emergencies and extraordinary payments, managed payout funds could help protect retirees from longevity risk without unduly reducing their living standard. This option could simplify decumulation choices in much the same way that automatic choices have simplified enrollment, contribution, and investment allocation decisions for millions of savers.

Chapter 12, "When Income Is the Outcome," takes on the challenge of increasing the ability of defined contribution savings to meet the income needs of retirees. The chapter explores legislative and regulatory reforms that could encourage workers to annuitize more of their 401(k) and other defined contribution balances upon retirement. The proposed changes would create an appropriately protective fiduciary safe harbor for plan sponsors that select annuity providers, increase the portability of annuities, and reform the required minimum distribution rules relating to retirement income.

Chapter 13, "Retirement Tontines," explores a new way to help retirees manage their retirement income. Tontines are investment pools to which members commit funds irrevocably and in which the assets of members who die are used to increase the retirement income of those who survive. These kinds of products were highly popular in the United States in the late nineteenth and early twentieth centuries, until they were effectively prohibited after they were involved in widespread insurance company mismanagement. Tontine-inspired products are receiving renewed attention in a number of countries as efficient, transparent ways to finance retirement income. Unlike commercial fixed income annuities, tontine pooling does not guarantee the amount of future payments but should pay more on average per dollar invested because it would avoid costly regulatory requirements applicable to commercial annuities.

Our private retirement system has helped millions of people augment their financial security in retirement, but it has also left substantial problems unaddressed. This volume proposes research-based policy solutions and reforms to address many of these problems and help Americans, especially moderate- and lower-income workers, better prepare for a financially secure retirement.

NOTES

1. Gale and John (2017).
2. Gale (2019); Social Security Administration, "Social Security Fact Sheet" (2020), https://www.ssa.gov/news/press/factsheets/basicfact-alt.pdf.
3. See Engen, Gale, and Uccello (1999); Scholz, Seshadri, and Khitatrakun (2006); Munnell, Hou, and Sanzenbacher (2018); Biggs (2020); and Bipartisan Policy Center (2016).
4. Federal Reserve (2020).
5. Iwry and John (2005).

REFERENCES

Biggs, Andrew G. 2020. "Two Decades Ago, Progressives Warned of a Retirement Crisis. It Didn't Happen." *Forbes*, May 29.

Bipartisan Policy Center. 2016. "Securing Our Financial Future: Report of the Commission on Retirement Security and Personal Savings." https://bipartisanpolicy.org/wp-content/uploads/2019/03/BPC-Retirement-Security-Report.pdf.

Engen, Eric M., William G. Gale, and Cori R. Uccello. 1999. "The Adequacy of Household Saving." *Brookings Papers on Economic Activity* 2: 65–187.

Federal Reserve. 2020. "Report on the Economic Well-Being of U.S. Households in 2019—May 2020." https://www.federalreserve.gov/publications/2020-economic-well-being-of-us-households-in-2019-retirement.htm.

Gale, William G. 2019. *Fiscal Therapy: Curing America's Debt Addiction and Investing in the Future.* New York: Oxford University Press.

Gale, William G., and David C. John. 2017. "State Sponsored Retirement Savings Plans: New Approaches to Boost Retirement Plan Coverage." Pension Research Council Working Paper. Wharton School, University of Pennsylvania. https://pensionresearchcouncil.wharton.upenn.edu/wp-content/uploads/2017/09/WP-2017-12-John-Gale.pdf.

Gallup. 2018. "Snapshot: Average American Predicts Retirement Age of 66." May. https://news.gallup.com/poll/234302/snapshot-americans-project-average-retirement-age.aspx.

Iwry, J. Mark, and David C. John. 2005. "Pursuing Universal Retirement Security through Automatic IRAs." In *Automatic: Changing the Way America Saves*, edited by William G. Gale, J. Mark Iwry, David C. John, and Lina Walker. Brookings.

Munnell, Alicia H., Wenliang Hou, and Geoffrey T. Sanzenbacher. 2018. "Trends in Retirement Security by Race/Ethnicity." Center for Retirement Research at Boston College.

Scholz, John Karl, Ananth Seshadri, and Surachai Khitatrakun. 2006. "Are Americans Saving 'Optimally' for Retirement?" *Journal of Political Economy* 114 (4): 607–643.

ONE

How Will Retirement Saving Change by 2050?

PROSPECTS FOR THE MILLENNIAL GENERATION

William G. Gale, Hilary Gelfond, and Jason J. Fichtner

How will changing demographic and economic factors affect households' ability to accumulate adequate resources for retirement over the next thirty years? Because the answers to this question are necessarily speculative, our goal in this chapter is to provide evidence that can help frame thinking about the issue. In particular, we (1) review what is known about the adequacy of retirement saving among current generations of retirees and near-retirees, (2) examine how economic factors that affect retirement saving seem likely to differ between prior generations and the millennials (who will be ages 54 to 69 in 2050), and (3) consider how the changing minority composition of the population will affect retirement saving.

We begin with a discussion of previous findings on the adequacy of retirement saving among current retirees or near-retirees. We highlight the conceptual issues in determining whether people are saving adequately and review previous studies. We document significant heterogeneity in how well members of Generation X and the Baby Boom have saved for retirement. These differences are not surprising given the widening income distribution of the past several decades and the uneven retirement preparation and plan participation shown in the data. The literature suggests that several significant subgroups of the population—including racial and ethnic minorities, women, those with income between the poverty level and the median, those with less than a college degree, individuals in poor health, and workers without a pension—are more vulnerable to retirement saving shortfalls than others.

We then explore a variety of issues that differentially affect the millennial generation relative to prior generations. The millennials have certain advantages over previous generations in saving for retirement; for example, they are the most educated generation in history. Furthermore, because of the evolution of the pension system toward defined contribution (DC) plans, they may well work longer than any previous generation, giving them additional years to save.

However, millennials also face numerous disadvantages. Their careers got off to a rocky start because of the financial crisis and Great Recession in 2007–2009 and the ensuing slow (but steady) recovery over the subsequent few years. They will be employed in contingent workforce jobs (which have weaker retirement benefits than traditional jobs) to a greater extent than previous generations. They have lower net worth and higher student debt burdens than earlier generations at the same age, and they are marrying, buying homes, and having children later. They will be required to manage and navigate their own retirement plans to a greater extent than previous generations, while also likely having longer lifespans.[1] They will face burdens from any eventual resolution of the government's long-term fiscal shortfalls in general, and from the financial imbalances in Social Security and Medicare in particular. They face an economic future with projections of lower rates of return and economic growth than in the past. These factors make accumulating sufficient funds for retirement more difficult for millennials than for previous generations.

We follow by examining the effects of the projected changes in the racial and ethnic composition of the population. The United States will be a "majority-minority" country by 2050, where minority is defined as any race other than non-Hispanic white. All races and ethnicities other than white are expected to grow as a share of the population. Using cross-section and pooled regressions from the 1989–2016 Surveys of Consumer Finances, we show that minority status is negatively associated with net worth, controlling for other household characteristics. The difference in wealth between Blacks and whites is growing over time, controlling for other factors.

These results have implications for millennials. The set of economic and social conditions that racial and ethnic minorities experience by 2050 will likely be different from those experienced by previous generations—including family and marital status, education, neighborhoods, discrimination, and job markets. Such differences in the future could serve either to raise or reduce wealth gaps between whites and minorities. That said, minorities in recent years faced different economic and social conditions than did minorities thirty years ago, yet wealth differences between whites and minorities, controlling for observable characteristics, have grown rather than fallen. If this trend continues, wealth inequality will continue to increase, which will make it that much harder for minorities to save adequately for retirement.

Ensuring the adequacy of saving presents enormous challenges and risks for individuals, government, and businesses. However, it also generates unique opportunities for creative public policies and innovative private markets to greatly improve people's lives.

THE ADEQUACY OF RETIREMENT SAVING[2]

Whether households are saving adequately for retirement is often addressed as a yes/no question. But even a moment's reflection will reveal that more interesting questions consider the share and characteristics of households that are and are not preparing adequately, as well as the extent to which they are undersaving. Framing the topic in this way inevitably leads to an emphasis on the importance of differences in how people and groups prepare for retirement. A one-size-fits-all answer to the question of how well people are doing is unlikely to characterize the problem clearly.

Conceptual Issues

The first task is to define the concept of adequate saving, which is surprisingly controversial.[3] For purposes of this paper, we define adequate saving as sufficient to provide a household with an expected standard of living in retirement that is commensurate with its standard of living during its working years. This definition has the advantage of conforming to people's "common sense" views of how they would like to live their lives.

But it comes with an important caveat. Our definition focuses on *expected* retirement living standards relative to preretirement living standards. Many things can go wrong between saving the right amount to maintain an expected standard of living and being able to maintain a standard of living in actuality. Individuals face numerous risks in preparing for retirement. Disability and layoffs may stop people from working as long as they had planned and hence reduce their ability to accumulate wealth. Assets may accrue less than the expected rate of return over time. A household may face disproportionate uninsured health care costs, including those associated with long-term care. People may face mental or physical declines that require expensive daily assistance. Household members may live longer than expected, which, while generally a good thing, has the side effect of generating higher saving needs to maintain preretirement living standards. Alternatively, a person may become widowed and thus lose important sources of income in retirement. Children may present unexpected financial burdens.

Many of these concerns relate to adequate *insurance* (for example, against risks associated with disability, rate of return, inflation, health care costs, health status, lifespan, and children's circumstances) as opposed to adequate saving, but the two issues are related and both are part of retirement *preparation*. Social Security, of course, is intended to cover only a portion of adequate retirement income, not all of it. In the absence of well-functioning insurance markets, people will to some extent need to save more in order to partially self-insure and be in a position to mitigate the negative consequences of adverse outcomes.

A definition of adequate *saving* that allows people to *self-insure* against *all* risks is probably an excessively high standard for all but the super-rich. But the distinction between saving enough to maintain expected living standards in retirement and saving enough to insure against all risks helps explain why there are different standards for "adequate saving."

One approach to measuring whether people are saving adequately is to compare their wealth accumulation behavior to that implied by an economic model that prescribes that people save optimally.[4] The standard economic approach is to equate the household's discounted marginal utility of consumption in each period. This approach has the advantage of being fully consistent with economic theory, but it is not always easy for people to translate this approach into practical advice, or to see where their preparations land them relative to the benchmark. And the results are sensitive to model specification, especially in the presence of major changes, such as those that occur in family size, marital status, or work status.[5]

A more common, intuitive, and flexible approach focuses on replacement rates. A replacement rate is a ratio of postretirement income to preretirement income. The *target* replacement rate that a household should aim for is one that will allow it to replicate its preretirement living standards in retirement. It is essential to emphasize that 100 percent is not a natural benchmark for an ad-

Table 1-1. *Calculating a Target Replacement Rate*
Dollars

	Preretirement	*Postretirement*
Wages	100	0
Health insurance	6	0
401(k) contributions	5	0
Mortgage payment	5	0
Work expenses	2.35	0
Payroll taxes	7.65	0
Federal and state taxes	12	8
Other consumption	62	62
Target replacement rate	—	**70**

Source: Authors' calculations.

equate replacement. The typical advice of financial planners is to target a replacement rate of between 70 and 85 percent, and some evidence suggests this is consistent with optimal models of saving.[6]

Table 1-1 provides an extremely stylized example of how target replacement ratios in this range might come about. Suppose a worker earns $100 in gross wages, and has $62 remaining after work expenses, mortgage costs, retirement saving contributions, health insurance premiums, payroll taxes, and federal and state income taxes. Suppose the worker reaches age 65, pays off the mortgage, and retires. The payments for work expenses, the mortgage, 401(k) contributions, payroll taxes, and health insurance stop (the last because the worker becomes eligible for Medicare) and taxes fall by one-third (because income declines and because there are currently benefits in the tax code for the elderly). That means the worker would only need $70 per year in retirement to replace the living standard that $100 provided during working years, or a 70 percent replacement rate.

This stylized example shows that adequate retirement income need not replace 100 percent of preretirement income and that there may be a sizable difference between saving enough and saving "a lot." For example, in the scenario just presented, if Social Security and a defined benefit plan replaced two-thirds of the worker's wages in retirement, very little additional saving would be required to maintain preretirement living standards in retirement.

Several qualifications are crucial. First, it is not clear what the "right" preretirement wage should be for purposes of the calculation. Oft-used measures include final earnings, an average of the highest three or five years of earnings, or average lifetime earnings. Empirical measures of the target replacement rate are sensitive to which measure is used as the denominator. Second, different households will have different target replacement rates. Factors such as the presence of children during working years or higher health care expenses during retirement years will influence how much spending is needed in retirement to maintain preretirement living standards. The target replacement rate would be higher to the extent that preretirement expenses on mortgages, health insurance, retirement contributions, and taxes were lower, or to the extent that postretirement health care needs or bequest motives were stronger. Third, different households may want to include different measures of assets as sources of available retirement income. Some might want to tap housing equity, while others may choose not to do so. For all of these reasons, the replacement rate needed to maintain preretirement living standards in retirement will vary across households.

Evidence

Previous studies tend to focus on current retirees and older workers, rather than the members of the younger generations, and have reached a wide variety of conclusions about the adequacy of saving. Many of these differences are traceable to different underlying assumptions.[7] Specifically, studies are likely to find a larger undersaving problem to the extent that they: use a target replacement rate based on the highest three-year earnings a worker achieved rather than career average earnings; minimize consumption needs during working years (for example, by excluding the role of children in household consumption); maximize consumption needs during retirement (for example, by expecting the household to self-insure against all risks); or assume that only narrow measures of net worth (for example, excluding housing wealth) can be used to fund retirement income.[8]

For example, to calculate the National Retirement Risk Index (NRRI), researchers at Boston College first estimate the projected replacement rate (with average lifetime income as the denominator) for each household in a nationally representative sample. They then calculate a target replacement rate (the rate necessary to maintain preretirement living standards in retirement) for each household and a projected actual replacement rate. The NRRI is the share of households whose projected actual replacement rates are more than 10 percent (not percentage points) below their target rates. In 2016, 50 percent of working-age households were classified as being at risk.[9]

In contrast, Scholz, Seshadri, and Khitatrakun (2006) develop an optimal savings model that compares households' optimal and actual wealth in order to ascertain whether they are saving enough for retirement. These authors implicitly use a measure of lifetime earnings, adjusted for family size, in the denominator of the replacement rate ratio. They find that most households are saving adequately for retirement, with only 15.6 percent having wealth that is less than their optimal targets.

Although previous research efforts reach different conclusions on the overall status of retirement saving adequacy, two robust conclusions emerge. First, groups differ in their retirement saving status. Members of racial and ethnic minorities are less likely to be saving adequately, as well as single-headed households, younger workers, those with fewer years of formal education, those without a retirement plan, and those with lower incomes.[10]

Second, while many households appear to be saving enough to *expect* to maintain preretirement living standards in retirement, virtually no one claims that many households are well insured against *all* risks. For example, Hurd and Rohwedder (2012) find that the risk of a health shock reduces the share of the population that is adequately prepared for retirement (by their definition) by 3 to 13 percentage points, depending on marital status and educational attainment. Poterba, Venti, and Wise (2015) find that even among those who amass significant wealth, a large health shock or death of a spouse can result in a significant decline in assets. VanDerhei (2014) cites longevity risk and health care costs as significant threats to retirement saving.[11]

INTERGENERATIONAL COMPARISONS

The millennial generation includes individuals born between 1981 and 1996.[12] Members of this group were between the ages of 22 and 37 in 2018. By 2050, they will be between the ages of 54 and 69. In 2019, millennials will become the largest living generation in the United States, overtaking the baby boomers, and will make up about a quarter of the population.[13] They are also more racially diverse than prior generations: 44 percent of millennials identify as a minority (a race or ethnicity other than non-Hispanic white); in 1985, by comparison, only 25 percent of individuals ages 21 to 36 did so.[14] Given the experience of prior generations, we now turn to examining how cross-generational differences affect millennials' retirement prospects.

Figure 1-1. **Median Net Worth among Young Households, 1989–2016**

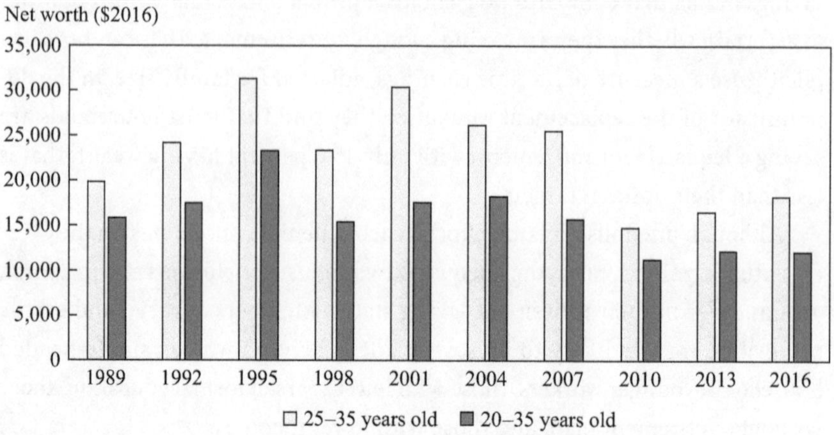

Source: Board of Governors of the Federal Reserve System (2017).

Current Status

Focusing first on their *current* status, today's young adults have accumulated less wealth than most previous generations at the same age. Figure 1-1 shows tabulations of Federal Reserve Board data from the triennial Survey of Consumer Finances (SCF), spanning the period 1989 to 2016. In the latter year, millennials were between the ages of 20 and 35. We examine net worth accumulation among 20–35-year-olds in each of the previous SCF years (with all wealth data reported in 2016 dollars). Because wealth accumulation patterns may not be particularly informative for people who are still in college, we also examine wealth patterns among 25–35-year-olds in each year.

The figure shows that, using either age-group comparison, median wealth among millennials in 2016 was lower than among similarly aged cohorts in any year from 1989 to 2007. The Great Recession of 2007–2009 significantly reduced household wealth, which has been slowly recovering since then. Median wealth among millennials was about 25 percent lower in 2016 than among households of similar ages in 2007. The percentage declines in mean wealth are even larger.[15]

Considering components of wealth (not shown), millennials had more debt than people of similar ages in 1989 but have about the same level as the 2001 cohort. The latter result may be surprising, given the well-publicized increase in student loan debt, but millennials have less credit card and other debt than prior generations.[16]

Figure 1-2. **DB and DC Plan Ownership among Cohort Aged 25–35, 1989–2016**

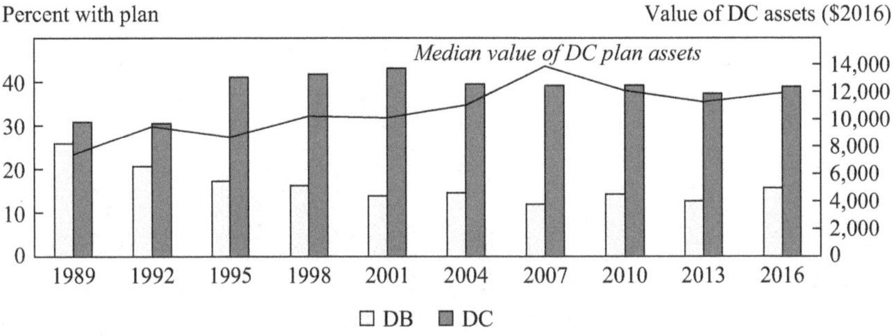

Source: Board of Governors of the Federal Reserve System (2017).

Retirement account assets include the value of IRAs, Keoghs, thrift-type accounts, and future and current account-type pensions.

Focusing on retirement wealth specifically, figure 1-2 shows that, relative to similarly aged people, millennials have about the same coverage rate for defined benefit pensions (DB) and defined contribution plans from 2004 on, but lower DC coverage than the 1995–2001 cohort and sharply lower DB coverage relative to that in the late 1980s. Median DC balances among account holders have fallen since 2007.[17]

All of the results mentioned above likely overstate the relative wealth position of millennials because of the interaction of three factors. First, the SCF does not survey dependent members of households, including millennials who live with their parents. Second, the share of millennials living with their parents is higher than the share of similarly aged people in prior generations. Among 25–34-year-olds, 16 percent lived with their parents in 2016, in comparison with 11 percent in 1990 and 10 percent in 2000.[18] Third, some formal evidence (as well as casual observations) suggests that young adults who are living in their parents' home are doing less well economically than other young adults. Among those 25–34 years of age and living at home in 2016, 26 percent were neither employed nor attending school.[19] Less educated people are less likely to live independently, and those with higher wages are more likely to do so.

Between 1989 and 2016, the distribution of wealth widened significantly (figure 1-3). For example, for 25–35-year-olds, average net worth in the bottom 25 percent of the distribution fell from about –$1,200 in 1989 to –$5,000 in

Figure 1-3. **Mean Net Worth by Percentile for Cohort Aged 25–35, 1989–2016**

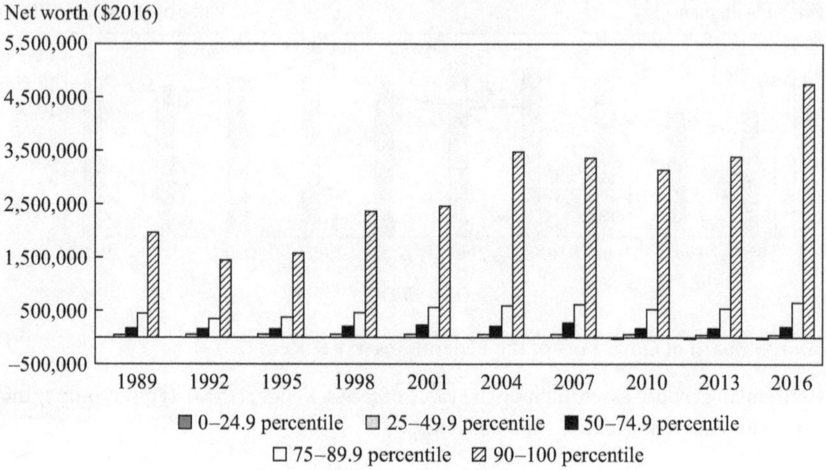

Source: Board of Governors of the Federal Reserve System (2017).

2007 and to –$20,000 in 2016. Over the same period, average wealth in the top 10 percent of the distribution skyrocketed, rising from $1.9 million in 1989 to $3.3 million in 2007 to $4.8 million in 2016. These patterns are consistent with the heterogeneity in preparation for retirement seen for other generations.

Future Status

Understanding the *future* saving behavior of the millennial generation will prove essential for addressing future retirement saving adequacy issues. Looking forward, millennials face a distinct set of issues and circumstances that will affect their ability to save for retirement, including both advantages and disadvantages in comparison with prior generations.

EDUCATION

Millennials start out with the advantage of having the most formal education of any generation in history. Over 60 percent of adult millennials have attended at least some college, compared to 46 percent of the baby-boomer generation when they were the same age.[20] Rising educational attainment among women drives this difference.[21]

Having more education will make it easier to save for retirement. First, the higher wages that come with higher education will give households more opportunities to save. Second, people with more education tend to save more of their income, controlling for income.[22] Third, people with higher education levels tend to have later retirement ages since they tend to have less physically demanding jobs, are healthier, and receive fringe benefits in addition to wages that may provide an incentive to stay in the labor force.[23] The overarching societal trend toward white-collar work may further increase average retirement ages for similar reasons. Good health status is also highly correlated with decisions to work longer.[24] Working longer, of course, makes it easier to finance adequate retirement saving.

On the other hand, higher education and income may make adequate saving more difficult to achieve in some ways. For example, Social Security benefits are progressive—replacing a smaller amount of average lifetime earnings as average lifetime earnings rise. And those who are better educated, and in better health, tend to live longer, meaning that they have a longer retirement period to finance, holding retirement age constant.

LONGER CAREERS

Since the 1980s, the share of people participating in defined benefit (DB) plans has decreased while participation in defined contribution (DC) plans has increased (figure 1-2). At the same time, the overall share of the workforce participating in any plan has remained relatively constant.[25]

This trend is expected to continue, implying that today's younger workers will have higher DC coverage than previous generations and lower DB coverage. As a result, millennials will likely retire later than previous generations, which would make it easier to accumulate funds necessary to finance retirement. Evidence suggests that DB plans often encourage comparatively early retirement through built-in incentives that maximize pension wealth at relatively early retirement ages.[26] Since the 1980s the average retirement age has risen after decades of decline, consistent with the decline of DB plans and rise of DC plans.[27]

As with better education, however, the shift to DC is not an unambiguous gain for retirement saving adequacy. Greater DC coverage and less DB coverage shifts much of the planning burden and investment risk from the employer to the employee.

EARLY-CAREER LABOR MARKET

Despite having some advantages relative to previous generations, the millennials face a variety of obstacles and concerns, including the early-career labor market they experienced. The millennial labor market has been dominated by the Great Recession and the tepid pace of recovery for several years after. The growth path of GDP has never recovered to the full-employment trend that existed before the Great Recession.[28] The weak job market and low overall labor force participation that existed at the beginning of their careers has probably adversely affected millennials' career earnings paths. Research shows that entering the labor force during an economic downturn depresses long-run earnings.[29] Evidence from the Great Depression further reveals that those who experience poor macroeconomic trends while they are young are less likely to take on significant financial risk, invest in the stock market, or own bonds.[30]

CONTINGENT JOBS

The evolution of the labor force toward contingent jobs will also complicate retirement saving for millennials.[31] In traditional employer-employee relationships, workers earn a salary or wage and receive fringe benefits, potentially including employer contributions to retirement plans. Contingent workers, on the other hand, work on an ad hoc basis and are paid based for each service or good they provide. They may or may not work full-time. Examples include Uber drivers, consultants, and contractors. Using a broad definition, there could be almost 20 million contingent workers in the United States.[32] Among full-time workers, these individuals have median weekly earnings about 30 percent lower than those of traditional workers and face numerous barriers to retirement saving. Conventional retirement savings mechanisms, such as payroll deductions and employer matching contributions, are not readily available. As a result, they are half as likely to have access to a work-provided retirement plan.[33] While non-employer-based retirement options such as IRAs are available to this group, only a small percentage participate.[34] Although a recent survey suggests that contingent work is not rising as fast as some had thought, it is nevertheless the case that millennials face higher probabilities of doing contingent work than previous generations.[35]

MORE DEFINED CONTRIBUTION PLANS

As noted, participants in DC plans tend to work longer than participants in DB plans. Other things equal, longer working careers should improve the adequacy of retirement saving. But other structural features of DC plans may lead to lower retirement incomes. First, to set up a DC plan, employees must make significantly more decisions regarding contribution levels, asset allocations, and asset drawdown. This freedom may actually serve to undermine retire-

Figure 1-4. **Share of Young Households Owning a Home, 1989–2016**

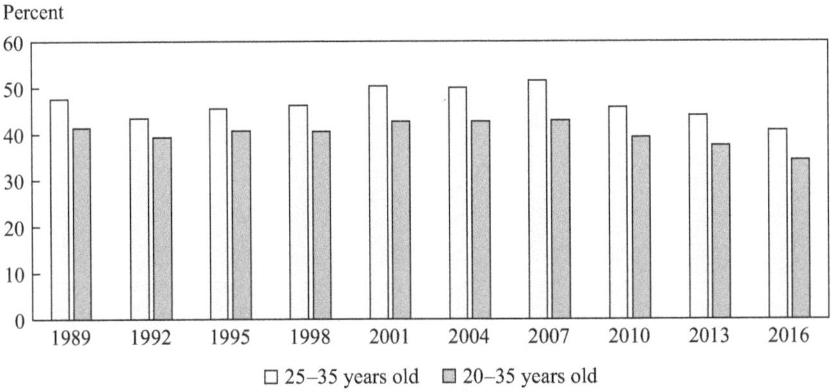

Source: Board of Governors of the Federal Reserve System (2017).

ment security if poor decisions are made.[36] Automatic mechanisms that govern enrollment, escalation of contributions, investment allocation, and rollovers can reduce these problems. Second, workers bear all of the investment risk in most DC plans.

DELAYED LIFE DECISIONS

Millennials are more likely than previous generations to delay homeownership, marriage, and childbearing. Young adults in 2016 had the lowest homeownership rate of any similarly aged generation since at least 1989 (figure 1-4). The average age of first marriage increased from age 21 for women (24 for men) in 1975 to age 27 (29) in 2016 (figure 1-5).[37] The age at which parents have their first child has increased over time as well, from 22 in 1975 to 26 in 2014.[38] The changes in these behavioral patterns are so large that there is debate over whether to label "emerging adulthood" as a new stage of life between childhood and adulthood.[39] These trends, in turn, may delay the onset of retirement saving if people feel the need to "get settled" by purchasing a house and raising children before beginning to think about saving for retirement.

INCREASING LIFESPANS

Just as delayed life choices may postpone substantial retirement saving, longer lifespans make it harder to maintain standards of living in retirement, other things equal. Over the past five decades, the average life expectancy at birth has increased from 67 to 76 for males and from 73 to 81 for females. These

Figure 1-5. **Median Age at First Marriage, 1970–2016**

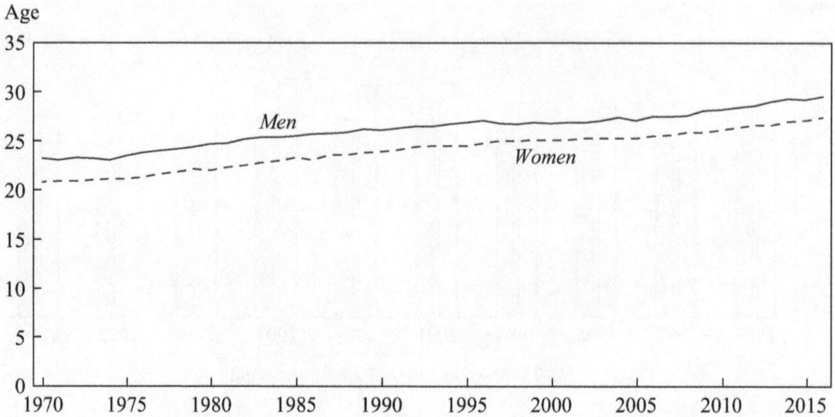

Source: US Census Bureau (2017).

increases are not borne equally, however. Those at the top of the income distribution account for almost all of the increase, while life expectancy for those at the bottom has remained constant or possibly even declined slightly.[40] If people live longer and plan to maintain their preretirement standard of living in retirement, they will either need to work longer or save more.

LONG-TERM FEDERAL FISCAL IMBALANCES

The federal government faces a long-term debt problem that will create pressure to cut spending and raise taxes. By the end of 2018, federal public debt will be 78 percent as large as gross domestic product (GDP), more than twice as large as the average ratio for the fifty years before the Great Recession. Under current policy assumptions, the ratio of public debt to GDP will exceed 106 percent by 2028 and 200 percent by 2048. Just to keep the debt-GDP ratio in 2048 at its current level would require a combination of immediate and permanent spending cuts or tax increases totaling 4.2 percent of GDP. This is equivalent to a 22 percent cut in noninterest spending or a 25 percent increase in tax revenue from current levels.[41] Even greater cuts would be required to lower the ratio to its fifty-year average rate. The longer policymakers wait to institute fiscal adjustments, the larger the adjustments will have to be in any given year, and the greater sacrifices millennials will have to make. Changes to Social Security, Medicare, and taxes will be particularly relevant in addressing the long-term fiscal imbalance. If such fiscal adjustments are made over the next few decades, it seems highly likely that millennials, who will then be in their prime earning years, will bear a significant amount of the burden.

LOW RATES OF RETURN

Real interest rates have fallen steadily from the mid-1990s. Many reasons have been put forward for the decline, and most of them suggest the low rates will persist somewhat.[42] One explanation, popularized by former Treasury secretary Lawrence Summers, involves a lack of aggregate demand due to the Great Recession and secular stagnation postrecession.[43] Other explanations include a worldwide savings glut and a flight to safety.[44]

To the extent that such trends continue or do not reverse, and result in lower overall asset returns, it will prove harder for millennials to accumulate sufficient retirement wealth.[45] With a given pattern of retirement contributions over time, a lower rate of return will result in a smaller accumulation of balances during the accumulation phase of retirement saving. With a given balance at the point of retirement, lower interest rates will result in smaller feasible payouts—for example, through an annuity—during the withdrawal phase of retirement saving.

Evidence

One early assessment (Johnson and others 2017) attempts to project future retirement income for older millennials and Generation Xers. The authors find that median income at age 70 for members of these groups will be higher than that of prior generations, though a smaller share of individuals will have enough to maintain their preretirement standard of living. These results, as the authors describe, are uncertain, given that today's young adults still have decades of work until their retirement.

WEALTH ACCUMULATION AND RACIAL AND ETHNIC MINORITIES

The projected growth of the minority population relative to the US population as a whole will present new challenges and opportunities for retirement saving. The literature on the adequacy of retirement saving shows significant intragenerational heterogeneity in preparation for retirement. Within generations, minorities appear to be at a disadvantage with regard to saving adequately for retirement compared to their non-minority counterparts. We provide further evidence on these issues in the following sections.

Table 1-2. *Projected Share of Population by Race and Hispanic Origin by Year, 2016–2050*

Percent

Year	*White*	*Hispanic*	*Black*	*Asian*	*2+ races*	*AIAN*[a]	*NHPI*[b]
2016	61.3	17.8	12.4	5.5	2.1	0.7	0.2
2020	59.7	18.7	12.5	5.8	2.3	0.7	0.2
2030	55.8	21.1	12.8	6.7	2.8	0.7	0.2
2040	51.7	23.5	13.0	7.5	3.4	0.7	0.2
2050	47.8	25.7	13.3	8.2	4.1	0.7	0.2

Source: Authors' calculations using data from US Census Bureau (2018).

Note: All percentages for a given race represent the share of that race that is not Hispanic. All Hispanics are captured in the Hispanic column.

[a] American Indian/Alaska Native.

[b] Native Hawaiian/Pacific Islander.

Projected Population Trends

Table 1-2 shows US Census Bureau (2018) projections of the composition of the future population. The United States will be a "majority-minority" country by 2050, where minority is defined as any race other than non-Hispanic white. The share of the population identifying as white only is projected to fall from 61.3 to 47.8 percent. As a share of the population, all races other than white are projected to grow or remain the same. The share of the population identifying as Hispanic is projected to increase from 17.8 to 25.7 percent. The Black-only share of the population is projected to increase from 12.4 to 13.3 percent; the American Indian and Alaska Native share is expected to stay relatively stable around 0.7 percent; the Asian share is expected to grow from 5.5 to 8.2 percent; the Native Hawaiian and Pacific Islander share is projected to stay steady around 0.2 percent; and the share of people of two or more races is projected to increase from 2.1 to 4.1 percent.[46]

Descriptive data

Appendix table 1A-1 reports characteristics of various racial and ethnic groups surveyed in the Federal Reserve's Survey of Consumer Finances. In general, the data show that whites have higher incomes than Blacks or Hispanics, who have roughly similar incomes on average. Whites have higher rates of college graduation than Blacks, who in turn have higher rates than Hispanics. Marriage is more prevalent among whites and Hispanics than Blacks. In the samples, whites tend to be somewhat older on average than Blacks, who in turn are older than Hispanics.

Whites are more likely than other groups to have a retirement account.[47] In 2016, 65.9 percent of whites, 37.8 percent of Blacks, 34.1 percent of Hispanics of any race, and 59.6 percent of people of other races had a retirement account. Overall, 56.5 percent of the population had a retirement plan.[48] Controlling for observable characteristics, Hasler, Lusardi, and Oggero (2018) show that whites are less likely to be "financially fragile," as they define it.

Regression specification

We estimate regression of the form

$$W = \alpha + \beta X + \gamma R + \varepsilon$$

where W is a measure of wealth, X is a vector of household characteristics, including education, marital status, sex (for singles), income and age categories, and R is a series of racial/ethnic indicators (Black, Hispanic, and nonwhite other, with white as the omitted category).[49] We employ cross-sectional data from each of the ten survey years the SCF has been administered (triennially from 1989 to 2016) and estimate least squares (LS) and median (least absolute deviation, or LAD) regressions, each with robust estimation techniques. Thompson and Suarez (2015) examine similar issues and provide wealth decompositions using the 1989–2013 SCFs.[50]

In the text, we present regressions using the level of wealth as the dependent variable. In the appendix, we present results that use the inverse hyperbolic sine of wealth as the dependent variable. We emphasize that the coefficient on race shows differences in wealth accumulation after controlling for various factors but should not be interpreted as an estimate of the impact of racial discrimination.

The LS regressions in table 1-3 show that Black households tend to have lower net worth than white households, controlling for other factors.[51] In the 2016 SCF, controlling for other factors, Black households had on average $124,000 less net worth than white households. This difference appears to have increased over time. The Black-white differences in wealth in the 1989, 1992, and 1995 cross-sections are smaller than the 2016 difference, with p values ranging from .035 to .105.

This finding should be qualified carefully. Certainly, reductions in Black-white differences over time in educational attainment and in wages should serve to *reduce* Black-white wealth differences. Our results address a different point. We show that—*controlling for* any changes in education, wages, and other household characteristics—the difference in wealth between Blacks and

Table 1-3. *Net Worth Regressions (Least Squares), 1989–2016*

	(1) *1989*	*(2)* *1992*	*(3)* *1995*	*(4)* *1998*	*(5)* *2001*	*(6)* *2004*	*(7)* *2007*	*(8)* *2010*	*(9)* *2013*	*(10)* *2016*
Black	−42,109* (23,206)	−40,433*** (13,804)	−56,846*** (18,309)	−66,146*** (19,132)	−96,659*** (31,543)	−97,979*** (27,485)	−78,393*** (29,495)	−141,470*** (26,428)	−83,542*** (23,857)	−124,142*** (37,193)
p-value, coefficient = 2016 value	0.061	0.035	0.105	0.166	0.573	0.572	0.335	0.704	0.358	n.a.[a]
Hispanic	−6,333 (26,919)	23,809 (24,879)	−34,760 (28,864)	29,801 (26,233)	−5,895 (38,400)	−25,377 (40,387)	70,958* (42,880)	−58,587** (29,682)	1,298 (28,004)	42,575 (37,425)
p-value, coefficient = 2016 value	0.289	0.676	0.102	0.780	0.366	0.217	0.618	0.034	0.377	n.a.
Nonwhite other	48,796 (89,674)	21,532 (49,493)	−20,803 (50,361)	−66,383 (91,136)	−160,583 (134,387)	−229,736*** (86,197)	−147,826 (115,956)	−279,171*** (87,955)	−69,021 (88,076)	−255,881** (105,779)
p-value, coefficient = 2016 value	0.028	0.018	0.045	0.175	0.577	0.848	0.491	0.866	0.175	n.a.
N	3,143	3,906	4,299	4,305	4,442	4,519	4,417	6,482	6,015	6,248
R-squared	0.114	0.084	0.088	0.094	0.131	0.102	0.104	0.099	0.093	0.071

Source: Board of Governors of the Federal Reserve (2017).

[a] n.a. = not available.

Control variables: Education level category (less than high school diploma, high school diploma, some college, bachelor's degree, graduate degree); Marital status; Sex of single heads of household; Income category ($0–19,999, $20,000–49,999, $50,000–99,999, $100,000–199,999, $200,000+); Age category (0–24, 25–34, 35–44, 45–54, 65–74, 75+).

Robust standard errors in parentheses.

*** $p < 0.01$, ** $p < 0.05$, * $p < 0.1$.

Table 1-4. *Pooled Net Worth Regressions (Least Squares)*

	(1) 1989–2016	(2) 1989–2007	(3) 2010–2016
Black	−90,972*** (8,626)	−71,877*** (9,386)	−117,903*** (17,292)
p-value, coefficient = 2016 value	n.a.[a]	0.012	n.a.
Hispanic	−7,845 (11,002)	3,575 (13,499)	−7,399 (18,635)
p-value, coefficient = 2016 value	n.a.	0.303	n.a.
Nonwhite Other	−112,807*** (29,078)	−70,197** (33,546)	−199,954*** (54,600)
p-value, coefficient = 2016 value	n.a.	0.045	n.a.
N	47,776	29,031	18,745
R-squared	0.091	0.102	0.082

Source: Board of Governors of the Federal Reserve (2017).
[a] n.a. = not available.
Control variables: same as in tables 1-3 and 1-5, plus year effects.
Robust standard errors in parentheses.
*** $p < 0.01$, ** $p < 0.05$, * $p < 0.1$.

whites may well have increased over time. Additional results presented below support this conclusion.

Households in which the head is of Hispanic origin do not generally have statistically significantly different net worth from whites, controlling for other factors.

Other nonwhite individuals, on average, had significantly lower net worth than whites in three of the SCF years (2004, 2010, and 2016). This difference appears to have increased over time, with the coefficients in the 1989, 1992, and 1995 regressions significantly smaller (in absolute value) than the coefficient in the 2016 regression.

In all of these regressions, however, the relevant sample sizes are fairly small, so precise estimation is difficult. To help address the concern with sample size, we also pool the data across survey years, adding a control for the survey year, with results shown in table 1-4.

As in the cross-section results, Blacks have lower net worth, controlling for other factors. The coefficients are larger in absolute value in the 2010–2016 specification than in the 1989–2007 specification, confirming the finding above about widening Black-white wealth differences, controlling for other factors.

Households in which the head is of Hispanic origin do not have a significantly different net worth in any of the specifications. Those who do not identify as white, Black, or Hispanic have significantly lower net worth than whites in each specification, and the difference has grown over time.

Since wealth tends to be distributed in a skewed manner, we also report LAD regressions to remove the impact of outliers. The regressions yield similar results to the LS findings, though of a smaller magnitude.

In cross-sectional results reported in table 1-5, the typical Black household had $43,262 less in wealth than the typical white household, controlling for other factors. The difference in wealth has increased over time, again conditional on observable factors.

The LAD regressions also show that the typical household with a head of Hispanic origin has less net worth than white households in several of the survey years, particularly in 2013 and 2016. The results suggest that wealth differences between whites and Hispanics may be increasing. Results are mixed for other nonwhite individuals, but the sample size for this group is relatively small, so precise estimation is difficult.

Table 1-6 reports LAD regressions using data pooled across survey years. The results are qualitatively similar to earlier findings. Black households have less wealth than white households, and the difference has grown over time, although it is smaller in the LAD regressions than in LS regressions.

Discussion

Our finding that differences in wealth between whites and minorities appears to have increased over time is consistent with a substantial body of literature.[52] The increase in the gap, at least over the past decade, appears to be due to the decline in housing wealth during the Great Recession, which affected low-wealth households more than high-wealth households.[53]

The implications of the results for the millennial generation are concerning. Chetty and others (2018) find that Black households have lower income, on average, than white households. Moreover, given parental income, they find that Black children have lower rates of upward mobility and higher rates of downward mobility than white children. Rates of upward mobility for Hispanics are lower than for whites but higher than for Black households. Their results suggest that closing the *income* gap over time between whites and

Table 1-5. *Net Worth Regressions (Least Absolute Deviations)*

	(1) *1989*	*(2)* *1992*	*(3)* *1995*	*(4)* *1998*	*(5)* *2001*	*(6)* *2004*	*(7)* *2007*	*(8)* *2010*	*(9)* *2013*	*(10)* *2016*
Black	−29,966***	−20,971***	−21,259***	−19,532***	−22,585***	−31,104***	−23,935***	−21,602***	−36,176***	−43,262***
	(4,534)	(3,181)	(3,719)	(3,123)	(3,890)	(6,478)	(5,844)	(4,480)	(2,927)	(3,019)
p-value, coefficient = 2016 value	0.019	<0.001	<0.001	<0.001	<0.001	0.113	0.010	<0.001	0.088	n.a.[a]
Hispanic	−25,656***	−8,703	−14,384***	−9,866	−9,010*	−5,346	−3,439	−6,724	−13,124***	−23,161***
	(9,338)	(5,808)	(5,113)	(6,065)	(5,043)	(5,973)	(6,960)	(4,466)	(3,823)	(4,457)
p-value, coefficient = 2016 value	0.665	0.028	0.237	0.053	0.024	0.017	0.025	0.004	0.069	n.a.
Nonwhite Other	−12,710	−11,955***	−23,216***	−23,200	−523.9	−25,554	−34,624***	−32,870***	−23,177	−8,501
	(9,025)	(3,212)	(6,717)	(17,139)	(30,931)	(19,163)	(11,401)	(9,290)	(15,789)	(6,512)
p-value, coefficient = 2016 value	0.786	0.611	0.052	0.438	0.741	0.287	0.192	0.049	0.382	n.a.
N	3,143	3,906	4,299	4,305	4,442	4,519	4,417	6,482	6,015	6,248
Pseudo R-squared	.180	.184	.143	.167	.166	.163	.158	.163	.168	.160

Source: Board of Governors of the Federal Reserve (2017).

[a] n.a. = not available.

Control variables: Education level category (less than high school diploma, high school diploma, some college, bachelor's degree, graduate degree); Marital status; Sex of single heads of household; Income category ($0–19,999, $20,000–49,999, $50,000–99,999, $100,000–199,999, $200,000+); Age category (0–24, 25–34, 35–44, 45–54, 65–74, 75+).

Robust standard errors in parentheses.

*** $p < 0.01$, ** $p < 0.05$, * $p < 0.1$.

Table 1-6. *Pooled Net Worth Regressions (Least Absolute Deviations)*

	(1) 1989–2016	(2) 1989–2007	(3) 2010–2016
Black	−26,419*** (1,171)	−23,339*** (1,394)	−33,809*** (1,714)
p-value, coefficient = 2016 value	n.a.[a]	<0.001	n.a.
Hispanic	−12,422*** (1,553)	−10,292*** (1,706)	−14,670*** (2,521)
p-value, coefficient = 2016 value	n.a.	0.129	n.a.
Nonwhite Other	−17,827*** (3,185)	−18,695*** (2,621)	−17,158*** (5,705)
p-value, coefficient = 2016 value	n.a.	0.643	n.a.
N	47,776	29,031	18,745
Pseudo R-squared	0.160	0.161	0.163

Source: Board of Governors of the Federal Reserve (2017).
[a] n.a. = not available.
Control variables: same as in tables 1-3 and 1-5, plus year effects.
Robust standard errors in parentheses.
*** $p < 0.01$, ** $p < 0.05$, * $p < 0.1$.

minorities will be difficult. Building off those results, our findings imply that minorities have less wealth than whites, *even after controlling for income* (and education, age, and marital status). Therefore, our results suggest that, even if the income gap between groups were eventually reduced or eliminated, that would not in itself be sufficient to ensure the adequacy of saving for minority households—there would still be a retirement saving gap between whites and minorities.

It is unclear, however, to what extent the wealth accumulation patterns of minorities in the past provides a reliable guide to their wealth accumulation patterns in the future. As the economy evolves, one can expect the economic experience of minorities to change. For example, relative to minorities in the past, minorities in the future may well reside in neighborhoods with different characteristics, go to different types of schools, and have different experiences with mentors, discrimination, marriage, childbearing, and so on. If these changes are advantageous, they could, in principle, help minorities accumulate more wealth relative to whites than in the past. However, the results above show that over the past thirty years the gap has widened, after controlling for observable characteristics.

A COMPLICATED FUTURE

Predicting retirement saving patterns in 2050 is an exercise in uncertainty. There is clearly cause for concern. First, many members of the current generation of retirees and near-retirees are not saving very much. Second, millennials will face a number of "headwinds" in accumulating enough saving to finance adequate retirement. Third, the projected rise in the minority population will reduce retirement saving adequacy, if current trends persist. On the other hand, millennials possess a few major advantages over previous generations in preparing for retirement, and it is not at all clear that the wealth accumulation patterns of minority households will remain constant if their economic situation changes.

APPENDIX

While the regressions in the text use the level of wealth (in 2016 dollars) as the dependent variable, the regressions in the appendix employ the inverse hyperbolic sine (IHS) of wealth. This transformation has been used in previous literature (for example, Gale and Pence 2006; Pence 2006; Thompson and Suarez 2015). The transformation approximates the logarithm of wealth for large positive values of wealth and is also able to address zero or negative values of wealth, which occur frequently in the data. The IHS transformation yields estimates of proportional differences in wealth, rather than the differences in levels generated by the regressions in the main text.

More formally, if θ is a scaling parameter and w is a measure of wealth, the inverse hyperbolic sine of wealth can be written as $\theta^{-1} \sinh^{-1}(\theta w) = \theta^{-1} \ln[\theta w + (\theta^2 w^2 + 1)^{1/2}]$. This symmetric function is linear around the origin but approximates the logarithm for larger values of wealth. To see this, note that if w is large, $\ln[\theta w + (\theta^2 w^2 + 1)^{1/2}] \approx \ln 2\theta + \ln w$, which is simply a vertical displacement of the logarithm. Following previous research, we set $\theta = 0.0001$.[54] When multiplied by this scaling parameter, coefficients from an inverse hyperbolic sine specification, like coefficients from a logarithmic specification, can be interpreted as the effect of a change in a given variable on the percentage change in wealth, for wealth values that are sufficiently large.[55]

Appendix tables 1A-2–1A-5 provide regression results using the IHS transformation of wealth that parallel tables 1-3–1-6 in the main text. Several patterns in the IHS estimates merit attention. First, controlling for demographic factors, Black-white wealth differences are large. In 2016, for example, controlling

Table 1A-1. *Demographic Characteristics by Year and Race/Ethnicity, 1989–2016*

A. Average age

Year	*Black*	*Hispanic*	*Other*	*White*
1989	47.3	42.5	41.9	49
1992	45.8	41.6	44.8	49.8
1995	45.8	40.2	45.4	49.7
1998	46	40.7	43.7	50.1
2001	45.4	40.7	45.5	50.6
2004	47.7	42.2	45.8	51
2007	45.7	41.3	44.4	52.2
2010	48.1	42.4	48.4	52.4
2013	48.8	44.2	45.9	53.1
2016	49.4	45.8	45	53.7

B. Share who are college grads (percent)

	Black	*Hispanic*	*Other*	*White*
1989	11.0	6.5	34.1	26.3
1992	17.0	6.5	31.6	30.8
1995	12.4	9.4	32.9	27.9
1998	14.0	12.1	32.7	29.9
2001	13.7	12.5	49.1	32.0
2004	20.1	8.9	51.6	34.0
2007	19.6	12.1	54.7	31.4
2010	19.9	15.3	48.6	34.1
2013	21.6	11.8	53.2	35.9
2016	22.1	17.2	54.3	38.1

C. Share who are married (percent)

Year	*Black*	*Hispanic*	*Other*	*White*
1989	28.0	60.5	57.9	63.0
1992	35.7	59.6	54.8	61.2
1995	35.8	69.7	62.0	61.3
1998	36.0	69.8	66.6	60.7
2001	38.2	61.8	61.7	64.1
2004	33.6	67.7	68.5	60.6
2007	41.3	68.4	66.4	60.2
2010	39.4	61.6	63.6	60.8
2013	36.6	63.0	63.6	60.1
2016	36.4	59.6	60.1	60.8

D. Average income (2016$)

	Black	*Hispanic*	*Other*	*White*
1989	36,815	39,742	58,884	86,229
1992	39,948	38,383	71,891	74,108
1995	36,206	47,993	72,883	77,506
1998	41,577	47,620	83,136	86,656
2001	50,495	52,716	83,761	105,968
2004	49,326	50,540	98,618	101,369
2007	53,087	55,349	104,161	110,394
2010	46,871	55,366	107,399	97,553
2013	43,785	47,123	95,831	105,203
2016	54,949	57,396	112,310	119,842

E. Share with retirement accounts (percent)

Year	*Black*	*Hispanic*	*Other*	*White*
1989	16.5	16.1	25.0	43.3
1992	24.2	19.2	28.5	45.2
1995	27.8	31.9	40.2	49.3
1998	34.5	22.4	46.0	54.3
2001	39.7	31.8	48.2	58.0
2004	32.3	25.7	51.7	55.9
2007	37.0	32.0	63.7	57.5
2010	32.6	27.8	51.9	57.3
2013	34.0	26.0	49.4	56.0
2016	34.0	31.2	55.6	59.6

F. Share of population (percent)[a]

Year	*Black*	*Hispanic*	*Other*	*White*
1989	12.8	8	4.4	74.8
1992	12.7	7.4	4.5	75.3
1995	12.8	5.7	4	77.6
1998	11.8	7.1	3.3	77.8
2001	13	7.9	2.8	76.3
2004	13.6	9.2	3.6	73.6
2007	12.6	9.4	4.1	73.9
2010	13.8	10.7	4.6	70.8
2013	14.6	10.6	4.7	70.1
2016	15.8	11.3	4.8	68

Source: Authors' calculations using Board of Governors of the Federal Reserve System (2017).

[a]Share of population is estimated by calculating the weighted share of observations in the SCF for each race in each year.

Table 1A-2. *Net Worth Regressions (Least Squares, Inverse Hyperbolic Sine Transformation)*

	(1) *1989*	*(2)* *1992*	*(3)* *1995*	*(4)* *1998*	*(5)* *2001*	*(6)* *2004*	*(7)* *2007*	*(8)* *2010*	*(9)* *2013*	*(10)* *2016*
Black	−0.452***	−0.402***	−0.435***	−0.352***	−0.445***	−0.452***	−0.413***	−0.453***	−0.552***	−0.537***
	(0.107)	(0.078)	(0.077)	(0.079)	(0.077)	(0.086)	(0.086)	(0.071)	(0.072)	(0.068)
p value, coefficient = 2016 value	0.185	0.014	0.052	0.001	0.076	0.120	0.029	0.090	0.746	n.a.[a]
Hispanic	−0.481***	−0.343***	−0.322***	−0.310***	−0.364***	−0.284***	−0.147	−0.292***	−0.323***	−0.322***
	(0.119)	(0.110)	(0.120)	(0.103)	(0.091)	(0.089)	(0.097)	(0.080)	(0.084)	(0.0766)
p-value, coefficient = 2016 value	0.059	0.818	0.996	0.886	0.596	0.644	0.064	0.702	0.991	n.a.
Nonwhite Other	−0.128	−0.102	−0.360***	−0.133	−0.335**	−0.156	0.047	−0.237**	0.009	0.051
	(0.149)	(0.113)	(0.139)	(0.165)	(0.202)	(0.135)	(0.124)	(0.123)	(0.113)	(0.116)
p-value, coefficient = 2016 value	0.322	0.330	0.006	0.341	0.050	0.218	0.983	0.059	0.802	n.a.
N	3,143	3,906	4,299	4,305	4,442	4,519	4,417	6,482	6,015	6,248
R-squared	0.548	0.509	0.490	0.499	0.555	0.528	0.523	0.454	0.501	0.522

Source: Board of Governors of the Federal Reserve (2017).

[a] n.a. = not available.

Coefficients have been multiplied by the scaling parameter for the inverse hyperbolic sine, 0.0001, and then transformed with $e^{\beta} - 1$. Statistical significance is calculated from the untransformed coefficients and standard errors.

Control variables: Education level category (less than high school diploma, high school diploma, some college, bachelor's degree, graduate degree); Marital status; Sex of single heads of household; Income category ($0–19,999, $20,000–49,999, $50,000–99,999, $100,000–199,999, $200,000+); Age category (0–24, 25–34, 35–44, 45–54, 65–74, 75+).

Robust standard errors in parentheses.

*** $p < 0.01$, ** $p < 0.05$, * $p < 0.1$.

Table 1A-3. *Pooled Net Worth Regressions (Least Squares, Inverse Hyperbolic Sine Transformation)*

	(1) 1989–2016	(2) 1989–2007	(3) 2010–2016
Black	−0.462*** (0.025)	−0.424*** (0.032)	−0.518*** (0.040)
p-value, coefficient = 2016 value	n.a.[a]	<0.001	n.a.
Hispanic	−0.323*** (0.030)	−0.326*** (0.039)	−0.315*** (0.046)
p-value, coefficient = 2016 value	n.a.	0.855	n.a.
Nonwhite Other	−0.124*** (0.042)	−0.160*** (0.054)	−0.064 (0.068)
p-value, coefficient = 2016 value	n.a.	0.203	n.a.
N	47,776	29,031	18,745
R-squared	0.508	0.521	0.492

Source: Board of Governors of the Federal Reserve (2017).

[a] n.a. = not available.

Coefficients have been multiplied by the scaling parameter for the inverse hyperbolic sine, 0.0001, and then transformed with $e^{\beta} - 1$. Statistical significance is calculated from the untransformed coefficients and standard errors.

Control variables: Same as in tables 1A-2 and 1A-4, plus year effects.

Robust standard errors in parentheses.

*** $p < 0.01$, ** $p < 0.05$, * $p < 0.1$.

for other factors, Blacks had more than 50 percent less wealth than whites at the mean and the median of the distribution. The estimates provide marginal support for the idea that the differences have grown over time in appendix tables 1A-2 and 1A-4 and strong support for the view in appendix tables 1A-3 and 1A-5. Second, the effects for Hispanics are smaller than for Blacks but the Hispanic coefficients under the IHS transformation are much more precisely estimated than under the level-of-wealth regressions in the main text. Third, the effects for "other" groups are smaller than for Blacks and Hispanics and are not precisely estimated.

Table 1A-4. *Net Worth Regressions (Least Absolute Deviations, Inverse Hyperbolic Sine Transformation)*

	(1) 1989	*(2)* 1992	*(3)* 1995	*(4)* 1998	*(5)* 2001	*(6)* 2004	*(7)* 2007	*(8)* 2010	*(9)* 2013	*(10)* 2016
Black	−0.418***	−0.393***	−0.461***	−0.376***	−0.486***	−0.409***	−0.462***	−0.483***	−0.558***	−0.559***
	(0.122)	(0.082)	(0.068)	(0.084)	(0.094)	(0.096)	(0.146)	(0.082)	(0.082)	(0.077)
p-value, coefficient = 2016 value	0.068	0.002	0.025	0.003	0.204	0.018	0.231	0.129	0.984	n.a.[a]
Hispanic	−0.529***	−0.365***	−0.385***	−0.286**	−0.395***	−0.330***	−0.065	−0.286***	−0.394***	−0.398***
	(0.155)	(0.128)	(0.132)	(0.151)	(0.088)	(0.103)	(0.091)	(0.073)	(0.091)	(0.093)
p-value, coefficient = 2016 value	0.142	0.761	0.877	0.292	0.960	0.408	0.001	0.136	0.961	n.a.
Nonwhite Other	−0.122	−0.167	−0.329***	−0.252	−0.318*	−0.071	0.045	−0.279**	−0.108	0.066
	(0.164)	(0.157)	(0.152)	(0.185)	(0.228)	(0.128)	(0.152)	(0.132)	(0.105)	(0.134)
p-value, coefficient = 2016 value	0.256	0.216	0.049	0.133	0.056	0.459	0.912	0.027	0.249	n.a.
N	3,143	3,906	4,299	4,305	4,442	4,519	4,417	6,482	6,015	6,248
Pseudo R-squared	.377	.353	.320	.341	.381	.362	.360	.336	.365	.368

Source: Board of Governors of the Federal Reserve (2017).

[a] n.a. = not available.

Coefficients have been multiplied by the scaling parameter for the inverse hyperbolic sine, 0.0001, and then transformed with $e^{\beta} - 1$. Statistical significance is calculated from the untransformed coefficients and standard errors.

Control variables: Education level category (less than high school diploma, high school diploma, some college, bachelor's degree, graduate degree); Marital status; Sex of single heads of household; Income category ($0–19,999, $20,000–49,999, $50,000–99,999, $100,000–199,999, $200,000+); Age category (0–24, 25–34, 35–44, 45–54, 65–74, 75+).

Robust standard errors in parentheses.

*** $p < 0.01$, ** $p < 0.05$, * $p < 0.1$.

Table 1A-5. *Pooled Net Worth Regressions (Least Absolute Deviations, Inverse Hyperbolic Sine Transformation)*

	(1) *1989–2016*	*(2)* *1989–2007*	*(3)* *2010–2016*
Black	−0.464***	−0.416***	−0.533***
	(0.030)	(0.038)	(0.045)
p-value, coefficient = 2016 value	n.a.[a]	<0.001	n.a.
Hispanic	−0.367***	−0.367***	−0.349***
	(0.034)	(0.047)	(0.050)
p-value, coefficient = 2016 value	n.a.	0.928	n.a.
Nonwhite Other	−0.138**	−0.174***	−0.116**
	(0.058)	(0.069)	(0.062)
p-value, coefficient = 2016 value	n.a.	0.491	n.a.
N	47,776	29,031	18,745
Pseudo R-squared	0.355	0.356	0.356

Source: Board of Governors of the Federal Reserve (2017).

[a] n.a. = not available.

Coefficients have been multiplied by the scaling parameter for the inverse hyperbolic sine, 0.0001, and then transformed with $e^{\beta} - 1$. Statistical significance is calculated from the untransformed coefficients and standard errors.

Control variables: same as in tables 1A-2 and 1A-4, plus year effects.

Robust standard errors in parentheses.

*** $p < 0.01$, ** $p < 0.05$, * $p < 0$.

NOTES

The authors thank Alec Camhi, Victoria Johnson, and Aaron Krupkin for expert assistance, and Karen Dynan, Douglas Holtz-Eakin, Alicia Munnell, and conference participants for helpful comments. This chapter was made possible by the US 2050 project, supported by the Peter G. Peterson Foundation and the Ford Foundation. The statements made and views expressed are solely the responsibility of the authors.

1. While living longer is obviously a good thing, having a longer retirement period (defined as the difference between lifespan and retirement age) makes it harder, other things equal, to finance adequate living standards in retirement.

2. Much of this section and the following section are based on Fichtner and Gale (2017).

3. For a recent review of the literature on the adequacy of retirement saving, see Mackenzie (2020).

4. Engen, Gale, and Uccello (1999); Scholz, Seshadri, and Khitatrakun (2006).

5. Dushi and others (2016).

6. Scholz and Seshadri (2009); Engen, Gale, and Uccello (1999).

7. Congressional Budget Office (2017).

8. Aon Hewitt (2012); Munnell, Hou, and Sanzenbacher (2016); Rhee (2013b).

9. For details of these calculations, see Munnell, Hou, and Sanzenbacher (2018a).

10. See, e.g., Butricia, Iams, and Smith (2012); Engen, Gale, and Uccello (1999); Hurd and Rohwedder (2012); John (2010); Pang and Warshawsky (2014); Rhee (2013a); Scholz, Seshadri, and Khitatrakun (2006); VanDerhei (2014); VanDerhei and Copeland (2010).

11. Studies that use administrative data often tend to find more income among retirees than studies that employ survey data with self-reported income. For example, based on a comparison of responses to the Current Population Survey Annual Social and Economic Supplement (CPS ASEC) and information from administrative records on earnings and income from Social Security and the Internal Revenue Service, Bee and Mitchell (2017) show that individuals underreport their income from defined benefit plans and retirement account withdrawals. Brady and others (2017) use Internal Revenue Service Statistics of Income panel data, supplemented by information returns, to show that individuals do not experience a reduction in disposable income after beginning to receive Social Security. However, Chen, Munnell, and Sanzenbacher (2018) find that the extent of understatement of wealth is minimal in the Health and Retirement Study and the Survey of Consumer Finances.

12. Dimock (2018). Various definitions of the millennial generation include those born between the early 1980s and the early 2000s. The Census Bureau (unofficially) defines millennials as the cohort born between 1982 and 2000 (US Census Bureau 2015).

13. Fry (2017a). The baby boomers are generally considered to include those born between 1946 and 1964.

14. Fry, Igielnik, and Patten (2018).

15. Dettling, Hsu, and Llanes (2018) provide further detail on wealth accumulation trends between 2007 and 2016.

16. Looney and Yannelis (2018).

17. Dettling and Hsu (2014) examine retirement saving trends for people 18–31 years of age in the successive SCFs. They find that millennials in 2013 were just as likely to have a defined contribution retirement account as similarly aged people in 2001. Millennials had higher median balances, conditional on ownership (by about $2,000), but they had lower participation in defined benefit plans.

18. Fry (2017b).

19. Fry (2017b).

20. Council of Economic Advisers (2014).

21. Johnson and others (2017).

22. Dynan, Skinner, and Zeldes (2004).

23. Burtless (2013).

24. Munnell (2015).

25. Gale and John (2017).

26. Kotlikoff and Wise (1984); Stock and Wise (1990).

27. Hou and others (2017); Morisi (2016); Munnell (2015). The rise in the average retirement age is also consistent with the gradual increase in the full retirement age in Social Security that was enacted in 1983 (Song and Manchester 2007) and more generally with the evolution of retirement incentives embedded in Social Security and private retirement plans (Coile 2018).

28. Congressional Budget Office (2018).

29. Welch (1979); Kahn (2010).

30. Malmendier and Nagel (2011).

31. Gale, Holmes, and John (2018); Harris and Krueger (2015); Katz and Krueger (2016).

32. Gale, Holmes, and John (2018).

33. Gale, Holmes, and John (2018).

34. US Government Accountability Office (2015).

35. US Bureau of Labor Statistics (2018).

36. Poterba (2014).

37. US Census Bureau (2017).

38. Matthews and Hamilton (2016); US Census Bureau (2017).

39. Vespa (2017).

40. National Academy of Sciences (2015).

41. Auerbach, Gale, and Krupkin (2018).

42. Elmendorf and Sheiner (2016).

43. Summers (2016).

44. Bernanke (2007, 2015).

45. Fichtner and Seligman (2017); Mitchell, Clark, and Maurer (2018).

46. By 2050, the foreign-born share of the population will increase from 13.6 to 16.8 percent. The share of the population 65 and older will rise from about 15.2 percent to 22.1 percent. The share of the population under 18 will decrease from 22.8 to 20.1 percent, and the share between 18 and 64 will decrease from 62 to 57.9 percent (US Census Bureau 2018).

47. The working-age population is defined as those 25 to 64 years of age. Ownership of a retirement account includes having a nonzero balance in any of the following, as defined by the SCF: IRAs, Keoghs, thrift-type accounts, and future and current account-type pensions. See also Rhee (2013b).

48. Harvey (2017). Statistics are for workers 18 to 64 who work in the private sector. In this case, CPS data are used as an illustrative example of disparities in retirement saving by demographics. Studies linking CPS survey data with administrative data find that Americans tend to underestimate their retirement income (Bee and Mitchell 2017). Many who receive such income fail to report it. Other studies suggest that self-reports of retirement plan participation are underestimated as well (Dushi and Honig 2015). Thus the estimates presented here may represent a lower bound of access to and participation in retirement plans.

49. Regressions using a variable called "normal income" instead of income yielded similar results.

50. Other studies of racial wealth gaps include those by Altonji and Doraszelski (2005); Barsky and others (2002); Masterson and others (2009); Pew (2011); Scholz and Levine (2003); and Shapiro, Meschede, and Osoro (2013).

51. Similarly, Emmons and Ricketts (2017) show that differences in observable variables cannot fully explain minorities' wealth accumulation relative to whites'.

52. See, e.g., Taylor and others (2011); Kochhar and Fry (2014); McKernan and others (2014); Shapiro, Meschede, and Osoro (2014); Thompson and Suarez (2015); and Wolff (2018). Munnell, Hou, and Sanzenbacher (2018b) show that differences in the proportion of households saving adequately for retirement (a different measure than the "wealth gap" measures used in the other studies cited here) fell for Blacks relative to whites from 2007 to 2016, but rose for Hispanics relative to whites. Hispanics were particularly hard hit by declines in housing prices in the Great Recession.

53. McKernan and others (2014); Shapiro, Meschede, and Osoro (2014); Wolff (2018).

54. Using maximum likelihood, Burbidge, Magee, and Robb (1988) find that 0.0000872 (or 0.0001, rounded) is the optimal value for the scaling parameter for net worth in their ordinary least squares specification; Pence (2002) finds that 0.0001 is the optimal value for her median regression specification. Kennickell and Sundén (1997) also use this parameter value for net worth.

55. See Pence (2006) for further exposition of this result and Burbidge, Magee, and Robb (1988) for more information on this transformation.

REFERENCES

Altonji, Joseph, and Ulrich Doraszelski. 2005. "The Role of Permanent Income and Demographics in Black/White Differences in Wealth." *Journal of Human Resources* 40 (1): 1–30.

Aon Hewitt. 2012. "The Real Deal: 2012 Retirement Income Adequacy at Large Companies." Ottawa, Canada.

Auerbach, Alan, William Gale, and Aaron Krupkin. 2018. "The Federal Budget Outlook: We Are Not Winning." *Tax Notes* (July 30): 617–28.

Barsky, Robert, John Bound, Kerwin Charles, and Joseph Lupton. 2002. "Accounting for the Black-White Wealth Gap." *Journal of the American Statistical Association* 97 (459): 663–73.

Bee, Adam, and Joshua Mitchell. 2017. "Do Older Americans Have More Income Than We Think?" SESHD Working Paper 2017-39. Washington, DC: US Census Bureau.

Bernanke, Ben. 2007. "Global Imbalances: Recent Developments and Prospects." Bundesbank Lecture, September 11.

———. 2015. "Why Are Interest Rates So Low, Part 3: The Global Savings Glut." *Ben Bernanke's Blog*, Brookings Institution, April 1.

Board of Governors of the Federal Reserve System. 2017. "Survey of Consumer Finances 2016." Washington, DC.

Burbidge, John B., Lonnie Magee, and A. Leslie Robb. 1988. "Alternative Transformations to Handle Extreme Values of the Dependent Variable." *Journal of the American Statistical Association* 83 (401): 123–27.

Burtless, Gary. 2013. "Can Educational Attainment Explain the Rise in Labor Force Participation at Older Ages?" Center for Retirement Research, Boston College.

Butricia, Barbara, Howard Iams, and Karen Smith. 2012. "This Is Not Your Parents' Retirement: Comparing Retirement Income across Generations." *Social Security Bulletin* 72 (1): 37–58.

Chen, Anqi, Alicia H. Munnell, and Geoffrey T. Sanzenbacher. 2018. "How Much Income Do Retirees Actually Have?" Center for Retirement Research, Boston College.

Chetty, Raj, Nathaniel Hendren, Maggie R. Jones, and Sonya R. Porter. 2018. "Race and Economic Opportunity in the United States: An Intergenerational Perspective." NBER Working Paper 24441. Cambridge, MA: National Bureau of Economic Research.

Coile, Courtney. 2018. "Working Longer in the U.S.: Trends and Explanations." NBER Working Paper 24576. Cambridge, MA: National Bureau of Economic Research.

Congressional Budget Office. 2017. "Measuring the Adequacy of Retirement Income: A Primer." Washington, DC.

———. 2018. "The Budget and Economic Outlook: 2018 to 2028." Washington, DC.

Council of Economic Advisers. 2014. "15 Economic Facts about Millennials." Washington, DC: The White House.

Dettling, Lisa, and Joanne Hsu. 2014. "The State of Young Adults' Balance Sheets: Evidence from the Survey of Consumer Finances." *Federal Reserve Bank of St. Louis Review, Fourth Quarter, 2014* (96) 4: 305–30.

Dettling, Lisa, Joanne Hsu, and Elizabeth Llanes. 2018. "A Wealthless Recovery? Asset Ownership and the Uneven Recovery from the Great Recession." FEDS Notes. Washington, DC: Board of Governors of the Federal Reserve System.

Dimock, Michael. 2018. "Defining Generations: Where Millennials End and Post-Millennials Begin." Washington, DC: Pew Research Center.

Dushi, Irena, and Marjorie Honig. 2015. "How Much Do Respondents in the Health and Retirement Study Know about Their Contributions to Tax-Deferred Contribution Plans? A Cross-Cohort Comparison." *Journal of Pension Economics and Finance* 14 (3): 203–39.

Dushi, Irena, Alicia H. Munnell, Geoffrey T. Sanzenbacher, Anthony Webb, and Anqi Chen. 2016. "Do Households Save More When the Kids Leave Home?" Center for Retirement Research, Boston College.

Dynan, Karen, Jonathan Skinner, and Stephen Zeldes. 2004. "Do the Rich Save More?" *Journal of Political Economy* 112 (2): 397–444.

Elmendorf, Douglas, and Louise Sheiner. 2016. "Federal Budget Policy with an Aging Population and Persistently Low Interest Rates." Hutchins Center Working Paper 18. Brookings.

Emmons, William, and Lowell Ricketts. 2017. "College Is Not Enough: Higher Education Does Not Eliminate Racial and Ethnic Wealth Gaps." *Federal Reserve Bank of St. Louis Review* 99 (1): 7–39.

Engen, Eric, William Gale, and Cori Uccello. 1999. "The Adequacy of Household Saving." *Brookings Papers on Economic Activity* 2: 65–187.

Fichtner, Jason, and William Gale. 2017. "Economic and Political Consequences of Inadequate Retirement Saving for the Millennial Generation." Mimeo.

Fichtner, Jason, and Jason Seligman. 2017. "Retirement Saving and Decumulation in a Persistent Low-Return Environment." Pension Research Council Working Paper. Wharton School, University of Pennsylvania.

Fry, Richard. 2017a. "5 Facts about Millennial Households." Washington, DC: Pew Research Center.

———. 2017b. "It's Becoming More Common for Young Adults to Live at Home—and for Longer Stretches." Washington, DC: Pew Research Center.

Fry, Richard, Ruth Igielnik, and Eileen Patten. 2018. "How Millennials Today Compare with Their Grandparents 50 Years Ago." Washington, DC: Pew Research Center.

Gale, William, and David John. 2017. "State Sponsored Retirement Savings Plans: New Approaches to Boost Retirement Plan Coverage." Pension Research Council Working Paper. Wharton School, University of Pennsylvania.

Gale, William, and Karen M. Pence. 2006. "Are Successive Generations Getting Wealthier, and If So, Why? Evidence from the 1990s." *Brookings Papers on Economic Activity* 1 (2006): 155–234.

Gale, William, Sarah Holmes, and David John. 2018. "Retirement Plans for Contingent Workers: Issues and Options." Brookings.

Harris, Seth, and Alan Krueger. 2015. "A Proposal for Modernizing Labor Laws for Twenty-First-Century Work: The 'Independent Worker.'" Hamilton Project. Brookings.

Harvey, Catherine. 2017. "Access to Workplace Retirement Plans by Race and Ethnicity." Fact Sheet. Washington, DC: AARP Public Policy Institute.

Hasler, Andrea, Annamaria Lusardi, and Noemi Oggero. 2018. "Financial Fragility in the US: Evidence and Implications." Global Financial Literacy Excellence Center, George Washington University School of Business.

Hou, Wenliang, Alicia Munnell, Geoffrey Sanzenbacher, and Yinji Li. 2017. "Why Are US Households Claiming Social Security Later?" Working Paper 2017-3. Center for Retirement Research, Boston College.

Hurd, Michael, and Susann Rohwedder. 2012. "Economic Preparation for Retirement." In *Investigations in the Economics of Aging*, edited by David Wise. University of Chicago Press.

John, David. 2010. "Disparities for Women and Minorities in Retirement Saving." Retirement Security Project. Brookings.

Johnson, Richard, Karen Smith, Damir Cosic, and Claire Wang. 2017. "Retirement Prospects for the Millennials: What Is the Early Prognosis?" WP 2017-17. Center for Retirement Research, Boston College.

Kahn, Lisa. 2010. "The Long-Term Labor Market Consequences of Graduating from College in a Bad Economy." *Labor Economics* 17 (2): 303–16.

Katz, Lawrence, and Alan Krueger. 2016. "The Rise and Nature of Alternative Work Arrangements in the United States, 1995–2015." NBER Working Paper 223667. Cambridge, MA: National Bureau of Economic Research.

Kennickell, Arthur B., and Annika Sundén. 1997. "Pensions, Social Security, and the Distribution of Wealth." Finance and Economics Discussion Series Paper 1997-55. Washington, DC: Board of Governors of the Federal Reserve System.

Kochhar, Rakesh, and Richard Fry. 2014. "Wealth Inequality Has Widened along Racial, Ethnic Lines since End of Great Recession." Washington, DC: Pew Research Center.

Kotlikoff, Laurence, and David Wise. 1984. "The Incentive Effects of Private Pension Plans." In *Issues in Pension Economics,* edited by Zvi Bodie, John Shoven, and David Wise, pp. 283–336. University of Chicago Press.

Looney, Adam, and Constantine Yannelis. 2018. "Borrowers with Large Balances: Rising Student Debt and Falling Repayment Rates." Brookings.

Mackenzie, George A. 2020. "Is There a Retirement Crisis? An Exploration of the Current Debate." Washington, DC: CFA Institute Research Center.

Malmendier, Ulrike, and Stefan Nagel. 2011. "Depression Babies: Do Macroeconomic Experiences Affect Risk-Taking?" *Quarterly Journal of Economics* 126 (1): 373–416.

Masterson, Thomas, Ajit Zacharias, and Edward Wolff. 2009. "Has Progress Been Made in Alleviating Racial Economic Inequality?" Levy Economics Institute Working Paper. Annandale-on-Hudson, NY.

Matthews, T. J., and Brady Hamilton. 2016. "Mean Age of Mothers Is on the Rise: United States, 2000–2014." NCHS Data Brief 32. US Department of Health and Human Services, National Center for Health Statistics.

McKernan, Signe-Mary, Caroline Ratcliffe, Eugene Steuerle, and Sisi Zhang. 2014. "Impact of the Great Recession and Beyond: Disparities in Wealth Building by Generation and Race." Washington, DC: Urban Institute.

Mitchell, Olivia S., Robert Clark, and Raimond Maurer, eds. 2018. *How Persistent Low Returns Will Shape Saving and Retirement.* Oxford University Press.

Morisi, Teri. 2016. "Why More People Ages 55+ Are Working." *US Department of Labor Blog*, November 18.

Munnell, Alicia H. 2015. "The Average Retirement Age—An Update." Center for Retirement Research, Boston College.

Munnell, Alicia H., Wenliang Hou, and Geoffrey T. Sanzenbacher. 2016. "How Much Does Housing Affect Retirement Security? An NRRI Update." Center for Retirement Research, Boston College.

———. 2018a. "National Retirement Risk Index Shows Modest Improvement in 2016." Center for Retirement Research, Boston College.

———. 2018b. "Trends in Retirement Security by Race/Ethnicity." Center for Retirement Research, Boston College.

National Academy of Sciences. 2015. "The Growing Gap in Life Expectancy by Income: Implications for Federal Programs and Policy Responses." Committee on the Long-Run Macroeconomic Effects of the Aging US Population. Washington, DC: National Academies Press.

Pang, Gaobo, and Mark Warshawsky. 2014. "Retirement Savings Adequacy of US Workers." *Benefits Quarterly* (First Quarter): 29–38.

Pence, Karen M. 2002. "401(k)s and Household Saving: New Evidence from the Survey of Consumer Finances." Finance and Economics Discussion Series Working Paper 2002–06. Washington, DC: Board of Governors of the Federal Reserve System.

———. 2006. "The Role of Wealth Transformations: An Application to Estimating the Effect of Tax Incentives on Saving." *Contributions to Economic Analysis and Policy* 5 (1): article 20.

Pew Research Center. 2011. "Twenty-to-One: Wealth Gaps Rise to Record Highs between Whites, Blacks, and Hispanics." Washington, DC.

Poterba, James. 2014. "Retirement Security in an Aging Society." NBER Working Paper 19930. Cambridge, MA: National Bureau of Economic Research.

Poterba, James, Steven Venti, and David Wise. 2015. "What Determines End-of-Life Assets? A Retrospective View." NBER Working Paper 21682. Cambridge, MA: National Bureau of Economic Research.

Rhee, Nari. 2013a. "Race and Retirement Insecurity in the United States." Washington, DC: National Institute on Retirement Security.

———. 2013b. "The Retirement Savings Crisis: Is It Worse than We Think?" Washington, DC: National Institute on Retirement Security.

Scholz, John Karl, and Kara Levine. 2003. "U.S. Black-White Wealth Inequality: A Survey." Institute for Research on Poverty, University of Wisconsin—Madison.

Scholz, John Karl, and Ananth Seshadri. 2009. "What Replacement Rates Should Households Use?" Michigan Center for Retirement Research Paper 2009–214. https://dx.doi.org/10.2139/ssrn.1513387.

Scholz, John Karl, Ananth Seshadri, and Surachai Khitatrakun. 2006. "Are Americans Saving Optimally for Retirement?" *Journal of Political Economy* 114 (4): 607–43.

Shapiro, Thomas, Tatjana Meschede, and Sam Osoro. 2013. "The Roots of the Widening Racial Wealth Gap: Explaining the Black-White Economic Divide." Institute on Assets and Social Policy Research Brief. Brandeis University.

———. 2014. "The Widening Racial Wealth Gap: Why Wealth Is Not Color Blind." In *The Assets Perspective*, edited by Reid Cramer and Trina R. Williams Shanks. New York: Palgrave Macmillan.

Song, Jae, and Joyce Manchester. 2007. "Have People Delayed Claiming Retirement Benefits? Responses to Changes in Social Security Rules." *Social Security Bulletin* 67 (2): 1–23.

Stock, James, and David Wise. 1990. "Pensions, the Option Value of Work and Retirement." *Econometrica* 58 (5): 1151–80.

Summers, Lawrence H. 2016. "The Age of Secular Stagnation: What It Is and What to Do about It." *Foreign Affairs*, February 15.

Taylor, Paul, Rakesh Kochhar, Richard Fry, Gabriel Velasco, and Seth Motel. 2011. "Wealth Gaps Rise to Record Highs between Whites, Blacks, and Hispanics." Pew Social & Demographic Trends. Washington, DC: Pew Research Center.

Thompson, Jeffrey P., and Gustavo A. Suarez. 2015. "Exploring the Racial Wealth Gap Using the Survey of Consumer Finances." Finance and Economics Discussion Series 2015–076. Washington, DC: Board of Governors of the Federal Reserve System.

US Bureau of Labor Statistics. 2018. "Contingent and Alternative Employment Arrangements—May 2017." Washington, DC: US Department of Labor.

US Census Bureau. 2015. "Millennials Outnumber Baby Boomers and Are Far More Diverse, Census Bureau Reports." Release CB15-113. Washington, DC.

———. 2017. "Table MS-2. Estimated Median Age at First Marriage, by Sex: 1890 to the Present." Washington, DC: US Department of Commerce.

———. 2018. "2017 National Population Projections Datasets." Washington, DC: US Department of Commerce.

US Government Accountability Office. 2015. “Contingent Workforce: Size, Characteristics, Earnings, and Benefits.” Washington, DC.

VanDerhei, Jack. 2014. “What Causes EBRI Retirement Readiness Ratings to Vary: Results from the 2014 Retirement Security Projection Model.” Issue Brief 396. Washington, DC: Employee Benefit Research Institute.

VanDerhei, Jack, and Craig Copeland. 2010. “The EBRI Retirement Readiness Rating: Retirement Income Preparation and Future Prospects.” Issue Brief 344. Washington, DC: Employee Benefit Research Institute.

Vespa, Jonathan. 2017. “The Changing Economics and Demographics of Young Adulthood: 1975–2016.” Current Population Reports. Washington, DC: US Census Bureau.

Welch, Finis. 1979. “Effects of Cohort Size on Earnings: The Baby Boom Babies’ Financial Bust.” *Journal of Political Economy* 87 (5): S65–S97.

Wolff, Edward N. 2018. “The Decline of African-American and Hispanic Wealth since the Great Recession.” NBER Working Paper 25198. Cambridge, MA: National Bureau of Economic Research.

TWO

Changing Wealth Accumulation Patterns

EVIDENCE AND DETERMINANTS

William G. Gale and Benjamin H. Harris

The patterns and determinants of household wealth accumulation have long been of interest to economists, with seminal contributions dating back at least to Modigliani and Brumberg ([1954] 2005), Friedman (1957), and Ando and Modigliani (1963). Recent work by Piketty (2014) and Saez and Zucman (2019) has sparked a new generation of research interest in this topic.

Wealth accumulation is of interest for several reasons. At the household level, wealth provides a source of future consumption, as well as insurance against adverse economic shocks. At the aggregate level, wealth finances domestic and foreign investment, affects current consumption spending, and influences the efficacy of monetary and fiscal interventions. More broadly, the sheer magnitude of changes in aggregate household wealth relative to gross domestic product (GDP) in recent decades merits attention.

Documenting and determining the causes of changes in the level and distribution of household wealth and its components across generations and over time is an extraordinarily ambitious goal. This chapter takes an initial step in that general direction, building on Gale, Gelfond, and Fichtner (2019) and Gale and Pence (2006). Using data from the Federal Reserve Board's Survey of Consumer Finances (SCF) we document how mean and median household wealth levels have changed for households of given ages across different birth cohorts and we explore the determinants of those changes.

Our main results can be summarized in three statements. First, the Great Recession in 2007–2009 reduced wealth in all age groups. Second, the broader long-term trend has been that the wealth of older age groups has increased, while the wealth of successive cross-sections of younger age groups has fallen. Third, a significant share of these changes, in both directions, can be explained by the evolution of household demographic and economic characteristics.

The rest of the chapter is organized as follows. We describe the SCF data, then follow with background data and context for the analysis. We then present descriptive data on mean and median net worth for constant-age categories across birth cohorts. We follow with an analytical framework for examining the determinants of wealth change. We then present the main empirical results and analysis, followed by a discussion of preliminary policy implications and how the analysis could be extended in future research.

SURVEY OF CONSUMER FINANCES

The SCF is a triennial household survey that is generally considered to provide the most reliable and complete survey-based measures of household wealth (or net worth, terms we use interchangeably below).[1] The surveys covering the period 1989 to 2016 follow a generally consistent methodology. Raw sample sizes vary from about 3,100 to about 6,200 in surveys during that period.

To capture how assets and debts are held broadly in the population, about two-thirds of the unweighted sample is drawn from a stratified, nationally representative random sample. The remainder of the sample is randomly selected from statistical records derived from tax returns, using a stratification technique that oversamples households likely to have substantial wealth. This sample design allows for more efficient and less biased estimates of wealth than are feasible through simpler designs. In particular, oversampling the wealthy is an important component of the survey, because wealth is so highly concentrated. All of the data presented in this chapter represent weighted statistics, using the sample weights provided by the SCF, which correct for selection probabilities and nonresponse.

The SCF covers all age groups and almost all household assets and liabilities, with two notable exceptions. First, the survey excludes households in the Forbes 400, which would be easily identifiable in the data. Second, because the SCF defines net worth as resources that a household has access to and can control immediately, the survey does not report defined benefit (DB) pension wealth—the present value of future income (minus future contributions) that households expect to receive from DB pension plans. To present a more complete analysis of household wealth, we add to the SCF definition of net worth a measure of the present value of DB wealth, following Sabelhaus and Volz (2019).

Our resulting wealth definition, like the SCF's, does not include future Social Security or Medicare benefits (or taxes), which often constitute a significant share of households' resources in retirement.[2]

The SCF also includes information on household demographic characteristics, income, attitudes, and current and past jobs. Some of the survey responses represent the head of household (e.g., age, gender, and level of education), while some represent the respondent (race and attitudinal feedback). Asset, debt, and income measures reflect the total value held by a household in certain categories.

The SCF uses a multiple imputation procedure to fill in missing data. Five implicates form an approximate distribution of the missing data, creating a sample that is five times larger than the actual sample. For descriptive statistics, we use all five implicates by dividing the sample weights by five. In our regressions, we use the first implicate only because using all five would inflate statistical significance.

For some purposes below, we divide household net worth into four mutually exclusive and exhaustive categories. Net financial assets include all financial assets except retirement accounts less unsecured debt (including student loans). Housing wealth is the difference between the value of the household's primary residence, if any, and the outstanding mortgage(s) against the primary residence. Retirement wealth is the sum of balances in defined contribution accounts, IRAs, and Keoghs, plus the present value of future defined benefit income (minus future contributions). Other wealth is the residual category and includes businesses, vehicles, second homes, and other items.

BACKGROUND AND CONTEXT

Aggregate household net worth rose from $20.6 trillion (3.7 times GDP) in 1989 to $89.2 trillion (4.8 times GDP) in 2016, the first and last years for which we have SCF data.[3] While macro factors clearly have affected the level of household wealth, micro factors may also play an important role (Gale and Pence 2006). A substantial share of the micro research on household saving and consumption focuses explicitly or implicitly on variations of the life-cycle/permanent income hypothesis, in which households equalize the marginal utility of consumption over time. The framework is quite flexible and can incorporate borrowing constraints, family formation, bequest motives, health shocks, uncertain income, and many other considerations. Most life-cycle models predict that households will accrue some debt before entering the labor market, will accumulate net wealth during their working life, and then spend down their assets to some extent in retirement (Browning and Crossley 2001; Fieveson and Sabelhaus 2019). Using a broad version of the life-cycle framework as motivation, this section provides background information on several factors that have changed over time and plausibly influenced the level or composition of household wealth accumulation between 1989 and 2016. The SCF-based statistics used below are reported in 2016 dollars and are summarized in table 2-1.

Aging

The population aged considerably between 1989 and 2016. For example, the share of households with heads age 45 and older rose from 50.4 percent in 1989 to 62.9 percent in 2016. This trend affects aggregate household wealth accumulation for the simple reason that wealth tends to rise with a household head's age, at least through the working years. For example, in 1989, average net worth among households headed by someone 55–64 years old was more than twice as large as for households headed by someone 35–44 years old. Multiplying the 2016 average net worth of each age category by the groups' 1989 population share shows that if the age distribution had not changed, average net worth in 2016 would have been about $705,000 (as opposed to the actual average of about $761,000). That is, the aging of the population alone explains about one-sixth of the difference in average household net worth between 1989 and 2016.

Student Loans

The prevalence and average size of student loan debt exploded between 1989 and 2016. For example, in 1989, 24 percent of households with heads 25–34 years of age held student debt, and the average balance among debtholders was about $12,000. By 2016, these figures had increased to 40 percent and $36,000.

The impact of rising student debt on wealth accumulation depends critically on why debt rose. To the extent that it is due to increases in high-quality educational attainment, rising student debt is financing investments in human capital that will be associated with higher lifetime earnings and could therefore raise lifetime wealth accumulation. In contrast, to the extent that it is due to lower public spending on higher education, or to spending on low-quality

Table 2-1. *Summary Statistics by Age and Year*

Variable	*Age*	*1989*	*2007*	*2016*
Population share (percent)	<25	5.8	5.4	4.9
	25–34	22.4	16.2	15.3
	35–44	21.5	19.6	16.8
	45–54	15.1	20.8	18.3
	55–64	13.9	16.8	19.2
	65–74	12.6	10.5	14.1
	75+	8.9	10.6	11.2
Mean net worth ($ thousands)	<25	23	55	95
	25–34	131	169	107
	35–44	335	469	378
	45–54	661	955	883
	55–64	731	1310	1,419
	65–74	659	1318	1,292
	75+	484	798	1,154
Has student debt (percent)	<25	24.0	30.7	40.2
	25–34	15.3	34.6	46.2
	35–44	10.9	14.7	34.3
	45–54	7.3	14.5	23.7
	55–64	4.1	10.6	12.9
	65–74	0.9	1.7	3.4
	75+	0.0	0.3	1.1
Average student loan debt, conditional on having student loans ($ thousands)	<25	7	18	22
	25–34	12	30	36
	35–44	9	22	35
	45–54	12	24	37
	55–64	6	21	34
	65–74	10	23	35
	75+	0	23	29
Homeownership (percent)	<25	11.7	12.2	11.2
	25–34	46.4	50.1	40.2
	35–44	66.1	66.1	57.8
	45–54	76.4	77.3	68.8
	55–64	80.1	81.0	73.7
	65–74	77.8	85.5	79.1
	75+	69.9	77.0	83.1

(*continued*)

Table 2-1. *(continued)*

Variable	*Age*	*1989*	*2007*	*2016*
Married (percent)	<25	29.5	42.7	34.7
	25–34	63.3	67.2	57.8
	35–44	66.5	63.8	63.9
	45–54	65.6	62.2	62.0
	55–64	60.5	59.0	58.2
	65–74	49.9	61.0	54.2
	75+	39.3	36.1	46.2
Defined benefit (DB) only (percent)	<25	4.4	4.9	2.2
	25–34	16.4	7.5	8.9
	35–44	27.6	7.7	9.7
	45–54	33.5	12.1	11.0
	55–64	40.9	27.0	21.9
	65–74	55.6	41.2	42.2
	75+	45.7	51.6	49.9
Defined contribution (DC) only (percent)	<25	4.8	19.8	19.3
	25–34	18.8	32.7	31.6
	35–44	17.7	31.2	36.1
	45–54	13.2	29.6	35.1
	55–64	10.4	22.6	22.2
	65–74	1.1	7.3	8.3
	75+	0.0	3.7	3.2
Both DB and DC (percent)	<25	1.3	0.5	0.5
	25–34	11.2	5.9	7.3
	35–44	19.5	14.4	9.0
	45–54	21.5	21.6	11.7
	55–64	11.8	15.1	15.5
	65–74	1.4	7.8	8.4
	75+	0.0	0.3	3.0
Neither DB nor DC (percent)	<25	89.5	74.9	78.0
	25–34	53.5	53.8	52.2
	35–44	35.2	46.7	45.2
	45–54	31.8	36.8	42.2
	55–64	37.0	35.2	40.5
	65–74	42.0	43.7	41.1
	75+	54.3	44.3	43.9

Source: Board of Governors of the Federal Reserve System (2017).

institutions, the rise in student debt is similar to a negative wealth shock and can be expected to reduce wealth accumulation trajectories across cohorts.

Evidence shows that the sharp increase in debt is due to a combination of rising gross and net tuition prices, changing composition of education (including increased attendance at for-profit schools and in graduate programs), and changing composition of student borrowers.[4] Recent analyses suggest that higher student debt may delay people's decisions to marry and buy a house and may affect early-career choice of occupation. Evidence regarding the impact on people's willingness to make retirement contributions is mixed.[5]

Homeownership

Primary residences are the largest asset for many households and a principal vehicle through which households accumulate wealth. Homeownership rates generally rose from 1989 to 2007, then fell significantly in the Great Recession. Since then, the aggregate homeownership rate has fallen back to 1989 levels. Controlling for age, however, the figures changed substantially. Relative to 1989, homeownership rates were substantially lower in 2016 for households under the age of 65 but higher for households age 65 and older. Housing values followed a similar time pattern as aggregate homeownership rates, rising from 1989 to 2007, falling sharply in the Great Recession, and recovering since then.[6] Mean age of first-time homeownership has risen by four years since the 1980s.

The decline in housing price growth, housing equity, and the rate of homeownership for younger households does not necessarily imply, in isolation, that aggregate wealth accumulation patterns are changing. In theory, households substitute housing investment with other forms of investment—financial assets in particular. However, the decline in ownership for younger households does not necessarily imply a rise in nonhousing saving; for example, Fisher and Gervais (2011) attribute the bulk of the long-term decline in younger household homeownership to a combination of delayed marriage and increased earnings risk.

RETIREMENT SAVING

The retirement saving landscape has undergone a massive shift over time from defined benefit plans to defined contribution plans. In 1989, more than 31 percent of households were covered by a DB plan but not a DC plan, a figure that fell below 21 percent in 2016. In contrast, the share covered by a DC plan but not a DB rose from about 12 to 24 percent. The share of households with no retirement plan remained roughly constant around 45 percent.

The switch from defined benefit pensions to defined contribution retirement plans can have subtle impacts on wealth accumulation. First, pension wealth accumulates in a back-loaded manner in DB plans relative to DC plans. Consider two workers who are identical in every way except one has a DB plan that pays $30,000 per year at retirement and the other has a DC plan that features contributions equal to a constant share of earnings and pays $30,000 per year at retirement upon conversion to an annuity. (Assume the employer makes all contributions to both accounts.) Because benefits accrue more slowly under the typical DB plan than under the DC plan, reported measures of wealth accumulation will show the first worker having less wealth than the second worker at any given age before retirement, even though the plans give the workers equal amounts of income in retirement.

A second factor is that households may consider DB plans to be less substitutable for ordinary saving than DC plans are. DC plans typically have provisions for hardship or early withdrawal, and workers typically have control over the level of contributions. Both factors make DC plans better substitutes for ordinary saving than DB plans are. To the extent that a tax-deferred saving vehicle is more substitutable for ordinary saving, contributions to that tax-deferred saving vehicle are less likely to represent net additions to saving (Engen, Gale, and Scholz 1996).

HOUSEHOLD FORMATION AND FERTILITY

Over time, the age of first marriage and the age when having one's first child have increased. For example, in 1989, 63 percent of household heads 25–34 years old were married, and 60 percent of all households in this age group had children. By 2016, these figures had fallen to 58 percent and 51 percent, respectively. The trends were different in older households, though. Among households age 65 and older, the share represented by married couples rose significantly over the same period. As a result, the share of all households that are married did not change very much over the sample period.

The delay in marriage among younger households likely reduces wealth accumulation at earlier ages. Marriage is associated with wealth building through several channels, including two-earner households, economies of scale, and higher rates of homeownership (Grinstein-Weiss and others 2008; Vespa and Painter 2011). While the precise impact of marriage per se is complicated by the potential for cohabitation, the substantial delay in marriage may well have an impact on the trajectory of wealth for younger households. In contrast, later-in-life childbearing and lower fertility rates may increase wealth accumulation (Scholz and Seshadri 2007).

Wages

SCF data show that average household wages (which aggregate the wages of married couples) rose by about 20 percent from 1989 to 2007 and were at about the same level in 2016 as in 2007. The data show increases in all constant-age groups and in particular in households in the 55–74 age group. The latter result may be due to changing female labor force participation and delayed retirement. Guvenen and others (2017) show that lifetime earnings were stagnant or fell for successive generations of males that reached age 25 in 1957 through 2013, but rose somewhat for females (from a very low base).

AGE-WEALTH PROFILES

Figure 2-1 shows median age-wealth profiles for constant-age groups over time. The data are scaled so that each generation's 1989 value is set to 100. The graph demonstrates two points. First, the Great Recession in 2007–2009 significantly reduced household wealth in all age groups. Second, younger age groups have been doing far worse than older age groups. For example, in 2016, all groups age 55 and older had more median wealth than their 1989 counterparts. Households in the 25–34 age group in 2016—roughly the millennial generation—held about 12 percent less wealth than did households of the same age in 1989.

Figure 2-2 shows scaled mean age-wealth profiles. Because of the growth of income and wealth at the top of the distribution, the mean increases exceed the median increases, but they follow the same general pattern, with wealth rising much more slowly for younger age groups than for older age groups.

Appendix tables 2A-1 and 2A-2 report median and mean net worth levels by age and year.

MODELING THE EFFECTS OF DEMOGRAPHIC CHANGES ON WEALTH

We analyze the influence of changes in demographic characteristics on wealth accumulation across cohorts by utilizing basic median and ordinary least squares regressions, in the absence and presence of demographic variables.

Figure 2-1. **Median Age-Wealth Profiles by Constant-Age Group (scaled, 1989 = 100)**

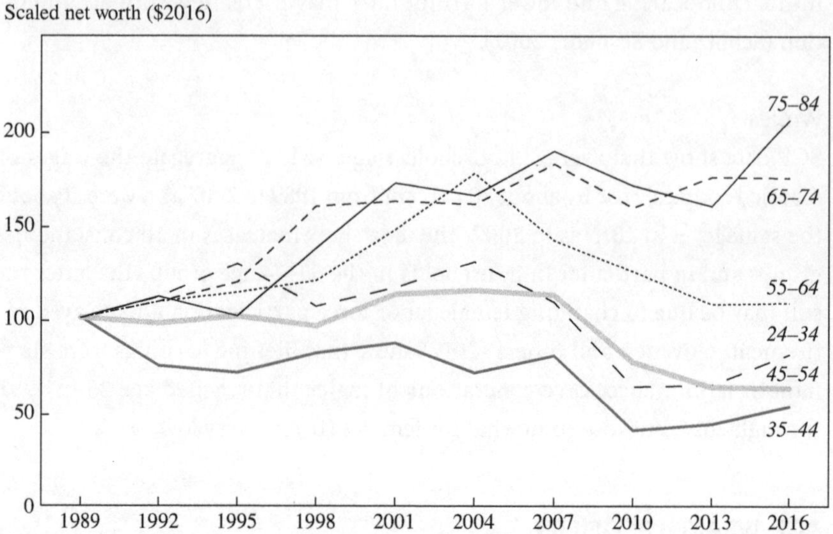

Source: Federal Reserve Board of Governors Survey of Consumer Finances (1989–2016), https://www.federalreserve.gov/econres/scfindex.htm.

Figure 2-2. **Average Age-Wealth Profiles by Constant-Age Group (scaled, 1989 = 100)**

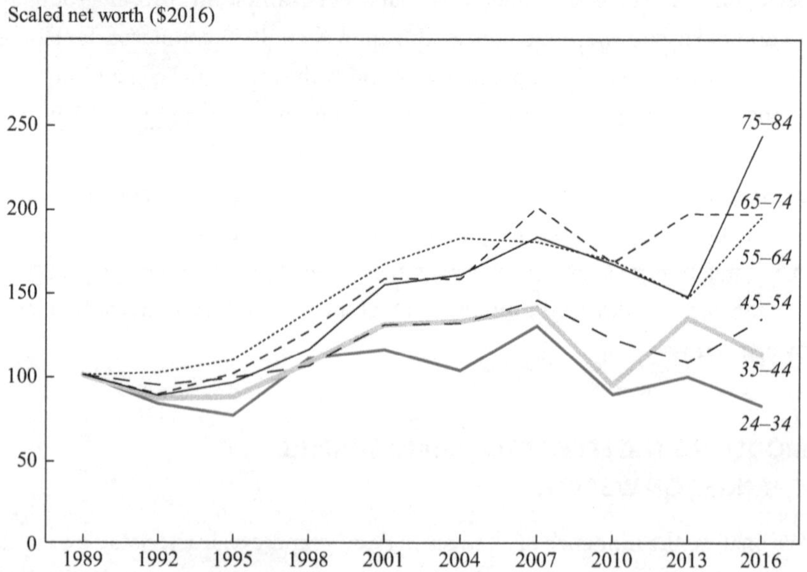

Source: Federal Reserve Board of Governors Survey of Consumer Finances (1989–2016), https://www.federalreserve.gov/econres/scfindex.htm.

Basic Regressions

We run median (least absolute deviation or LAD) regressions and ordinary least squares regressions, pooling data from the 1989 and 2016 SCFs. We break the data into four age-category subsets, one for 25–34-year-olds, one for 35–44-year-olds, one for 45–54-year-olds, and one for 55–64-year-olds. For each household *i* in each age category *k*, we specify wealth as a function of a constant and a survey year indicator variable:

$$w_{k1} = \alpha_{k1} + \beta_{k1}(\text{year} = 2016)_i + \varepsilon_{k1i} \tag{2-1}$$

In this model, the coefficient β_{k1} captures the change in median or mean wealth between the 1989 and 2016 samples of each age category.

In a second basic regression specification, we add a vector of demographic indicators, denoted by *X*. This demographic specification is described in detail below.

$$w_{k2} = \alpha_{k2} + \beta_{k2}\,(\text{year} = 2016)_i + \gamma_{k2}\,Xi + \varepsilon_{k2i} \tag{2-2}$$

If demographic changes explain most of the difference in wealth between 1989 and 2016 for age category *k*, β_{k2} should be close to zero, and the coefficients for the variables in the demographic vector should be statistically significant.

The specifications above assume that the relationship between wealth and demographic characteristics is the same in both years (other than a shift in the intercept), an assumption that does not apply to the mean-based decomposition described below.

Specification of Demographic Characteristics

Each of the analyses we describe above uses a vector of demographic variables, denoted as *X*. This vector is constructed from SCF data, which are constrained in a few important ways. First, the survey respondent and the household head are not necessarily the same person. The SCF designates the household head as the man in a mixed-gender relationship and the older partner in a same-gender relationship, while the respondent is (supposed to be) the person most familiar with the family's finances. The SCF reports the race of the survey respondent, not of the household head. Similarly, it reports the educational attainment of only the household head.

As a result, demographic characteristics do not always map neatly onto households, our unit of observation. For instance, in the 2001 SCF, mixed-gender partnerships accounted for 87 percent of responses, but an estimated

46 percent of respondents from mixed-gender partnerships were female; the respondent and the household head were different in at least 40 percent of surveyed households (Lindamood, Hanna, and Bi 2007). And while partners are often people of similar demographic characteristics, this is not always the case, so demographic insights must be constrained to reflect this uncertainty.

A second constraint on demographic insights is sample size. Because we are analyzing changes among age groups within years, our sample sizes are fairly limited, ranging from 452 to 1,446 people per age group per year. Notably, 2016 sample sizes for each age group are about two to three times the size of the sample sizes of the same age groups in 1989. The uncertainty this introduces will manifest in standard errors and significance levels, which are reported in our results.

Our demographic vector includes the following characteristics: race, marital status, sex, educational attainment, and income category.[7]

Race, as described above, applies to the race of the respondent, and is reported as indicator variables over each of the four categories: non-Hispanic white, Black, Hispanic, or other (including those of Asian and Native descent). Non-Hispanic white is the omitted category.

Marital status reflects whether the household consists of a single financially independent adult or two financially interdependent adults. Importantly, the survey does not distinguish between two financially interdependent unmarried people living together and a married couple. We use an indicator for "marriage" to describe those households with two financially interdependent adults. Single households are the omitted category.

We control for the sex of the household head. But, as described above, the household head is either a man, a single female head of household, or the older member of a same-sex female couple, so it is more accurately interpreted as the presence or absence of a man in the primary economic unit. Single male is the omitted category.

The educational attainment variable reflects the maximum educational attainment of the household head. This is represented through indicators for each of the following categories: less than a high school diploma, high school diploma, some college, bachelor's degree, and graduate degree. Less than a high school diploma is the omitted category.

We also include an income category variable to reflect the household's reported income level, with an indicator for each level. The income cutoffs are $20,000, $50,000, $100,000, and $200,000. Less than $20,000 is the omitted category.

Specification of the Dependent Variable

We employ two different wealth specifications, one that uses the level of wealth, and one that uses the inverse hyperbolic sine transformation of wealth. The results derived from the level-of-wealth analysis describe absolute changes in wealth over the period, while the results from the inverse hyperbolic sine specification describe proportional changes in wealth over the period. We use this transformation, instead of the more traditional logarithmic transformation, because it approximates the logarithm while remaining defined for the nonpositive values common in wealth data.

More formally, if θ is a scaling parameter and w is a measure of wealth, the inverse hyperbolic sine of wealth can be written as $\theta^{-1}\sinh^{-1}(\theta w) = \theta^{-1} \ln\left[\theta w + (\theta^2 w^2 + 1)^{\frac{1}{2}}\right]$. This symmetric function is linear around the origin but approximates the logarithm for larger values of wealth. To see this, note that if w is large, $\ln\left[\theta w + (\theta^2 w^2 + 1)^{\frac{1}{2}}\right] \approx \ln 2\theta + \ln w$, which is simply a vertical displacement of the logarithm. Following previous research and our own prior methodology, we set $\theta = 0.0001$.[8] When multiplied by this scaling parameter, coefficients and standard errors from an inverse hyperbolic sine specification, like logarithmic coefficients and standard errors, can be interpreted as the percentage change in wealth implied by a change in a particular demographic characteristic, assuming that wealth values are sufficiently large.[9]

Results

Table 2-2 reports results from median regressions. The first specification follows equation 2-1 in the chapter, explaining the level of household wealth as a function only of a constant and an indicator for whether the observation occurred in 2016. The constant term replicates the 1989 median age-wealth profile shown in appendix table 2A-1. The 2016 indicator shows that median wealth was substantially lower in 2016 than in 1989 for households age 35–44 and 45–54—by about \$77,000 and \$97,000, respectively. Median wealth for 25–34-year-olds and 55–64-year-olds was not significantly different in the two sample years.

The effects shown in table 2-2 could be due to changes in the general economic environment and/or to changes in specific household characteristics. To isolate the impact of these two groups of determinants, the second specification includes several household-level demographic variables, following equation 2-2.

The results show that changes in household characteristics reduced wealth for households in the 25–54 age group in 2016 relative to 1989 but raised wealth

Table 2-2.

Pooled (Least Absolute Deviations), 1989–2016

	(1) *25–34*	*(2)* *35–44*	*(3)* *45–54*	*(4)* *55–64*
Constant	28,344*** (4,933)	165,024*** (17,388)	267,826*** (27,166)	303,986*** (31,336)
Year 2016	−3,504 (5,971)	−77,124*** (19,188)	−96,826*** (31,389)	14,777 (39,818)
Observations	1,250	1,712	1,848	2,015

Robust standard errors in parentheses.
*** $p < 0.01$, ** $p < 0.05$, * $p < 0.1$.

Pooled (Least Absolute Deviations), 1989–2016

	(1) *25–34*	*(2)* *35–44*	*(3)* *45–54*	*(4)* *55–64*
Constant	3,920 (3,190)	30,074*** (11,528)	65,327*** (13,574)	79,198*** (13,388)
Year 2016	−5,593*** (1,851)	−15,531*** (4,845)	−54,126*** (4,273)	−28,942** (13,631)
Black	−3,455 (2,494)	−26,437*** (7,304)	−39,108*** (10,299)	−48,274*** (12,695)
Hispanic	−3,828 (2,548)	−30,169*** (8,094)	−48,019*** (16,030)	−50,256*** (16,682)
Other race	3,614 (13,758)	9,675 (17,545)	−9,410 (43,261)	−186,183 (122,426)
Married	5,531 (3,471)	13,188 (11,361)	27,567* (14,096)	35,934* (19,371)
Female head of household	−91.99 (2,430)	−3,637 (9,633)	−17,308** (7,494)	−30,924*** (10,544)
High school	−373.2 (1,290)	858.3 (5,730)	11,117 (8,802)	1,908 (17,342)
Some college	3,143 (2,458)	1,191 (5,337)	41,406*** (15,508)	37,743 (26,406)
Bachelor's degree	7,435 (6,183)	5,598 (17,855)	69,355** (33,578)	124,374*** (46,634)
Graduate degree	−10,080 (7,310)	53,990 (33,056)	191,573*** (39,322)	353,881*** (40,847)

(continued)

Table 2-2. *(continued)*

Pooled (Least Absolute Deviations), 1989–2016

	(1) 25–34	(2) 35–44	(3) 45–54	(4) 55–64
Income \$20,000–\$49,999	8,814*** (2,210)	15,755*** (3,608)	27,701*** (9,801)	77,470*** (15,622)
Income \$50,000–\$99,999	61,027*** (8,297)	105,037*** (12,188)	138,641*** (17,915)	250,679*** (31,010)
Income \$100,000–199,999	192,005*** (18,780)	330,295*** (29,884)	440,104*** (37,589)	931,367*** (81,094)
Income 200,000+	552,695*** (63,712)	692,671*** (126,735)	1.762e+06*** (210,929)	3.320e+06*** (387,076)
Observations	1,250	1,712	1,848	2,015

Source: Board of Governors of the Federal Reserve System (2017).
Robust standard errors in parentheses.
*** $p < 0.01$, ** $p < 0.05$, * $p < 0.1$.

for households in the 55–64 age group over the same period. For example, for households aged 35–44, the coefficient on the 2016 indicator was about –\$54,000, compared to about –\$97,000 in the first specification. This implies that changes in household characteristics explain about 45 percent of the decline in wealth for this age group over time.

Likewise, for households aged 35–44, the 2016 effect reduced wealth by \$77,000 when demographic variables were excluded but by only \$15,000 when demographic variables were included. Thus more than 80 percent of the decline in wealth for that group can be explained by demographic factors.

In contrast, for households aged 55–64, the coefficient on the 2016 indicator is about –\$29,000, which is lower (algebraically) than the coefficient in the first equation—which is about \$15,000—but not significantly different from zero.

The coefficients on the demographic variables are consistent with much prior work. Households that are Black or Hispanic have lower wealth than other households, even after controlling for observables. Households in which the head has more formal education and/or higher income accumulate more wealth. To some extent, married households have more wealth and female-headed households often have lower wealth.

Table 2-3 repeats the exercise using mean (ordinary least squares) regressions. The first specification shows that average wealth rises substantially in the 45–54 and 55–64 age groups. Coupled with the changes in median wealth

Table 2-3.

Pooled (Least Squares), 1989–2016

	(1) 25–34	(2) 35–44	(3) 45–54	(4) 55–64
Constant	137,580***	324,112***	642,123***	720,288***
	(19,883)	(21,669)	(43,958)	(50,043)
Year 2016	−29,057	51,286	239,161***	678,944***
	(21,870)	(34,665)	(72,015)	(85,037)
Observations	1,250	1,712	1,848	2,015
R-squared	0.001	0.000	0.001	0.003

Robust standard errors in parentheses.
*** $p < 0.01$, ** $p < 0.05$, * $p < 0.1$.

Pooled (Least Squares), 1989–2016

	(1) 25–34	(2) 35–44	(3) 45–54	(4) 55–64
Constant	39,433	116,867**	288,633***	90,083
	(26,654)	(48,669)	(86,452)	(79,836)
Year 2016	−45,801	23,300	86,261	228,623***
	(29,179)	(32,799)	(64,748)	(82,572)
Black	−31,235**	−72,481***	−158,248***	−117,262***
	(13,747)	(24,152)	(50,633)	(42,454)
Hispanic	−1,583	−70,476***	−223,419***	−98,899
	(18,388)	(22,248)	(73,088)	(114,311)
Other race	96,456	88,757	−312,730	−176,079
	(114,685)	(102,032)	(198,873)	(208,243)
Married	−16,724	−81,212	−63,855	32,847
	(40,366)	(69,203)	(78,603)	(97,075)
Female head of household	−68,678*	−108,210**	−184,932***	−183,642**
	(39,782)	(50,805)	(64,980)	(85,200)
High school	22,449	−2,743	−49,880	−39,510
	(18,222)	(24,304)	(69,432)	(72,367)
Some college	52,286**	492.3	−77,073	64,189
	(23,852)	(24,963)	(78,077)	(93,117)
Bachelor's degree	81,266**	102,380**	158,422	453,799***
	(31,810)	(43,964)	(124,104)	(154,877)

(continued)

Table 2-3. *(continued)*

Pooled (Least Squares), 1989–2016

	(1) 25–34	(2) 35–44	(3) 45–54	(4) 55–64
Graduate degree	125,120 (104,349)	86,950 (67,423)	274,424 (187,570)	815,027*** (223,226)
Income \$20,000–\$49,999	33,828 (30,250)	25,129 (16,272)	2,574 (43,827)	15,576 (40,098)
Income \$50,000–\$99,999	74,576*** (20,560)	153,071*** (28,784)	146,827** (61,597)	196,780*** (65,308)
Income \$100,000–\$199,999	227,544*** (37,855)	426,417*** (41,490)	554,695*** (91,061)	921,836*** (110,392)
Income \$200,000+	749,899*** (128,048)	1.788e+06*** (219,066)	3.984e+06*** (340,753)	5.878e+06*** (405,410)
Observations	1,250	1,712	1,848	2,015
R-squared	0.078	0.023	0.118	0.109

Source: Board of Governors of the Federal Reserve System (2017).
Robust standard errors in parentheses.
*** $p < 0.01$, ** $p < 0.05$, * $p < 0.1$.

shown in table 2-2, these figures suggest a substantial widening of the distribution of wealth in those age groups over time.

The second specification shows, again, that changes in household demographic variables served to raise wealth substantially in the 55–64 age group. More than two-thirds of the increase in wealth in that age group documented in the first specification can be explained by changes in demographic characteristics in the second specification.

The impacts of the individual demographic variables are qualitatively similar to those found in the median regressions in table 2-2: minorities and female-headed households have less wealth; households in which the head is married or has more formal education, or in which income is higher, tend to have higher wealth.

Appendix tables 2A-1 and 2A-2 provide regression results using the hyperbolic sine of wealth as the dependent variable and generate broadly similar conclusions.

POLICY IMPLICATIONS

This chapter aims to document and explain changing wealth levels across the life cycle. There is good reason to believe that the path of wealth accumulation is changing for American households. The economics literature suggests that many determinants of wealth accumulation are shifting later in life. Young workers are more frequently entering their working years with substantial student debt, including in particular higher debt for those who attended for-profit institutions. The mean age of entering into homeownership—one of the most prominent forms of wealth accumulation—has increased by four years since the early 1980s. The ongoing transformation from defined benefit plans to defined contribution plans can, for some workers, mean diminished retirement savings through middle-age. Marriage—also a determinant of wealth—typically takes place about seven years later than it did in the 1950s. And while wages are rising for all groups, mean increases are higher for older workers.

Not all trends suggest that wealth accumulation should be occurring later in life. For example, Americans are increasingly choosing to have children later in life, which can depress middle-age wealth accumulation. On the whole, however, the bulk of the evidence provides support for the view that wealth accumulation trends should be shifting later in life.

Indeed, we find empirical support for this view. Our analysis suggests that while the Great Recession reduced wealth in all age groups, we also find a longer-term trend of increasing wealth in older age groups paired with falling wealth among younger households. We show that a significant share of these changes can be attributed to the evolution of household demographic and economic characteristics.

This topic is primed for future study. To start, future research can address changing wealth patterns by race, sex, educational attainment, and marital status. Given that many of the changing wealth determinants can be expected to have differential impact along these margins, further studying trends along these lines is an important extension of the research on wealth accumulation. In addition, this research can be extended to address the lack of a lifelong, high-quality panel dataset measuring changes in wealth and incorporating multiple waves of respondents. One potential strategy for addressing this concern is to construct a synthetic microdata set that allows for the comparison of wealth accumulation patterns across successive birth cohorts. In addition, more research is needed to quantify the changing relationship between various determinants of wealth and observed wealth accumulation, including the wealth determinants we discuss above and others not identified in this chapter. Last, further attention can be directed at determining the impact of changing wealth trajectories on aggregate wealth inequality. If wealth accumulation is indeed occurring later in life, this trend (all else equal) could increase cross-sectional wealth inequality without necessarily increasing inequality across the life cycle.

We conclude by noting that shifts in wealth trajectories may well be linked to explicit policy decisions. The rise in early-life student debt can be linked, for example, to an accommodative stance by policymakers regarding for-profit universities and fiscal decisions by state legislatures to shift a greater share of the public university funding burden to students and families. Sharp cuts in the estate tax since 2001 have made the after-tax cost of bequests cheaper than *inter vivos* giving (transferring property during one's lifetime). And a growing preference by policymakers to provide greater benefits to families than to single taxpayers, coupled with an upward shift in childbearing ages, means that tax breaks are increasingly targeted toward those later in middle age. While it is difficult to isolate the precise impact of policy decisions on observed shifts in wealth determinants, the incentives for later-in-life wealth accumulation often correspond to the empirical patterns.

Policymakers have an array of options for countering the shift in wealth accumulation; we raise several potential options:

One, the structure of the up-front exclusion on contributions to retirement accounts could be converted to a flat-rate credit (Gale, John, and Smith 2012). For example, one revenue-neutral option would be to replace the current exclusion for contributions to a retirement account with a tax credit of approximately 25 percent. Such a reform would weaken the link between the present value of retirement saving contributions and marginal tax rates, which disproportionately benefits older workers, without forgoing the inside buildup benefit, which disproportionately benefits younger savers.

Two, tax rates could be a function of age, in addition to income and filing status. As suggested by Weinzierl (2011), lowering tax rates for saving-constrained younger workers can result in a welfare gain equal to 0.6 to 1.5 percent of consumption.

Three, the Saver's Credit—a tax credit that benefits low-income savers—could be substantially expanded, by including a more generous maximum credit amount, a more generous matching rate, and a higher eligibility threshold. Evidence from field experiments suggests that such a reform can significantly boost saving rates (Duflo and others 2006).

Four, a first-time homebuyer's tax credit can replace the current itemized deduction for mortgage interest expense. Such a reform would benefit younger savers, who often take on excess mortgage debt exclusively due to the tax subsidy. A first-time homebuyer tax credit could potentially boost housing prices and more progressively distribute tax incentives for homeownership (Harris, Steuerle, and Eng 2013).

Five, the formula for determining Social Security benefits can be made more progressive. This reform may seem counterintuitive because Social Security benefits are not typically received until beneficiaries reach retirement age. However, to the extent that Social Security benefits are *accumulated* throughout workers' careers, the timing of the benefit receipt is immaterial. A more progressive benefit formula would disproportionately benefit younger workers, who typically have lower wages than their older counterparts.

Six, lifetime benefits for defined contribution accounts could be limited. In President Obama's FY2014 budget, he proposed to equalize the lifetime benefit limit for pensions by introducing a limit on the amount in 401(k)-type plans (Department of the Treasury 2013).

Seven, the estate tax breaks in the 2017 Tax Cuts and Jobs Act could be repealed, and estate tax parameters could be amended to match the tax's structure in earlier years, such as 2009, when the top rate was 45 percent and the per-person exemption was $3.5 million. Similarly, the stepped-up basis—whereby all capital gains held until death are excluded from tax—could be repealed. Both provisions would encourage more *inter vivos* giving relative to end-of-life bequests, which would increase the receipt of wealth during beneficiaries' lifetime.

APPENDIX

Table 2A-1.

Pooled (Least Absolute Deviations), Inverse Hyperbolic Sine

	(1) *25–34*	*(2)* *35–44*	*(3)* *45–54*	*(4)* *55–64*
Constant	4.840*** 0.172	32.036*** 0.113	52.581*** 0.203	59.813*** 0.120
Year 2016	−0.116 0.224	−0.466*** 0.153	−0.361*** 0.141	0.049 0.146
Observations	1,250	1,712	1,848	2,015

Robust standard errors in parentheses.
*** $p < 0.01$, ** $p < 0.05$, * $p < 0.1$.

Table 2A-1. *(continued)*

Pooled (Least Absolute Deviations), Inverse Hyperbolic Sine

	(1) *25–34*	*(2)* *35–44*	*(3)* *45–54*	*(4)* *55–64*
Constant	0.264 (0.161)	1.266*** (0.182)	1.588*** (0.190)	4.877*** (0.256)
Year 2016	−0.207*** (0.093)	−0.184** (0.082)	−0.313*** (0.009)	−0.121 (0.102)
Black	−0.204*** (0.117)	−0.469*** (0.129)	−0.398*** (0.136)	−0.515*** (0.162)
Hispanic	−0.204** (0.109)	−0.493*** (0.091)	−0.3478*** (0.135)	−0.427** (0.270)
Other race	0.198 (0.330)	0.085 (0.201)	0 (0.165)	−0.472* (0.427)
Married	0.367*** (0.128)	0.089 (0.169)	0.104 (0.137)	0.004 (0.098)
Female head of household	−0.007 (0.131)	−0.169 (0.171)	−0.204* (0.144)	−0.432*** (0.178)
High school	0 (0.126)	0.092 (0.103)	0.513*** (0.147)	0.146 (0.142)
Some college	0.193 (0.128)	0.129 (0.127)	0.839*** (0.171)	0.594*** (0.138)
Bachelor's degree	0.196 (0.143)	0.234 (0.158)	1.132*** (0.173)	0.760*** (0.147)
Graduate degree	−0.063 (0.259)	0.544*** (0.162)	1.458*** (0.187)	1.259*** (0.138)
Income \$20,000–\$49,999	1.213*** (0.128)	2.073*** (0.196)	3.2060*** (0.195)	5.006*** (0.265)
Income \$50,000–\$99,999	7.789*** (0.169)	11.945*** (0.114)	12.48*** (0.146)	12.335*** (0.255)
Income \$100,000–199,999	23.360*** (0.159)	28.702*** (0.138)	24.230*** (0.159)	27.148*** (0.272)
Income \$200,000+	70.215*** (0.103)	51.876*** (0.210)	88.423*** (0.232)	77.086*** (0.280)
Observations	1,250	1,712	1,848	2,015

Source: Board of Governors of the Federal Reserve System (2017).
Robust standard errors in parentheses.
*** $p < 0.01$, ** $p < 0.05$, * $p < 0.1$.

Table 2A-2.

Pooled (Least Squares), Inverse Hyperbolic Sine

	(1) *25–34*	*(2)* *35–44*	*(3)* *45–54*	*(4)* *55–64*
Constant	5.325***	19.080***	37.974***	40.484***
	(0.102)	(0.098)	(0.105)	(0.110)
Year 2016	−0.316***	−0.378***	−0.358***	0.127
	(0.132)	(0.125)	(0.129)	(0.131)
Observations	1,250	1,712	1,848	2,015
R-squared	0.009	0.013	0.011	0.001

Robust standard errors in parentheses
*** $p < 0.01$, ** $p < 0.05$, * $p < 0.1$.

Pooled (Least Squares), Inverse Hyperbolic Sine

	(1) *25–34*	*(2)* *35–44*	*(3)* *45–54*	*(4)* *55–64*
Constant	0.863***	1.946***	3.892***	6.331***
	(0.246)	(0.220)	(0.194)	(0.178)
Year 2016	−0.329***	−0.300***	−0.433***	−0.281***
	(0.109)	(0.095)	(0.093)	(0.089)
Black	−0.333***	−0.453***	−0.391***	−0.459***
	(0.146)	(0.155)	(0.139)	(0.135)
Hispanic	−0.217	−0.336***	−0.335***	−0.437***
	(0.177)	(0.128)	(0.155)	(0.163)
Other race	0.172	0.408**	−0.070	−0.417**
	(0.239)	(0.179)	(0.217)	(0.276)
Married	0.189	0.079	0.076	0.219
	(0.156)	(0.164)	(0.125)	(0.131)
Female head of household	−0.270**	−0.311**	−0.201*	−0.335***
	(0.158)	(0.191)	(0.13)	(0.142)
High school	0.111	0.159	0.262*	0.226*
	(0.189)	(0.141)	(0.149)	(0.121)
Some college	0.262	0.072	0.484**	0.784***
	(0.203)	(0.143)	(0.170)	(0.131)
Bachelor's degree	0.256	0.235	0.957***	1.090***
	(0.244)	(0.168)	(0.174)	(0.157)

(continued)

Table 2A-2. *(continued)*

Pooled (Least Squares), Inverse Hyperbolic Sine

	(1) 25–34	(2) 35–44	(3) 45–54	(4) 55–64
Graduate degree	−0.216 (0.315)	0.229 (0.216)	1.143*** (0.203)	1.381*** (0.167)
Income \$20,000–\$49,999	0.841*** (0.169)	1.337*** (0.167)	1.582*** (0.176)	2.426*** (0.148)
Income \$50,000–\$99,999	3.875*** (0.210)	6.189*** (0.183)	6.028*** (0.185)	6.561*** (0.160)
Income \$100,000–\$199,999	13.457*** (0.273)	21.143*** (0.198)	16.959*** (0.206)	16.582*** (0.171)
Income \$200,000+	46.418*** (0.366)	52.861*** (0.226)	66.627*** (0.241)	54.813*** (0.194)
Observations	1,250	1,712	1,848	2,015
R-squared	0.301	0.436	0.490	0.584

Source: Board of Governors of the Federal Reserve System (2017).
Robust standard errors in parentheses.
*** $p < 0.01$, ** $p < 0.05$, * $p < 0.1$.

NOTES

This chapter was prepared for the Conference on Measuring and Understanding the Distribution and Intra/Inter-Generational Mobility of Income and Wealth, March 5–6, 2020. We thank John Sabelhaus for sharing wealth data and Grace Enda and Claire Haldeman for outstanding research assistance.

1. The SCF is conducted by the nonpartisan and objective National Opinion Research Center (NORC) at the University of Chicago on behalf of the Federal Reserve Board and with the cooperation of the Department of Treasury.

2. Social Security provides about 90 percent or more of the income for one-third of retirees and 50 percent or more of the income for two-thirds of retirees (Social Security Administration 2019).

3. Board of Governors of the Federal Reserve System (2017).

4. Akers and Chingos (2014) find that over half of the change in mean debt between 1989 and 2010 was due to higher tuition, and that roughly one-quarter was due to greater educational attainment. Similarly, Looney and Yannelis (2015) attribute much of the increase in debt between 2000 and 2011 to a soaring rise in "nontraditional" borrowers—namely students at for-profit institutions and in two-year degree programs.

5. See Givecha (2016) on marriage, Mezza and others (2020) on home purchases, and Rothstein and Rouse (2011) on early career choices. Elliott, Grinstein-Weiss, and Nam (2013) and Rutledge, Sanzenbacher, and Vitagliano (2018) obtain contrasting results on the impact of student debt on retirement contributions.

6. Federal Reserve Bank of St. Louis (2020).

7. In the dataset, these variables correspond to categorical variables RACE, MARRIAGE, HHSEX, an EDCL categorical variable adjusted with information from EDUC to provide more granularity with less than high school and graduate school specifications, and a household income category variable generated from INCOME, all as defined in "Changes in U.S. Family Finances from 2013 to 2016," *Federal Reserve Bulletin* 103 (3), https://www.federalreserve.gov/publications/files/scf17.pdf. See also "Definition of SCF Bulletin Asset and Debt Categories in Calculation of Net Worth," https://www.federalreserve.gov/econres/files/Networth%20Flowchart.pdf.

8. Burbidge, Magee, and Robb (1988) find the optimal value of θ to be 0.0000872 (within rounding distance of our choice). Pence (2002) finds that 0.0001 is the optimal value of θ, a value also used by Kennickell and Sundén (1997). See Gale and Pence (2006) for Gale's prior work conforming to this methodology.

9. See Pence (2006) for further explanation of the logarithmic approximation; see Burbidge, Magee, and Robb (1988) for more information about the inverse hyperbolic sine transformation itself.

REFERENCES

Akers, Beth, and Matthew M. Chingos. 2014. "Is a Student Loan Crisis on the Horizon?" Brookings.

Ando, Albert, and Franco Modigliani. 1963. "The Life Cycle Hypothesis of Saving: Aggregate Implications and Tests." *American Economic Review* 53 (1): 55–84.

Blinder, Alan S. 1973. "Wage Discrimination: Reduced Form and Structural Estimates." *Journal of Human Resources* 8 (4): 436–55.

Board of Governors of the Federal Reserve System. 2017. Distributional Financial Accounts. https://www.federalreserve.gov/releases/efa/efa-distributional-financial-accounts.htm.

Browning, Martin, and Thomas F. Crossley. 2001. "The Life-Cycle Model of Consumption and Saving." *Journal of Economic Perspectives*, 15 (3): 3–22.

Burbidge, John B., Lonnie Magee, and A. Leslie Robb. 1988. "Alternative Transformations to Handle Extreme Values of the Dependent Variable." *Journal of the American Statistical Association* 83 (401): 123–27.

Congressional Budget Office. 2019. Historical Data and Economic Projections. https://www.cbo.gov/about/products/budget-economic-data#7.

Department of the Treasury. 2013. "General Explanations of the Administration's Fiscal Year 2014 Revenue Proposals." Washington, DC: Government Printing Office.

Duflo, Esther, William Gale, Jeffrey Liebman, Peter Orszag, and Emmanuel Saez. 2006. "Saving Incentives for Low- and Middle-Income Families: Evidence from a Field Experiment with H&R Block." *Quarterly Journal of Economics* 121 (4): 1311–46.

Elliott, William, Michal Grinstein-Weiss, and Ilsung Nam. 2013. "Student Debt and Declining Retirement Savings." CSD Working Paper 13–34. Center for Social Development, Washington University.

Engen, Eric M., William G. Gale, and John Karl Scholz. 1996. "The Illusory Effects of Savings Incentives on Saving." *Journal of Economic Perspectives* 10 (4): 113–38.

Federal Reserve Bank of St. Louis. 2020. Average Sales Price of Houses Sold in the United States (updated October 26). https://fred.stlouisfed.org/series/ASPUS.

Feiveson, Laura, and John Sabelhaus. 2019. "Lifecycle Patterns of Saving and Wealth Accumulation." Finance and Economics Discussion Series 2019–010. Washington, D.C.: Board of Governors of the Federal Reserve System (U.S.).

Fisher, Jonas D. M., and Martin Gervais. 2011. "Why Has Homeownership Fallen among the Young?" *International Economic Review* 52 (3): 883–912.

Friedman, Milton. 1957. *A Theory of the Consumption Function.* Princeton University Press.

Gale, William G., and Karen M. Pence. 2006. "Are Successive Generations Getting Wealthier, and If So, Why? Evidence from the 1990s." *Brookings Papers on Economic Activity* 2006 (1): 155–234.

Gale, William, Hilary Gelfond, and Jason Fichtner. 2019. "How Will Retirement Saving Change by 2050? Prospects for the Millennial Generation." Brookings.

Gale, William G., David C. John, and Spencer Smith. 2012. "New Ways to Promote Retirement Saving." Washington, DC: AARP Public Policy Institute.

Givecha, Dora. 2016. "Student Loans or Marriage? A Look at the Highly Educated." *Economics of Education Review* 53: 207–16.

Grinstein-Weiss, M., Lung-Sook Lee, Johanna Greeson, Chang-Keun Han, Yeong Yeo, and Kate Irish. 2008. "Fostering Low-Income Homeownership: A Longitudinal Randomized Experiment on Individual Development Accounts." *Housing Policy Debate* (19) 4: 711–39.

Guvenen, Faith, Greg Kaplan, Jae Song, and Justin Weidner. 2017. "Lifetime Incomes in the United States over Six Decades." NBER Working Paper 23371. Cambridge, MA: National Bureau of Economic Research.

Harris, Benjamin H., C. Eugene Steuerle, and Amanda Eng. 2013. "New Perspectives on Homeownership Tax Incentives." *Tax Notes*, Special Report, December 23.

Kennickell, Arthur B., and Annika Sundén. 1997. "Pensions, Social Security, and the Distribution of Wealth." Finance and Economics Discussion Series Paper 1997–55. Washington, DC: Board of Governors of the Federal Reserve System, October.

Lindamood, Suzanne, Sherman D. Hanna, and Lan Bi. 2007. "Using the Survey of Consumer Finances: Some Methodological Considerations and Issues." *Journal of Consumer Affairs* 41 (2): 195–214.

Looney, Adam, and Constantine Yannelis. 2015. "A Crisis in Student Loans? How Changes in the Characteristics of Borrowers and in the Institutions They Attended Contributed to Rising Loan Defaults." *Brookings Papers on Economic Activity* (Fall).

Mezza, Alvaro A., Daniel R. Ringo, Shane M. Sherlund, and Kamila Sommer. 2020. "Student Loans and Homeownership." *Journal of Labor Economics* 38 (1): 215–60.

Modigliani, Franco, and Richard Brumberg. (1954) 2005. "Utility Analysis and the Consumption Function: An Interpretation of Cross Section Data." *The Collected Papers of Franco Modigliani.* MIT Press.

Oaxaca, Ronald. 1973. "Male-Female Wage Differentials in Urban Labor Markets." *International Economic Review* 14 (3): 693–709.

Pence, Karen M. 2002. "401(k)s and Household Saving: New Evidence from the Survey of Consumer Finances." Finance and Economics Discussion Series Working Paper 2002–06. Washington, DC: Board of Governors of the Federal Reserve System (January).

———. 2006. "The Role of Wealth Transformations: An Application to Estimating the Effect of Tax Incentives on Saving." *Contributions to Economic Analysis and Policy* (5)1: Article 20.

Piketty, Thomas. 2014. *Capital in the Twenty-First Century.* Belknap Press of Harvard University Press.

Rothstein, Jesse, and Cecilia Rouse. 2011. "Constrained after College: Student Loans and Early-Career Occupational Choices." *Journal of Public Economics* 95 (1–2): 149–63.

Rutledge, Matthew S., Geoffrey T. Sanzenbacher, and Francis M. Vitagliano. 2018. "Do Young Adults with Student Debt Save Less for Retirement?" IB#18-13. Center for Retirement Research, Boston College.

Sabelhaus, John, and Alice Henriques Volz. 2019. "Are Disappearing Employer Pensions Contributing to Rising Wealth Inequality?" *FEDS Notes.* Washington, DC: Board of Governors of the Federal Reserve System.

Saez, Emmanuel, and Gabriel Zucman. 2019. *The Triumph of Injustice: How the Rich Dodge Taxes and How to Make Them Pay.* New York: W.W. Norton.

Scholz, John Karl, and Ananth Seshadri. 2007. "Children and Household Wealth." Michigan Retirement Research Center Paper WP 2007-158. https://dx.doi.org/10.2139/ssrn.1083829.

Social Security Administration. 2019. "Fact Sheet." https://www.ssa.gov/news/press/factsheets/basicfact-alt.pdf.

Vespa, Jonathan, and Matthew Painter. 2011. "Cohabitation History, Marriage, and Wealth Accumulation." *Demography* 48 (3): 983–1004.

Weinzierl, Matthew. 2011. "The Surprising Power of Age-Dependent Taxes." *Review of Economic Studies* 78 (4): 1490–1518.

THREE

How Does Gender Equality Affect Women in Retirement?

Grace Enda and William G. Gale

In the 100 years since the ratification of the 19th Amendment, women have made substantial and well-publicized gains—both in absolute terms and relative to men—in educational attainment, employment, and earnings. Their status in retirement, however, has received far less attention.

Variations across individuals or groups in economic status in retirement can be traced to differences in labor market earnings, retirement saving derived from those earnings, and other factors including marital status, life expectancy, risk aversion, and financial acumen.

These factors help explain women's resources in retirement. For a variety of reasons, women earn less on average over the course of a lifetime than men do.[1] Lower lifetime earnings make it harder for women to save for retirement. Exacerbating these differences, women are on average longer lived, more risk averse, less financially literate, and more likely to have greater caregiving responsibilities than men.[2]

Public policies that aim to boost women's status in retirement should focus on the ways women participate in the labor market and in wealth accumulation programs, as well as on specific retirement programs and benefits.

EARNINGS

For several interrelated reasons, average lifetime earnings are substantially lower for women than for men.[3] One primary reason is that women provide a majority of unpaid family caregiving, which can lead them to interrupt their careers, seek part-time jobs in the market, or work in low-wage occupations to maintain flexibility.[4] Caregiving provided during women's twenties and thirties, when careers are formed and when age-earnings profiles are relatively steep, creates career-long earning losses.[5] One study found that a woman with one child earns 28 percent less on average over her career than a woman without children, partially as a result of time out of the workforce.[6] (In sharp contrast, becoming a father typically does not reduce a man's earnings.) Each additional child reduces average women's earnings by another 3 percent. Women are also more likely than men to care for their aging parents—a responsibility that predominantly falls on women over the age of 50.[7] People who leave the labor force early to care for a parent or other elderly relative lose an average of $142,000 in wages.[8]

Even within occupations, however, women receive unequal pay for similar work. Among full-time, year-round workers in 2018, median women's earnings equaled 81.1 percent of median men's earnings. Controlling for age, education, job tenure, occupation, job title, location, and industry, the figure rises to 94.6 percent.[9] Because this estimate controls for job title and occupation, it obscures important facets of gender inequality—the social constraints and biases that limit women's opportunity for career advancement (i.e., promotions) and pressure women into lower paying jobs. The wage differential varies across occupations but is almost always to women's detriment.

Progressive income taxation of *family* income provides significant disincentives for married women to work in the paid labor force. By taxing the first dollar of a second earner's income at the same marginal tax rate as the last dollar of the primary earner's income, the tax system discourages work among married women.[10]

FROM EARNINGS TO RETIREMENT WEALTH

Lower lifetime earnings lead to lower retirement wealth. The most important link is through Social Security, which provides over half of family income to 52 percent of the elderly and at least 90 percent of income to 25 percent of the elderly.[11] Women receive Social Security benefits that are, on average, 80 percent of those men receive.[12] Benefits are based on a person's 35 highest earning years. Women with long career interruptions risk not having 35 years with positive earnings, and the wage gaps noted above further reduce women's benefits. The motherhood penalty applies here, too: having a first child reduces a woman's Social Security benefits (through reduced earnings) by an average of 16 percent.[13] Each additional child increases the gap by 2 percent. Women who leave work to care for an elderly family member not only lose wages; they also lose an average of $131,000 in lifetime Social Security benefits.[14] Spouses (or ex-spouses, if the marriage lasted more than ten years) can choose to receive benefits based on their own earnings history or to receive half of their spouse's benefit. Given the trends in employment, earnings, and marriage, women are increasingly choosing to receive their own benefits.

Lower lifetime earnings also reduce the amount of wealth women can accumulate from employer-sponsored retirement plans, which come in two forms—defined benefit (DB) and defined contribution (DC) plans. Typically, in a DB plan, retirement benefits are paid as an annuity and depend on the worker's job tenure and salary. In DC plans, an employee contributes funds to an individual account (to which some employers make a matching or other contribution). DC plan benefits come from the contributions and returns that accrue over time. Over the past several decades, DC plans (including 401(k)s) have increasingly replaced DB plans, which are common now only for government and unionized workers.[15]

The shift away from DB plans has helped women in a key sense: DB plans are designed for those with long, uninterrupted careers. Benefits usually do not vest immediately and are usually "back-loaded."[16] That is, they require several years of job tenure before the employee is eligible to receive any benefit, and long job tenure is rewarded with disproportionately larger benefits. Although the gap between job tenure for men and women has fallen over time, men still have longer job tenure on average. DB plans were designed to benefit workers with career jobs (who, several decades ago, were almost exclusively men). As a result, retired women are two-thirds less likely to be receiving annuity and employer-based pension income, and among recipients, women's benefits average two-thirds of the average for men.[17]

DC plans tend to be less structured around job tenure and are portable. Workers are immediately vested in their own contributions and can take their accounts with them at job separation, which better fits women's work patterns. As of 2012, men and women working full-time, year-round in the private sector had nearly equal access to DC plans (45 and 46 percent, respectively) and equal take-up rates (81 percent).[18] Vanguard data show that in 2016 the average account balance for women was two-thirds the average for men, but almost all of the difference was the result of wage differences rather than saving behavior, given earnings.[19]

But managing DC accounts poses some new obstacles too. First, women, on average, express more risk aversion and tend to hold overly conservative portfolios, which reduces the returns they earn on savings.[20] In practice, the prevalence of target-date funds as default investments has helped women assume similar levels of risk (and returns) as men.[21]

Second, DC plans often require participants to make active decisions about their contribution, investment, withdrawal, distribution, and rollovers. Automatic approaches to enrollment, escalation, investment allocation, and other decisions have helped people manage these accounts, but workers are still responsible for ensuring the adequacy of their own savings. As a group, however, women are less financially literate than men, though their financial literacy increases after their husbands' deaths.[22]

Third, DC plans rarely pay benefits in the form of a stable monthly income stream. This hurts women, who have longer life expectancies than men. Under a DB plan, women and men with identical earnings histories receive equal monthly payments, even though women are expected to live longer.[23]

FROM RETIREMENT WEALTH TO RETIREMENT SECURITY

For a given amount of wealth, women face several obstacles relative to men in maintaining living standards in retirement.

Women tend to live longer than men and thus often have to draw down their retirement wealth over a longer period of time. In 2020, average life expectancy at age 65 is 21.1 years for women and 18.6 years for men. (The gap between men and women is fairly consistent across racial and ethnic groups.) As a result, for a given level of retirement wealth at age 65, women can afford to consume about 7 percent less per year than men. Women are more likely to run out of retirement savings, especially because older women are more likely to be the surviving partner, living on less Social Security income and with their partner's medical bills. Perhaps in response, women over the age of 55 are increasingly remaining in the workforce.[24] (Older men are too, but the increase is smaller.) Working longer gives people more time to save for retirement and reduces time they need to depend exclusively on retirement savings.

Poverty rates for women rise with age—from 8.6 percent among women aged 65 to 69 to 13.5 percent among women aged 80 or older—and are closely tied to family circumstances.[25] In 2017, among elderly women, the poverty rate was 4.3 percent for those who were married, 13.9 percent for widows, 15.8 percent for divorced women, and 21.5 percent for never-married women. More and more women reaching retirement are divorced or unmarried. In every marital status group, women with children had higher poverty rates than women without children, a pattern that does not hold for men.

POLICY OPTIONS

Although gender inequality is a pervasive problem with deep cultural roots, narrow economic policies can help reduce disparities between men and women. But fixing a retirement system that was not designed to accommodate women's experiences will require significant changes, not just in retirement policy but in labor market practices and policies as well.[26]

Making paid work more amenable to women is a key step. First, a robust federal paid family and medical leave program would let people save for retirement and earn Social Security credits while providing care to children and relatives.[27] Under such a program, employers would be required to provide employees a certain amount of paid time off for caregiving, parental leave, and periods of illness. Eight states and the District of Columbia already have such programs.[28] Second, under a Social Security caregiver credit, the government would assign a value to caregiving work that would be used as part of Social Security benefit calculations. The United Kingdom, France, Germany, and Sweden provide caregiver credits for public pensions, and both President Trump and former Vice President Biden have called for the United States to adopt a version of this policy.[29] Third, subsidizing high-quality childcare would enable more mothers to remain in the workforce.[30] Fourth, reforming the tax code either to provide a second-earner tax credit or to tax individuals rather than families would increase incentives for married women to work.

The retirement saving system presents many opportunities for reform. Although more and more women are working for employers that offer retirement plans, women still constitute a majority of the estimated 55 million US workers who are not eligible for or covered by an employer-sponsored plan.[31] Adoption of a nationwide Automatic Individual Retirement Account (Auto IRA) program could make most of these workers (as well as other part-time and lower-wage workers) eligible to participate in a tax-preferred workplace retirement program. Already, several states have launched their own Auto IRAs.[32] Expanding the Saver's Credit (a tax credit for low-income savers) to make it refundable and to provide higher effective matching rates would raise the return to saving for women with low and moderate incomes.

Strengthening the social safety net is a third major component ripe for reform. For example, boosting Supplemental Security Income benefits to close the gap between Social Security income and the poverty threshold could lift nearly 5 million elderly people, a majority of whom are women, out of poverty.[33] Increasing the support from Medicare and Medicaid for end-of-life care could alleviate the stress on widows. Finally, a thorough reexamination and reform of divorce laws could help women be more adequately prepared to meet their financial needs.

Although the differences in economic outcomes between men and women are sizable, they have grown smaller over time. Policymakers can accelerate that change and help bring about gender equity.

NOTES

1. Social Security Administration (2015).
2. Arias and Xu (2019); Eckel and Grossman (2008); Board of Governors of the Federal Reserve System (2020); National Alliance for Caregiving and AARP Public Policy Institute (2015).
3. Jacobsen, Khamis, and Yuksel (2014).
4. OECD (2020); Women's Bureau (2016); Tucker and Patrick (2017).
5. Kleven, Landais, and Søgaard (2017).
6. Rutledge, Zulkarnain, and King (2017).
7. Bureau of Labor Statistics (2019b).
8. MetLife Mature Market Institute (2011).
9. Chamberlain (2016).
10. Kearney and Turner (2013).
11. Dushi, Iams, and Trenkamp (2017).
12. Social Security Administration (2019).
13. Rutledge, Zulkarnain, and King (2017).
14. MetLife Mature Market Institute (2011).
15. Bureau of Labor Statistics (2017, 2018).
16. Tax Policy Center (2020).
17. McDonnell (2008).
18. Brown and others (2016).
19. Young and Young (2019).
20. MassMutual (2019); Brown and others (2016).
21. Young and Young (2019).

22. Board of Governors of the Federal Reserve System (2020); Hsu (2016).
23. Munnell (2019).
24. Bureau of Labor Statistics (2019a).
25. Li and Dalaker (2019).
26. John (2010).
27. Mathur and Sawhill (2018).
28. National Conference of State Legislatures (2020).
29. Government of the United Kingdom (2020); Jankowski (2011); Keith (2019); Biden for President (2020).
30. Whitehurst (2017).
31. Brown and others (2016); Koenig and John (2014).
32. National Conference of State Legislatures (2018).
33. Li and Dalaker (2019).

REFERENCES

Arias, Elizabeth, and Jiaquan Xu. 2019. "United States Life Tables, 2017." *National Vital Statistics Reports* 68 (7): 1–65. Hyattsville, MD: National Center for Health Statistics.

Biden for President. 2020. "The Biden Agenda for Women." https://joebiden.com/womens-agenda/#.

Board of Governors of the Federal Reserve System. 2020. "Report on the Economic Well-Being of U.S. Households in 2019, Featuring Supplemental Data from April 2020." https://www.federalreserve.gov/publications/files/2019-report-economic-well-being-us-households-202005.pdf.

Brown, Jennifer Erin, Nari Rhee, Joelle Saad-Lessler, and Diane Oakley. 2016. "Shortchanged in Retirement: Continuing Challenges to Women's Financial Future." Washington, DC: National Institute on Retirement Security.

Bureau of Labor Statistics. 2017. "Three Quarters of State and Local Government Workers Were in Defined Benefit Pension Plans in 2016." Washington, DC. https://www.bls.gov/opub/ted/2017/three-quarters-of-state-and-local-government-workers-were-in-defined-benefit-pension-plans-in-2016.htm.

———. 2018. "51 Percent of Private Industry Workers Had Access to Only Defined Contribution Retirement Plans." Washington, DC. https://www.bls.gov/opub/ted/2018/51-percent-of-private-industry-workers-had-access-to-only-defined-contribution-retirement-plans-march-2018.htm.

———. 2019a. "Civilian Labor Force Participation Rate by Age, Sex, Race, and Ethnicity." Washington, DC. https://www.bls.gov/emp/tables/civilian-labor-force-participation-rate.htm.

———. 2019b. "Unpaid Eldercare in the United States—2017–2018: Data from the American Time Use Survey." Washington, DC. https://www.bls.gov/news.release/pdf/elcare.pdf.

Chamberlain, Andrew. 2016. "Demystifying the Gender Pay Gap: Evidence from Glassdoor Salary Data." Mill Valley, CA: Glassdoor. https://www.glassdoor.com/research/app/uploads/sites/2/2016/03/Glassdoor-Gender-Pay-Gap-Study-3.pdf.

Dushi, Irena, Howard M. Iams, and Brad Trenkamp. 2017. "The Importance of Social Security Benefits to the Income of the Aged Population." *Social Security Bulletin* 77 (2): 1–12. Woodlawn, MD: Social Security Administration.

Eckel, Catherine C., and Philip J. Grossman. 2008. "Men, Women and Risk Aversion: Experimental Evidence." In *Handbook of Experimental Economics Results*, vol. 1, edited by Charles Plott and Vernon Smith, pp. 1061–73. New York: Elsevier.

Government of the United Kingdom. 2020. "Carer's Credit." London. https://www.gov.uk/carers-credit.

Hsu, Joanne W. 2016. "Aging and Strategic Learning: The Impact of Spousal Incentives on Financial Literacy." *Journal of Human Resources* 51 (4): 1036–67.

Jacobsen, Joyce P., Melanie Khamis, and Mutlu Yuksel. 2014. "Convergences in Men's and Women's Life Patterns: Lifetime Work, Lifetime Earnings, and Human Capital Investment." IZA Discussion Paper 8425. Bonn: Institute of Labor Economics.

Jankowski, John. 2011. "Caregiver Credits in France, Germany, and Sweden: Lessons for the United States." *Social Security Bulletin* 71 (4): 61–76. Woodlawn, MD: Social Security Administration.

John, David C. 2010. "Disparities for Women and Minorities in Retirement Saving." Brookings. https://www.brookings.edu/testimonies/disparities-for-women-and-minorities-in-retirement-saving/.

Kearney, Melissa S., and Lesley J. Turner. 2013. "Giving Secondary Earners a Tax Break: A Proposal to Help Low- and Middle-Income Families." Hamilton Project Discussion Paper 2013–07. Brookings.

Keith, Tamara. 2019. "Paid Parental Leave: How Republicans Learned to Love a Democratic Priority." National Public Radio. https://www.npr.org/2019/12/13/787631029/paid-parental-leave-how-republicans-learned-to-love-a-democratic-priority.

Kleven, Henrik J., Camille Landais, and Jakob Egholt Søgaard. 2017. "Children and Gender Inequality: Evidence from Denmark." https://www.henrikkleven.com/uploads/3/7/3/1/37310663/kleven-landais-sogaard_gender_feb2017.pdf.

Koenig, Gary, and David C. John. 2014. "Workplace Retirement Plans Will Help Workers Build Economic Security." Fact Sheet 317. Washington, DC: AARP Public Policy Institute.

Li, Zhe, and Joseph Dalaker. 2019. "Poverty among Americans Aged 65 and Older." Report R45791. Washington, DC: Congressional Research Service.

MassMutual. 2019. "Closing the Retirement Gender Gap: What Your Clients Need to Know about Women and Investing." Springfield, MA: Massachusetts Mutual Life Insurance Company.

Mathur, Aparna, and Isabel V. Sawhill. 2018. "A Path Forward on Paid Family Leave." Brookings. https://www.brookings.edu/blog/up-front/2018/09/10/a-path-forward-on-paid-family-leave/.

McDonnell, Ken. 2008. "Retirement Annuity and Employment-Based Pension Income among Individuals Age 50 and Over: 2006." *EBRI Notes* 29 (1): 2–6. Washington, DC: Employee Benefit Research Institute.

MetLife Mature Market Institute. 2011. "Caregiving Costs to Working Caregivers Double Jeopardy for Baby Boomers Caring for Their Parents." https://www.caregiving

.org/wp-content/uploads/2011/06/mmi-caregiving-costs-working-caregivers.pdf.

Munnell, Alicia H. 2019. "Should Annuities Pay Out the Same for Men and Women?" *Market Watch*, Opinion, May 6.

National Alliance for Caregiving and AARP Public Policy Institute. 2015. "Caregiving in the U.S." https://www.aarp.org/content/dam/aarp/ppi/2015/caregiving-in-the-united-states-2015-report-revised.pdf.

National Conference of State Legislatures. 2018. "State-Facilitated Retirement Savings Programs for Private Sector Workers." Washington, DC. https://www.ncsl.org/research/fiscal-policy/state-facilitated-retirement-savings-programs-for-private-sector-workers.aspx.

———. 2020. "Paid Family Leave Resources." Washington, DC. https://www.ncsl.org/research/labor-and-employment/paid-family-leave-resources.aspx.

Organization for Economic Cooperation and Development (OECD). 2020. "Time Spent in Paid and Unpaid Work, by Sex." https://stats.oecd.org/index.aspx?queryid=54757.

Rutledge, Matthew S., Alice Zulkarnain, and Sara Ellen King. 2017. "How Much Does Motherhood Cost Women in Social Security Benefits?" WP 2017–14. Chestnut Hill, MA: Center for Retirement Research.

Social Security Administration. 2015. "Education and Lifetime Earnings." Woodlawn, MD: Social Security Administration. https://www.ssa.gov/policy/docs/research-summaries/education-earnings.html#:~:text=Research%2C%20Statistics%20%26%20Policy%20Analysis&text=Men%20with%20bachelor's%20degrees%20earn,earnings%20than%20high%20school%20graduates.

———. 2019. "Fact Sheet: Social Security Is Important to Women." Woodlawn, MD: Social Security Administration. https://www.ssa.gov/news/press/factsheets/women-alt.pdf.

Tax Policy Center. 2020. "What's the Difference between Front-Loaded and Back-Loaded Retirement Accounts?" In *Tax Policy Center Briefing Book*. Washington, DC: Urban-Brookings Tax Policy Center.

Tucker, Jasmine, and Kayla Patrick. 2017. "Low-Wage Jobs Are Women's Jobs: The Overrepresentation of Women in Low-Wage Work." Washington, DC: National Women's Law Center. https://nwlc.org/wp-content/uploads/2017/08/Low-Wage-Jobs-are-Womens-Jobs.pdf.

Whitehurst, Grover J. 2017. "Why the Federal Government Should Subsidize Childcare and How to Pay for It." Brookings.

Women's Bureau. 2016. "Percent Distribution of Workers Employed Full-Time and Part-Time by Sex." Washington, DC: US Department of Labor. https://www.dol.gov/agencies/wb/data/latest-annual-data/full-and-part-time-employment

Young, Galina, and Jean A. Young. 2019. "Women versus Men in D.C. Plans." Arlington, VA: Vanguard Research.

FOUR

A Retirement Dashboard for the United States

David C. John, Grace Enda, William G. Gale, and J. Mark Iwry

Navigating the American retirement system is not easy for many people. Because most workers change jobs (and hence retirement plans) multiple times during their career, developing a comprehensive picture of one's retirement preparations can be challenging. In addition, successful retirement saving strategies can be undone rapidly if funds are withdrawn before or soon after retirement begins, even if there are good reasons for such withdrawals. More generally, planning for retirement is a complicated and uncertain exercise, and unbiased information is often difficult to identify.[1]

Workers across the world face similar problems. To help address these issues, several governments and pension providers have created pension registries—websites where people can see all their retirement benefits, including Social Security, employer-sponsored or "occupational" plans, and individual retirement accounts, and find contact information for the administrator of each plan or account. Other countries have gone further to develop national, online retirement "dashboards"—websites that not only include a registry or tracking system but also offer expanded functions such as recovering and consolidating lost accounts, projecting estimated future income, expanding financial literacy, and providing unbiased financial advice to users.

In this chapter, we discuss the possibilities for a retirement dashboard for the United States. While it would not address systemic problems such as coverage, a dashboard could reduce the strain that a complex retirement system imposes on households. An effective dashboard could help employees and other savers, employers, record-keepers, asset managers, plan providers, and the government, all of whom have an interest in ensuring that workers understand and manage their retirement savings appropriately.

The private sector does not currently provide such a dashboard and is unlikely to be able to do so. Fintech applications typically help retrieve only those accounts the user is already aware of and often charge for their services. Some applications can search databases, but record-keepers and asset managers may be reluctant to allow access to possible competitors. Moreover, we believe a national online retirement dashboard should have standard features, avoid conflicts of interest, and be easy to find and available to everyone free of charge. For-profit providers are unlikely to provide dashboards without charge—especially not to people who are not their clients—and keeping private sector dashboards conflict-free and with standard features would be a challenge. Accordingly, while the private sector could conceivably provide a dashboard, we believe it would be most effectively and reliably provided through a website sponsored or co-sponsored by the federal government that is designed exclusively to serve savers' interests.

In this chapter we first discuss how a retirement dashboard could help with some of the retirement saving challenges American workers face. Then we consider the major objectives and desirable features of a US dashboard. We follow with a brief overall assessment and review four significant potential challenges to the creation of a dashboard. In the appendix we review other countries' experience with retirement dashboards, including screenshots illustrating how the Danish dashboard presents information.

MEETING THE CHALLENGES OF RETIREMENT PLANNING

People must make decisions about their retirement income far in advance of retirement, but because each person passes through life only once, everyone is a novice in preparing for retirement, and any insights must be gleaned from the actions or advice of others. This section reviews several ways a dashboard could help by providing unbiased, practical information during people's working years as they accumulate retirement savings.[2]

Finding and Consolidating Lost Accounts

The most common purpose of a retirement dashboard is to include a registry showing users all their retirement benefits and enabling them to find lost or missing accounts from previous jobs. The US Bureau of Labor Statistics reports that people between ages 56 and 63 in 2016–2017 held an average of more than twelve jobs in their lives, including, on average, nearly five jobs between ages 35 and 52.[3] As a result, workers may have to keep track of multiple retirement plans from past jobs, some of which may date back several decades.

Accounts can be lost for any of several reasons. Former employees may leave checks uncashed or change postal and email addresses. Former employers may terminate plans, change providers, go out of business, be acquired, or change the company's name. The result is often lost or missing benefits to the worker or lost or missing participants from the provider's perspective. Plan sponsors' widespread implementation of automatic enrollment over the past two decades has proven to be a major improvement in the private pension system, although it has generated a side effect: many more small accounts belonging to former employees, who, in many cases, are unaware that the account exists because it was established without requiring them to take any action.

Finding lost or missing accounts and participants is not easy. Each of the three federal pension agencies and the Social Security Administration offer resources that can be helpful, but—separately and in the aggregate—they are far from comprehensive and their information cannot be accessed from one central location. The Social Security Administration (SSA) and the IRS formerly offered letter-forwarding services plan sponsors could use to locate participants who were no longer their employees, but both services have been discontinued.[4]

On the other hand, the IRS does have a form that serves as a registration statement of participants in plans covered by the Employee Retirement Income Security Act (ERISA) who are no longer employed by the plan sponsor but who still have vested benefits in the plan. Every year, plan administrators are required to report this information to the IRS. The IRS then transmits it to SSA, which uses it to notify applicants for Social Security benefits that they may be entitled to benefits from a prior employer's plan.[5]

In addition, the Department of Labor (DOL) actively audits plan sponsors to ensure compliance with requirements to search diligently for missing participants. Although DOL guidelines do not expressly apply to ongoing plans,[6] they do provide that sponsors of terminating DC plans have a fiduciary responsibility under ERISA to make reasonable efforts to find missing plan participants, including checking plan and employer records, contacting designated beneficiaries, and using certified mail and internet search tools. If these efforts are unsuccessful, the plan is obligated to pursue additional search methods such as commercial locator services, credit reporting agencies, or information brokers that could charge for their services, provided that the cost would be justified in view of the size of the balance and likelihood of success. If a participant cannot be found, the plan must transfer the benefits to an IRA in the name of the missing participant or make another appropriate disposition of the benefits.[7] Sponsors of terminated plans can resort to commercial locator services, at least one of which lets employers register inactive DC plans and lets former employees search the registry for their accounts.[8] However, it has been estimated that each search, whether successful or not, costs plan sponsors an average of $40.[9]

Both DOL, through the Employee Benefits Security Administration (EBSA), and the Pension Benefit Guaranty Corporation (PBGC) administer programs that help people find their defined benefit (DB) pensions from former jobs. PBGC maintains an online "Unclaimed Pensions" database that participants can search but that for years was limited to terminated DB plans that PBGC administers. Following congressional authorization to expand this program to cover other terminating plans, PBGC allows, but does not require, terminating defined contribution (DC) and other plans to send it lost account or benefit information for safekeeping while plan officials and PBGC look for the owner.[10] The program, however, applies only to terminating plans.

Another option for plan participants is to search states' unclaimed property databases. Accounts can be located there, but often these benefits were invested by the state in a money market account where they likely will have earned a lower rate of return than in most investment plans. Mukherjee (2020) studies retirement savings that appear in these databases and estimates that Americans in 2016 owned about 70,000 such accounts holding $38 million. She finds that the vast majority of these accounts remain unclaimed up to a decade after being reported to state unclaimed property authorities.

Because there is no centralized reporting of missing participants or lost benefits, and because some lost benefits are uncashed checks, there are only a few rough estimates of the number of lost accounts or the associated balances. PBGC estimates that 80,000 former participants in DB pension plans have so far failed to claim $400 million in vested benefits, but it is unknown what portion of these benefits are or will be permanently unclaimed or lost.[11]

Similarly, a 2014 Government Accountability Office (GAO) report found that in the previous nine years, workers had left about $8.5 billion in their previous employers' plans in more than 16 million accounts of $5,000 or less.[12] Including larger accounts, GAO estimated that workers had left behind 25 million accounts but did not estimate the lost balances.[13]

GAO recommended (as have others) that a national pension registry be established to inform participants of their DB and DC plan benefits, including benefits at former employers' plans, and to help participants track all of those benefits on a single website. This recommendation was shared with DOL, which said it would evaluate creating a task force to explore the possibility of a national pension registry even though it lacked the authority to develop and host a registry site. DOL has not acted, however, even though in 2018 and 2019 GAO placed the registry on its list of six high-priority open recommendations to DOL.[14]

How a Dashboard Could Help

Helping recover and consolidate lost accounts is one of the most basic functions of a dashboard. In the United States, improving account portability could prevent many accounts from being lost in the future, but would not help locate accounts that are already lost. Meanwhile, American workers could more easily find and recover lost accounts if an easily navigable website housed a database listing all their accounts and their current location and explained how to claim and consolidate the accounts. To that end, proposed bipartisan legislation, the Retirement Savings Lost and Found Act, would create an online national "lost and found" data registry and search tool to help savers locate inactive accounts, including current contact information for the plan administrator maintaining the account.[15] If enacted, the bill could create a data source for a national dashboard.

Combining accounts can simplify people's portfolios and save fees, especially on small or inactive accounts. These accounts tend to be harder for people to track and are more complicated to manage in an integrated, coherent fashion. In addition, fees and expenses are often proportionately higher on smaller balances because they do not benefit from economies of scale that apply to larger-balance customers. Inactive accounts might also have higher expenses if they date back to a time that was technologically less advanced and when fee consciousness was less acute. A dashboard could help savers compare account fees and expenses by requiring a standard format for disclosing them, building on existing DOL regulations. But investors can be deterred from consolidating accounts because investment firms may be reluctant to lose the assets under management.[16]

Reducing Preretirement Leakage

The loss of retirement income from preretirement withdrawals that are not rolled over to another plan or IRA can be quite large. Annual leakage from the retirement saving system of just 1.5 percent of asset balances reduces the ultimate value of a 401(k)-type plan by 25 percent in comparison with an account without such withdrawals.[17] Preretirement withdrawals in the aggregate appear to be large. A study by researchers for the Joint Committee on Taxation found that, in 2014 alone, 20 percent, or $65.5 billion, of withdrawals from DC plans and IRAs went to people of preretirement age.[18] Another study found that, each year, about 22 percent of participants under age 55 take a distribution from their retirement plan or IRA accounts.[19]

The plan qualification rules generally are intended to discourage leakage and promote portability of savings. When employees leave their jobs and decide to take their benefits from a DC plan, the default form of payout from a DC plan is a "direct rollover" of the balance to another plan or IRA. Participants who instead take the balance as a lump-sum payout face a 20 percent mandatory withholding tax and will usually face an additional 10 percent tax for early withdrawal.

Nevertheless, participants often need or want use of the funds immediately, especially low-marginal-rate individuals who are less sensitive to tax consequences. According to a 2009 GAO report, 89 percent of leakage occurs because of cash-outs at termination of employment.[20] Accounts with small balances are more frequently cashed out, in part because only balances over $1,000 are protected from involuntary cash-out by plan administrators and in part because owners of smaller balances often see them as inconsequential—too small to contribute appreciably to their future retirement security.[21] In addition, people who are younger, have lower income or wealth, or have changed jobs more frequently are more likely to cash out balances before retirement.[22]

Preretirement withdrawals of retirement savings can, of course, be necessary or desirable in some circumstances. Some liquidity encourages plan participation by assuring potential savers that they can access their retirement savings in the event of financial hardship. One study found that, at any given time, 20 percent of DC plan participants have plan loans outstanding.[23] Most plan loans are repaid with interest through payroll withholding, but about 10 percent of borrowers default when their employment terminates and payroll withholding stops before the loan has been fully repaid.

Because most leakage occurs at job changes, reforming the rollover rules and practices—including expansion of automatic rollovers and automatic portability—would likely have the greatest impact on leakage.[24] Dashboards, however, could play a meaningful supporting role in reducing leakage by helping people understand the short- and long-term consequences of cashing out and how to preserve savings through retention or rollover. A dashboard that directs savers to the correct forms they need to combine accounts and helps them complete and send the forms to the right place could also help people move their savings directly to their new employer's plan. In many cases, this would be preferable to rolling the money into an IRA, which would often have higher fees and a less professionally curated investment menu.

As a matter of behavioral finance, a comprehensive website presentation of a saver's accounts and benefits can drive home the fact that even balances that seem small when viewed in isolation can grow over time and be combined with other accounts to provide meaningful additional security in retirement. In addition to providing information, a dashboard—especially if it promotes data standardization—might conceivably be used in the future to facilitate or simplify rollovers and transfers by connecting providers and financial institutions.[25]

Providing Useful and Unbiased Financial Information

The shift in the retirement system from pensions to 401(k) retirement savings arrangements has placed a heavy burden on savers to make key financial decisions. The spread of automatic 401(k) enrollment, escalation, reenrollment, investment, rebalancing, and rollovers has eased this burden for many people.[26] But a 401(k) with automatic features is not a replacement for financial literacy or for all retirement-related financial advice. People still need advice on saving, investing, paying down debt, making decisions relating to job transitions and rollovers, drawing benefits, and related issues. Without financial literacy and unbiased financial advice, many people will make poor choices. And because financial literacy is lower among groups that have less access to financial resources, including Blacks, Latinx, and women, focusing on financial literacy may also help address racial, ethnic, and gender disparities in wealth.[27]

Financial advisers often add value for retirement savers. However, too many brokers, insurance agents, and other for-profit financial advisers have allowed their own or their firm's financial interests to conflict with clients' interests and to bias their advice. Against their clients' interests, some advisers have benefited from pushing plans and investments with excessive and nontransparent fees and expenses, steering clients to investments that particularly benefit the adviser, or churning accounts to increase commissions.

DOL has promulgated rules intended to ensure that advisers providing individualized investment advice do so solely in the investor's best interests—unaffected by any financial interests of the adviser. The DOL rules treat many of these investment advice activities as being subject to fiduciary duties under ERISA.[28] However, DOL's 2016 fiduciary rule issued during the Obama administration was later overturned by a court and effectively reversed by DOL during the Trump administration. And even if reinstated in some form, this effort will likely continue to focus more on preventing conflicted advice than on expanding the availability of sound advice. Therefore, a considerable need for more unbiased and widely available retirement planning advice remains. This is particularly true because many financial advisers are not interested in serving clients lacking substantial net worth. While many advisers serve middle-income households, personalized advice is not—or seems not to be—affordable for tens of millions of moderate- or lower-income people who often lack the financial capability to save, invest, and plan wisely for retirement on their own.[29]

The United States offers more types of retirement information programs than any other country in the Organization for Economic Cooperation and Development.[30] These include websites, awareness campaigns and events, comparison tools, pension statements, calculators, simulators, retirement planning seminars, and counseling services. The Treasury Department heads up a twenty-two-agency federal government–wide Financial Literacy and Education Commission.

Collecting these resources, or links to these resources, on a single site that also contains an individual's personal financial information could improve access to them and make them more likely to be used. Currently, a "*my* Social Security" account with the Social Security Administration (SSA) gives people personalized estimates of their future Social Security benefits.[31] DOL's Employee Benefits Security Administration has thorough savings fitness worksheets anyone can use. The Treasury Department supports a financial literacy website that includes links to additional resources. The SEC has a "roadmap to saving and investing." The Consumer Financial Protection Bureau (CFPB) has a tool, Planning for Retirement, that allows users to simulate future decisions and provides concise information relevant to a user's choices.

Outside of government, nonprofits and other organizations have developed useful financial education and retirement planning materials. A dashboard could use or link to such information as well. Other possibilities include providing search capabilities and chat functions enabling users to locate and connect with nonprofits or other unbiased sources of advice.

AN AMERICAN DASHBOARD

As described in the appendix and summarized in table 4-1, other countries have already built retirement dashboards with particular objectives in mind. A US version of a dashboard should seek to address certain demonstrated problems in our retirement system. Here we provide an ambitious list of objectives, ranging from core functions to more aspirational possibilities, showing that a dashboard could help make the retirement system easier for savers to navigate.

Objectives

Policymakers may reasonably choose to prioritize specific problems, addressing the most urgent first and phasing in solutions for other issues over time. Having the larger goals in mind can inform the process of designing a dashboard and its features.

HELP PEOPLE FIND AND RETRIEVE INACTIVE ACCOUNTS AND LOST BENEFITS

A first and fundamental objective of a dashboard should be to enable savers to find and view all their benefits and accounts in one location. This would require a central registry of all lost accounts as proposed by GAO or a similar "lost and found" database as proposed by the Retirement Savings Lost and Found Act. It should also incorporate the existing PBGC online search tool for unclaimed pension benefits.

PROVIDE A COMPREHENSIVE PICTURE OF ALL RETIREMENT BENEFITS

By showing savers all their benefits and accounts, a dashboard can present a comprehensive picture of their retirement resources. Including estimated payments from DB pension plans and estimated Social Security benefits

Table 4-1. *Retirement Dashboards and Similar Facilities in Other Countries*

Country	*User access*	*Data access*	*Objective*	*Functions*	*Financial support*
Australia	Digital ID	Central database	Finder service	Rollovers, consolidation	Government general revenue; pension industry tax
Belgium	Digital ID	Information	Finder service	Projections	Government general revenue
Denmark	Digital ID	Live requests	Information	Projections	Pension providers voluntarily
Israel	Credit card number	Data clearing-house	Finder service	Document transfer, update contact information, private financial advice	Government general revenue; participant charges
The Netherlands	Digital ID	Live requests	Information	Projections	Pension providers, per participant
Sweden	Digital ID	Central database	Information	Information sharing, projections (new features in development)	Government general revenue; pension providers

Sources: Government Accountability Office (2014); UK Department for Work and Pensions (2018); Lindley (2019).

would enable workers to understand what their potential total retirement income could be. At the very least, this would help savers to understand that their retirement income would come from several sources, what those sources are, and how those sources might be expanded to produce additional income or savings in retirement. If a retirement dashboard also allowed individuals to add their other assets and personal savings outside of the retirement system, the information would be even more complete, although this would require further cooperation from the financial services industry. For the industry, the dashboard could have the advantage of increasing user engagement.[32] Realistically, however, providers might be reluctant to alert inactive account holders to the existence of high-fee accounts and to their ability to consolidate accounts, since doing so could reduce the providers' assets under management and fees.

FACILITATE CONSOLIDATION OF ACCOUNTS WHERE APPROPRIATE

A tool that made it easy to consolidate IRAs and 401(k) accounts into a single retirement vehicle, such as a current employer's plan, would be very useful. At the least, a dashboard should include simple instructions on how to combine accounts to simplify management and potentially use consolidation to eliminate high-cost or inactive accounts that no longer serve the investor's purposes. It should also include a step-by-step guide with links to appropriate forms and the ability to send them electronically or provide a mailing address.

Several years ago, some of the authors viewed a demonstration of a prototype European dashboard that automated and handled the process of combining accounts. A similar mechanism, with appropriate safeguards, could help the saver better evaluate the implications of moving accounts by warning of existing accounts with higher fees or other distinctive attributes. Making it easier to move former accounts directly into a new employer's plan would reduce the chance that the money would go to an IRA with higher fees and suboptimal investments.

At the same time, it would be important to provide sufficient safeguards to prevent anyone from taking or causing unauthorized actions, such as pressuring account holders to consolidate in or transfer to a particular plan or account.

SERVE AS A CENTRAL SOURCE OF EDUCATIONAL MATERIAL AND OTHER UNBIASED INFORMATION

As discussed above, too many American households lack adequate financial literacy and affordable, unbiased financial advice. Accordingly, many are confused or uninformed about the financial decisions they need to make to prepare for retirement. These issues include how and how much to save, how to invest, when to retire, whether to continue working part-time, when to claim Social Security benefits, when and how much to withdraw and spend, the effect of taxes and Medicare premiums on retirement income, how various investment and retirement income products work, and their advantages and disadvantages for people in various situations.

The dashboard could serve as a trusted source of usable information on these and related questions. Recognizing that most people are ill-equipped to undertake complex financial planning and that financial literacy tends to increase overall well-being, a dashboard could prove helpful in this regard.[33] With a better understanding of their financial needs and resources, people could make more effective plans and decisions about saving, investing, and spending. Retirement plan providers would benefit from better-educated customers and might find that it is more efficient for them to direct savers to the dashboard than to spend time and money developing that information themselves.

One value of a central dashboard sponsored or co-sponsored by the federal government would be to prevent private sector providers from using a US dashboard to market or cross-sell other financial products or services. Such a practice should be explicitly prohibited and the United States could follow the example set in the UK, where a similar rule has been proposed. Preventing solicitation by private sector providers could also clarify to users that the dashboard provides reliably unbiased information.

In addition to providing general "educational" information, a separate question is how close a national dashboard could or should come to providing individualized financial advice.[34] Depending on the circumstances, investment advice could be treated under ERISA as subject to fiduciary duties and standards. Even if it avoids providing investment or other financial advice, a retirement dashboard could refer users to sources of unbiased and affordable personalized financial planning advice, such as certain qualified nonprofits. But determining which for-profit advisers should be considered sufficiently impartial and qualified for this purpose would likely involve difficult line-drawing issues and questions about implicit (or explicit) government endorsement.

HELP PEOPLE PLAN

People often, and understandably, struggle to determine how much to save and how much income to expect in retirement. A dashboard should include calculators that allow savers to understand how much income their savings could generate through a variety of mechanisms and products. The SECURE Act should help considerably by requiring 401(k) and other DC plan benefit statements to include appropriate retirement income projections. These projections, however, would apply only to savings in the individual plan providing the statement. A dashboard could help savers make a consolidated projection of benefits from all their retirement plans as well as Social Security. In addition, participants need to be able to understand the effects on future income of continuing to contribute at the same or a different rate, taking withdrawals, changing their investments, and other actions. Interactive features that enable savers to simulate the retirement-related decisions they will have to make in the future and providing helpful, expert advice could significantly reduce financial anxiety and errors.[35]

HELP REDUCE LEAKAGE

Hardships can necessitate preretirement withdrawals, but some flows out of the retirement systems are unnecessary and may result from limited financial literacy. A dashboard could include information to help evaluate the tradeoff between withdrawing retirement savings for immediate needs and leaving these savings to accumulate on a tax-favored basis for future income. A person considering an early withdrawal could instantly calculate and visualize the impact, including tax effects, that a withdrawal could have on future retirement income and could estimate the amount of additional contributions that would be needed to offset the withdrawal. A dashboard could provide the projections illustrating how even relatively small balances from each of a series of employer plans could accumulate on a tax-deferred basis and add up to a meaningful total at retirement if not previously cashed out and spent. This could help discourage ill-considered decisions to dissipate retirement savings.

Key Attributes of an Effective Retirement Dashboard

To work effectively, a retirement dashboard should have certain key attributes. First, it should be easy to find and access. Accordingly, financial providers and advisers should be encouraged or, if need be, required to provide a prominent link to the dashboard as well as a quick explanation of what it is and how it can be used.

Second, all retirement plan providers should be required to participate in the dashboard, as they are in most other countries with dashboards. Plans and providers would report all benefits and accounts to an online registry that people can search through the dashboard.

Third, a dashboard needs to be available to all free of charge. Charging people to access the dashboard would defeat the purpose of having as many people as possible use it.

Fourth, it should require data standardization. Information from financial providers must be sent to the dashboard in the same format so that it can be compiled and uniformly presented to users. In addition, the process of creating a dashboard should require a standard methodology for valuation, estimation, and projection methods and assumptions for valuing assets, converting balances to estimated future retirement income, and projecting future contributions and income.[36]

Fifth, the dashboard should be secure. Trust in the dashboard's data security will improve engagement among both the financial industry and users.[37] This will require all providers to comply with cybersecurity standards as they evolve.

Sixth, the dashboard should present information in a user-friendly manner. While enabling one-stop shopping, a dashboard must avoid overwhelming users with too much information. Striking this balance will be challenging, but centralizing information, resources, and tools in a single location would be worth the effort. The combined materials must be curated, coordinated, and consolidated so that they are as easy as possible to use—inviting rather than daunting.[38]

In its 2014 report, GAO recommended that a national dashboard be a governmental undertaking, involving, at the very least, the US Departments of Labor, Commerce, and the Treasury. The government would need to ensure participation and cooperation by all providers to provide data on all benefits and accounts, whether as a standing database or on a temporary basis responding to requests from users. It would also need to enforce data standardization; enforce disinterested cooperation by asset managers, record-keepers, and plan providers in facilitating transfers, rollovers, and consolidation when requested by the account owner; supervise the operation of the dashboard; and provide sufficient oversight to give users and providers confidence in the security of the data. None of this requires that the government host the site—in some other countries, for example, organizations formed by public-private collaboration host the dashboards. And private sector organizations could be heavily involved in carrying out other dashboard functions as partners with the government or as government contractors. Without extensive federal government involvement, a dashboard with the functions, attributes, and reliability contemplated here would not be feasible.

ASSESSING THE DASHBOARD PROPOSAL AND ASSOCIATED CHALLENGES

There is to date little formal evidence regarding retirement dashboards' effects on outcomes for users.[39] In Sweden, for example, 48 percent of dashboard users reported having enough understanding of their pension benefits to make active management decisions; only 13 percent of non-dashboard users felt similarly competent, but the causal effect is unclear: people who are more financially literate or familiar with retirement planning may have a greater tendency to use a dashboard, or using a dashboard may increase understanding.[40] In any event, half of the working population of Sweden uses the dashboard minPension, and a remaining third of nonusers lack internet access.[41]

The experiences to date with dashboards in other countries (as summarized in the appendix) suggest that dashboards could help alleviate some of the difficult problems that retirement savers face. That said, establishing a dashboard would entail significant challenges, albeit ones we believe can be surmounted. We focus here on four.

Scale and Complexity

The US private retirement system is much larger and more diverse than those in countries that currently have dashboards.[42] The establishment of a US retirement dashboard will therefore be more difficult, especially given the need for universal participation among plan sponsors, record-keepers, asset managers, investment firms, and others.

The dashboard could operate from a single central data repository or as a finder or tracking service that sends out data requests to plan providers when a customer logs in and then compiles a report of responses with their name and other identifying information. A central database would require collecting and storing data, updating it regularly, and ensuring its accuracy and safety. A finder service, on the other hand, must be able to reach all potential sources of relevant data quickly and accurately, and then produce a report that users can understand and act upon. Given the size and complexity of the US retirement system, neither system will be easy to create or inexpensive.

One way to deal with this complexity would be to establish the dashboard in stages, starting by building a retirement registry or tracking service, before moving on to more complex functions. Rather than deciding on the next stage on an ad hoc basis, however, it would be important to have a comprehensive but flexible plan to clarify what additional features will be provided and how they will fit into the whole.

Industry Opposition

Efforts to develop a dashboard should continually invite input from all stakeholders and carefully consider legitimate concerns. A major challenge will be political opposition to a retirement dashboard that goes beyond a registry and its basic tracking and locating services. Recent efforts to reform the US private pension system to better serve the interests of American workers by facilitating rollovers and account consolidation and making investment advice clearer and less conflicted faced well-financed political opposition from sectors of the financial services industry. Many in the industry will feel threatened by such changes and by the government involvement needed to bring them about. Efforts to standardize data, advice, formats, and functionality in a dashboard will conflict with competitive branding and product differentiation and will likely be criticized as a "one size fits all" approach that stifles market creativity and restricts choice.

Accordingly, the needed cooperation from record-keepers and asset managers will not be easily achieved. The more a dashboard departs from the more basic registry model and approaches something akin to a marketplace model—facilitating consumer apples-to-apples comparisons of product features, fees and expenses, enabling individuals to easily carry out transfers, consolidations, or other transactions, and helping users obtain unbiased financial advice—the more opposition it will draw.[43] Witness the bitter and protracted political battles between industry on the one hand and government and consumer advocates on the other, as well as in Congress, over DOL's fiduciary rule intended to reduce conflicts of interest in investment advice and over the establishment of the CFPB and the scope of its functions.

Moreover, for a dashboard to recommend or refer users to impartial financial advisers would inevitably raise industry concerns about "government picking winners and losers" among competing advisers or other providers in the market. And any attempt to have the dashboard itself dispense investment advice, as opposed to more limited and noncontroversial "information" or "education," could trigger attacks on asserted government interference with free market competition and encroachment on established private sector functions and longstanding adviser-client relationships.

The UK's continuing difficulty in developing a national retirement dashboard also suggests the potential for a major push from the financial services industry to allow multiple commercial dashboards sponsored by vendors instead of or in addition to a free, noncommercial national dashboard sponsored or co-sponsored by government. Multiple commercial dashboards listing an individual's benefits and accounts with private sector vendors and the government would raise additional issues of confidentiality, security, conflicts of interest, coordination, and reliability.

Cybersecurity

A third major challenge will be providing cybersecurity safeguards that protect the personal financial information held on a dashboard. The alarming and pervasive nature of recent data breaches—and the fact that they seem to continue successfully penetrating the largest, most sophisticated firms and public sector organizations—suggests that centralization of each individual's entire portfolio of retirement assets and benefits in a single repository might provide too tempting a target for theft of information. It would not be unfair, therefore, to ask whether such centralization in a dashboard is worth the data security risk.

We think it is, when there is sufficient ground for confidence that cybersecurity safeguards and related consumer protections will be effective. Such safeguards and protections are obviously essential and are being vigorously pursued wholly apart from the need for a dashboard. In addition, though, dashboards in other countries have illustrated that the risk of aggregating so much financial data in a single repository can be circumvented. An alternative is for the dashboard to send user-initiated information requests to all participating providers or other information sources and quickly assemble a comprehensive picture of the individual's resources, including income projections, on a temporary basis. Once the user has reviewed and perhaps copied or transmitted the information to a secure, personal destination, the information would disappear from the dashboard website.

Covering the Costs

Funding the dashboard is another challenge.[44] Adhering to compulsory data standardization and security standards will involve expense for plan providers, who will have to staff this operation and develop internal guidelines to meet the dashboard regulations. Especially at the outset, government may have to subsidize some of these costs with temporary tax credits or other approaches to defray the costs. Because use of the dashboard can be expected to increase gradually, costs per user might be high at first but, with robust marketing, usage should grow, and per-user costs can reasonably be expected to decline over time.

A dashboard could also reduce costs for some plan sponsors and providers, who might view it as making their own financial education or financial literacy programs redundant. Others might retain those programs insofar as they are intended to serve commercial purposes.

PUTTING SAVERS FIRST

Our private pension system—a market-based public-private joint venture often driven by the financial interests of competing investment and record-keeping firms—needs to place a higher priority on making life easier for savers. While automatic features have made huge strides in simplifying enrollment, saving, and investing, the retirement system remains fragmented and complex and requires decisions that most people are not equipped to make.

Savers could benefit from a retirement dashboard—a single website that they can be confident is operated solely in their interest. The emergence and popularity of dashboards in other countries facing similar issues, and the compelling need to assist savers in managing their own retirement planning, suggest that US policymakers should make it a priority to develop a retirement dashboard for American workers. Of course, the lengthy delays and obstacles encountered by the UK in its efforts to establish such a facility could be instructive as the United States designs and builds its own version. As a first step, a feasibility task force, like the one GAO recommended to DOL, could build relationships with the teams that built and manage foreign dashboards.[45]

APPENDIX: EXAMPLES OF RETIREMENT DASHBOARDS IN OTHER COUNTRIES

Many countries have addressed issues with their retirement income systems in part by establishing dashboards, registries, or similar comprehensive retirement record-keeping facilities. Table 4-1 highlights key design features in several countries. Reviewing other countries' facilities, which we broadly refer to here as dashboards but which they refer to by a variety of terms, shows a range of purposes and design options. Other countries' experiences also demonstrate that dashboards commonly go through several stages of development, often starting as simpler information sites or registries, and build up over time by adding features and capabilities.

Australia

Australia's dashboard resulted from an effort to reduce the number of savers with duplicate accounts. At one point, an estimated 40 percent of Australians had more than one account, resulting in an estimated 10 million unnecessary duplicate accounts and costing participants an estimated A$2.6 billion each year in unnecessary fees.[46]

In Australia, the government manages the dashboard and provides a single access point. Using their myGov accounts, which provide access to several government services, Australians connect to the dashboard from the Australian Tax Office site. Pension providers cannot embed the dashboard into their own sites, and only pensions created within the Australian government's superannuation ("super") system are linked to the dashboard.[47] The Australian Tax Office acts as a clearinghouse, directing employer contributions through the SuperStream, the government's mechanism for transmitting super funds between employers, participants, and the government. Because these contributions are made through the same government agency that manages the dashboard, the data behind the dashboard are already standardized. The primary objective of the dashboard is to reunite people with all their retirement plans. From the dashboard site, users can consolidate their savings into one super-account, which reduces plan fees and simplifies their retirement asset portfolio. The dashboard is financed with government funds and a pension industry tax.

Belgium

Belgium has developed a facility to allow users to see their public and occupational pension benefits. Sigedis, a nonprofit established by the government, manages the site by aggregating public and private pension information. Just over 200 insurance companies and pension funds manage over 100,000 private plans.[48] Users access this facility using their e-card, a form of digital ID. The Belgian government's goal was to improve understanding of pension rights for residents approaching retirement. The facility is updated to reflect retirement policy changes so that users have an easier time understanding how policy changes affect their retirement income. In 2014, its purpose was expanded to include responsibility for maintaining information on inactive accounts, something pension providers had been doing. In 2016 and 2017 the facility was visited more than 6.7 million times.[49] Funding comes from government general revenues.[50]

Denmark

Denmark's pension dashboard, first launched in 1999 and made fully comprehensive in 2013, is managed by a consortium that relies on bank, pension provider, and government participation. People access the dashboard with their digital ID. The dashboard, known as PensionsInfo, saw 1.3 million unique users (among a population of 4.4 million adults) in 2017.[51] The occupational pensions in Denmark are typically sector-wide, cover a vast majority of workers through collective labor agreements, and, for the most part, are DC plans.[52] Denmark's dashboard relies on voluntary participation by pension providers—an approach that did not make the dashboard comprehensive until 14 years after its introduction. The dashboard is designed to work like a search engine, sending providers a request for information when users log in. It does not maintain a central data repository. Through the PensionsInfo site, users can view their accrued benefits, understand their pension's fee, simulate the impact of retirement decisions, project future payout amounts under various scenarios, and consult with an adviser from their pension provider. Pension providers voluntarily fund the dashboard project.

Screenshots of the Danish dashboard (Figure 4A-1) show how users see their pensions and can navigate through the site to access more detailed information about their retirement income. The screenshots show how a user can explore the effects of retiring at a certain age, becoming eligible for disability, or combining retirement income with their partner. In addition, the dashboard has features that help identify inactive accounts for potential consolidation.

Israel

Israel has a facility, built with data from a government-owned clearinghouse, accessible from a noncommercial site and from private sector sites. The project began in 2010 after receiving government authorization. The clearinghouse, operated by a third party, provides a finder service and Israelis can consent to share their data with private sector dashboards managed by pension advisers and insurance agents.[53] Legislation requires all providers to share their data with the clearinghouse. The government also requires plans to disclose their charges so that users can see whether switching plans would save them money.

Netherlands

The Netherlands has a "Pensioenregister" which, like Sweden, provides information about public and occupational pensions, but not about individual pension products.[54] Employees in industries with occupational pensions must participate in the pensions, which include sector pension funds (e.g., for construction employees) and occupational pension funds (e.g., for notaries). Occupational pensions are provided by 319 pension funds, a majority of which are single-employer plans.[55] In addition to the nearly universal public pension, 94 percent of Dutch employees are covered by an occupational DB plan. Though DB plans have been the dominant retirement system in the Netherlands, a 2020

Figure 4A-1. **Danish Dashboard: Overview by Page Account with an Estimation of Payments in the First Year**

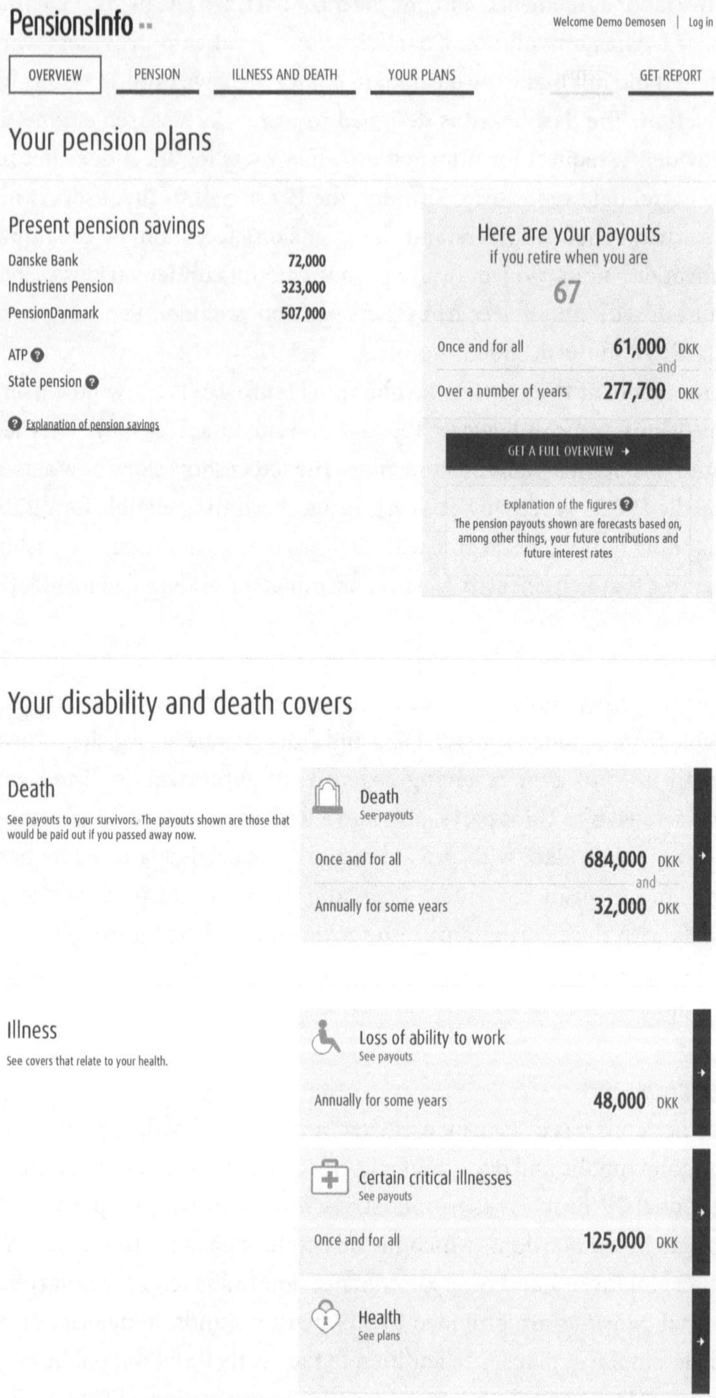

Source: Pensioenregister (2020).

Figure 4A-1. (***continued***)

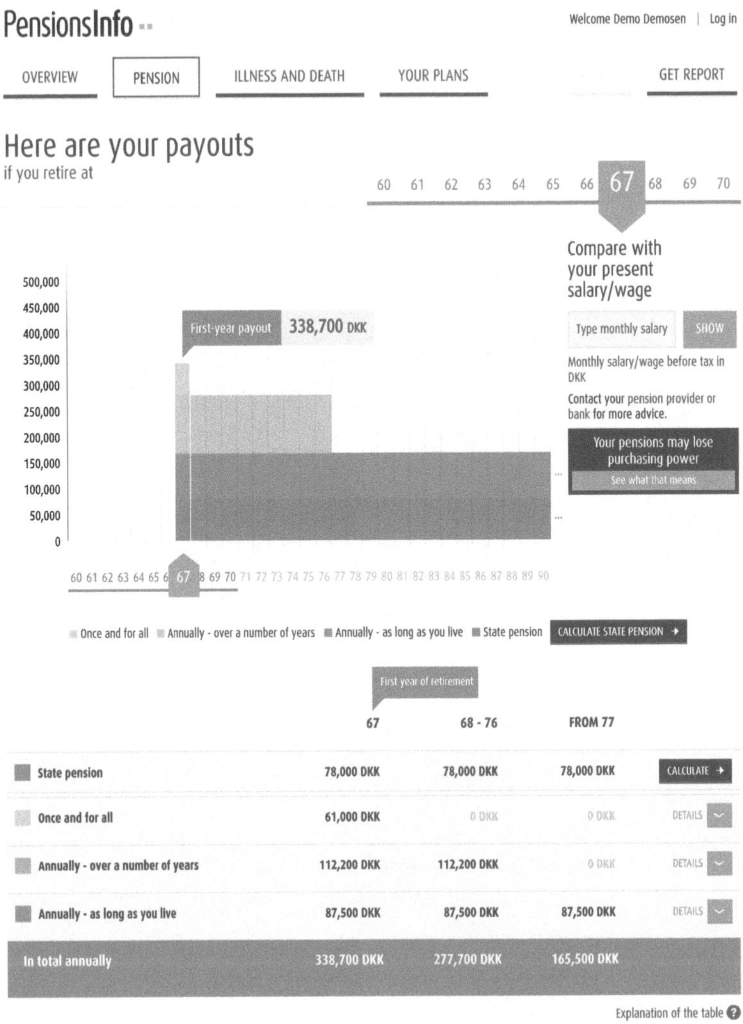

(***continued***)

agreement between the government, employers, and labor unions will see it transition into a form of DC plan by 2026.

The pension registry's primary objective is to increase awareness of pension rights and saving. Accessed by a digital ID, it shows information on the public and occupational pensions at the user's request. Because consumers' data can be more vulnerable in an aggregate repository, the Dutch avoid the use of a permanent database. When the user exits, the data are no longer available to the dashboard. The registry resembles a dashboard insofar as users can simulate their own future decisions, such as selecting a retirement age, and

Figure 4A-1. (*continued*)

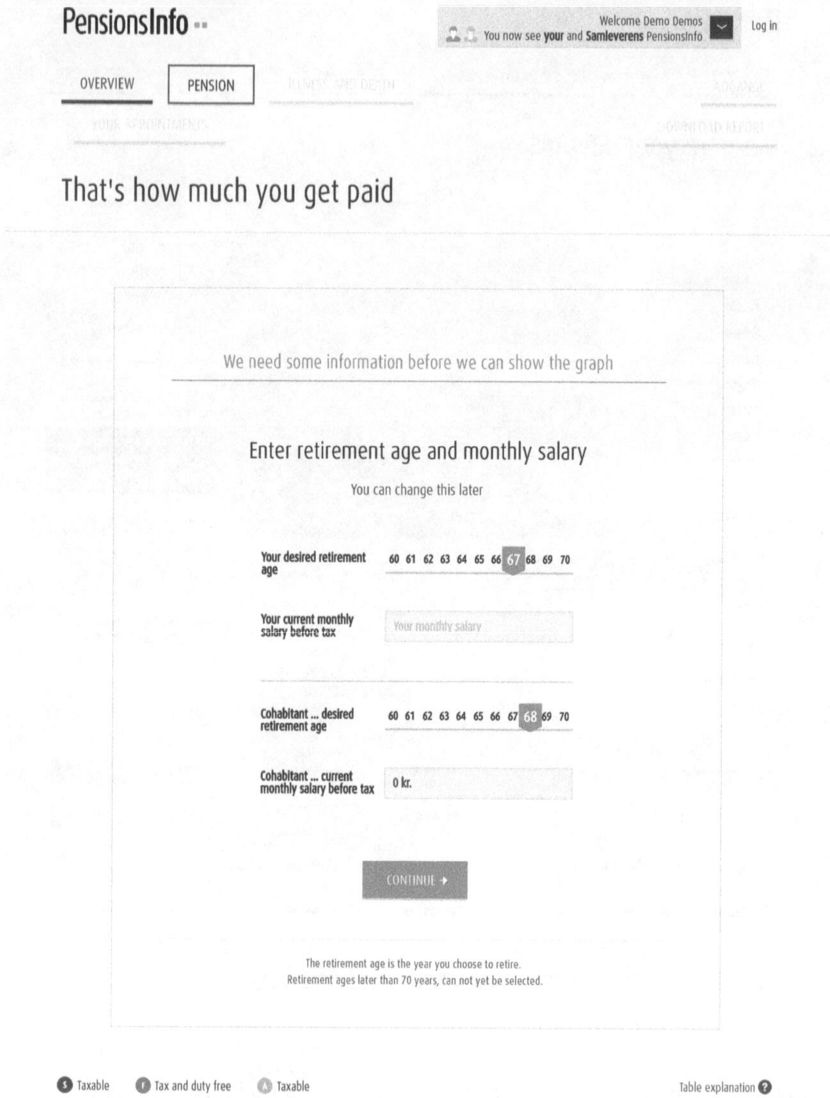

(*continued*)

view how that will affect their expected benefits, but are referred to their providers' sites to make changes to their plans. The dashboard, implemented by the Pension Register Foundation in 2011, is a joint initiative of the Dutch pension funds, pension insurers, and the Social Insurance Bank; as a public project, it is free to use.[56] The government made provider participation mandatory, and providers finance the dashboard.

Figure 4A-1. (***continued***)

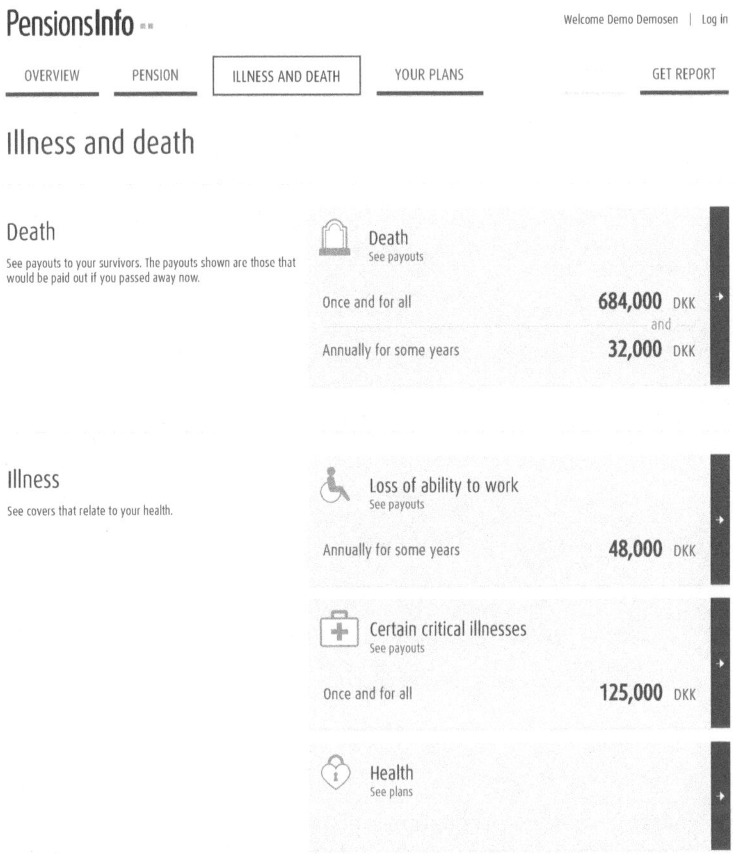

Sweden

Like the Australian dashboard, the Swedish dashboard is available through a single site accessed by digital ID. The Swedish government and pension providers voluntarily worked together to provide a dashboard through the nonprofit organization minPension. The collaboration allows for coverage of both government and private pensions. There is no standing data repository. Instead, when a user logs in, minPension sends an information request to the state pension and to the nearly thirty participating pension providers. Within minutes, minPension compiles all the pension information—public, occupational, and private—and the user can see a comprehensive, current summary of their retirement benefits and a visualization of their anticipated income. A fairly uniform pension system—nearly all workers receive the public pension and

Figure 4A-1. (*continued*)

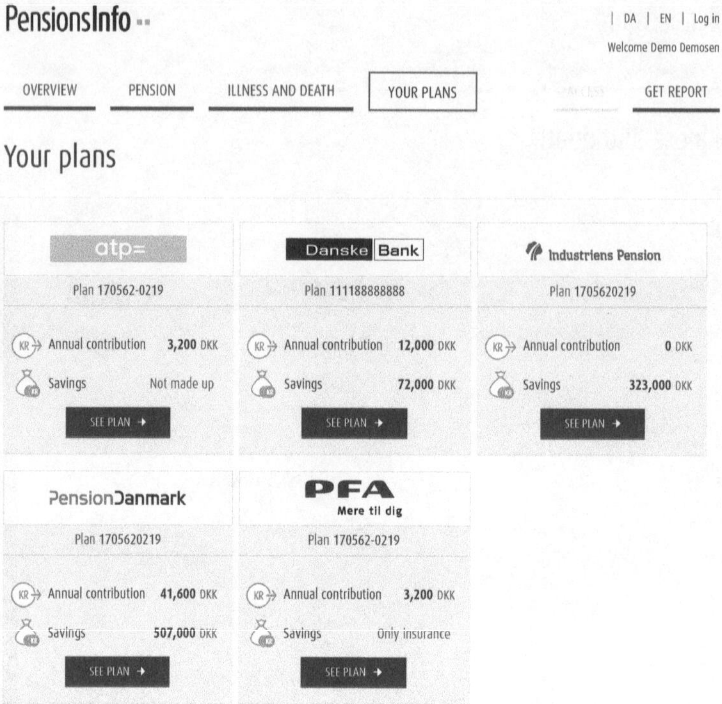

90 percent are covered by occupational pensions, which are mandatory for employees working under certain collective agreements—facilitates collaboration and integration.[57]

Sweden's dashboard began primarily as an information-sharing tool. Before minPension's 2004 launch, the government's pension agency began sending out an annual notice of accrued benefits from the public pension and the government-mandated individual pension (known as a premium pension fund)—and sent it in a distinctive bright orange envelope. The dashboard built on this effort to share important pension information with participants and reflected an increased commitment by the Swedish government to encourage people to be knowledgeable about their pensions.

A popular feature of the Swedish dashboard is the pension forecast tool, which allows users to project their benefits on the assumption that their earnings and contributions continue at the current rate until retirement.[58] In addition, the forecast tool enables users to simulate how changing jobs, receiving a different salary, withdrawing contributions, or changing benefits will affect their future pension.[59] Users can expand their profiles to see more in-depth information, but the initial view is clean and high-level.[60] MinPension reports that the dashboard has 3.8 million users out of an adult population of 8.15 million, who in turn generate over 26 million forecasts a year.[61]

United Kingdom

The UK has been working for some years to develop a pension dashboard. Unlike some of the other countries with dashboards or registries that have essentially universal public pensions and a few large occupational pensions, the UK—much like the United States—has a decentralized pension system (apart from its first-pillar mandatory State Pension). The work process the UK government has established and the challenges the initiative has faced offer useful lessons for developing a US retirement savings dashboard.

The UK dashboard is intended to "enable individuals to access their pensions information online, securely and all in one place, thereby supporting better planning for retirement and growing financial wellbeing. Dashboards will provide clear and simple information about an individual's multiple pension savings, including their State Pension. They will also help them to reconnect with any lost pension pots."[62]

As of 2020, the UK is planning for multiple commercial dashboards and a free, noncommercial dashboard built on data from pension providers and the State Pension. To use the dashboard system, pension plan participants will have to provide consent to their pension providers for the inclusion of their information in the dashboard database.

The government's 2016 budget initially committed to launching a dashboard by 2019. Almost immediately, controversies developed about the number of dashboards that would be allowed, what would be included on them, and other issues. While Parliament and consumer groups have pushed for a dashboard, segments of the pensions industry have resisted. As a result, the agencies responsible for creating the dashboard's digital architecture have struggled to access all the necessary data and establish a timeframe for the pension industry and elected officials. Among the controversies was whether the UK would have one dashboard or many individual ones. Those supporting many dashboards have prevailed, but one of the questions before Parliament is whether to ban the dashboards of individual companies from marketing unsuitable products to users.

At this writing, Parliament is completing legislation that would set a structure for UK dashboards, including data standards. The government's latest report states the launch date has yet to be determined, but many structural details have been worked out. Some of those specifics were developed by the Pension Dashboard Prototype Project, which finished its work in October 2018, and can be seen on its website.[63] More recently, the Pensions Dashboards Programme, established by the Money and Pensions Service, is designing and implementing an infrastructure, working closely with the industry, regulators, and government.[64] It is also developing a dashboard for the Money and Pensions Service.[65] Because the United States' retirement system is more like the UK's system than the systems of some other countries with pension dashboards, insights from the ongoing development of a UK dashboard could facilitate the process here.

NOTES

This chapter was made possible through generous support from Arnold Ventures. The views expressed here are solely those of the authors and should not be attributed to any other person or any organization.

Disclosure: Iwry provides, through J. Mark Iwry, PLLC, policy and legal advice to plan sponsors and providers, nonprofit organizations, trade associations, fintechs, private equity firms, other investment firms, and financial institutions regarding retirement and savings policy, pension and retirement plans, and related issues. Iwry is a member of the American Benefits Institute Board of Advisors, the Board of Advisors of the Pension Research Council at the Wharton School, the Council of Scholar Advisors of the Georgetown University Center for Retirement Initiatives, the Panel of Outside Scholars of the Boston College Center for Retirement Research, the CUNA Mutual Safety Net Independent Advisory Board, and the Aspen Leadership Forum Advisory Board. He also periodically serves as an expert witness in federal court litigation relating to retirement plans. The authors did not receive any financial support from any firm or person for any views or positions expressed or advocated in this document. They are currently not an officer, director, or board member of any organization that has compensated or otherwise influenced them to write this paper or to express or advocate any views in this paper. Accordingly, the views expressed here are solely those of the authors and should not be attributed to any other person or any organization.

1. For example, in a recent Federal Reserve Board (2020) survey, only about 37 percent of nonretired adults thought that their retirement savings were "on track" (as they defined it). About 44 percent said their savings were not on track, and the remaining 26 percent were not sure.

2. Dashboards could also help people navigate the process of converting retirement savings into income, a topic we leave to future research.

3. US Bureau of Labor Statistics (2019).

4. See Internal Revenue Service (2020); Internal Revenue Service (2012).

5. This particular information reporting does not, however, extend to benefits that have been paid out of a plan to a missing or unresponsive participant, even if the intended recipient has not received them, has failed to cash a benefits check, or is unaware that they have been automatically rolled over to an IRA in the individual's name.

6. See Advisory Council on Employee Welfare and Pension Benefit Plans (2019).

7. DOL Field Assistance Bulletin 2014-01. The IRS has similar guidance in Revenue Procedure 2018–52, section 6.02(d)(5), requiring plan administrators to take reasonable actions to search for missing participants who are entitled to benefits but do not respond to a mailing to their last known address.

8. EBSA's Abandoned Plan Program helps plan participants obtain their benefits from retirement plans abandoned by their employer sponsors. When an employer abandons a plan, this program facilitates the termination process by requiring participant notification, maintaining a searchable database, and providing a fiduciary safe harbor for missing participants in terminating abandoned plans. Employee Benefits Security Administration (2009).

9. Missing Participants Rule (2017).

10. Missing Participants Rule (2017).

11. Pension Benefit Guaranty Corporation (2020).

12. Government Accountability Office (2014). Benefits left behind in a previous employer's plan would seem to be at greater risk of becoming lost over time than benefits that are transferred to a new employer plan or to an IRA. On the other hand, benefits maintained in an employer plan have advantages over IRAs, such as fiduciary protection for participants and, usually, lower costs.

13. A 2017 TIAA survey found that about one-third of employees had left a retirement plan at a former employer rather than roll it into an IRA or the plan of their next employer. The reasons they cite for doing so are revealing. While 30 percent said that they were satisfied with their former employer's plan, 17 percent did not know that they could move their money, another 17 percent did not know what to do, 13 percent did not have the time to do a rollover, and another 9 percent found the rollover process too complicated.

14. Government Accountability Office (2019a).

15. The bill was introduced most recently in the Senate as S.2474 by Elizabeth Warren (D-MA) and Steve Daines (R-MT), and in the House of Representatives as H.R.6540 by Suzanne Bonamici (D-OR) and Jim Banks (R-IN). It had previously been introduced in both 2016 and 2018. It includes a requirement that plan administrators update the registry annually on changes in the location of employees' retirement benefits. Although this bill is intended to reduce the number of lost accounts, a provision toward the back of the bill would actually increase the $5,000 cap on the size of distributions that plans can distribute unilaterally to an IRA in the name of an unresponsive participant.

16. Of course, whether consolidation of accounts is in the account holder's interest in any given case will depend on a variety of factors, such as whether any of the accounts are inactive, whether some are in plans of former or current employers or in IRAs, the comparative costs to the account holder of maintaining the accounts with or without consolidation, how many accounts there are, how they are invested, liquidity, and other specific terms of the accounts.

17. Munnell and Webb (2015) estimate an annual leakage rate of 1.5 percent using leakage data from Vanguard; their data represent a small portion of all plans. Bryant, Holden, and Sabelhaus (2011) find an annual leakage rate of 2.5 percent for participants under the age of 60, and observe that about 15 percent of DC and IRA contributions ultimately leak out as penalized withdrawals.

18. Goodman and others (2019).

19. Argento, Bryant, and Sabelhaus (2015).

20. Government Accountability Office (2009).

21. Savings Preservation Working Group (2019); Alight (2019).

22. See Bryant, Holden, and Sabelhaus (2011); Burman and others (2012); Burman, Coe, and Gale (1999).

23. Lu and others (2017). Government Accountability Office (1997), Mitchell, Utkus, and Yang (2005), and Holden and VanDerhei (2001) conclude that plans offering loans tend to have higher employee participation and contributions.

24. "Automatic rollover" means that, if an employee's employment with a plan sponsor terminates with a vested benefit between $1,000 and $5,000, the balance is automatically rolled over tax-free to an IRA established in the employee's name unless the employee directs otherwise or the plan sponsor chooses to retain the benefit in the plan (Internal Revenue Code sections 401(a)(31), 402(c)). The IRAs usually invest the benefits in principal preservation funds such as money market funds because DOL regulations limit safe harbor treatment to such investments, but the Retirement Savings Lost and Found bill referred to above would allow investment in target date funds with a view to reducing the likelihood that the IRA balances will shrink as fees exceed returns. "Automatic portability" refers to a newer procedure whereby, in these circumstances, if a departing employee takes a new job and participates in the new employer's plan but does not direct a rollover, the former employer's plan and new employer's plan (or more likely their record-keepers on their behalf) can provide an intermediary entity the information needed to complete an automatic rollover to the new plan unless the participant directs otherwise. The rollover can automatically go directly to the new plan or, if the departing employee is not yet a participant in a new employer plan, it can go to an IRA and later automatically roll from the IRA to the new plan. See DOL PTE 2019–02, 84 Fed. Reg. 37337 (July 31, 2019). Norway announced in 2020 that it will require autoportability on somewhat similar terms (Nordahl 2020).

25. The Retirement Savings Lost and Found bill includes a provision that would transfer, when participants change jobs, plan balances of $1,000 or less to the Treasury Department. Participants could then claim the benefits from the Treasury. Section 3(b)(2). It might be worth exploring whether this process could be directed through a dashboard and whether companies could be required to refer employees to a dashboard with a view to reducing at least some leakage.

26. See, e.g., Orszag, Iwry, and Gale (2006); Gale and others (2009).

27. Federal Reserve Board (2020).

28. Employee Benefits Security Administration (2020) and *US Chamber of Commerce* v. *US Department of Labor* (2018). The Securities and Exchange Commission (SEC) has also issued a regulation defining the duties under the securities laws of broker dealers as well as registered investment advisers that provide investment advice;

see SEC, "Regulation Best Interest," https://www.sec.gov/info/smallbus/secg/regulation-best-interest.

29. In fact, some studies suggest that many people with financial advisers do worse than those who invest on their own. Bergstresser, Chalmers, and Tufano (2009), Nanda, Wang, and Zheng (2009).

30. OECD (2016).

31. Social Security Administration (2020).

32. Misiri (2017).

33. Lusardi and Mitchell (2014).

34. Another alternative is being pursued in the UK (see appendix), which has gone further and established a financial advice agency, the Money and Pension Service. If the United States were to attempt something similar, perhaps within the CFPB, such an entity might be accessed through the dashboard.

35. Half of retired households cannot maintain the level of spending from their first five years of retirement into later years. While some reduction in spending is associated with the tapering off of certain expenses for older households (e.g., they travel less), some of the reductions result from not saving enough or spending savings too quickly, indicating that retirees need help to better understand how to pace their distributions over their later years (see Consumer Financial Protection Bureau 2020).

36. As required by Congress, DOL is expected to publish by around the end of 2020 final regulations protecting plan sponsors from liability if they provide retirement income illustrations. For further discussion, see Gale and others (2008, p, 20).

37. Presumably, user information and any reports that users produce or are created for them would not be retained on the dashboard after they log off, but users would be able to send a secure copy to their own email address or personal website.

38. This process would need to draw on the most advanced and effective techniques of web content design, including appropriate linking, layering, and other packaging of information, to give users an accessible range of choices from concisely hitting the high points to diving more deeply. Regular market testing of alternative presentations on consumers could also be useful.

39. UK Department for Work and Pensions (2018). A UK survey found that a significant majority of respondents across gender and age groups expressed an interest in having a pension dashboard if one were established. B&CE (2015).

40. UK Department for Work and Pensions (2018).

41. Moss (2016).

42. Private pensions and retirement plans hold more than $28 trillion in assets for the benefit of over 90 million individuals. About two-thirds of retirement assets are held among more than 700,000 401(k), pension, and other employer-sponsored retirement plans, while the remaining third is held in some 46 million individual retirement accounts. Investment Company Institute (2019, 2020); Employee Benefits Security Administration (2018).

43. Among other concerns that will be raised will be the risk that ease of transfer and consolidation via dashboard might make it "too easy" for savers to close accounts without careful deliberation and to put all of their eggs in a single basket. It will be argued that if savers could transfer and consolidate accounts without necessarily

communicating directly with the "losing" financial providers in such a transaction, aggressive providers competing to manage all of a saver's retirement assets would pressure individuals into making unduly hasty or ill-considered decisions, including consolidation in a suboptimal account. The potential concern is that this might exacerbate the impact of the intense advertising that currently urges employer plan participants to roll over from their "old" 401(k) into an IRA, even when (as is often true in the case of the federal Thrift Savings Plan, for example) retention of the assets in the former employer's plan is probably in the participant's best interests.

44. A 2019 report by the US Treasury Department estimated that the federal government spends $273 million a year on financial literacy and financial education. Department of the Treasury (2019).

45. Government Accountability Office (2019b).

46. Plastow (2018).

47. The Superannuation Guarantee is funded by an employer contribution, currently 9.5 percent of workers' salaries, and additional individual contributions.

48. Actuarial Association of Europe (2015).

49. Rust (2017).

50. Belgian officials interviewed by GAO staff projected the cost of the fully functioning dashboard to be 3.5 million euro annually; see Government Accountability Office (2014, p. 77).

51. UK Department for Work and Pensions (2018).

52. Van Dam and Anderson (2008).

53. Lindley (2019); Shamah (2013).

54. Royal London (2018).

55. OECD (2017).

56. Pensioenregister (2020).

57. European Commission (2020); OECD (2017).

58. Royal London (2018).

59. MinPension (2020).

60. Larsson, Paulsson, and Sundén (2011); Misiri (2017).

61. MinPension (2020).

62. Pensions Dashboards Programme (2020).

63. UK Department for Work and Pensions (2018).

64. The UK's Money and Pensions Service was established in 2019 as a merger of the Money Advice Service, Pensions Advisory Service, and Pension Wise with a view to improving the financial capabilities of UK citizens.

65. Pensions Dashboards Programme (2020).

REFERENCES

Actuarial Association of Europe. 2015. "Report on Key Issues for Setting Up National Pension Tracking Services in Six EU Countries." Brussels, Belgium.

Advisory Council on Employee Welfare and Pension Benefit Plans. 2019. "Voluntary Transfers of Uncashed Checks from ERISA Plans to State Unclaimed Property Programs." Report to the Honorable Eugene Scalia, United States Secretary of Labor.

Alight. 2019. “What Do Workers Do with Their Retirement Savings after They Leave Their Employers?” Lincolnshire, IL: Alight Solutions.

Argento, Robert, Victoria Bryant, and John Sabelhaus. 2015. “Early Withdrawals from Retirement Accounts during the Great Recession.” *Contemporary Economic Policy* 33 (1): 1–16.

B&CE. 2015. “Public Attitudes towards a Pension Dashboard.” Crawley, UK: Building & Civil Engineering Holidays Scheme Management Limited.

Bergstresser, Daniel, John M. R. Chalmers, and Peter Tufano. 2009. “Assessing the Costs and Benefits of Brokers in the Mutual Fund Industry.” *Review of Financial Studies* 22 (10): 4129–56.

Bryant, Victoria, Sarah Holden, and John Sabelhaus. 2011. “Qualified Retirement Plans: Analysis of Distribution and Rollover Activity.” Working Paper 2011-01. Philadelphia: Pension Research Council.

Burman, Leonard E., Norma Coe, and William G. Gale. 1999. “Lump Sum Distributions from Pension Plans: Recent Evidence and Issues for Policy and Research.” *National Tax Journal* 52 (3): 553–62.

Burman, Leonard E., Norma Coe, Michael B. Dworsky, and William G. Gale. 2012. “Effects of Public Policies on the Disposition of Pre-Retirement Lump-Sum Distributions: Rational and Behavioral Influences.” *National Tax Journal* 65 (4): 863–87.

Consumer Financial Protection Bureau. 2020. “Financial Decision-Making: Research Brief.” Washington, DC: CFPB Office of Financial Protection for Older Americans.

Department of the Treasury. 2019. *Federal Financial Literacy Reform: Coordinating and Improving Financial Literacy Efforts.* July 15. https://home.treasury.gov/news/press-releases/sm729.

Employee Benefits Security Administration. 2009. *Fact Sheet: Abandoned Individual Account Plan Final Regulations and Class Exemption.* Washington, DC: US Department of Labor. https://www.DOL.gov/agencies/ebsa/about-ebsa/our-activities/resource-center/fact-sheets/abandoned-individual-account-plan.

———. 2018. *Private Pension Plan Bulletin.* Washington, DC: US Department of Labor.

———. 2020. “Financial Factors in Selecting Plan Investments.” 85 Fed. Reg. 39113. June 22, 2020 (codified as 29 C.F.R. pt. 2550).

European Commission. 2020. *Sweden—Old-Age Pension.* European Commission Directorate-General for Employment, Social Affairs, and Inclusion. https://ec.europa.eu/social/main.jsp?catId=1130&langId=en&intPageId=4814.

Federal Reserve Board. 2020. “Report on the Economic Well-Being of U.S. Households in 2019, Featuring Supplemental Data from April 2020.” Washington, DC: Board of Governors of the Federal Reserve System.

Gale, William G., J. Mark Iwry, David C. John, and Lina Walker. 2008. “Increasing Annuitization in 401(k)s with Automatic Trial Income.” Brookings.

———. 2009. *Automatic: Changing the Way America Saves.* Brookings.

Goodman, Lucas, Kathleen Mackie, Jacob A. Mortenson, and Heidi R. Schramm. 2019. “The Evolution of Leakage and Retirement Asset Flows in the U.S.” Washington, DC: Joint Committee on Taxation, US Congress.

Government Accountability Office. 1997. “401(k) Pension Plans: Loan Provisions Enhance Participation but May Affect Income Security for Some.” US HEHS-98-5.

———. 2009. "401(K) Plans: Policy Changes Could Reduce the Long-term Effects of Leakage on Workers' Retirement Savings." US GAO-09-715.

———. 2014. "401(k) Plans: Greater Protections Needed for Forced Transfer and Inactive Accounts." US GAO-15-73.

———. 2019a. "Department of Labor Priority Recommendations." US GAO-19-395SP Priority Recommendations. Department of Labor.

———. 2019b. "Retirement Accounts Federal Action Needed to Clarify Tax Treatment of Unclaimed 401(k) Plan Savings Transferred to States." US GAO-19-88.

Holden, Sarah, and Jack VanDerhei. 2001. "Contribution Behavior of 401(K) Plan Participants." Issue Brief 238. Washington, DC: Employee Benefit Research Institute.

Internal Revenue Service. 2012. "Revenue Procedures 2012-35." 26 CFR 601.601. https://www.irs.gov/pub/irs-drop/rp-12-35.pdf.

———. 2020. *Missing Participants or Beneficiaries.* https://www.irs.gov/retirement-plans/missing-participants-or-beneficiaries.

Investment Company Institute. 2019. "The Role of IRAs in US Households' Saving for Retirement." *ICI Research Perspective* 25 (10).

———. 2020. *Retirement Assets Total $28.7 Trillion in First Quarter 2020.* https://ici.org/research/stats/retirement/ret_20_q1.

Larsson, Paul, Arne Paulsson, and Annika Sundén. 2011. "Customer-Oriented Services and Information Experiences from Sweden." In *Priority Challenges in Pension Administration*, edited by Noriuki Takayama. Tokyo: Maruzen.

Lindley, Dominic. 2019. "Delivering Pensions Dashboards in the Public Interest." The People's Pension. https://2ihxox21inu92ajbbx2yez7v-wpengine.netdna-ssl.com/wp-content/uploads/2019/01/Pension-Dashboard-report.pdf.

Lu, Timothy (Jun), Olivia S. Mitchell, Stephen P. Utkus, and Jean A. Young. 2017. "Borrowing from the Future? 401(k) Plan Loans and Loan Defaults." *National Tax Journal* 70 (1): 77–110.

Lusardi, Annamaria, and Olivia Mitchell. 2014. "The Economic Importance of Financial Literacy: Theory and Evidence." *Journal of Economic Literature* 52 (1): 5–44.

MinPension. 2020. *See What You Get in Retirement.* https://www.minpension.se/allt-om-pensioner/pensionsprognos/se-vad-du-far-i-pension.

Misiri, Talya. 2017. Interview with Patrik Malmquist. *European Pensions* (April/May): 40–41.

Missing Participants Rule. 2017. Pension Benefit Guaranty Corporation. 82 Fed. Reg. 60800. Jan. 22, 2017 (codified as 29 C.F.R. pts. 4000, 4001, 4003 and 4041).

Mitchell, Olivia, Stephen P. Utkus, and Tongxuan (Stella) Yang. 2005. "Turning Workers into Savers? Incentives, Liquidity, and Choice in 401(k) Plan Design." *National Tax Journal* 60 (3): 469–89.

Moss, Gail. 2016. "Communication: Lessons from Scandinavia." *IPE Magazine*, June.

Mukherjee, Anita. 2020. "Frictions in Saving and Claiming: An Analysis of Unclaimed Retirement Accounts." University of Wisconsin-Madison.

Munnell, Alicia, and Anthony Webb. 2015. "The Impact of Leakages from 401(k)s and IRAs." Working Paper 2015–2. Center for Retirement Research, Boston College.

Nanda, Vikram K., Z. Jay Wang, and Lu Zheng. 2009. "The ABCs of Mutual Funds: On the Introduction of Multiple Share Classes." *Journal of Financial Intermediation* 18 (3): 329–61.

Nordahl, Bjoern-Erik. 2020. *Norway: New Law Automatically Consolidates Employee DC Accounts.* Willis Towers Watson, May 29.

Organization for Economic Cooperation and Development (OECD). 2016. "OECD Pensions Outlook 2016." Paris.

———. 2017. "OECD Pensions at a Glance 2017: Country Profiles—Netherlands." OECD and G20 Indicators. Paris.

Orszag, Peter R., J. Mark Iwry, and William G. Gale. 2006. *Ideas to Improve Retirement Security in America.* New York: Century Foundation Press.

Pensioenregister. 2020. *Pension Overview for All Citizens with Pension Entitlements in the Netherlands.* https://pensioenregister.nl/.

Pension Benefit Guaranty Corporation. 2020. *Search Our List of Missing Participants.* https://www.pbgc.gov/wr/missing-participants.

Pensions Dashboards Programme. 2020. *Vision.* https://www.pensionsdashboards programme.org.uk/vision/.

Plastow, Killian. 2018. "The Avoidable Super Fees Stinging Almost Half Australia's Workforce." *New Daily.* https://thenewdaily.com.au/finance/superannuation/2018/10/09/how-to-consolidate-super/.

Royal London. 2018. "Pension Dashboards around the World." Royal London Policy Paper.

Rust, Susanna. 2017. *Belgium Adds Functionality to Online Pension Portal.* IPE. https://www.ipe.com/belgium-adds-functionality-to-online-pension-portal-/10021941.article.

Savings Preservation Working Group. 2019. "Cashing Out: The Systemic Impact of Withdrawing Savings before Retirement." Issue Brief Volume 1. https://tsretirement.com/wp-content/uploads/2020/02/cashing-out-issue.pdf.

Shamah, David. 2013. "Online Service Aims to Clean up Israel's Pension Mess." *Times of Israel*, April 20.

Social Security Administration. 2020. *My Social Security: What Is an Account?* https://www.ssa.gov/myaccount/what.html.

TIAA. 2017. "Lack of Understanding Linked to Low IRA Ownership." https://www.tiaa.org/public/about-tiaa/news-press/press-releases/pressrelease668.html.

UK Department for Work and Pensions. 2018. "Pensions Dashboards Working Together for the Consumer." Presented to Parliament by the Secretary of State for Work and Pensions by Command of Her Majesty.

US Bureau of Labor Statistics. 2019. "Number of Jobs, Labor Market Experience, and Earnings Growth: Results from a National Longitudinal Survey." Washington, DC: US Department of Labor.

US Chamber of Commerce v. US Department of Labor. No. 17-10238 (5th Cir. 2018).

Van Dam, Rein, and Erik Brink Anderson. 2008. *Risk-Based Supervision of Pension Institutions in Denmark.* Washington, DC: World Bank.

FIVE

Retirement Plans for Contingent Workers

ISSUES AND OPTIONS

William G. Gale, Sarah Holmes Berk, and David C. John

In the traditional employer-employee relationship, workers earn a salary or hourly wage and receive fringe benefits. Today, however, a wide variety of workers have alternative work arrangements. These workers may be full-time, part-time, or seasonal. They range from independent contractors and white-collar consultants to blue-collar workers such as security guards and maintenance professionals. The rise of the so-called gig economy—which allows people to hail cabs through Lyft, find household help through TaskRabbit, and book lodging through Airbnb, among other applications—has brought these workers into the spotlight. But similar issues have been present for the past several decades, as employers have increasingly substituted independent contractors or firms employing them for traditional employees. Contingent workers now account for a significant and, by most estimates, growing share of the US workforce, and their role in labor markets is expected to continue to rise.

This chapter examines retirement saving policy for contingent, or independent, workers, terms we use interchangeably. It also covers gig workers, a subset of this group who work usually temporary, flexible jobs for an online entity. Contingent workers face many challenges in preparing for retirement. On average, they earn less than traditional employees and have more volatile income, giving them less disposable income available to save and making it harder to set aside regular saving amounts.

The current employer-focused private retirement system was not designed with these workers in mind. As a result, contingent workers have less access to and coverage under work-provided retirement plans than traditional workers. Thus they also tend to miss out on provisions that encourage retirement wealth accumulation, such as payroll deduction contributions, automatic enrollment, and employer matching contributions. In addition, under the current system, job changes create an unnecessarily high likelihood of pension leakage. However well or poorly it serves the needs of traditional workers, the current retirement system does not meet the needs of contingent workers, who plausibly have less job stability than traditional workers; it is also inadequate for those who switch back and forth between contingent and traditional jobs.

Of course, anyone with earnings can contribute to an Individual Retirement Account (IRA), but only a small percentage of people do so on a regular basis. Moreover, because IRAs have lower annual contribution limits than 401(k) plans and cannot accept employer matches, the amount that can be accumulated is limited. For the most part, automatic payroll deductions deposited into an IRA exist in only a handful of states that have implemented Automatic IRAs.

To help contingent workers save for retirement, we propose several changes, ranging from using fintech more effectively, to expanding and developing automatic payroll deduction IRAs, to judiciously expanding tax incentives for retirement saving.

We also present a more comprehensive solution—which we call employer-facilitated accounts—that would decouple retirement saving plans from the employer. Individuals would have retirement accounts—much like their Social Security accounts—that follow them when they change employers and work arrangements. This new retirement saving vehicle would provide contingent workers with access to payroll deductions and employer matches and would have contribution limits consistent with other existing plans. It would accommodate the diversity of the contingent workforce and the resulting diversity of needs for new retirement saving. Importantly, it would provide stable retirement saving arrangements for people who move back and forth over the course of their careers between traditional jobs and contingent positions. It would reduce leakage from retirement accounts when they changed jobs, and it would eliminate the dependence of workers on employer choices to offer retirement plans. Although we propose the plan as a way to improve retirement saving for contingent workers, we believe that once employer-facilitated plans are established, both employers and employees in traditional jobs may well prefer the new vehicle to existing retirement accounts.

We begin by providing background on the contingent workforce and the characteristics of contingent workers, then follow with an exploration of several options for improving independent workers' retirement security.

THE CONTINGENT WORKFORCE

In traditional employment situations, workers are salaried, or they work specific hours or shifts for an hourly wage. In contrast, contingent workers work on an ad hoc basis and are paid by the service or good they provide. In theory, contingent workers have more flexibility than their traditionally employed peers and may be able to choose when and from where they work. For example, a Lyft driver need not commit to driving eight hours per day or at specific times of day. However, many other contingent workers are at the mercy of their employers and earn income only when they are needed. Some have regular hours, but others are on call and get work sporadically. These workers could arrive at their job to find that the employer's needs have changed and that they will not be able to work or receive pay for that day.

Many contingent workers occupy a nebulous space between "employee" and "independent contractor." The Internal Revenue Service offers three criteria employers must consider when determining a worker's status: (1) the extent to which the employer controls how a worker does his or her work; (2) the extent to which the business aspects of the work are controlled by the employer; and (3) the existence of written contracts and benefits, as well as the nature of the employer-worker relationship and the importance of the work to the employer (IRS 2015a). The Department of Labor (2015) issued guidelines saying that workers who rely on a single stream of income should be formally considered employees, though the Department of Labor (2017) later withdrew those guidelines.

Some recent cases at the state level have been more in line with the guidelines initially issued by the Department of Labor (2015) in classifying gig workers as employees. The Supreme Court of California (2018) set a precedent that employers should classify independent contractors and employees according to the "ABC test." Using this standard, a worker should be classified as an independent contractor "only if the hiring entity establishes: (A) that the worker is free from the control and direction of the hirer in connection with the performance of the work, both under the contract for the performance of such work and in fact; (B) that the worker performs work that is outside the usual course of the hiring entity's business; and (C) that the worker is customarily engaged in an independently established trade, occupation, or business of the same nature as the work performed for the hiring entity." Other states, including New Jersey, Illinois, and Massachusetts, use similar tests (Wiessner 2018).

Some contingent workers, however, have characteristics of an employee *and* a contractor; this is especially true for gig workers. For example, a dog walker who uses Rover as an intermediary can choose when to work and what to charge (like an independent contractor) but must still provide walks of a certain basic length and quality (like an employee). Harris and Krueger (2015) propose to address these issues by creating a new category of worker—"independent workers"—for people who are neither fully employees nor fully contractors.

The narrowest measure of the contingent workforce includes only workers with temporary employment arrangements and excludes self-employed workers. The Bureau of Labor Statistics (BLS 2018) estimates that about 1.3 percent of the working labor force fell into this category in 2017. The broadest definition includes all workers with nonstandard work arrangements, from day laborers and agency temps to consultants and independent contractors. Just over 40 percent of all workers—including seasonal and part-time workers—fell into this category in 2010 (GAO 2015).

Between those two extremes lies a definition that includes those who have either a contingent job or an alternative work arrangement as their primary job. The BLS (2018) found that 15.5 million people, representing 10.1 percent of the workforce, had an alternative work arrangement in 2017. About 5.9 million people, accounting for 3.8 percent of the workforce, had contingent jobs. In total, after adjusting for people who had both a contingent job and an alternative work arrangement, the BLS (2018) identified 19.8 million people (12.8 percent of the workforce) who were independent workers in their primary job.

These figures were slightly down from 2005 when the BLS surveyed labor market conditions (BLS 2005). Most other estimates, however, such as those by Katz and Krueger (2016), the JP Morgan Chase and Co. Institute (2016b), and QuickBooks (2016), show an increase in the number of independent workers over this period. The BLS surveys count people who have independent work as their primary job, and thus do not capture what appears to be vast growth in independent work as an individual's second (or third) job.

While it receives a great deal of publicity, the gig economy accounts for only a small portion of contingent work. For example, JP Morgan Chase estimates that only around 1 percent of adults earn money through the online on-demand economy.[1]

CHARACTERISTICS OF CONTINGENT WORKERS

There are two broad views of contingent workers and contingent work. Some people see contingent work as an opportunity for people who have full-time jobs to generate supplemental income or for people to have work that is flexible in time and location. In this view, the increase in contingent work is supply-driven; more people have become contingent workers because they want to be. An alternative view is that contingent work represents the further erosion of basic standards and protections that workers have had in the past. In this view, the increase in contingent work is demand-driven, as employers find new ways to cut costs. Given the diversity of contingent workforce arrangements, there is clearly some truth in both interpretations.

According to the Bureau of Labor Statistics (2018), in 2017, relative to traditional workers, contingent workers were more likely to be young (under 25), more likely to have less than a high school education, and slightly more likely to hold a bachelor's degree. Just under half of traditional and contingent workers were female. About 22 percent of contingent workers and 16 percent of noncontingent workers were Hispanic. Contingent workers were concentrated in professional and related occupations and were more likely than traditional workers to be in the construction, extraction, education, and health industries. They were less likely to work in retail trade or manufacturing.

Contingent workers have lower earnings than traditional workers. BLS (2018) reports that, among full-time workers, median weekly earnings for noncontingent workers were about 30 percent higher than for contingent workers ($886 versus $685, respectively). The difference reflects a combination of age, experience, industry, and occupation effects, as well as any inherent differences in compensation between contingent and traditional work. Katz and Krueger (2016) find significant variation in wages across types of contingent workers, with independent contractors most likely to fall into the highest earning quintile and temporary workers most likely to fall into the lowest earning quintile. They also find that contingent workers are more likely to work part-time, tend to work fewer hours per week, and are more likely to have multiple jobs than traditional workers. Contingent workers are also more likely to live in poverty and to receive public assistance (GAO 2015).

Differences in benefits between traditional and contingent jobs parallel the differences in wages and income. Coverage rates for employer-provided health insurance plans are twice as high for traditional workers as for contingent workers (BLS 2018). Most important for this chapter, employer-provided retirement plans were offered to only half as many contingent workers (23 percent) as to traditional workers (48 percent). Participation rates were even more skewed—18 percent for contingent workers and 43 percent for traditional workers. As with wages, the differences in retirement plan coverage and access between contingent and traditional workers represents the net effect of many factors. Beyond this basic information on retirement accounts, however, there is little specific evidence about the retirement security preparedness of contingent workers.

Non-employer-sponsored retirement solutions are available, but Internal Revenue Service (2018) Statistics of Income Data show that fewer than 3 million people (1.8 percent of all tax filers) made a tax-deductible contribution to an IRA in 2015. Even if contingent workers contributed to IRAs at the same rate as the general population—which seems unlikely, given their lower-than-average income—relatively few would have any significant balances in them.

IMPROVING CONTINGENT WORKERS' RETIREMENT SECURITY

Independent workers almost always lack access to an employer-sponsored retirement account that makes saving easy through mechanisms such as payroll deduction, employer contributions, and automatic enrollment and automatic escalation of contributions.[2] Without this access—or other alternatives—this population may face retirement with little more than Social Security.[3] To improve contingent workers' retirement security, we consider several different approaches that may have some promise.

New Technology and Automatic Transfer

Some contingent workers are not paid through a corporate payroll system or on a regular schedule. For example, Lyft drivers have the option to "cash out" their earnings immediately, instead of waiting for a weekly paycheck (Lyft 2018). In other cases, a worker is paid after a task via a payment platform such as Stripe (Fitchard 2013). Independent contractors who work a different number of hours each week may have an income stream that varies considerably over time. None of these situations make it easy for the worker to use a traditional payroll deduction retirement saving model.

Recent technological advances and savings apps may provide an answer, however. Lyft drivers are offered payroll deduction IRAs through the fintech firm Honest Dollar. Other fintech firms offer similar saving opportunities. For instance, Uber has partnered with Betterment to provide its drivers with access to an IRA and financial counseling, with the first year free for its drivers and a discount in subsequent years (Marte 2016). To compensate for irregular payment amounts and schedules, savers can choose to save a preset amount each month, save a percentage of each payment, or save only when a payment is over a certain amount. Another option leaves it to the saver to decide when and how much to save but sends text messages to encourage saving and reminders when deposits have not been made on schedule.

In addition, Digit and other similar fintech companies offer smartphone applications that analyze a participant's bank account. When the app detects that the account contains money that is not needed for immediate expenses, it automatically sweeps it into a savings account. Finally, some employers offer workers the option to split their pay between a checking account and a retirement savings account by specifying that either a set amount or a percentage of income is saved. Honest Dollar has submitted a patent application for a service that would allow individuals to save for several individually chosen goals and receive regular updates on their progress toward meeting the goal.

These and other automated systems could allow contingent workers to save routinely without having to take any specific action. A key feature is the workers' ability to choose the system that best meets their circumstances and income stream. These benefits would be intensified if the workers were also automatically enrolled in the system when hired. As online employment platforms for contingent workers continue to develop, they could include either benefits or the opportunity to have them as a feature of their systems.

These models do require the contingent worker to have a retirement account. Workers with preexisting IRAs or other accounts can simply connect to the account in the same way they direct payments to their checking accounts. Workers without such an account would have to set up a new account or have their employer or the fintech provider do so. Fortunately, technology makes this an easy task. Honest Dollar (2018), for example, advertises that it can quickly sign up gig and contingent workers with an IRA that offers a variety of investment choices. In general, an increase in fintech companies and users can be expected to continue to increase the availability of these accounts and to drive down the costs of these services.

State-Sponsored Plans

Contingent workers will be able to take advantage of group retirement plans such as the new state-sponsored proposals being developed by states for workers who do not have an employer-sponsored retirement saving or pension plan. These accounts could take the form of Automatic IRAs or Multiple Employer Plans (MEPs). Initially, state-sponsored plans were offered through employers, but some states are also making them available to contingent workers as well.

As of 2018, California, Illinois, Oregon, Maryland, New York, and Connecticut are setting up plans based on the Automatic IRA (Gale and John 2017). OregonSaves is beginning to make accounts available to contingent workers, while both California and Illinois are beginning to test their systems (Bradford 2018). In addition, Washington State's Small Business Retirement Marketplace is offering prescreened plans through private providers; the plans are simple, low-cost accounts that are available to contingent, part-time, and gig workers.

The Automatic IRA model allows workers without access to a 401(k) or other employer-sponsored plan to nonetheless benefit from automatic enrollment, payroll deduction, and sensible default investments. New hires automatically start making contributions to an IRA unless they actively opt out. These contributions are usually made via direct deposit and sent to a single IRA provider, thus easing the administrative burden for the employer.

As of 2018, Vermont is implementing an MEP, but under existing law it is only available to traditional employees. MEPs are a type of group 401(k) plan that allows several employers to join together to offer a plan with more features and consumer protections than a typical Automatic IRA. MEPs have lower administrative costs and a simpler regulatory structure than a 401(k) and could be offered to independent workers as well as traditional employees if Congress and regulators approve. Currently, MEPs can only be offered through state plans, but Congress could also allow them to be offered by private providers. If it does so, it could also open them to independent workers (Bradford 2018).

Improved Tax Benefits

While the tax system may have a limited effect on households' overall level of saving, two simple changes to tax benefits would enable independent workers to increase their retirement balances. The most direct way would be to modify the Saver's Credit, which helps low- and moderate-income workers build retirement savings.

Currently, the Saver's Credit is little known and largely ineffective. Only about three out of every ten American workers know about the Saver's Credit (Transamerica Center for Retirement Studies 2015). In 2015, individuals with earnings of $30,500 or less, and married couples with incomes of $61,000 or less, were eligible for up to $1,000 or $2,000, respectively, if they made contributions to a retirement account. In 2012, the mean Saver's Credit was only $127 for individuals and $215 for married couples (IRS 2014). This is largely due to the credit's nonrefundability; it can be used to reduce a filer's tax liability to zero, but any "extra" is lost to the filer.

Making the credit refundable and having it deposited directly into the taxpayer's retirement account would make it much more salient for many taxpayers (Brown and John 2017). Another reform, described by Gruber, Orszag, and Gale (2006) and proposed in both legislation and early Obama administration budgets, would change the credit to a government match; instead of receiving the credit as part of their refund (where it is likely to be spent), individuals' contributions would be matched (up to a certain threshold) and deposited directly into their retirement account. The rest of their refund would be treated just as it is currently. In addition, the Saver's Credit should be able to be claimed on all tax forms. Currently, it is only available on longer tax forms that are not widely used by its target population. The restructured Saver's Credit would encourage retirement saving and help people who qualify for it to build their retirement balances faster than they could otherwise.

A second tax change that could benefit independent workers would be to ensure that spouses who are employed could contribute the full amount to a retirement account regardless of marital status. Currently, individuals may contribute up to $5,500 per year to an IRA ($6,500 per year for individuals age 50 and older) (IRS 2015c). Traditional IRA contributions—but not Roth IRA contributions—are deductible, but if an individual or his/her spouse has an employer-sponsored retirement plan, these deductions may be limited (IRS 2015b).

The net effect of tax incentives is subject to debate. Chetty and others (2013), using data on households from Denmark, find that reducing the tax benefits in one tax-preferred saving account caused high-income households to deposit saving into a different tax-preferred saving account rather than reduce their overall saving. Research that focuses on low-income households, however, generally finds larger impacts of saving incentives on net saving.[4] In addition, if the Saver's Credit is reformed so that it is refundable directly into the account, its value would be as much to improve savings balances for eligible taxpayers as to encourage participation.

Employer-Facilitated Retirement Accounts

We now turn to a more far-reaching idea, restructuring retirement accounts so that they follow workers from job to job. We refer to these as employer-*facilitated* accounts, as opposed to the current system, which features employer-*sponsored* accounts.

This idea is motivated by several factors. First, the current retirement system depends critically on employer-sponsored plans, and that dependence can create problems. For example, most payroll deduction retirement saving plans are offered to workers through their employers. This effectively leaves out independent contractors, gig workers, most part-time employees, and many others. If an employer chooses not to offer such a plan, even the firm's full-time workers are denied access to this effective retirement saving method. They have the option to open an IRA, but few will contribute regularly in the absence of payroll deduction.

Second, under the current system, job changes can discourage retirement saving. In many cases, when an employee leaves a job with a retirement savings account, the funds are either rolled into an IRA, which may have significantly higher fees than the 401(k) plan the worker just left, or the funds are cashed out.[5] Research suggests that there are significant amounts of preretirement withdrawals (Argento, Bryant, and Sabelhaus 2014). In an increasingly mobile and diverse workforce, these results are likely to be suboptimal for workers.[6]

Third, it is likely that in the future, an increasing number of individuals will spend time as both an employee and an independent or contingent worker, and their retirement arrangements should function effectively for both types of employment status.

A sweeping way to address all of these issues would be to attach the retirement account to the worker rather than depending on the employer to offer a retirement benefit. In an employer-facilitated model—as opposed to the current employer-sponsored model—every person would have a retirement savings account that travels with him or her from job to job. Employers, including those that use contingent workers, would be required to provide workers the ability to make payroll deduction contributions to their retirement accounts (and to have state and federal tax withheld). This requirement would apply to full- and part-time employees as well as contingent workers of all types. Employers would not be required to offer their own retirement account, although they could decide to do so to attract and keep the kind of workforce they desire, just as they do now.[7]

This idea is a departure from the current system, which relies on employer-sponsored accounts. At the same time, the idea of an account that travels with the worker from job to job, and that is able to receive employer contributions, should be quite familiar, since Social Security has those features.[8] Others have proposed similar models, such as the Universal Retirement Security Account (URSA), as a way to reduce costs and simplify the retirement savings paradigm (Friedman 2015). In addition, some, including the Aspen Institute's Future of Work Initiative (2016), have called for a universal, portable, and prorated system that works with—rather than against—the frequent job and career changes workers make today.[9]

Under an employer-facilitated account, at the time of hire, the worker would supply a Social Security number for tax purposes, a bank account number for direct deposit of the paycheck, and a retirement account number. The worker would also indicate how large the desired "employee" contribution would be.[10] Workers with volatile incomes may not want to commit to a retirement contribution amount in advance. To remedy this concern, these workers could be offered the option to connect to the retirement account through a savings app such as offered by Digit or a similar provider. They could have the option to make contributions by committing to contribute a set amount each month, an amount conditional on earnings, or on a discretionary basis rather than through automatic payroll deduction.[11]

An open question is to what extent the account should change to conform with the plan in place at a worker's firm.

Under one approach (the "fixed approach"), the employee's account would remain fixed in form and contribution limit when he or she changes jobs. In a second approach (the "adjustable approach"), the account could be adjusted so that when the worker is employed by a firm with a 401(k) plan, the account would be subject to all 401(k) rules, with the same contribution limit, withdrawal rules, and other account features, along with whatever employer match that company offers. As with the first approach, when the employee moves to a company that does not offer a 401(k), the account would become a payroll deduction IRA with all of the rules currently attached to that type of account.

Under a third approach (the "intermediate approach"), the employee's account would adjust the contribution limits and ability to receive an employer match to conform with the plan the employer offers, but otherwise, all employee accounts would have uniform rules. In this approach, the account would be adjusted so that when the worker is employed by a firm with a 401(k) plan, it would be subject to 401(k) contribution limits along with whatever employer match the company offers.[12] When a firm that does not offer another type of retirement account employs the worker, the retirement account would be a payroll deduction IRA with the same contribution limits that apply to that type of account.

The fixed approach would be the simplest option for workers, but it could be disruptive to the existing retirement savings system as it would create one uniform contribution limit and enable these accounts to receive an employer contribution even when the account is not part of a 401(k)-type plan. This approach may also discourage some employers from deciding to offer a 401(k) plan that offers additional features to a payroll deduction IRA. Indeed, it may encourage some companies that now offer a 401(k) to drop that plan in favor of the simpler employer-facilitated alternative.

Relative to the fixed approach, the adjustable approach is less disruptive to the existing retirement savings system and might provide more encouragement to employers to offer a 401(k)-type plan with employer matching contributions. Most employees contribute less than the $5,500 annual IRA contribution limits, but the higher contribution limits for 401(k) plans make them more attractive to senior management. The higher limits for a 401(k)-type account would encourage employers to start such a plan. In order to take advantage of those higher limits, 401(k) antidiscrimination tests require that the plan be offered to lower-paid employees also.[13]

The intermediate approach could be both less disruptive to the current retirement savings system than the first approach and easier for both employers and employees to administer than the second approach. We expect the intermediate approach would be most acceptable to both employers and employees.

Under any approach, contingent workers and regular employees who prefer to have a 401(k) plan would continue to be able to seek jobs at companies that offer them, but would be able to avoid a break in employee contributions if they moved to a job without an employer plan. In addition, all types of workers would be able to avoid the hassle of combining different accounts of potentially different types from several employers over the course of a career. Workers would enjoy the benefit of having one account throughout their careers without accidental leakage or periods without contributions when employed by firms without a plan.

Employers would have the flexibility to offer whatever type of retirement plan they believe is necessary to attract and retain the type of employee they need to be competitive. Each approach also retains the private sector nature of the retirement savings system. Private account management firms would handle employees' accounts, and private entities would continue to be able to offer different types of plans to employers. However, the two functions would be separate: account management firms would serve only individual savers, and plan managers would serve only employers. This would enhance consumer protections by avoiding potential conflicts of interest. Although different from the current system, the new structure would also likely eliminate hidden charges and subsidies present in today's combined system.[14] Otherwise, transitioning to the new system would be fairly simple.[15]

Workers could either choose an investment management firm when they start their career, or more likely, be assigned a provider whose accounts meet certain specifications at random through an automatic enrollment arrangement using either a national or state mechanism.[16] In order to ensure that savers are not charged high fees or placed in inappropriate investments, the initial investment choice would have certain fee requirements and would invest in low-cost index funds, probably as part of a target-date fund.[17] Workers would always be free to change investments or investment management firms, but in order to promote safe decision making, they would be encouraged to stay with low-cost, buy-and-hold strategies. Consumer protections would help keep workers' nest eggs safe for the duration of their careers. The Consumer Financial Protection Bureau and US Treasury Department would be natural candidates, along with the Department of Labor, to serve as regulators, ensuring respectively that savers have a reasonable menu of portfolios to choose from and that account management carries out its fiduciary responsibility (Friedman 2015).

We believe that an employer-facilitated account structure has the flexibility to serve both traditional employees and contingent workers and would provide them with better retirement security than the existing fragmented structure in which a saver has a different account from each employer. Ultimately, what concerns a retiree is how much money he or she has available in retirement rather than the structure of the account where it is located. A single account that travels with the worker from job to job regardless of the employment relationship reduces the chance that accounts and the money they contain will be lost or cashed out when jobs end. It also eliminates the complex and confusing rules that govern rollovers. If an account can accept contributions from both 401(k) plans and payroll deduction IRAs while retaining the same underlying investments, the total will likely grow faster than if the money went into individual, smaller accounts at each employer.

THE IMPORTANCE OF EXPANDED ACCESS

As the American workforce ages, it will be even more important that everyone has the opportunity to build a retirement nest egg to supplement Social Security benefits. Currently, less than half of Americans are enrolled in a workplace retirement savings or pension plan. There are a number of efforts to expand this proportion, but almost all of them focus solely on workers who are classified as employees. Efforts to help other types of workers save for retirement are not as common.

As the number of contingent workers grows, making retirement saving easier and more financially rewarding for these workers, who are largely left out of the current retirement system, becomes ever more compelling.

The problems in the current system and the characteristics of growing contingent employment are reasons to consider decoupling retirement saving plans from employers. The reform we discuss would enable every worker to have one retirement plan and carry it from employer to employer, just like Social Security. It would still enable employers to select the type of retirement plan they need to attract and retain good quality employees, it would reduce leakage when workers change jobs, and it would preserve the private sector nature of the US retirement system.

As more researchers focus on these issues and with continuing rapid advances in technology, we anticipate that additional solutions will be developed. For example, Harris and Krueger's (2015) proposal to create a new category of "independent workers" could pave the way toward improved retirement security for certain contingent workers. Similarly, Choitz and Conway (2015) have proposed policies that include using state-sponsored retirement saving plans to improve contingent and lower-income workers' retirement outcomes. In any case, as the number of contingent workers grows and the average American lifespan extends, it is essential to begin to address these issues quickly.

NOTES

We thank Alec Camhi for research assistance and Debbie Chalfie, Derek Dorn, Jason Fichtner, John Friedman, Hilary Gelfond, Joshua Gotbaum, Catherine Harvey, Aaron Krupkin, Robert Toth, and Christian Weller for helpful comments. We thank the Laura and John Arnold Foundation for funding this work. The findings and conclusions are the responsibility of the authors and do not necessarily reflect positions or policies of the Brookings Institution, its funders, or any other organization.

1. JP Morgan Chase & Co. Institute (2016a) estimates that the gig economy comprised 2.5 million workers in September 2015. This is probably an underestimate because the calculation is based only on Chase bank account holders who earned income from among thirty different gig platforms. Chase does not offer a truly free checking account and so may miss lower-income households, and the list of thirty platforms is likely to be nonexhaustive. QuickBooks (2016) estimates there were 3.2 million gig economy workers in 2015. This is probably an overestimate, since it is based on an online survey, and both respondents and gig economy workers are likely to be more tech savvy than average. Manyika and others (2015) and Katz and Krueger (2016) obtain smaller numbers than the other studies, but they count only labor platform workers, not capital platform workers.

2. Madrian and Shea (2001); Benartzi and Thaler (2007).

3. And unfortunately, even those benefits may be lower for contingent workers than they are for traditional employees owing to low tax compliance and a variety of other factors (Schreur and Veghte 2018).

4. Benjamin (2003); Engen and Gale (2000).

5. The Department of Labor's now defunct fiduciary rule may have had have some effect on the fees charged to IRA owners, but since its demise, it is uncertain if those changes will remain. In addition, rollovers from a 401(k) plan are likely to remain higher than those charged by the plan. An important distinction is that a payroll deduction IRA will not have the same fee structure as a retail IRA because it is a group product with a simple structure and index fund investments.

6. According to Munnell and Webb (2015), a leakage occurs when funds are permanently withdrawn from a 401(k) or IRA before retirement.

7. Implementing this proposal would require that the IRS definition of "employee" change so that providing access to a retirement savings account, regardless of type, would not in itself turn a contingent worker into an employee. The effect of these changes could be significant but are outside of the scope of this chapter.

8. Of course, there are also many differences between Social Security, a public, defined benefit, pay-as-you-go system, and the idea considered here, which would apply to private, defined contribution, fully funded accounts.

9. The concept of prorating in this context is simple: it means that the amount workers contribute to their retirement is determined by the number of hours they work, dollars they earn, or some combination thereof (Foster, Nelson, and Reder 2016). See also Harkin (2014).

10. This notification could be a form from the past employer that includes both the routing number and the level of past contributions. That way the level of contributions would be at least the same from employer to employer. We believe that employee contributions should be greater than the 3 percent level often found in many of today's automatic enrollment plans and encourage employers with a 401(k)-type plan to use automatic escalation to increase the initial employee contribution level to a higher amount. We use the term "employee contributions" here to mean contributions from any worker's pay.

11. In such a case, the employee's retirement account would be directly connected to his or her checking account, and the employer would not be forwarding retirement

saving. However, if the employee later has a job that provides a steady income stream, the contributions would come through the employer's payroll system.

12. Legally, a 401(k)-type plan would continue to be defined as an employer-sponsored plan since it would be offered at the employer's discretion. As is the case today, an employer would not be required to offer such a plan. A key difference would be that employers would no longer be responsible for investment choices; those would be made by the employees and would apply to their accounts regardless of where they were employed. However, antidiscrimination tests would still be applied and would be expanded to cover both those who qualify as employees and those who are contingent workers.

13. When workers change employers, all of the accounts would continue to receive the same type of tax treatment that they had received before. Individuals would have the opportunity to choose which type of tax treatment when they are first employed or be automatically enrolled in one type of account or the other. Employees who choose a traditional account that deducts contributions from taxable income could move to a Roth IRA simply by paying back the tax preference, just as they can today.

14. This change has the advantage that the account manager would be working directly for the saver—the ultimate customer—rather than indirectly through the saver's employer. In the process, the responsibilities and administrative burdens for employers that offer a 401(k)-type account would be sharply reduced. Savers could be protected against predatory fees and inappropriate investment choices through safe harbors and appropriate default funds.

15. In the initial stages of the transition, employers that do not offer another retirement savings or pension plan would automatically enroll their existing employees in a payroll deduction IRA; neither employers that do offer such a plan nor their employees would be affected. However, all employers would also enroll contingent employees, and we would encourage them to re-enroll existing employees who are not participating in the plan. Once all accounts have an individual routing number so that they could accept direct transfers of deposits, the new system could go fully into effect.

16. New savers could be placed in state-sponsored retirement saving plans in the state in which they reside or use a national mechanism that places savers randomly with a provider that meets specified standards for fees and investment choices. New Zealand's KiwiSaver plan uses such a system. Of course, savers could also choose their own provider or change providers at any time.

17. Of course, upper-income and high-balance retirement savers could always choose to have a more sophisticated or actively managed investment choice. Our reform would allow investment firms that prefer these savers to serve them only rather than having to accept a mixture of balances, as they do through the current system. However, they would have to meet suitability standards to ensure that higher cost investments are not sold to savers who will not benefit from them. We anticipate that investment options would be commodity-like standardized funds that all have the same basic elements. One option to keep costs low would be to use professionally managed pooled funds. Savers would retain the option to have more actively managed investments.

REFERENCES

Argento, Robert, Victoria L. Bryant, and John Sabelhaus. 2014. "Early Withdrawals from Retirement Accounts during the Great Recession." *Contemporary Economic Policy* 33 (1): 1–16.

Benartzi, Shlomo, and Richard H. Thaler. 2007. "Heuristics and Biases in Retirement Savings Behavior." *Journal of Economic Perspectives* 21 (3): 81–104.

Benjamin, Daniel J. 2003. "Does 401(k) Eligibility Increase Saving? Evidence from Propensity Score Subclassification." *Journal of Public Economics* 87: 1259–90.

Bradford, Hazel. 2018. "Efforts to Help Gig Economy Workers Save for Retirement Gaining Ground." *Pensions & Investments*, July 9.

Brown, Jennifer Erin, and David C. John. 2017. "Improving the Saver's Credit for Low- and Moderate-Income Workers." Washington, DC: AARP Public Policy Institute, September 25.

Bureau of Labor Statistics (BLS). 2005. "Contingent and Alternative Employment Arrangements—February 2005." www.bls.gov/news.release/archives/conemp_07272005.pdf.

———. 2018. "Contingent and Alternative Employment Arrangements—May 2017." www.bls.gov/news.release/pdf/conemp.pdf.

Chetty, Raj, John N. Friedman, Soren Leth-Petersen, Torben Heien Nielsen, and Tore Olson. 2013. "Active v. Passive Decisions and Crowd-Out in Retirement Savings Accounts: Evidence from Denmark." www.rajchetty.com/chettyfiles/crowdout.pdf.

Choitz, Vickie, and Maureen Conway. 2015. "The Future of Work for Low-Income Workers and Families." *Working Poor Families Project* (Fall/Winter). www.workingpoorfamilies.org/wp-content/uploads/2015/12/WPFP-Fall_Winter-2015-Brief.pdf.

Department of Labor. 2015. "Administrator's Interpretation No. 2015-1." July 15. www.dol.gov/whd/workers/Misclassification/AI-2015_1.htm.

———. 2017. "US Secretary of Labor Withdraws Joint Employment, Independent Contractor Informal Guidance." June 7. https://www.dol.gov/newsroom/releases/opa/opa20170607.

Engen, Eric, and William Gale. 2000. "The Effects of 401(k) Plans on Household Wealth: Differences across Earnings Groups." NBER Working Paper 8032. Cambridge, MA: National Bureau of Economic Research.

Fitchard, Kevin. 2013. "Braintree Launches Marketplace, a Payments System for Collaborative Consumption Apps." *GigaOM*, August 14.

Foster, Natalie, Greg Nelson, and Libber Reder. 2016. "Portable Benefits Resource Guide." Washington, DC: Aspen Institute, July 13.

Friedman, John N. 2015. "Building on What Works: A Proposal to Modernize Retirement Savings." Hamilton Project. Brookings, June 23.

Future of Work Initiative. 2016. "Toward a New Capitalism: A Policy Agenda to Restore the Promise of Work." Washington, DC: Aspen Institute.

Gale, William G., and David C. John. 2015. "Two Important New Retirement Savings Initiatives from the Obama Administration." *TaxVox*. Washington, DC: Urban-Brookings Tax Policy Center, November 19.

———. 2017. "State Sponsored Retirement Savings Plans: New Approaches to Boost Retirement Plan Coverage." PRC WP2017. Pension Research Council, Wharton School, University of Pennsylvania. https://pensionresearchcouncil.wharton.upenn.edu/wp-content/uploads/2017/09/WP-2017-12-John-Gale.pdf.

Government Accountability Office (GAO). 2015. "Contingent Workforce: Size, Characteristics, Earnings, and Benefits." April 20. www.gao.gov/assets/670/669766.pdf.

Gruber, Jonathan, Peter R. Orszag, and William G. Gale. 2006. "Improving Opportunities and Incentives for Saving by Middle- and Low-Income Households." Brookings, April 1.

Harkin, Tom. 2014. "HELP Chairman Tom Harkin Introduces the USA Retirement Funds Act—Bill Summary." US Senate: Health, Education, Labor and Pensions Committee.

Harris, Seth D., and Alan B. Krueger. 2015. "A Proposal for Modernizing Labor Laws for Twenty-First Century Work: The 'Independent Worker.'" Hamilton Project. Brookings, December 7.

Honest Dollar. 2018. "How Do I Get Started with Honest Dollar?" https://help.honestdollar.com/hc/en-us/articles/360000091188-How-do-I-get-started-with-Honest-Dollar.

Internal Revenue Service (IRS). 2014. "Plan Now to Get Full Benefit of Saver's Credit; Tax Credit Helps Low- and Moderate-Income Workers Save for Retirement." November 3.

———. 2015a. "Independent Contractor (Self-Employed) or Employee?" https://www.irs.gov/Businesses/Small-Businesses-&-Self-Employed/Independent-Contractor-Self-Employed-or-Employee.

———. 2015b. "IRA Deduction Limits." https://www.irs.gov/Retirement-Plans/IRA-Deduction-Limits.

———. 2015c. "Retirement Topics - IRA Contribution Limits." https://www.irs.gov/Retirement-Plans/Plan-Participant,-Employee/Retirement-Topics-IRA-Contribution-Limits.

———. 2018. "Table 2. Individual Income and Tax Data, by State and Size of Adjusted Gross Income, Tax Year 2015." https://www.irs.gov/pub/irs-soi/15in54cm.xlsx.

JP Morgan Chase & Co. Institute. 2016a. "Paychecks, Paydays, and the Online Platform Economy." New York, February.

———. 2016b. "Paychecks, Paydays, and the Online Platform Economy." New York, November.

Katz, Lawrence F., and Alan B. Krueger. 2016. "The Rise and Nature of Alternative Work Arrangements in the United States, 1995–2015." http://krueger.princeton.edu/sites/default/files/akrueger/files/katz_krueger_cws_-_april_26_2016.pdf.

Lyft. 2018. "Express Pay—Lyft Help." https://help.lyft.com/hc/en-us/articles/115012923167-Express-Pay.

Madrian, Bridgette C., and Dennis F. Shea. 2001. "The Power of Suggestion: Inertia in 401(k) Participation and Savings Behavior." *Quarterly Journal of Economics* 116 (4): 1149–87.

Manyika, James, Susan Lund, Kelsey Robinson, John Valentino, and Richard Dobbs. 2015. "A Labor Market That Works: Connecting Talent with Opportunity in the Digital Age." McKinsey Global Institute, June.

Marte, Jonnelle. 2016. "Uber Is Tackling One of the Biggest Challenges for Workers in the Gig Economy." *Washington Post,* August 24.

Munnell, Alicia H., and Anthony Webb. 2015. "The Impact of Leakages of 401(k)/IRA Assets." No. 15-2. Center for Retirement Research, Boston College. crr.bc.edu/wp-content/uploads/2015/01/IB_15-2.pdf.

QuickBooks. 2016. "Dispatches from the New Economy: The On-Demand Workforce." www.slideshare.net/IntuitInc/dispatches-from-the-new-economy-the-ondemand-workforce-57613212/4-the_majority_of_ondemand_economyproviders.

Schreur, Elliot, and Benjamin W. Veghte. 2018. "Improving Social Security Coverage and Retirement Benefits for Independent Contractors." Washington, DC: National Academy of Social Insurance, June.

Supreme Court of California. 2018. *Dynamex Operations West, Inc., Petitioner, v. The Superior Court of Los Angeles County, Respondent; Charles Lee et al., Real Parties in Interest.* www.courts.ca.gov/opinions/documents/S222732.PDF.

Transamerica Center for Retirement Studies. 2015. "16th Annual Transamerica Retirement Survey: A Compendium of Findings about American Workers." www.transamericacenter.org/docs/default-source/resources/center-research/16th-annual/tcrs2015_sr_16th_compendium_of_workers.pdf.

Wiessner, Daniel. 2018. "GrubHub Case Could Be Barometer for New Rules on Independent Contractors." Reuters, May 6.

SIX

Supplemental Transition Accounts for Retirement

A PROPOSAL TO INCREASE RETIREMENT INCOME SECURITY AND REFORM SOCIAL SECURITY

Gary Koenig, Jason J. Fichtner, and William G. Gale

Social Security is arguably the most successful federal program in US history. The program has substantially reduced senior poverty, enabled millions of older Americans to live independently, and provided vital support to families who lose income because a loved one dies or is too ill or injured to work. With rising life expectancy and the shift away from traditional pension plans, Social Security's inflation-protected lifelong benefits are likely to become increasingly important for old-age economic security in the decades ahead.

Despite Social Security's successes, the program could do more to improve the financial health of older Americans by facilitating the delayed claiming of benefits. Between the ages of 62 and 70, monthly Social Security benefits increase by 7–8 percent for each *one-year delay* in claiming, holding work history constant. This increase is reflected in higher monthly benefits for the life of the beneficiary. To the extent that delayed claiming leads to longer working lives, it can raise benefits for that reason as well. Delayed claiming can also result in higher benefits for surviving spouses.

In this chapter, we propose Supplemental Transition Accounts for Retirement (STARTs) to serve as a bridge to receiving Social Security benefits. STARTs would be mandatory add-on savings accounts funded by employees, employers, and a progressive government contribution. STARTs would be fully integrated into the Social Security program. Every individual with a START would be required to exhaust the account's assets before receiving retired-worker benefits, or age-based spousal or survivor benefits. For many people, STARTs would serve to raise the age at which Social Security benefits are first paid. Thus our proposal reduces the total actuarial reduction or increases the delayed retirement credits (DRCs) that would apply, resulting in higher monthly benefits for the life of the beneficiary.

The Urban Institute, using its microsimulation model DYNASIM (dynamic simulation of income model), estimates that by 2065 this innovation would increase per capita mean net cash income, on average, by 4.4–6.7 percent for people age 62 and older (with the median increase between 8.2 and 10.3 percent). The range of estimates reflects different assumptions about whether participants would reduce other retirement plan contributions in response to START. People age 62 and older in the lowest lifetime earnings quintile would see the biggest percentage increase in income, on average about 10 percent (a median increase of 15.4 percent), and the highest income quintile would see the smallest increase, on average between 1.4 and 4.9 percent (a median increase of 2.5 percent). Those increases in income would be achieved while reducing Social Security's seventy-five-year actuarial deficit from 2.68 percent of taxable payroll to 2.48 percent.

Importantly, this innovation would increase monthly benefits without affecting beneficiaries' expected actuarial lifetime Social Security benefits or limiting their access to essential income at early retirement ages. This proposal builds on Social Security's comparative advantage to mitigate the key factors that undermine economic security at older ages: longevity risk, market risk, and inflation risk.

ADEQUACY OF SOCIAL SECURITY BENEFITS

Researchers have long recognized the role Social Security benefits play in contributing to a secure retirement.[1] Social Security retirement benefits provide income security for tens of millions of Americans. In 2014, 85 percent of married couples and 84 percent of nonmarried people age 65 or older received Social Security benefits. About 61 percent of all aged beneficiary units rely on Social Security for 50 percent or more of their income, and 33 percent rely on

Social Security for 90 percent or more of their income (Social Security Administration 2016a).[2] Not surprisingly, reliance on Social Security benefits increases with age. Research using the Current Population Survey shows that while 33 percent of people 65–69 years of age rely on Social Security for 50 percent or more of their family income, that number climbs to almost 56 percent for those age 80 and older (Shelton 2016). Social Security was never designed to be the only source of income for people in retirement. For an average worker, Social Security replaces about 40 percent of annual preretirement earnings, with additional income coming from an employer-provided pension and personal savings.

Social Security's full retirement age (FRA), currently 66 and 2 months, is in the process of rising from age 65 and will reach 67 for people born in 1960 or later.[3] With that increase, the actuarial reductions for claiming Social Security benefits early at a given age are increasing, and the program's replacement rates are falling. That is, raising the full retirement age reduces annual and lifetime benefits. Over the period that the FRA is increasing, average longevity is also expected to rise. An increase in average longevity results in greater lifetime benefits, holding annual benefits constant. The actuarial reductions are designed so that lifetime benefits, on average, are roughly the same regardless of the age at which a person claims benefits. The total reduction, however, often results in a monthly benefit that is inadequate, especially for those who live to or beyond the average life expectancy. Raising the FRA further—a possible component of any future Social Security reform effort—will only make a bad situation worse for many by increasing the actuarial reductions and, therefore, reducing the monthly benefit amount for those who claim Social Security retirement benefits early.

Roughly half of beneficiaries who first claimed retirement benefits in 2014 were age 62, the earliest eligibility age (EEA).[4] More than two-thirds were younger than the FRA. One way to increase the adequacy of Social Security benefits (and income for longer lifespans) is for people to delay claiming retirement benefits. As noted earlier, between age 62 and FRA, monthly Social Security benefits increase by 7–8 percent for each one-year delay in claiming (see table 6-1).

For example, consider someone who turns 62 in 2022 and whose current full retirement age is 67. Assume that person would be eligible for a $1,300 monthly benefit at the full retirement age. If that person waited until age 70 to begin taking benefits, the monthly benefit would be 24 percent higher, or

Table 6-1. *Percentage Increase in Social Security Retirement Benefits by Claim Age*[a]
Percent

Claim age	*Monthly benefit as percentage of full retirement age (67) benefit*	*Increase in monthly benefit with a one-year delay*	*Cumulative increase if not claimed at age 62*
62	70		
63	75	7.1	7.1
64	80	6.7	14.3
65	86.67	8.3	23.8
66	93.33	7.7	33.3
67	100	7.1	42.9
68	108	8.0	54.3
69	116	7.4	65.7
70	124	6.9	77.1

Source: Social Security Online, "Social Security Benefits: Early or Late Retirement?" https://www.ssa.gov/OACT/quickcalc/early_late.html.

[a] Full retirement age for this example is 67; assumes annual earnings at age 62 and after are not large enough to change benefit amount (i.e., the earnings are not among the worker's thirty-five highest annual earnings).

$1,612 per month; claiming early, at age 62, would result in a monthly benefit of only $910, or 30 percent less. Note that delaying claiming until age 70 results in a monthly benefit amount that is 77 percent greater than the benefit at age 62.[5]

STARTs could complement efforts to educate people about the benefits of delaying claiming. But education efforts alone may have only limited success. Many people cannot afford to delay. Others may be reluctant to give up current income for what they perceive as a small increase in their lifetime monthly benefit.

Because Social Security benefits act as inflation-protected annuities, those who delay claiming are essentially purchasing an additional inflation-protected annuity benefit.[6] In the private sector, most companies that sell annuities adjust their payouts and make them less generous when lifespans increase or when interest rates decrease in order to maintain the lifetime value of annuity payouts. In contrast, Social Security does not adjust monthly benefits this way—its benefit formula and age adjustments are fixed by law. As longevity increases, on average, and interest rates fall, the lifetime value of benefits for any given claim age increases as well. This also means that if lifespans continue to increase and the economy continues to sustain low interest rates, delaying the initial Social Security claim will become more financially valuable over time. The START program would encourage individuals to take advantage of this provision.

Further, the movement away from defined benefit plans to defined contribution plans, by both private and public sector employers, has shifted much of the burden and risk of paying for retirement onto the individual, increasing the relative importance of monthly Social Security benefits in retirement.

BARRIERS TO DELAYING SOCIAL SECURITY RETIREMENT BENEFITS

Research published by AARP's Public Policy Institute used the Health and Retirement Study (HRS) to analyze those who claimed Social Security benefits at age 62 and those who claimed later. Those claiming benefits at age 62 had lower earnings, were less educated, were more likely to work in physically demanding jobs, and, importantly, were likely to be less healthy (Li, Hurd, and Loughran 2008). According to the research, one in five early claimers (19 percent) reported that they had a work-limiting condition at the time of claiming early Social Security retirement benefits.

Research published by the University of Michigan Retirement Research Center finds evidence that those with physically demanding jobs face many challenges and barriers to extending their working careers (Neumark and Song 2012). Further, workers who develop cognitive impairment in their later working years may face significant barriers to working throughout their 60s. A Boston College Center for Retirement Research report, referencing data by the Alzheimer's Association, states, "over half the cases of mild impairment progress to dementia, which erodes all cognitive functions irreversibly." While the incidence of Alzheimer's disease (the most common type of dementia) in one's 50s and early 60s is low (less than 4 percent of people under age 65), it rises to 15 percent of 65–74 year olds" (Belbase and Sanzenbacher 2016).

Additional research by the Boston College Retirement Research Center notes that the bottom third of the income distribution, those who tend to have lower employment skills and higher levels of unemployment as they approach retirement, face significant barriers to working later in life and extending work past normal retirement age (Munnell, Sanzenbacher, and Sass 2009). As the authors note, "The bottom line is that working longer may not be realistic or desirable for all members of society, and this possibility merits careful consideration when it comes to reforming the US retirement income system."

The retirement landscape is changing, and the likely reality is that people will need to save more and work longer, either retiring later or working for pay during retirement. Any barrier to extending one's working career will likely create additional financial stress on the ability to save for and have enough financial resources in retirement. Retirement policy reforms that increase the ability of workers to delay claiming Social Security benefits, thereby mitigating the effects of actuarial reductions for claiming early and potentially allowing workers to gain additional monthly Social Security benefits through the delayed retirement credits, would increase the financial security of millions of Americans in retirement.

SUPPLEMENTAL TRANSITION ACCOUNTS FOR RETIREMENT

The goal of STARTs is to allow a worker to delay claiming Social Security benefits for two to three years from the date the worker would have otherwise claimed benefits. This delay increases monthly Social Security benefits by 14 to 25 percent, depending on the original claim age. Importantly, monthly Social Security benefits would increase without limiting access to essential income at early retirement ages.

In essence, the proposal effectively increases the early eligibility age for Social Security retired-worker benefits, spousal benefits, and widow(er) benefits to mitigate the impact of actuarial reductions and to increase monthly benefits, which will help future retirees finance consumption over a longer lifespan. By design, the increase in the EEA is flexible depending on the amount of assets a person has in his or her START.

Our proposal helps workers receiving Social Security Disability Insurance (SSDI) whose benefits are not subject to actuarial reductions or DRCs. While the rules governing STARTs are generally similar for recipients of SSDI and other beneficiaries, these differences are important. First, we adjust the benefits of a DI beneficiary up by an actuarially fair factor to reflect the time period that START assets were used instead of DI trust fund assets. Second, we allow a DI beneficiary with a severe medical condition that meets any of the conditions set forth in the Social Security Administration's Compassionate Allowances program to take a lump-sum distribution from START regardless of age.[7] The special rules for DI beneficiaries are discussed in further detail below.

Our START proposal differs from other mandatory private savings account proposals in some important ways. First, our proposal would not require that assets in the START be used to purchase a private sector annuity. Rather,

START assets would be used to purchase additional inflation-protected annuitized income through the Social Security program. As noted above, the annuities provided by higher Social Security benefits are superior to those offered by the private sector in several ways. Second, we do not reduce Social Security benefits for money distributed from the account. Our focus is on improving benefit adequacy for longer lifespans, not on solvency, although our proposal does modestly reduce the long-term funding shortfall in Social Security. Policymakers should make changes to Social Security to address the program's seventy-five-year financing deficit. We believe, however, that any adjustment to Social Security benefits to achieve solvency should not be related to START assets so as not to reduce public support for START or penalize those with higher START assets.

Funding

START contributions would be required for all workers with taxable earnings covered under Social Security and who have not reached their full retirement age. Required contributions would not apply to earnings beginning on January 1 in the year a worker reaches full retirement age. To take advantage of compounding for younger workers, we would not impose a minimum age requirement.

Each worker and employer would contribute 1 percent of earnings (2 percent combined), up to the annual maximum subject to Social Security payroll tax ($127,500 in 2017), to the worker's START. The self-employed would make required contributions as both employer and employee.[8]

The Social Security Administration would enroll all Social Security–covered workers in START. START contributions would be collected in the same way and on the same schedule as payroll taxes. For employees, a worker's employer would submit the employer and employee contributions with other payroll taxes. Self-employed workers would also submit START contributions with their payroll taxes. This typically occurs through quarterly estimated tax payments and is reconciled on the tax return.

The tax character of START contributions is the same as for Social Security payroll taxes. Employer contributions are pretax, while worker contributions are after tax. The self-employed would be allowed to deduct half of their START contributions from taxable income, just as the self-employed can deduct payroll taxes.[9]

The federal government would contribute to the STARTs of low-income workers. The maximum government contribution would be 1 percent of earnings for married couples filing jointly with adjusted gross income (AGI) less

Table 6-2. *Social Security as a Percentage of Career Average Earnings, Age 62 in 2022*

Earnings (dollars)	*Replacement rate (percent)*
Very low earnings (11,922)	56.1
Low earnings (21,459)	40.7
Medium earnings (47,687)	30.2
High earnings (76,299)	25.0
Steady max earnings (116, 123)	19.8

Source: Social Security Administration, "Replacement Rates for Hypothetical Retired Workers," https://www.ssa.gov/oact/NOTES/ran9/an2016-9.pdf.

than $40,000, single filers with AGI less than $20,000, and head-of-household (HOH) filers with AGI less than $30,000. The government contribution would be phased out over an AGI range of $10,000, $7,500, and $5,000 for joint filers, HOH filers, and single filers, respectively. For example, the government contributions for joint filers with AGI of $42,500 would be 0.75 percent and with AGI of $45,000 would be 0.5 percent. Workers in low-income households would receive a total START contribution of up to 3 percent of earnings. The government contribution would be treated like an employer contribution and would not be included in current taxable income.

The progressive government contribution is needed to replicate the progressive structure of the Social Security benefit formula. As shown in table 6-2, Social Security replaces a higher percentage of career average earnings of low-lifetime earners than of high-lifetime earners. Because distributions from START assets will equal the Social Security benefits that would have otherwise been paid, lower earners need higher START assets as a percentage of their earnings than higher earners to "buy" an equivalent amount of delay. For example, low-earning workers who turn 62 in 2022 would need START assets equal to 40.7 percent of their career average earnings to "buy" one year of delay; in comparison, medium earners would need START assets of 30.2 percent of career average earnings.

For married couples, total contributions (employer, employee, and government) to each spouse's START would be split equally between the spouses based on the married couple's combined earnings (what we refer to as "deposit splitting"). Deposit splitting would occur regardless of whether the spouse had Social Security taxable earnings or not. We take this approach because women are more likely to have years without earnings than men, often to fulfill caregiving responsibilities. Further, the additional annuitized income that comes from delayed claiming is particularly important for women who, on average, live longer than men and rely on Social Security for a higher percentage of income. Finally, this approach makes administering the accounts easier because there is no need to split the assets at divorce or retirement.[10]

Distributions

START assets must be distributed and exhausted before an individual begins receiving Social Security benefits that are subject to actuarial reductions.[11] Social Security benefits that meet these conditions include retired worker benefits and spousal benefits of a retired or disabled worker, which a person can claim as early as age 62, and survivor benefits of an aged widow or widower, which a person can claim as early as age 60.[12]

An individual could elect to begin receiving START benefits at the earliest age of eligibility but would not be required to do so. The amount that any individual could withdraw in a given year would be limited to the Social Security benefit payable under today's Social Security rules.[13] The annual cost-of-living adjustment applicable to Social Security benefits would also apply to START benefits once distributions from the accounts began.

Social Security benefits would begin once a person exhausted his or her START assets or reached FRA and elected to stop receiving START distributions. The Social Security benefit would be subject to actuarial reductions and delayed retirement credits, if applicable, as under current law. Individuals could access START assets without restrictions and without any effect on Social Security benefits beginning at FRA and until age 70. This would include taking the full amount of START assets as a lump-sum distribution. At age 70, beneficiaries would be required to liquidate the accounts either by taking a full lump-sum distribution, or rolling the assets into a qualified plan or IRA or a beneficiary's START.

Consider the example of someone whose FRA is 67, but decides to claim benefits at age 62. If her monthly benefit at FRA was $1,300, her monthly benefit at age 62 would be $910. Under our proposal, the Social Security Administration (SSA) would pay $910 per month funded from her START assets beginning at age 62. Once SSA distributed all of the START assets, it would begin paying Social Security benefits. If the START assets were sufficient to cover just two years of delayed claiming, SSA would pay this beneficiary $1,040 per month, or a benefit that is 14 percent higher.

Any START assets remaining at the time of the account owner's death would go to her designated beneficiaries. These assets could be transferred to the beneficiary's START or paid directly as a lump-sum distribution. A lump-sum distribution would be included in the beneficiary's taxable income. Assets transferred to a START, however, would only become taxable when the beneficiary began taking distributions. The tax character of START assets (pretax and after tax) would transfer from the original account holder to the beneficiary.

Special Rules for Social Security Disability Insurance

Social Security disability benefits are not subject to actuarial reductions or delayed retirement credits, so workers who become disabled get no benefit from delaying claiming. Nonetheless, our goal for START is to increase economic security at older ages for all workers through the Social Security system. Consistent with this goal, the START rules for DI beneficiaries would be similar for retired workers, with two important exceptions. First we discuss the similarities.

Like retired workers, DI beneficiaries would have unrestricted access to their START assets beginning at their FRA. Also like retired workers, DI beneficiaries who apply for and receive disability benefits between age 62 and FRA would be required to first exhaust their START assets before receiving Social Security payments from the DI trust fund.[14] We take this approach to ensure that our proposal does not change the relative value of claiming disability benefits compared to retired-worker benefits between age 62 and FRA.[15]

After a beneficiary exhausts her START assets or reaches FRA and elects to stop receiving START distributions, the Social Security Administration would begin paying monthly benefits that reflect actuarially fair credits for the time the beneficiary received START assets instead of Social Security.[16] SSA would need to determine the actuarially fair credit, which provides that benefits paid over the life of the beneficiary, on average, are about the same regardless of whether a person's SSDI benefits had been suspended and temporarily replaced with START assets. For purposes of modeling the distributional effects of this proposal, we asked the Urban Institute to use the delayed retirement credit—two-thirds of 1 percent for each month delay, or 8 percent annually—to adjust SSDI benefits.[17]

Because of the unique circumstances of workers with a disability, we allow them greater flexibility in accessing their START assets than retired workers. First, a DI beneficiary who has a condition on the compassionate allowance list would have unrestricted access to her START assets regardless of age. SSA's compassionate allowance program identifies diseases and serious medical conditions that clearly meet Social Security's definition of disability and allow for an expedited approval process. SSA adds new conditions to the list annually. We take this approach to balance the need for financial resources that often accompanies a serious disability against the underlying goal of our proposal to improve financial security at older ages. Second, DI beneficiaries in pay status when they turn 62 could elect to use their START assets to "purchase" additional Social Security annuity income but would not be required to do so.

Consider the example of a beneficiary who first receives SSDI at age 59 equal to $1,000 per month. Let's assume $24,000 in START assets at age 62. Beginning at age 62, the beneficiary could elect to receive the $1,000 monthly payment from START assets instead of Social Security. The START assets would replace two years of SSDI payments. Beginning at age 64, this person would receive SSDI benefits again, but the payment after adjusting for inflation would be $1,160 (16 percent more) to reflect the actuarially fair credit (for this example, we used the DRC).

Account Structure and Administrative Considerations

STARTs would be professionally managed in a pooled account with an emphasis on keeping administrative fees as low as possible. An independent board would serve as the fiduciary. The board would select the private investment firm(s) responsible for managing START assets and set the investment guidelines for the pooled assets.[18] Individuals would not be allowed to select investments.

We expect the investment guidelines to structure the accounts at the participant level like target-date funds. The independent board would set the glide path, to manage longevity and market risks, as well as provide guidance on allocations across and within investment classes. The board could elect to use the federal Thrift Savings Plan (TSP) target-date funds as a model. For purposes of the dynamic simulations discussed below, we used TSP's target-date funds as the investment for START assets.

Because STARTs would be integrated with Social Security, SSA could use existing systems and benefit from economies of scale in administrating these accounts.[19] SSA's tasks would include maintaining account records, such as tracking individual account balances and transactions, communicating with participants, and answering their questions. More generally, SSA would be responsible for educating participants about how STARTs work and how they interact with Social Security. We recognize that administering START accounts would be a significant undertaking for the SSA and that the agency would require additional funding to carry out its new responsibilities, the costs of which could be funded by a small administrative fee on the START assets.

Tax Treatment of START Distributions

Distributions from STARTs, including amounts rolled into a qualified plan or IRA, would be included in taxable income to the extent they represent pretax contributions and earnings. Revenue from the taxation of START distributions would be credited to the Social Security trust funds, and would be more than adequate to cover the seventy-five-year cost of the government contributions.

DYNASIM ANALYSIS

This section discusses and highlights results from DYNASIM, the Urban Institute's dynamic microsimulation model. The model projects income and assets through the year 2090 by age, gender, race and ethnicity, lifetime income and earnings quintile, education, and a number of other characteristics. DYNASIM is well suited to model the changes in income and assets from START, which is highly dependent on the asset value of the accounts at older ages—a process that will take many years.

The Urban Institute (2018) ran four sets of START simulations reflecting two assumptions regarding benefit levels (scheduled benefits and payable benefits) and two assumptions on the effect of START on participants' contributions to defined contribution plans (no offset, and dollar-for-dollar offset). The scheduled benefit baseline assumes that current-law Social Security benefits will continue to be paid in full even after the Social Security trust funds are exhausted. The payable benefits baseline assumes that once the Social Security trust funds are exhausted the amount payable will be limited to current revenue coming into the system (mainly payroll taxes). The two sets of assumptions regarding benefit levels and offsets to other savings are intended to represent extremes, so the four scenarios bound the range of plausible outcomes.

Each simulation projects the distributional effects of START for the years 2025, 2035, 2045, 2055, and 2065. The Urban Institute did not model any change in labor force participation.

Below, we detail the effects of our proposal on poverty and income. First, we make some general observations from the simulations.

First, STARTs would raise the income of low-income older Americans. Mean and median increases in net per capita cash income are about 10 and 15 percent in 2065. Not surprisingly, the effect increases substantially over time as the accounts receive more contributions and the assets grow.

Second, the proposal is fully funded by employee and employer contributions and by crediting the Social Security trust funds with the revenue from taxing START distributions. The last item more than offsets the cost of the government contributions, thereby reducing Social Security's seventy-five-year actuarial deficit from 2.68 percent of taxable payroll to 2.48 percent.

Third, the overall average increase in net per capita income depends on whether workers reduce their other retirement savings in response to START contributions. However, the different overall results are driven by higher-income households, which are much more likely than lower-income households to be making contributions to an existing retirement plan. The change in average income for low-income households and overall poverty rates is almost identical under the assumptions regarding saving behavior.

And finally, STARTs would reduce poverty by less and raise income by less for people age 80 and older than for those age 70–79. This is a transition issue: older participants in 2065 would have had fewer years to accumulate assets in STARTs. Someone age 85 in 2065 who left the labor force at age 65 in 2045, for example, would have had only about twenty-six years to contribute to her START (for contributions made from 2019 until 2045). A 75-year-old in 2065 who retired at age 65 would have contributed for 36 years (2019 through 2055).

Poverty

START would reduce poverty significantly for people age 62 and over (see figure 6-1). The reduction is due to the higher monthly Social Security retirement benefit people would receive by delaying claiming.

Under the scheduled benefit scenario, STARTs would reduce poverty for people age 62 and over from 7.4 percent to 7.0 percent in 2045; and from 5.6 percent to 5.0 percent in 2065.

STARTs would reduce poverty by even more under the payable benefits scenario. For people age 62 and over, poverty would fall from 10.4 percent to 9.0 percent in 2045 and from 8.1 percent to 6.3 percent in 2065.

Focusing on estimates for 2065 under the scheduled benefit scenario, STARTs would reduce poverty rates in all age groups age 62 and over, all racial categories, and all marital status categories (see figure 6-2).

Income

STARTs would raise net per capita cash income considerably among people age 62 and over. Assuming there is full offset of START contributions with reductions in other retirement savings, average household income in 2065 would still rise in each quintile, with the lowest quintile exhibiting the greatest proportional increase—9.7 percent (see figure 6-3a). The proportionally bigger

Figure 6-1. **Poverty Rates for People Age 62+, 2045, 2055, 2065**

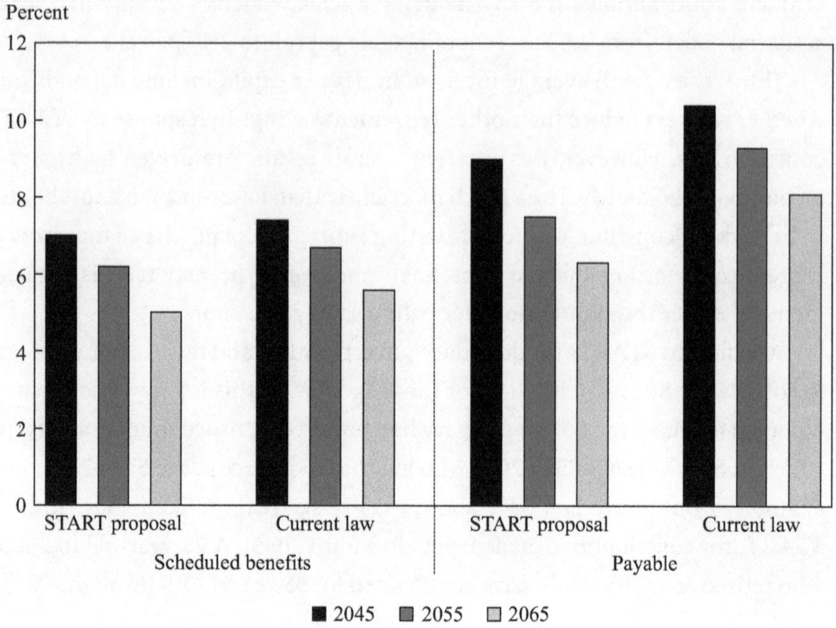

Source: Urban Institute (2018).

Figure 6-2. **Poverty Rates for People 62+ by Selected Characteristics, 2065**

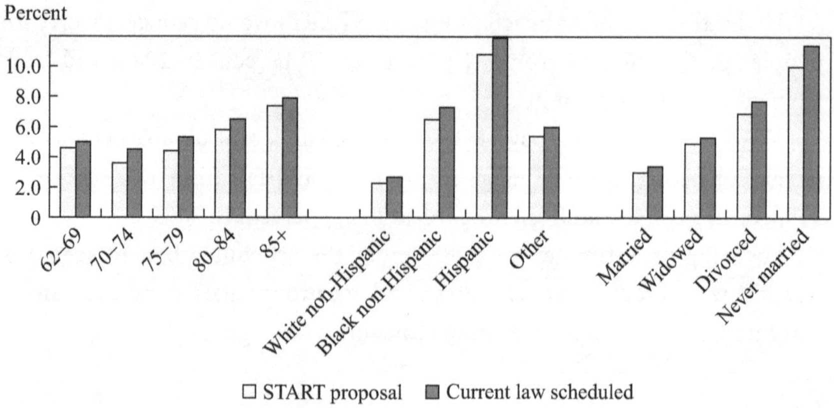

Source: Urban Institute (2018).

Figure 6-3a. **Percentage Change in Average per Capita Net Cash Income among Individuals Age 62 and Older by Shared Lifetime Earnings in Selected Years**

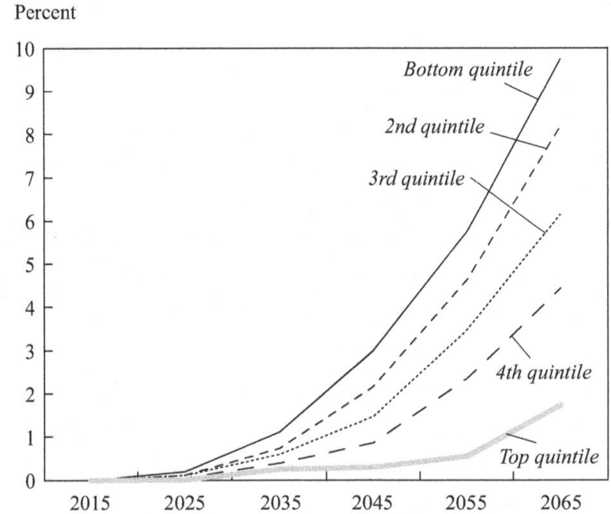

Source: Urban Institute (2018).

Figure 6-3b. **Percentage Change in Average per Capita Net Cash Income among Individuals Age 62 and Older by Shared Lifetime Earnings in Selected Years (No Offset)**

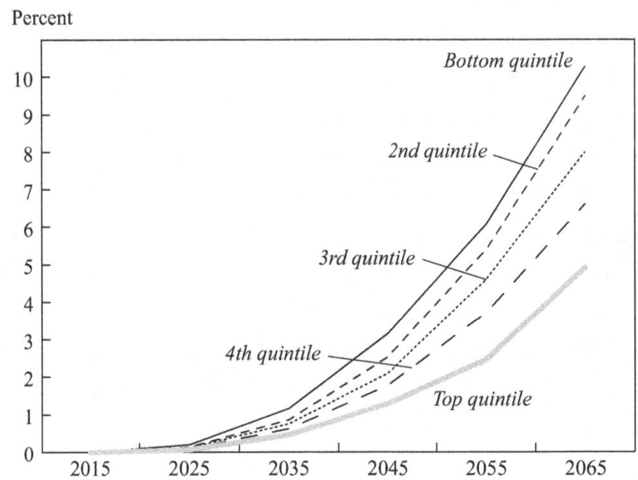

Source: Urban Institute (2018).

increase in income for low-lifetime earners reflects their greater reliance on Social Security income. Higher earners are more likely to have other sources of retirement income than Social Security, so a 10 percent increase in that group's Social Security benefits, for example, would represent a smaller percentage increase in cash income than it would for low earners whose only source of income is Social Security.[20]

Figure 6-3b shows similar data as figure 6-3a, but here we assume that there is no reduction in private saving as a result of START contributions. Under this assumption, the percentage change in average net cash income is higher for all quintiles than under the full-offset assumption shown in figure 6-3.

Average net cash income also rises for households in each marital category for those age 62 and over. Figure 6-4 presents the results assuming a full dollar-for-dollar offset; figure 6-4b assumes no offset.

Figures 6-5a (offset) and 6-5b (no offset) provide similar results by age category for those age 62 and over. START raises net per capita cash income the most for people in the 70–79 age group. The increases for those age groups represent the most accurate picture of the full potential of our proposal on economic security at older ages. As mentioned earlier, people age 80 and older in 2065 would have less than a full career of START contributions and asset accumulation. Further, many individuals age 62–69 would receive smaller START benefits than the adjusted Social Security benefits they will receive.

The increase in cash income as a result of STARTs would significantly improve the retirement security of the aged.

Table 6-3 provides a summary side-by-side comparison of the percent and dollar increase in net per capita cash income of people age 62 and over by selected characteristics, based on the Social Security scheduled benefits scenario (no reduction in benefits due to trust fund depletion). The results show the effects under the two assumptions about whether START contributions displace contributions to an employer-provided retirement saving plan or not.

The Urban Institute projections show that women and men experience similar increases in income under our proposal, but there are notable differences by education and race/ethnicity. For example, Blacks and Hispanics would have larger percentage increases in cash income than whites, on average, but smaller dollar increases. The average percentage increase in cash income falls as educational attainment rises.

Figure 6-4a. **Percentage Change in per Capita Net Cash Income among Individuals Age 62 and Older by Marital Status in Selected Years**

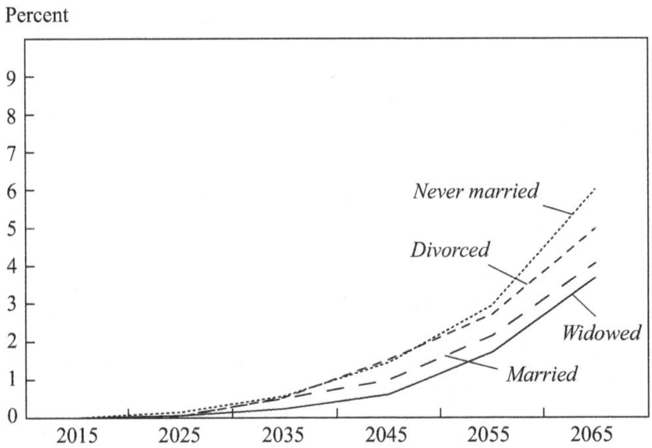

Source: Urban Institute (2018).

Figure 6-4b. **Percentage Change in per Capita Net Cash Income among Individuals Age 62 and Older by Marital Status in Selected Years (No Offset)**

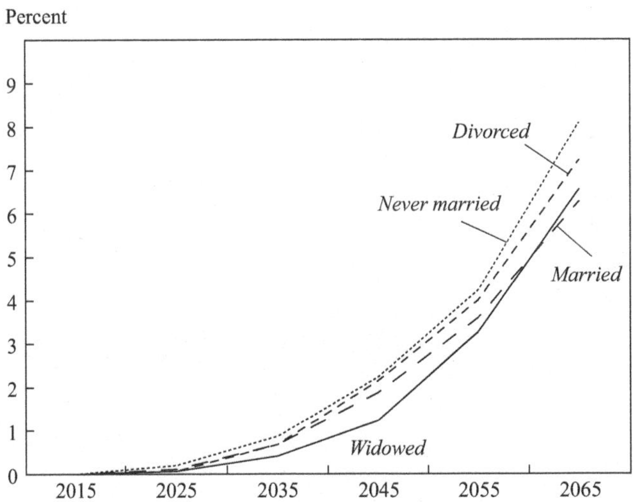

Source: Urban Institute (2018).

Figure 6-5a. **Percentage Change in Average per Capita Net Cash Income among Individuals Age 62 and Older in Selected Years by Age**

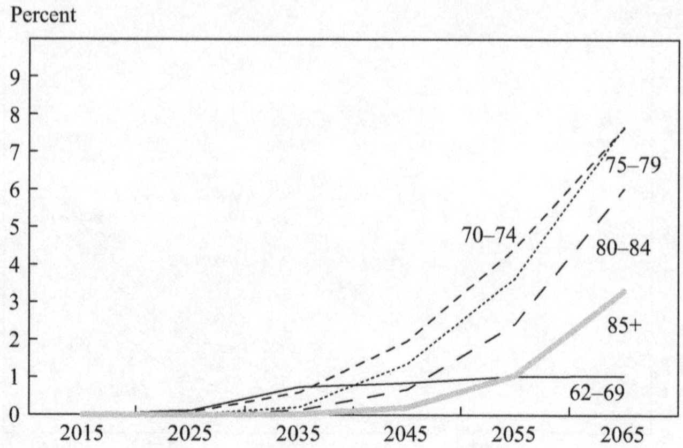

Source: Urban Institute (2018).

Figure 6-5b. **Percentage Change in Average per Capita Net Cash Income among Individuals Age 62 and Older in Selected Years by Age (No Offset)**

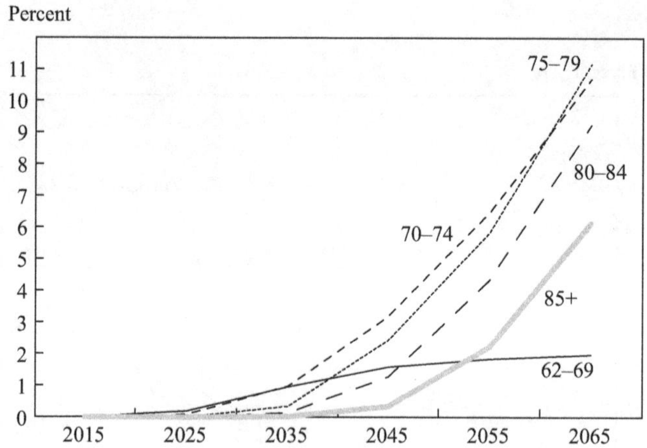

Source: Urban Institute (2018).

Table 6-3. *Increase in Net per Capita Cash Income of People Age 62 and Older by Selected Characteristics, 2065*
Percent

	With offset		*No offset*	
Scheduled benefits	*Percent*	*$2015*	*Percent*	*$2015*
All	4.4	1,884	6.7	2,874
Age				
62–69	1.0	511	2.0	970
70–74	7.6	3,543	10.7	4,955
75–79	7.7	3,142	11.2	4,566
80–84	6.0	2,210	9.2	3,388
85+	3.3	1,097	6.1	2,035
Sex				
Female	4.5	1,899	6.8	2,884
Male	4.3	1,868	6.6	2,862
Education				
No high school diploma	7.7	1,474	9.3	1,775
High school graduate	5.5	1,862	7.7	2,612
Some college	4.6	1,940	7.0	2,961
College graduate	3.5	1,990	5.9	3,347
Race or ethnicity				
White non-Hispanic	4.0	1,958	6.4	3,139
Black non-Hispanic	5.5	1,924	8.0	2,808
Hispanic	5.3	1,774	7.2	2,414
Other	4.1	1,656	6.2	2,472

Source: Urban Institute. https://www.urban.org/dynasim4-projections-birth-cohort.

Labor Force Participation

The proposal also has the potential to increase retirement security more broadly by encouraging work, for two main reasons. First, START benefits would not be subject to the retirement earnings test (RET). The RET is a widely misunderstood feature of the Social Security program that most beneficiaries view as a pure tax (Government Accountability Office 2016). As a result, researchers have found some evidence that it discourages work (Engelhardt and Kumar 2014). Second, the proposal could provide additional incentives for working longer through its unrestricted access to START assets at full retirement age, including a lump-sum distribution. While this could have a positive effect on the labor supply of workers who otherwise would have left the labor force before FRA, it could encourage people who otherwise would have left employment after FRA to leave sooner.

In a separate study, the Urban Institute estimated that for each additional year of work, annual consumption in retirement would increase by 9 percent. And the benefits to working longer would be larger for lower-income households. One additional year of work could increase annual consumption at retirement for the bottom lifetime earnings quintile and the second quintile by 16 percent and 12 percent (Butrica, Smith, and Steuerle 2006). People who work longer would not only receive higher Social Security benefits but would also have more retirement savings and fewer years of retirement that have to be covered by those savings. In addition, the longer people work, the better the financial position of the Social Security program will be because the additional work will increase payroll taxes.

A NECESSARY BRIDGE

The retirement landscape has evolved over the past few decades. A movement away from defined benefit plans to defined contribution plans, by both private and public sector employers, has shifted much of the burden and risk of paying for retirement onto the individual.

Financial security in retirement is still obtainable. However, the likely reality is that people will need to save more on their own and work longer, either retiring later or working for some paid income during retirement. Social Security's inflation-protected annuity feature could help millions of Americans achieve a more financially secure retirement by facilitating later claiming of Social Security retirement benefits in order to maximize the inflation-protected annuity value that Social Security provides.

Supplemental Transition Accounts for Retirement (START) accounts would provide the necessary bridge and allow individuals to delay claiming Social Security benefits. This, in turn, would mitigate the effects of actuarial reductions for claiming early and potentially allow workers to gain delayed retirement credits. The result would be higher monthly Social Security benefits—on average, 5–7 percent overall and 10 percent for the lowest-income workers—that cannot be outlived or eroded by inflation.

NOTES

This chapter represents the views of the authors and does not necessarily reflect the views of any of the organizations with which they are affiliated. The authors thank the Urban Institute's Karen Smith, who modeled the effects of our proposal; Sita Slavov;

and participants at the AARP Public Policy Institute's innovation roundtable for helpful comments.

1. For a summary of research in this area, see Burkhauser and others (2009).

2. An aged unit is either a married couple living together or a nonmarried person, which also includes persons who are separated or married but not living together. A married couple's age is defined as the age of the older spouse. The example in this chapter refers to aged units that are 65 years of age or older. See "Income of the Aged Population," https://www.ssa.gov/policy/docs/chartbooks/fast_facts/2008/fast_facts08.html#agedpop.

3. US Social Security Administration, "Retirement Benefits," https://www.ssa.gov/planners/retire/retirechart.html.

4. Authors' calculation based on table 6.B5 of the Annual Statistical Supplement to the Social Security Bulletin (Social Security Administration, 2016a). The percentages exclude disability conversions at FRA.

5. Social Security Administration, "When to Start Receiving Retirement Benefits," https://www.ssa.gov/pubs/EN-05-10147.pdf.

6. Social Security Administration, "When to Start Receiving Retirement Benefits."

7. Social Security Administration, "Compassionate Allowances Conditions," https://www.ssa.gov/compassionateallowances/conditions.htm.

8. Contributions made on earnings in excess of the taxable maximum ($127,500 in 2017) are treated in the same way as Social Security payroll taxes. The employee portion of the overpayment would be refunded to the worker through his or her tax return. The employer portion is not refunded, and this amount would be credited to the Social Security trust funds.

9. The self-employed would be able to deduct half of their START contributions from taxable income, just as employees would not include their employers' START contributions in taxable income.

10. Note, this approach means that spouses working in uncovered employment (e.g., certain state and local government workers not covered under Social Security) would have contributions made to a START in their name.

11. This provision differs from benefits based on a disability or caring for a child beneficiary.

12. For a description of the types of Social Security beneficiaries, see Social Security Administration, "Types of Beneficiaries," https://www.ssa.gov/oact/progdata/types.html.

13. If a worker did not qualify for Social Security, he or she would still have access to START assets without restriction beginning at age 62.

14. The payments may not come directly from the START, but rather the Social Security Administration would continue to pay DI benefits and be reimbursed from the worker's START.

15. Owing to the actuarial reduction factors associated with early claiming of Social Security retirement benefits, there exists a perverse financial incentive to apply for disability benefits before the full retirement age because DI benefits are not subject to actuarial reductions for age. Proposals that would increase the full retirement

age would increase this perverse incentive. For a more detailed discussion see Fichtner and Seligman (2016, p. 140).

16. Under current law, SSA converts DI beneficiaries to OASI (Old-Age and Survivors Insurance) at FRA. This conversation has no implications for the benefits received by the beneficiary, but it does change the trust fund from which benefits are paid from the DI trust fund to the OASI trust fund.

17. Our intention is to have the Social Security Administration determine an actuarial fair rate based on the life expectancy of DI beneficiaries. One possibility would be to use the DRC rate of 8 percent or the rates associated with the actuarial reductions for claiming early.

18. The board could choose to distribute participants' assets among multiple fund managers to mitigate against the risk that participants' asset returns will vary by fund manager.

19. For a full discussion of administrative and record-keeping issues associated with individual accounts related to Social Security, see Whitman (2006).

20. The Urban Institute's measure of income includes Social Security, defined benefit pensions, interest, dividends, rental income, retirement account withdrawals, and means-tested and non-means-tested benefits.

REFERENCES

Belbase, Anek, and Geoffrey Sanzenbacher. 2016. "Cognitive Aging and Ability to Work." Research Brief 16-18. Center for Retirement Research, Boston College.

Burkhauser, Richard, Alan Gustman, John Laitner, Olivia S. Mitchell, and Amanda Sonnega. 2009. "Social Security Research at the Michigan Retirement Research Center." *Social Security Bulletin* 69 (4). https://www.ssa.gov/policy/docs/ssb/v69n4/v69n4p51.html.

Butrica, Barbara A., Karen E. Smith, and C. Eugene Steuerle. 2006. "Working for a Good Retirement." Retirement Security Project Discussion Paper #06–03. Washington, DC: Urban Institute. http://www.urban.org/sites/default/files/publication/50566/311333-Working-for-a-Good-Retirement.PDF.

Engelhardt, Gary, and Anil Kumar. 2014. "Taxes and the Labor Supply of Older Americans: Recent Evidence from the Social Security Earnings Test." *National Tax Journal* 67 (2): 443–58.

Fichtner, Jason, and Jason Seligman. 2016. "Enhancing U.S. Retirement Security through Coordinated Reform of Social Security Disability." *Journal of Retirement* (Summer 2016): 131–47.

Government Accountability Office. 2016. "Social Security: Improvements to Claims Process Could Help People Make Better Informed Decisions about Retirement Benefits." GAO-16-786. Washington, DC. http://www.gao.gov/assets/680/679747.pdf.

Li, Xiaoyan, Michael Hurd, and David S. Loughran. 2008. *The Characteristics of Social Security Beneficiaries Who Claim Benefits at the Early Entitlement Age*. Research Report 2008–19. Washington, DC: AARP Public Policy Institute. http://assets.aarp.org/rgcenter/econ/2008_19_beneficiaries.pdf.

Munnell, Alicia, Geoffrey Sanzenbacher, and Steven Sass. 2009. "Can the Bottom Third Work Longer?" Research Brief 9-1. Center for Retirement Research, Boston College.

Neumark, David, and Joanne Song. 2012. "Barriers to Later Retirement: Increases in the Full Retirement Age, Age Discrimination, and the Physical Challenges of Work." Research Brief 265. University of Michigan Retirement Research Center. www.mrrc.isr.umich.edu/publications/briefs/pdf/rb265.pdf.

Shelton, Alison. 2016. "Social Security: Who's Counting on It?" Fact Sheet. Washington, DC: AARP Public Policy Institute. http://www.aarp.org/ppi/info-2015/social-security-who-is-counting-on-it.html.

Social Security Administration. 2016a. "The Annual Statistical Supplement to the Social Security Bulletin, 2015." SSA Publication 13-11700. Washington, DC. https://www.ssa.gov/policy/docs/statcomps/supplement/2015/supplement15.pdf.

———. 2016b. "Relative Importance of Social Security, 2014." *Fast Facts & Figures*, August 2016. https://www.ssa.gov/policy/docs/chartbooks/fast_facts/2016/fast_facts16.html#page5.

———. 2017. "When to Start Receiving Retirement Benefits, 2017." https://www.ssa.gov/pubs/EN-05-10147.pdf.

Urban Institute. 2018. Results of DYNASIM Model. Unpublished study. Washington, DC.

Whitman, Debra. 2006. "The Structure of Social Security Individual Account Contributions and Investments: Choices and Implications." CRS Report for Congress. May 1, 2006. Congressional Research Service. http://research.policyarchive.org/2819.pdf.

SEVEN

State-Sponsored Retirement Saving Plans

NEW APPROACHES TO BOOST RETIREMENT PLAN COVERAGE

William G. Gale and David C. John

Americans face a serious and continuing problem in building retirement security to supplement their Social Security benefits. The share of the workforce covered by a retirement saving plan has remained relatively flat in recent decades. In 1987, about 51 percent of private sector workers age 21–64 had access to a retirement saving or pension plan through their employer. The share rose to 59 percent by 2000, but then fell gradually back to 51 percent as of 2013 (Copeland 2014).

The low-return investment environment (as of 2017) makes it harder for people to accumulate a given amount of wealth in retirement, especially if the onset of retirement saving is delayed. As a result, bringing people into the retirement system and having them initiate contributions to retirement accounts as early as possible remains an important priority (Byrne and Reilly 2017).

Recent federal policy has not had a significant effect on coverage rates. The Pension Protection of Act (PPA) of 2006 encouraged automatic enrollment in defined contribution (DC) plans. This policy raised participation rates among those workers who were already offered a plan, but it did little to expand coverage rates. In 2014, an Obama administration executive order established the myRA, which is available nationally as a starter retirement savings account, but it has generated only very limited participation. Federal legislation creating an Automatic IRA and open Multiple Employer Plans (MEPs) has been introduced but not enacted.[1]

In the wake of stagnant coverage trends, and in the absence of more comprehensive federal legislation, several states have acted on their own. Five states (California, Connecticut, Illinois, Maryland, and Oregon) have enacted Secure Choice plans based on the Automatic IRA (AARP 2017). In these plans, states sponsor a simple, low-cost payroll deduction plan managed by private sector providers. The structure is similar to Section 529 college saving plans. With some exceptions, employers are required to participate in the plan if they do not offer workers another type of retirement plan. Eligible workers are automatically enrolled. In addition, two states (Washington and New Jersey) are developing retirement savings marketplaces, state-sponsored websites that enable small businesses to find retirement plans that are prescreened to meet certain criteria. Many other states are considering Secure Choice plans, marketplaces, or other options, such as Vermont's decision to start an open Multiple Employer Plan. The best plan for a particular state will depend on its economic needs, political constraints, and other factors.

Although federal legislative action has been lacking, 2016 federal regulations by the Department of Labor temporarily eased the implementation of state actions, by confirming conditions under which state-sponsored retirement saving plans are exempt from federal pension regulation (81 F.R. § 92639).[2] In the first half of 2017, however, Congress used the Congressional Review Act to overturn the relevant regulations and to prohibit agencies from issuing similar rulings in the future without advance congressional approval. While reversing these regulations will hamper state-sponsored plans, it will not necessarily end them.[3]

This chapter evaluates models and features used in state-sponsored retirement saving plans. These plans have the potential to raise the number of Americans with access to payroll-deduction retirement saving plans, and thus to reduce the number of retirees with few financial resources other than Social Security benefits. They could also improve the sponsoring states' fiscal outlooks by reducing the extent to which future retirees depend on taxpayer-financed government services.[4]

Our main conclusion is that, regardless of which approach is taken—Secure Choice, open MEP, marketplace, or other—plans that boost coverage most will feature two characteristics: required provision of a retirement saving plan by

Figure 7-1. **Access and Participation in US Private Sector Employer-Sponsored Retirement Plans, 1987–2013 (workers age 21–64)**

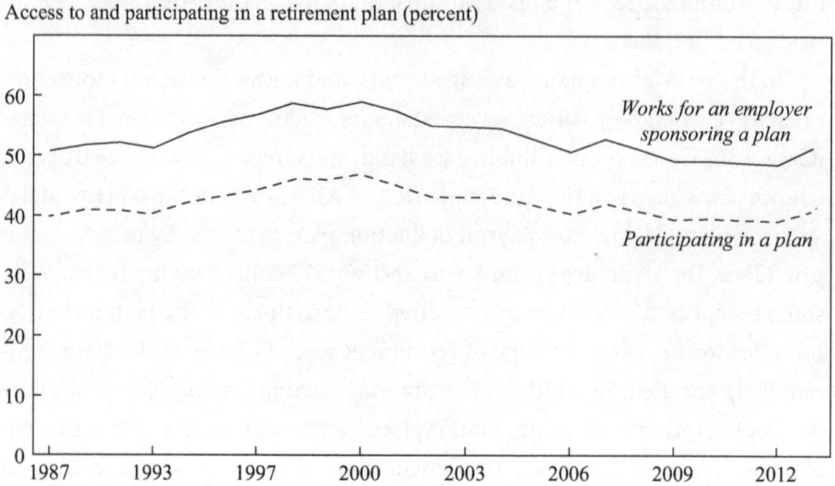

Source: Copeland (2014).

the firm, and automatic enrollment of eligible workers. Yet we also note that under current legal and regulatory conditions Secure Choice is the only model that enables states to require that employers provide a plan.

This chapter provides background on workers' access to retirement saving plans, describes actions that states have taken and other actions they could pursue, and evaluates the importance of coverage mandates on firms and automatic enrollment of workers.

WORKERS' ACCESS TO RETIREMENT SAVING PLANS

As stated earlier, the proportion of US private sector workers with access to an employer-sponsored payroll deduction retirement saving plan or pension has remained stagnant for several decades. Figure 7-1 shows the share of private sector workers covered by a retirement saving or pension plan between 1987 and 2013.[5] Both coverage rates and plan participation remained relatively constant over the twenty-six-year period. Despite a slight peak in the late 1990s, coverage in 2013, as shown in figure 7-1, was the same as it was in the 1980s.

Access to a retirement plan varies by workers' demographic characteristics and firm size, as shown in figure 7-2. In 2012, coverage rates rose with the worker's income, from 23 percent in the lowest quartile to 81 percent in the

Figure 7-2. **US Private Sector Retirement Plan Access by Selected Demographics**

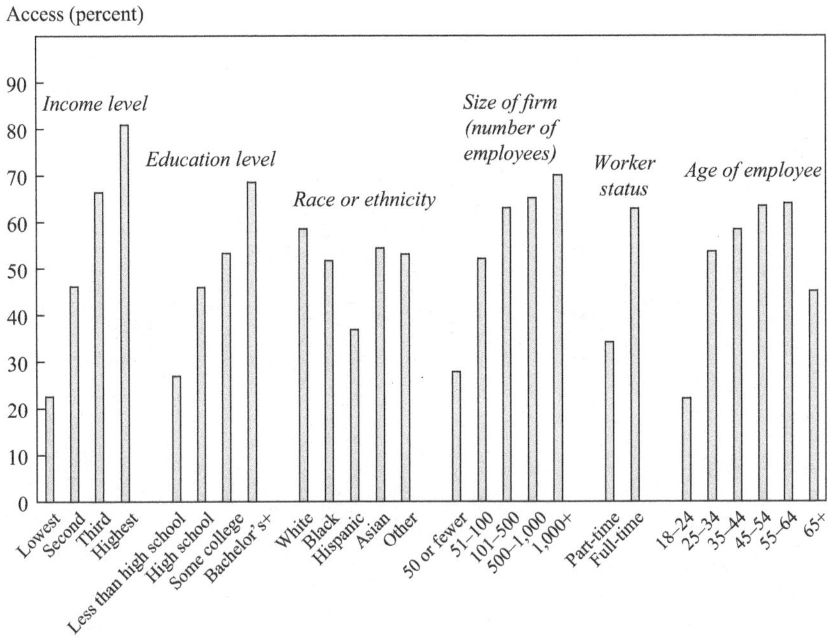

Source: GAO (2015) analysis of 2012 SIPP data.

Note: Access is defined as working for an employer who offers a retirement plan and being eligible for that plan.

highest quartile.[6] They also rose with the worker's educational attainment. Only 27 percent of workers with less than a high school degree were covered, in comparison with 69 percent of those with a bachelor's degree or more education. Coverage rates are fairly constant by age once workers reach age 25, varying from 54 to 64 percent for workers age 25 to 64. More full-time workers are covered than part-time workers, and more white workers are covered than workers of other racial and ethnic groups. Coverage rates also increase with firm size. Among firms with fifty or fewer or workers, only 28 percent of workers have access to a retirement saving plan. Among firms with 1,000+ employees, 70 percent have access to a plan.

Participation rates in 2012, given coverage, were fairly high, as shown in figure 7-3. Conditional participation rates exceeded 72 percent for all worker characteristics and firm sizes, except in three categories: workers age 18–24, workers in the lowest earnings quartile, and high school dropouts. Even in

Figure 7-3. **Participation in a US Private Sector Retirement Plan Conditional on Access, 2012**

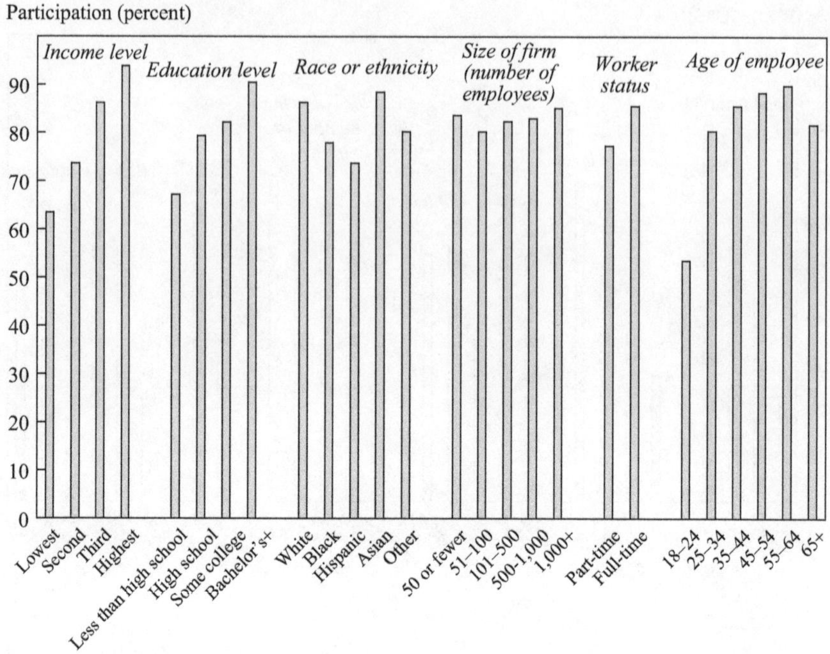

Source: GAO (2015) analysis of 2012 SIPP data.

those categories, conditional participation rates exceeded 50 percent. Likewise, the time-series data in figure 7-1 show that conditional participation rates were high and relatively steady—between 79 percent and 81 percent—since 1987. These facts suggest that expanding coverage will expand participation as well.

Lack of access to workplace pensions matters because it impedes the accumulation of retirement wealth. In a 2016 EBRI study, about 61 percent of employees with access to an employer-sponsored plan held more than $25,000 in overall (nondefined benefit) savings balances, and 35 percent held $100,000 or more. By contrast, among those without access to a plan, 87 percent held less than $25,000, and only 5 percent held $100,000 or more (Helman and others 2016).[7]

Meeting the Needs of Small Business Employees

Two principal models have been used, though others may be considered in the future. Table 7-1 describes each of the major approaches, and table 7-2 summarizes several advantages and disadvantages of each option. A successful plan

Table 7-1. *Comparison of State Retirement Plan Structures*

	Auto IRA	*Open MEP*	*Marketplace*	*MyRA*
Account structure	Payroll deduction IRA (traditional or Roth)	401(k) or other defined contribution plan	Varies. May include SIMPLE IRAs, Auto IRAs, Roth IRAs, 401(k), myRA	Roth IRA
Employer participation requirement	Yes	No	No	No
Employer contribution	No	Allowed	Allowed	No
Contribution limits	$5,500 annually ($6,500 if over 50)	Same as for a 401(k): $18,000 annually ($24,000 if over 50)	Depends on account type	$5,500 annually ($6,500 if over 50). After $15,000 must roll over into private Roth IRA
ERISA coverage?	No	Yes	Marketplace itself is not covered, but individual plans may be	No

Source: Authors' compilation.

Table 7-2. *Advantages and Disadvantages of Retirement Plan Types*

	Secure Choice (Auto IRA)	*Open Multiple Employer Plan (MEP)*	*Marketplace*	*MyRA*
Advantages	• Simple and low cost • Employers have virtually no regulatory burden or fiduciary responsibility • Easy to change contribution amounts • Employees do not need to take action to participate and maintain complete control over their account	• Allows employer contributions • Higher contribution limits • ERISA protection • More likely to have additional investment and financing options • Lower regulatory burden for employers • Streamlined compliance at the state level • Can use auto-enrollment	• Allows the state to prescreen retirement plans to ensure they meet certain standards • Can provide high-quality information about retirement alternatives • Employers can choose their level of involvement • State does not have any involvement with ERISA	• Good way for new savers to get in the habit of saving • Simple and easy to understand • Limited to no risk of loss • No fees • National program available to everyone
Disadvantages	• Low contribution limits • No employer matches • Strength of employee protections depends on state law • Plans in different states may have different rules	• May impose higher costs and more responsibilities on employers than IRAs • Employer must ensure fiduciary responsibilities are handled by provider	• No direct incentive for employers to adopt a retirement saving plan (will do little to raise coverage) • Does nothing to simplify retirement saving or reduce regulatory burdens for small employers • Needs an enforcement mechanism to ensure that plans continue to be adequate	• Low maximum size • No real potential for contributions to grow • No mechanism to roll over account to a private provider once maximum size is reached • Uncertain political future

Source: Authors' compilation.

will be practical for small businesses and the state to implement, and will meet the needs of affected employees.

Secure Choice (Auto IRA)

Five states (California, Connecticut, Illinois, Maryland, and Oregon) have enacted Secure Choice programs based on the Automatic IRA (AARP 2017; Iwry and John 2009). Under these plans, states would sponsor a simple and low-cost plan using a payroll deduction IRA. The programs could be offered to employees by employers who offer no other retirement saving or pension plan. Employers would face few regulatory burdens, no fiduciary responsibility, and no contribution responsibilities. Most employers already use either an outside payroll provider or payroll processing software, so the cost of setting up the deduction and forwarding contributions would be minimal. Employees would be enrolled automatically and could opt out or adjust their contribution level. Contributions would be invested into a target-date fund or similar vehicle, unless employees chose to allocate funds to one of a few other basic investment options. Investment management and record-keeping could be contracted to a private provider. States would handle fiduciary responsibilities and consumer protections.

Secure Choice plans were developed to meet the needs of small businesses and their employees. One criticism of payroll deduction IRAs is that contribution limits are significantly lower than in 401(k) plans. In 2017, workers under 50 could contribute up to $18,000 annually to 401(k) plans but only $5,500 to an IRA. Small-business employees, however, are likely to have lower median earnings than those of larger firms, suggesting lower optimal targets for wealth accumulation.[8] In addition, the significant gap in contribution limits between IRAs and 401(k)s would help minimize the extent to which the program encourages firms to drop their existing 401(k)s in favor of a Secure Choice plan. Secure Choice plans are not covered by the Employee Retirement Income Security Act (ERISA), the major federal law covering employee benefits. Thus the strength of employee protections in Secure Choice plans depends on state laws and may differ from the extensive protections guaranteed under ERISA.

The Illinois Secure Choice Savings Program was enacted in January 2015 and with plans for a pilot program beginning in 2018. The plan applies to all employers with at least twenty-five employees, who have been in business for at least two years, and who do not currently provide a qualifying saving plan.

Smaller employers can voluntarily participate (Illinois State Treasurer 2016). Employees will be automatically enrolled in a Roth IRA with a 3 percent default contribution rate.

The Oregon Saves program was enacted in 2015 and set to be expanded in 2018. The plan requires all Oregon employers to either join the state Oregon Saves plan or offer their own qualified retirement plan (State of Oregon 2017). Employees are to be automatically enrolled in a Roth IRA with a 5 percent default contribution rate.

California's Secure Choice program was enacted in September 2016 for a phase-in starting in 2019. The program requires employers who have five or more employees and who do not otherwise offer a retirement plan to automatically enroll their employees in a state-sponsored IRA overseen by the Secure Choice Retirement Savings Investment Board. As enacted in 2016, the default contribution rate begins at 3 percent of workers' payroll, with the option for the board to implement an automatic escalation policy (automatically increase contributions by 1 percent per year, capped at a rate of 8 percent). Initially, funds were invested in low-risk securities such as Treasury bonds, with more investment options made available over time (California State Treasury 2017). While the low-risk investments reduce the chance of loss, they also make it difficult for California savers to build significant retirement balances.

The Connecticut Retirement Security Program was enacted in 2016 to take effect in 2018. The plan requires employers with five or more employees and who do not provide a retirement saving option to join the state plan. Employees are automatically enrolled in a Roth IRA with an initial 3 percent default contribution rate (Act Creating the Connecticut Retirement Security Program 2016). A public-private oversight board, the Connecticut Retirement Security Authority, was established to oversee the implementation of the program.

The Maryland Small Business Retirement Savings Program and Trust was enacted in 2016, with plans to take effect in 2017. The plan requires private employers who do not currently offer a retirement saving plan and who have been in business for the past two years to enroll their employees in an Automatic IRA. The program is required if an employer uses an outside payroll provider or a payroll software program. Businesses that comply with the law will receive a waiver on an annual $300 business report filing fee (Maryland General Assembly 2016). The Small Business Retirement Savings Board oversees the program and selects Auto IRA plans and contribution rates.

Marketplaces

As of 2017, two states (Washington and New Jersey[9]) are in the process of implementing retirement savings marketplaces (table 7-3). A marketplace is a state-sponsored website that enables small businesses to find retirement saving or pension plans. The marketplace displays a diverse array of plans—including payroll deduction IRAs, Savings Incentive Match Plan for Employees (SIMPLE) IRAs, open MEPs, myRA, and perhaps even 401(k) plans and defined benefit plans—offered by several different providers. The state prescreens retirement plans, ensuring that the options presented to employers meet certain standards (regarding fees, for example) and provide unbiased information about retirement plan options. Because the marketplace merely lists plan options, a state has no potential ERISA liability and does not take on any of the employer's legal responsibilities. The marketplace design enables employers to determine which type of plan best meets their and their employees' needs, including whether they prefer an ERISA-covered plan. A marketplace could be coupled with a requirement that employers provide coverage, as discussed in the next section. But by itself, a marketplace does nothing to simplify retirement saving or to reduce the regulatory burdens and fiduciary responsibilities that would be placed on smaller employers.

Washington's Small Business Retirement Marketplace, enacted in 2015, was fully operational in 2017. Employers with fewer than 100 employees are eligible to participate but are not required to do so. The law permits the government to provide incentives for employers to do so. The marketplace contains a variety of low-cost savings options provided by financial services firms (SIMPLE IRA and payroll deduction IRAs, for example) and investment choices, as well as access to the federal myRA.

New Jersey enacted a marketplace plan in 2016 based on Washington's model. It is to be available to companies with fewer than 100 employees, and participation is voluntary. The marketplace must offer a similar variety of low-cost savings options, at least two investment choices, and access to myRA (Bernard 2016).

Open Multiple Employer Plans

Beyond Secure Choice plans and marketplaces, states can also choose to operate an open Multiple Employer Plan (MEP).[10] In 2017, Vermont approved legislation establishing a MEP, and the New York City Comptroller's Office proposed a variation of an open MEP in 2016 as part of a larger retirement saving plan (Office of the New York City Comptroller 2016). As of 2017, Philadelphia

Table 7-3. *Comparison of State Retirement Plan Actions*

	California	*Illinois*	*Oregon*	*Maryland*	*Connecticut*	*Washington*	*New Jersey*
Date enacted	September 29, 2016	January 5, 2015	June 25, 2015	May 10, 2016	May 27, 2016	May 18, 2015	January 19, 2016
Date to be implemented	Bill effective January 1, 2017. Implementation in 2018 or later.	Effective June 1, 2017. Participants must be able to enroll within two years and employers have nine months after that to set up automatic payroll deposits. Phased enrollment	Individuals may begin to make contributions beginning July 1, 2017	Act takes effect July 1, 2016	January 1, 2018	January 1, 2017	Not specified
Plan type	Auto IRA	Roth IRA	Roth IRA	At least one payroll deposit IRA	Roth IRA	Marketplace containing selection of: SIMPLE IRA, myRA, Auto IRA and/or "life insurance plans for retirement purposes"	Marketplace containing selection of: SIMPLE IRA, myRA, Auto IRA and/or "life insurance plans for retirement purposes"
Automatic enrollment	Yes	Yes	Yes	Yes	Yes	Not required	Not required
Default contribution rate	3% (Board can adjust from 2% to 5%), option for auto-escalation at no more than 1% per year until rate reaches 8%	3%	5% standard rate, 1% minimum and no maximum	Not specified	3%	None specified	None specified

Source: AARP (2017).

is also considering an open MEP for that city's small businesses (City of Philadelphia Office of the Comptroller 2017). Federal regulations require employers participating in private sector MEPs to have a common bond (such as being in the same industry). State-sponsored MEPs do not face this restriction; they may cover workers from firms without a common bond. Under an open MEP, several small businesses join together to offer a common type of account to each employer's workforce. The common plan structure reduces the compliance burden and places most fiduciary responsibilities on the plan administrator. State-sponsored open MEPs can be open to any small business in the state that wants to offer its employees a retirement plan. Like the Secure Choice model, these open MEPs would use services that are contracted out to private sector providers.

Wealth accumulation can be higher in a MEP because the plans contain higher contribution limits and employers can make contributions. MEPs are also more likely to offer loan provisions and more diverse investment choices. For small employers, both MEPs and Secure Choice plans entail lower administrative costs than comparable retirement plans. But MEPs may impose higher administrative costs and greater responsibilities on employers than IRA-based plans, since MEPs typically offer more services and employers must meet certain fiduciary and regulatory responsibilities under ERISA. Participation in a state-sponsored MEP is voluntary, as states are not allowed to require employers to offer ERISA-regulated plans.

myRA

Another option states can pursue is to encourage workers to sign up for myRA accounts.[11] Established by executive order by the Obama administration in 2015, the myRA is a Roth IRA offered through the US Treasury, designed to be a simple starter account available to all workers. Roth IRA income limits apply, however, and myRA savers who also have other retirement accounts face overall contribution limits. The program has no fees. Funds are invested exclusively in Treasury bonds, which at low interest rates allow savers to do little more than to keep up with inflation.

These accounts can be offered through an employer using payroll deduction, or individuals can participate on their own using automatic debit from a checking account. Savers can also direct all or a portion of their income tax refunds directly into a myRA. myRAs can travel with workers from job to job if a new employer offers the program or if the saver converts it into an individual account. When the myRA balance reaches $15,000, the account holder must transfer the funds to a private sector Roth IRA in order to continue contributing. By 2017, however, no mechanism exists to facilitate these transfers, which hampers the usefulness of the myRA. In addition, the myRA faces an uncertain political future with the Trump administration ending the program. Because of the limited reach of the myRA, participation has been limited thus far.

Other State and Local Actions

Legislation has been introduced in more than half of the remaining states to either establish state-sponsored retirement programs or to create a commission to study them (Georgetown University Center for Retirement Initiatives 2017). In 2017 alone, legislators in over ten states proposed legislation to enact state-sponsored retirement saving plans or create a feasibility study. In 2012, Massachusetts enacted the Connecting Organizations to Retirement Program (CORE), a voluntary 401(k) plan for nonprofit firms with fewer than twenty employees, where the state controls administrative costs. States are also experimenting with different plan features. For example, West Virginia and Utah have proposed Automatic IRA plans without a mandate that employers participate.

In addition, cities such as New York City, Seattle, and Philadelphia expressed interest in creating retirement plans for local private sector workers. New York City has proposed creating a voluntary marketplace to access easy-to-use 401(k) plans, including the publicly funded Empire City 401(k) MEP, Simplified Employee Pension (SEP) IRAs, and SIMPLE IRAs. Employers who do not offer a plan on their own or through the marketplace would be mandated to enroll employees in a new NYC Roth IRA in which the first $15,000 is invested in a myRA account and anything above that would be put in more conventional investment vehicles (Office of the New York City Comptroller 2016). The overturning of DOL regulations that would have enabled cities to establish Auto IRAs complicates the implementation of much of this plan. Philadelphia created a working group to develop a plan, as well as a series of outreach efforts with the local community (City of Philadelphia Office of the Controller 2016). As mentioned, these efforts resulted in the recommendation that the city establish an open MEP (City of Philadelphia Office of the Controller 2017).

Small-Business Needs

A key factor in designing a successful state-sponsored plan is understanding why small businesses do not offer plans and what reform features they support. In order for these plans to attract sufficient political support, it is imperative for small businesses to believe that a state proposal is feasible and de-

Figure 7-4. **Reasons Small- and Medium-Sized Businesses Do Not Offer Retirement Plans**

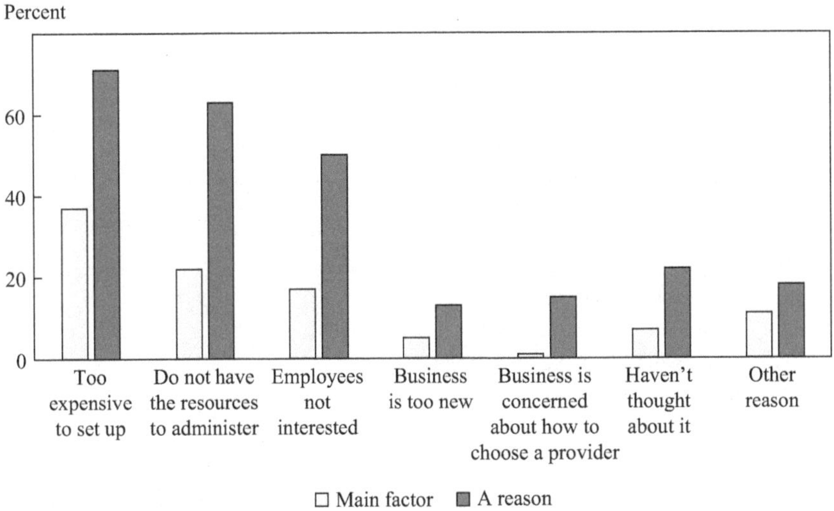

Source: Pew Charitable Trusts (2017, figure 1).

Note: Survey data are from the attributed source. The study authors surveyed owners of small- and medium-sized businesses without a retirement plan in place about their views on implementing such a plan.

signed to meet the needs of their workers. At the same time, the state needs to understand how small businesses will react to the proposal, and what proportion of employers required to offer a plan will use the state plan instead of starting their own.

Expense and complexity are major reasons why employers fail to offer small-business retirement plans. On an asset-weighted basis, the smallest existing private sector retirement saving plans can cost up to four times as much as larger plans (Steverman 2017). In a 2017 survey, 37 percent of small businesses that do not offer plans said that the main reason was because it was too expensive to set up. About 71 percent cited expense as one of the factors contributing to their decision, as shown in figure 7-4. Another 22 percent said the main reason was that the company did not have the resources to administer a retirement plan, with a total of 63 percent mentioning this as a reason. The focus on cost was reinforced later in the survey when small- and medium-sized business owners were asked what would motivate them to offer a retirement plan; the answer that drew the largest support was an increase in profits, followed by the provision of a business tax credit for starting a plan (Pew

Table 7-4. *Individual Features of an Auto IRA That Business Owners Support*

Feature	*"Somewhat Support" or "Strongly Support" (percent)*[a]
Businesses' only responsibility would be to withhold money from participating employees' paychecks and send it to the retirement account on their behalf.	79
Businesses would not be required to contribute to the plan.	83
Businesses would not have any legal responsibility for their employees' retirement accounts.	86
Employees who do not have access to a retirement saving plan at their work would be offered the chance to participate in one.	92
By default, workers would contribute to the retirement savings account unless they took action to opt out of the program.	72
Employees could stop or change their contributions at any time.	92
As a starting point, participating employees would contribute a set amount of 3 percent of their paychecks to the retirement account.	79
As a starting point, participating employees would contribute a set amount of 6 percent of their paychecks to the retirement account.	69
Employees could withdraw their own contributions to the account at any point without a penalty.	82

Source: Derived from Pew Charitable Trusts (2017), table 1.

[a]Survey data from Pew Charitable Trusts (2017). The study authors surveyed owners of small- and medium-sized businesses without retirement plans in place about their views on implementing such a plan. For this question, employers were asked to indicate their support for features of a hypothetical retirement plan similar to an Auto IRA that would be sponsored by an outside organization and not a business like theirs.

Charitable Trusts 2017, p. 3). Interestingly, the survey found that the creation of a retirement plan with fewer administrative requirements and the availability of easy-to-understand information would have almost no effect on plan offerings; over half of the small-business respondents said that those factors would make them no more likely to offer a plan.

By contrast, small businesses responded positively in the survey to a mandatory retirement saving plan with features like those found in the Automatic IRA, as shown in table 7-4. About 92 percent of small- to medium-sized em-

Figure 7-5. **US Employers' Attitudes toward Auto IRA Plans**

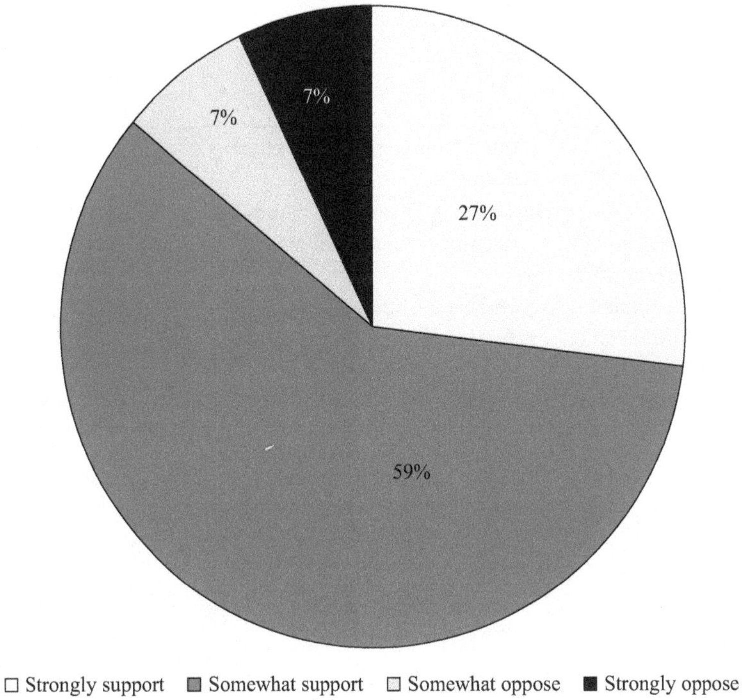

Source: Pew Charitable Trusts (2017), figure 3.

Note: Survey data are directly from the attributed source. The study authors surveyed owners of small- and medium-sized businesses without a retirement plan in place about their views on implementing such a plan.

ployers expressed some level of support for enabling employees who lacked a workplace retirement plan to participate. Further, 79 percent supported the idea that employers would only have the responsibility to withhold money from an employee's pay and send it to the retirement account, and 83 percent supported employers not being required to contribute. Overall, 86 percent of surveyed employers expressed some level of support for an Automatic IRA–based program. Yet that support was less than enthusiastic, with 59 percent "somewhat" supportive, as shown in figure 7-5.

Features of an open MEP are also popular with small- to medium-sized employers: 88 percent of employers would support allowing both employers and employees to contribute, and 85 percent would favor the reduced legal liability found in an open MEP (table 7-5).[12] Employers also supported a marketplace, with almost 86 percent saying that it would be helpful to improve

Table 7-5. *Individual Features of a Multiple Employer Plan (MEP) That Business Owners Support*

Feature	*"Somewhat Support" or ""Strongly Support" (percent)*[a]
Several businesses could adopt a group retirement saving plan run by their state treasurer's office.	55
Both employers and employees could make contributions.	88
Employers and employees have some choice in how to invest their contributions.	92
The state would handle record-keeping, financial reporting, and communication for the plan.	57
Employers would have less legal liability than if they operated their own plan.	85

Source: Derived from Pew Charitable Trusts (2017), figure 5.

[a]Survey data from Pew Charitable Trusts (2017). The study authors surveyed owners of small- and medium-sized businesses without retirement plans in place about their views on implementing such a plan. For this question, employers were asked to indicate their support for features of a hypothetical retirement plan similar to a Multiple Employer Plan (MEP) that would be sponsored by an outside organization and not a business like theirs.

retirement savings. Yet, this contrasted with earlier answers stating that easy-to-understand information and a plan with reduced administrative requirements would make employers no more likely to start a plan.

EVALUATING STATE-SPONSORED PLANS

The two features most essential to the success of state-sponsored retirement saving plans are, first, requiring an employer to offer a retirement saving option, and second, automatic enrollment of workers in the plan.

An effective state-sponsored plan will generate several results. In addition to raising coverage and generating high participation rates among the newly covered workers, it should also induce significant contributions, provide safe and rewarding investments, impose low fees, and induce responsible withdrawal patterns. Luckily, the states that have enacted Secure Choice plans have already included provisions that address fees and initial investment choices. Several of them recognize the need for an appropriate level of contributions and have taken steps in that direction. Others have discussed responsible withdrawal options, but have recognized that this discussion must come after the plan is established.

State-sponsored plans may also reduce the amount that states and the federal government must spend in the future to support retirees with inadequate resources (Trostel 2017). For states, these savings would be due primarily to reductions in Medicaid costs and certain housing programs. The amount of saving per state would depend on the size of the low-income population and the scope of assistance provided through public programs. Federal savings would come from reductions in demand for other means-tested programs (such as SSI), as well as from the federal share of Medicaid funding.[13] It is also possible that state-sponsored retirement savings programs will increase state revenues. If the state taxes retirement income, then any increase in retirement savings will eventually lead to higher revenue. In addition, higher retirement income might lead retirees to spend more money, which could result in higher sales and corporate tax revenue.

Boosting Coverage through Mandatory Provision

Requiring employers to offer a plan would be the most effective way to increase coverage.[14] Most mandatory provision rules require that all companies offer some type of retirement saving or pension plan to their workers. Firms that offer 401(k)s or DB pension plans already meet this requirement. Those that do not would have to either establish such a plan or offer their employees access to a state-sponsored retirement saving plan. Under federal law, required coverage can only apply to an IRA-based retirement plan; states are forbidden from requiring employers to establish an ERISA-regulated retirement plan.

There is some evidence that a state-sponsored plan without mandatory provision is less likely to significantly increase coverage rates. For example, at the end of 2016, only about 20,000 people had enrolled in the nationwide myRA program (Lobosco 2016). Even with much more promotion, a voluntary program is unlikely to encourage employers who are mainly concerned with running a business to establish a retirement plan for their employees.

Small businesses do have concerns about state government involvement in retirement saving, expressing much stronger support for a plan sponsored and administered by a private sector provider such as an insurance company or mutual fund than for a plan administered by the federal government or a state government. As a result, employers split almost 50–50 between those who would participate in the state-sponsored plan and those who would start their own retirement plan (Pew Charitable Trusts 2017, p. 8).

Nevertheless, we do not believe that it would be effective for states to require small- and medium-sized businesses to offer a payroll deduction IRA or their own plan and then to leave it to the private sector to provide the plans from its usual offerings.[15] The plans would initially have high prices, undermining support for the program early on, although the entry of competition in the later years would eventually decrease prices to some extent. Therefore, pairing a low-cost state-sponsored payroll deduction plan with a mandatory provision requirement is most likely to both increase coverage and provide employers with a low-cost savings vehicle.

Boosting Participation through Automatic Enrollment

In a traditional DC plan or IRA, individuals must sign up to participate, designate a contribution level, and allocate contributions to investment vehicles before they can begin saving. Under automatic enrollment, eligible workers are placed in the plan and save a predetermined amount in a preset investment option unless they decide otherwise. Savers always have complete control and can choose at any point to opt out or change their contribution levels or investment allocations. Automatic enrollment is essential to create the needed participation by newly covered employees. Studies in the United States and other countries show the value of automatic enrollment, but adoption of the feature is voluntary for employers, and automatic enrollment is offered primarily by larger companies.[16]

A new UK retirement savings program offers data on the potential effects of a universal automatic enrollment system.[17] Under the UK reforms, all employers will eventually be required to offer a retirement plan that automatically enrolls workers and meets minimum contribution levels. These reforms were phased in over several years ending in 2019, and experience with them will be valuable for understanding the potential effects of state-sponsored retirement plans. Specifically, an early evaluation of these reforms shows a substantial increase in both retirement plan coverage and participation at all incomes, ages, genders, employer sizes, and among both full-time and part-time workers (Department for Work and Pensions 2016). Through October 2016, almost 7 million UK workers had been automatically enrolled in retirement plans at almost 300,000 different employers. Some 265,000 employees who opted out the first time have been re-enrolled.

Initial participation was very high, but varied by age, working hours, and employer size (James 2017). Opt-out rates ranged from about 8 percent at the largest employers to roughly 11 percent at firms with 50–99 employees; the proportion climbed to 17 percent for the smallest firms having nineteen employees or fewer. About 90 percent of full-time employees participated, but only an average of 82 percent of part-time workers. About 93 percent of employees under age 30 participated, 91 percent of those age 30–49, and only 77 percent of workers over age 50. Estimates suggest that, controlling for other factors, automatic enrollment was responsible for a 37 percentage point increase in overall participation (Cribb and Emmerson 2016).

Automatic enrollment was especially effective in increasing participation among younger workers, with a 52 percentage point increase in workers age 22–29, and 37 percent in workers age 30–39. It also had a major effect on low- to moderate-income workers, with an increase in participation of 54 percentage points among those with earnings in the lowest earnings quartile and 46 percentage points among those in the second quartile.

These findings, combined with surveys of automatically enrolled workers in the United States, show wide support for the mechanism, even among those who have opted out. Thus, a compelling case can be made for including the mechanism in state-sponsored retirement saving plans (Retirement Made Simpler 2009).

COVERAGE FOR EVERY WORKER

There is near-universal agreement that pension coverage rates for American workers are lower than they could be, yet state-sponsored retirement saving plans are only just starting up. By 2017, five states have Secure Choice plans, one has a MEP, and two have marketplaces. These numbers are expected to grow in the near future as other states add state-sponsored plans. The most important determinants of the programs' ability to reach their full potential are straightforward: requiring firms to offer either the state plan or their own plan and automatically enrolling workers. In principle, these two features matter more than whether the underlying account is an IRA or a 401(k). As a practical matter, however, federal regulations forbid states from requiring employers to offer ERISA-regulated plans, making an IRA-based state program the only option consistent with mandatory provision.

Enabling all Americans to save for retirement from the day they go to work until the day that they fully retire is an idea that has been discussed for decades. The new plans being implemented offer great potential to raise coverage, participation, and retirement wealth accumulation among a broad swath of the American workforce.

NOTES

1. For example, the Obama administration included an Automatic IRA proposal in every proposed budget. The last Automatic IRA proposal by that administration would have required employers with more than ten employees in operation for over two years to enroll employees in a Roth IRA with a 3 percent default contribution rate. Employers with fewer than 100 employees who did so would receive a temporary tax credit of $1,000 for up to three years in addition to an annual credit of $25 per employee (up to $250) for six years (Office of Management and Budget 2017). Members of Congress also proposed bills mandating employers to offer an Automatic IRA in each of the preceding six years. More recently, the American Savings Account Act of 2017 (H.R. 1083) would have automatically enrolled private sector workers lacking access to a retirement saving plan into a newly created American Savings Account, similar to the Thrift Savings Plan currently offered to federal government employees. During 2017, members of Congress also proposed legislation to decrease barriers to open MEPs in the private sector (H.R. 854; H.R. 6396) and to authorize the creation of state-sponsored MEPs (S. 3389).

2. Additional DOL regulations gave certain cities similar powers. Seattle, Philadelphia, and New York City wrote letters of interest to the DOL asking whether their 2015 ruling that cleared the way for states to enact state-sponsored retirement plans also applied to cities. DOL responded by clarifying that political subdivisions qualify if they meet three criteria: (1) state law gives them the authority to require employers' participation in payroll deduction savings programs; (2) the political subdivision has a population that is at least the size of the least populous state (currently Wyoming, with 600,000 residents); and (3) the state in which the subdivision is located cannot already have a statewide retirement program for private sector employees. These additional regulations were final in January 2017, but were overturned by a Congressional Review Act resolution that was passed by Congress and signed by the president later that year.

3. The regulations clarify that if states offer an Auto IRA under certain conditions, the plans do not fall under the Employee Retirement Income Security Act (ERISA). Although states now working on such a plan believe that the regulations are helpful in avoiding a legal challenge, they also believe that they have legal authority under earlier, less explicit laws and regulations.

4. A study by Segal Consulting estimated that if all states sponsored a retirement savings program, taxpayers would save $5 billion over the first decade in Medicaid costs and that these savings would continue to increase over time. Fifteen states have the potential to save over $100 million each over the first decade (Segal Consulting 2017).

5. The Current Population Survey measured coverage between 1987 and 2013. After 2013 the survey was redesigned, and the accuracy of its later results has been questioned. For this reason, we do not include post-2013 data.

6. Participation and coverage information presented in this section is adapted from a Government Accountability Office (2015) analysis of data from the Census Bureau's Survey of Income and Program Participation (SIPP). We define retirement plan coverage (synonymous with access) as the availability of an employer-sponsored retirement plan to an employee age 18 or older. Since GAO does not report trends in coverage, we use data from Copeland (2014). This EBRI report presents Current Pop-

ulation Survey data on retirement plan participation and coverage over time for workers ages 21 to 64.

7. EBRI defines "having a retirement plan" as having an Individual Retirement Acocount (IRA), defined benefit plan (DB), or defined contribution plan (DC). The value of assets reported contains all investments except for the value of the respondent's primary residence and DB plan assets. Although workers without an employer-based plan can contribute to IRAs, very few do.

8. In California, research shows that employees without access to a retirement plan have a median income of $23,000 (Overture Financial 2016).

9. The New Jersey marketplace was later repealed and was never implemented.

10. MEPs can be either open or closed. Under a closed MEP, all businesses that enter the plan must have some common interests (such as being in the same industry). An open MEP has greater flexibility in the types of businesses that it includes. All MEPs considered by the states are open MEPs because they allow any business that employs residents of that state to join.

11. The myRA was ended by the Trump administration and is no longer available.

12. Although the employers like the ability to contribute if they so choose, they do not want to be required to do so. This preference is reflected in the Automatic IRA question.

13. These estimates assume that the retirement plans being examined increase the retirement income of low-income workers such that they would not qualify for public assistance programs. It also assumes that the individual will not need those supports before retirement and that retirement savings do not fall under the program's maximum allowed asset level. This last assumption is especially questionable since, under current federal law, the only program that completely exempts retirement assets from its asset test is the Supplemental Nutritional Assistance Program (SNAP).

14. Whether this requirement would apply to all employers in the state or only to employers with more than a certain number of employers is a political decision.

15. Similarly, the United Kingdom found that relying on competition alone to reduce fees and create effective retirement products would not be effective because many employers would not have enough information to choose a provider that offered good value. See Office of Fair Trading (2013).

16. See, for example, Madrian and Shea (2001); Chetty and others (2013).

17. A key difference is that the United Kingdom is also phasing in the contribution level. Initially, employers and employees contribute only 1 percent of earnings each. This 2 percent total initial contribution is close to the usual 3 percent initial contribution in the United States. As of April 2019, the annual total can be 8 percent of earnings. Also, the UK system exempts the lowest-income workers from automatic enrollment and does not collect contributions on the first £113 of weekly earnings.

REFERENCES

AARP. 2017. "State Retirement Savings Plans." Washington, DC: State Retirement Savings Resources Center. http://www.aarp.org/ppi/state-retirement-plans/savings-plans/.

Act Creating the Connecticut Retirement Security Program. 2016. Connecticut sHB 5591.

American Savings Account Act of 2017. HR 1083, 115th Congress.

Bernard, T. 2016. "New Jersey Creates Retirement Savings Plan, Modified by Christie." *New York Times*, January 19.

Byrne, A., and C. Reilly. 2017. "Investing for Retirement in a Low Returns Environment: Making the Right Decision to Make the Money Last." https://pensionresearchcouncil.wharton.upenn.edu/wp-content/uploads/2017/04/PRC-CP-2017-08-Reilly-and-Byrne.pdf.

California State Treasury. 2017. "California Secure Choice: Making Workplace Retirement Savings Possible for Millions of Californians." http://www.treasurer.ca.gov/scib/.

Chetty, Raj, J. Friedman, S. Petersen, T.H. Nielsen, and T. Olsen. 2013. "Active vs. Passive Decisions and Crowd-Out in Retirement Savings Accounts: Evidence from Denmark." *Quarterly Journal of Economics* 2014: 1141–219.

City of Philadelphia Office of the Controller. 2016. "Retirement Security in Philadelphia: An Analysis of Current Conditions and Paths to Better Outcomes." Philadelphia, PA.

———. 2017. "Retirement Security for All Philadelphians." Philadelphia, PA.

Copeland, Craig. 2014. "Employment-Based Retirement Plan Participation: Geographic Differences and Trends." Issue Brief 45. Washington, DC: Employee Benefit Research Institute.

Cribb, J., and C. Emerson. 2016. "What Happens When Employers Are Obliged to Nudge? Automatic Enrolment and Pension Saving in the UK." London: Institute for Fiscal Studies.

Department for Work and Pensions. 2016. *Automatic Enrolment Evaluation Report 2016*. Ad Hoc Research Report 45. London: Department for Work and Pensions.

Georgetown University Center for Retirement Initiatives. 2017. "State Initiatives Transforming the Retirement Savings Landscape." Georgetown University Center for Retirement Initiatives (updated March 7, 2017). http://cri.georgetown.edu/states/.

Government Accountability Office (GAO). 2015. "Retirement Security: Federal Action Could Help State Efforts to Expand Private Sector Coverage." GAO-15-556. Washington, DC.

Helman, R., Greenwald & Associates, C. Copeland, and J. VanDerhei. 2016. "The 2016 Retirement Confidence Survey: Worker Confidence Stable, Retiree Confidence Continues to Increase." EBRI Issue Brief 422. Washington, DC: Employee Benefit Research Institute.

Illinois State Treasurer. 2016. "Secure Choice" (updated 2016). http://illinoistreasurer.gov/Individuals/Secure_Choice.

Iwry, J. Mark, and David C. John. 2009. "Pursuing Universal Retirement Security through Automatic IRAs." Brookings.

James, H. 2017. "The Impact of Automatic Enrolment in the UK as at 2016." Briefing Note 87. London: Pension Policy Institute.

Lobosco, K. 2016. "After One Year, 20,000 People Are Saving for Retirement with Obama's MyRA." *CNN Money*, December 16.

Madrian, B., and D. Shea. 2001. "The Power of Suggestion: Inertia in 401(k) Participation and Savings Behavior." *Quarterly Journal of Economics* 116 (4): 1149–87.

Maryland General Assembly. 2016. "Maryland Small Business Retirement Savings Program and Trust." Fiscal and Policy Note SB 1007. Annapolis, MD.

Office of Fair Trading. 2013. "Defined Contribution Workplace Pension Market Study." OF1505. London. http://webarchive.nationalarchives.gov.uk/20131101164215/http:/www.oft.gov.uk/shared_oft/market-studies/oft1505.

Office of Management and Budget. 2017. "Analytical Perspectives." Budget of the US Government Fiscal Year 2017. Washington, DC.

Office of the New York City Comptroller. 2016. "The New York City Nest Egg: A Plan for Addressing Retirement Security in New York City." New York.

Overture Financial. 2016. "Final Report to the California Secure Choice Retirement Savings Investment Board." RFP CSCRSIB03-14. www.treasurer.ca.gov/scib/report.pdf.

Pew Charitable Trusts. 2017. "Small Business Views on Retirement Savings Plans." Washington, DC.

Retirement Made Simpler. 2009. "Fact Sheet: 2009 Survey of Employee Sentiments on Saving for Retirement." Washington, DC: AARP.

Retirement Security for American Workers Act of 2016. HR 6396, 114th Congress.

Retirement Security for American Workers Act of 2017. HR 854, 115th Congress.

Segal Consulting. 2017. "State Retirement Savings Initiatives Do More Than Enhance Retirement Security for Private Sector Workers." *Data: Practical Research on Public Sector Benefits* (Winter).

State of Oregon. 2017. "Oregon Saves." State of Oregon (updated 2017). http://www.oregon.gov/retire/Pages/index.aspx.

State Retirement Savings Act of 2016. S. 3389, 114th Congress.

Steverman, B. 2017. "Two-Thirds of Americans Aren't Putting Money in Their 401(k)." Bloomberg, February 21.

Trostel, P. 2017. "The Fiscal Implications of Inadequate Retirement Savings in Maine." https://mcspolicycenter.umaine.edu/wp-content/uploads/sites/122/2017/03/final-aarp-report.pdf.

USA Retirement Funds Act of 2016. HR 6136, 114th Congress.

EIGHT

Structuring State Retirement Saving Plans

A GUIDE TO POLICY DESIGN AND MANAGEMENT ISSUES

David C. John and William G. Gale

Many American workers do not have access to employer-sponsored payroll deduction plans for retirement saving. Groups with low rates of access include younger workers, members of minority groups, and those with low-to-moderate incomes.[1] Small-business employees are especially at risk. Only about 14 percent of businesses with 100 or fewer employees offer their employees a retirement plan, leaving between 51 and 71 percent of the roughly 42 million people who work for a small business without access to an employer-administered plan (Government Accountability Office 2013).

Lack of access makes it difficult to build retirement wealth. A study by the Employee Benefit Research Institute (2014) shows that 62 percent of employees with access to an employer-sponsored plan held more than $25,000 in savings balances and 22 percent had $100,000 or more. In contrast, among those without access to a plan, 94 percent held less than $25,000 and only 3 percent held $100,000 or more. Although workers without an employer-based plan can contribute to Individual Retirement Accounts (IRAs), very few do.[2] But employees at all income levels tend to participate at high rates in plans that are structured to provide guidance about the decisions they should make (Wu and Rutledge 2014).

With these considerations in mind, many experts and policymakers have advocated for increased retirement plan coverage. Although a national approach would be desirable, there has been little legislative progress. States, however, are acting. By 2015, three states had already created state-sponsored retirement saving plans for small-business employees, and twenty-five were in some stage of considering such a move (Pension Rights Center 2015).

This chapter highlights a variety of issues that policymakers will need to address in creating and implementing an effective state-sponsored retirement saving plan. It begins with a discussion of policy design choices and is followed by a discussion of management issues faced by employers, employees, and states administering such a plan.

PLAN DESIGN

State-sponsored plans can be either defined contribution plans or defined benefit plans, although defined contribution plans are more common. A third option, the marketplace model, can be used with either type of plan and provides a way to connect firms and providers. Each option has advantages and disadvantages. The optimal choice for a specific state will depend on its own political, historical, and economic factors. Because most workers hold several jobs during their working life, state-sponsored plans need to be compatible with those offered through private sector employers.

Defined Contribution Retirement Saving Plans

There are a number of considerations important to structuring state-sponsored defined contribution retirement plans.

TYPES OF PLANS

States have explored two types of plans most often—Automatic IRAs and Multiple Employer Plans (MEPs)—though sometimes they are called by different names.

Under an Automatic IRA, employers automatically enroll workers in a payroll deduction IRA (Iwry and John 2009). Employees have complete control and can choose to opt out, save more or less than the default amount, and choose their investment option. Their contributions are placed in one of only a few investment options, with those who do not choose otherwise contributing to a target-date fund or similar investment. Savers receive regular statements.

The Automatic IRA is a simple, easy-to-understand, low-cost retirement saving plan for small businesses and aims to replicate the benefits of automatic enrollment seen in 401(k) plans (Madrian and Shea 2001). It was designed as a federal retirement savings initiative with bipartisan support and was included in every Obama administration budget, but never approved by Congress. However, the Automatic IRA is equally suitable for state-sponsored retirement saving plans. Because it is not an Employee Retirement Income Security Act (ERISA) plan, and because all investment options are specified by the state, employers face minimal if any regulatory burdens. The Automatic IRA is likely to boost retirement plan participation substantially, but its effect on retirement saving balances depends on how old employees are when they start to save and how much they contribute (VanDerhei 2015).

Under a Multiple Employer Plan (MEP), several small businesses join together to offer the same type of account to each employer's workforce. In the state context, states would create a MEP for their small businesses. As ERISA-regulated plans, MEPs can be 401(k) plans or accounts with features similar to 401(k)s, including allowing for employer contributions. But MEPs are simpler: the common plan structure reduces the compliance burden and places most fiduciary responsibilities on the plan administrator. As the regulations stand in 2015, the Department of Labor requires all employers participating in a MEP to have a common bond such as being in the same industry, but a regulatory change or pending federal legislation could make MEPs less restrictive. If states are allowed to offer MEPs, it is uncertain if they could also require a small business to offer its employees such a plan, as ERISA appears to prohibit states from requiring employers to offer an ERISA plan.

In addition to the Automatic IRA and the MEP, some states are considering other defined contribution accounts ranging from the SIMPLE IRA (SIMPLE = Savings Incentive Match Plan for Employees) to the then available federal myRA to more complex models containing features that are closer to the 401(k). Because the SIMPLE IRA is covered by ERISA, states cannot require an employer to offer it, but they can include the accounts as an option in a voluntary marketplace model. The myRA, which was created during the Obama administration and ended in 2017, was essentially a Roth IRA, and explicitly outside of ERISA. It had a maximum size of $15,000 and could only be invested in government bonds. This requirement made it suitable as a starter account, but it needed to be supplemented with another type of account so that funds could be transferred once the balance limit was reached.

TAX TREATMENT

Traditionally, retirement saving plans have exempted contributions and accruals from taxation and taxed withdrawals as income. This treatment provides an immediate deduction for contributions, a benefit that is visible on the payroll stub. However, the deduction is worth less to those who have less income and thus face a lower marginal tax rate. In addition, a withdrawal before age 59½ imposes income tax and in many cases an additional 10 percent penalty. The penalty is waived in cases of hardship and, for an IRA, if the money is used for certain purposes. When savers change employers, traditional retirement account balances can be moved to a traditional 401(k) or a traditional IRA.

Roth IRAs and 401(k)s embody an alternative tax treatment: the contribution is made from after-tax income, and accrual and withdrawals (after age 59½) are not taxed. Because Roth contributions are made with income that has already been taxed, payroll stubs do not show any tax benefit. But savers may withdraw all or part of their contributions at any time without having to pay any additional tax. This feature makes them more suitable for lower-income savers, who are less likely to benefit from a traditional tax treatment and may have a greater need to withdraw money for financial emergencies. The Roth tax treatment is available to IRA savers at all income levels and to 401(k) savers with income below $116,000 for single taxpayers and $183,000 for those who are married and filing jointly.[3] At higher income levels, the benefit phases out. Roth accounts have more limited rollover options.[4]

AUTOMATIC ENROLLMENT

In a traditional retirement saving plan, workers are not enrolled unless they choose to sign up. In automatic-enrollment plans, workers are automatically enrolled unless they opt out, taking advantage of savers' tendencies toward inaction. Automatic enrollment has been shown to raise participation rates among eligible workers of all ages, genders, racial and ethnic groups, and income levels (Madrian and Shea 2001). While savers always have complete control and can always choose to opt out, automatic enrollment provides guidance that many savers find valuable.[5] If a state-sponsored plan uses automatic enrollment, employers merely have to offer automatic payroll deduction, sign the workers up for the plan, distribute information to employees, and collect forms from those who wish to opt out.[6] Each pay period, as the employer sends deductions for income taxes, state taxes, and payroll taxes to their respective destinations, it also deducts an amount for the retirement savings contribution and sends that amount to the account administrator.

States that choose to require automatic enrollment are likely to see higher participation levels. However, the ERISA treatment of automatic enrollment in an IRA is a gray area, as we discuss later. As of 2015, forthcoming regulatory guidance from the Department of Labor may resolve this question. An alternative currently considered by some states would require an active enrollment decision. Under this mechanism, employees must indicate in writing that they want to participate. Requiring an employee to opt in in this way does not produce the same participation rates as automatic enrollment, but it has produced better results than a traditional opt-in approach in a 401(k) setting (Carroll and others 2009).

CONTRIBUTION LEVELS

Most state-sponsored plans include a default contribution level, and plans with automatic enrollment must specify a default contribution level. Many retirement saving plans, including some planned state-sponsored plans, follow the lead of federal legislation and use a contribution level of 3 percent of earnings. This level, however, is not high enough to create retirement balances sufficient to replace much preretirement earnings, especially if workers begin contributions when they are older.[7] Allowing a higher initial contribution of 5 or 6 percent might be preferable. In automatic enrollment plans, participation rates are not particularly sensitive to the initial contribution level (Chandler and Mottola 2014). Lower-income savers are less likely to opt out of default levels, even if those levels are not economically advantageous to them (Beshears and others 2013). Initial contribution levels should be set with those employees in mind.

Automatic escalation, in which the share of earnings contributed rises over time, is popular with employees. Typically, the contribution rate rises each time an employee receives a raise. Workers are often willing to commit to higher contribution amounts in the future when this feature is added to the plan (Thaler and Benartzi 2004). Employers, however, have raised concerns that dealing with each employee's contribution level individually is administratively difficult. An alternative would be to phase in higher contribution levels for all participants gradually over time.

INVESTMENT OPTIONS

Most state-sponsored plans have a small number of investment choices, with one designated as the default fund that savers will be placed in unless they choose another. The likelihood of worker participation in a plan declines as the number of investment choices rises (Iyengar, Jiang, and Huberman 2003).

Federal law allows plan sponsors to adopt either of two methods when developing a default investment choice. Sponsors can choose a mix of investments that accounts for "the characteristics of the group of employees as a whole, rather than each individual"; or the sponsor can consider each participant's age, retirement date, and life expectancy. These standards usually allow a choice of balanced funds, target-date funds, and managed accounts.

Initially, states may wish to use passive index funds, as those usually perform as well as actively managed funds at a much lower average cost. However, if the experience of state-sponsored plans follows that of the federal Thrift Savings Plan (TSP), as the plans grow, purveyors of other types of assets such as real estate funds may seek to have their products added to investment options. These funds often prove to be more expensive than other investment options and carry a higher risk to savers.

Target-date funds are a diversified mixture of investments designed to be the workers' only investment choice. The mix of investments changes automatically as the account holder ages, thus freeing the worker from having to think about investment allocation over time. A target-date fund is usually invested in a high proportion of equities or other risky assets when the worker is young, moving to a less risky investment mix as retirement gets closer. Target funds are especially useful for workers who do not wish to be involved in decision making (Chalmers and Reuter 2012).

The United Kingdom's National Employment Savings Trust (NEST) uses a different strategy, placing contributions in a stable value fund for the first two years after a worker joins. This protects savers from principal losses in the first two years and may encourage continued participation. After the two years, NEST moves the existing balance and all new contributions to the appropriate target-date fund, given the worker's age. This system is more complex than a standard target fund, but state-sponsored funds may wish to consider it.

Friedman and Stein (2014b) propose yet another strategy: using a single pool of diversified investments. The pool would be professionally managed and could offer low administrative fees because of its size and simplicity. The chosen strategy would be structured to meet the specific needs of the overall population using the state-sponsored plan and would not be tailored to individual workers' characteristics. Diversified pooled investments would be suitable for either a defined contribution or a hybrid pension plan.

RATE-OF-RETURN GUARANTEES

Some states are considering guarantees that would protect individual savers from investment losses or ensure at least a certain level of return. To a large extent, interest in this type of provision comes from the high losses suffered by some retirement savers during the financial crisis that started in 2008. Supporters believe that a guarantee would protect state-sponsored plan participants at a low cost.

The benefits of a guarantee will depend on the overall share of wealth that is guaranteed, the level of the guarantee, and the saver's risk aversion (Gale, John, and Kim 2015). The level of costs will depend mainly on what is guaranteed. A guarantee against principal losses is less expensive than a guarantee that a portfolio will earn at least a specified positive return. Including inflation protection adds more expense. Insuring "bond-like" returns backed with "equity-like" assets is quite expensive. The allocation of costs is equally important. Savers can pay for guarantees explicitly through premium payments or implicitly through caps on how much they can earn (with returns above that amount accruing to the plan provider) or restrictions on the portfolio. Insurance companies will not bear the burden of the costs—they will pass it along to workers. Governments may show small budgetary costs, but these costs do not account for the economic resource value of the guarantee, which can be quite large, even if expected outlays are small.

WITHDRAWAL OPTIONS

A state-sponsored plan could include an immediate annuity upon retirement, a longevity annuity that begins making payments a number of years after retirement, or a target-date fund that begins to convert retirement balances into an annuity during workers' careers (Kahn and Strakosch 2015). However, an annuity-like product that is purchased before retirement may lose value when converted back into cash for a rollover. Until annuity costs come down, conversions become less complex, and such features are commonly found in the private sector plans, it may be prudent for states to resist the temptation to require them. The market for annuities is changing rapidly, however, and better lifetime income options may well emerge.

Defined Benefit Plans

A second model for state-sponsored plans is to offer small-business employees the opportunity to join a defined benefit (DB) plan. The program can be managed by the state's public employee pension plan or a subsidiary of that plan or by a private entity. A DB plan can provide workers with a predictable level of lifetime income if they remain in the plan until they retire, but it also has drawbacks.

For example, in the Secure Choice Pension (SCP) plan, small-business employees are enrolled in a hybrid defined benefit plan that converts into an annuity upon retirement (Kim 2011).[8] Contributions are managed in a separate but parallel fund with those of the state employee pension plan, with both funds managed in the same way. The private employees would benefit from the expertise and economies of scale of the state employee plan. But using the same investment strategy might not make sense if the two workforces differ. Small-business employees, for example, are likely to be more mobile than state employees. An investment strategy that stresses long-term growth may see small-business employees who belong to the plan for only a few years lose out on certain market gains. Further, tying the state-sponsored plan to a state employee pension plan that is underfunded or has political liabilities could undermine support for the small-business plan. And upon retirement, a defined benefit plan with an automatic annuity provides safe lifetime income, but that retirement income option may be less suitable for savers with lower incomes and relatively high Social Security benefits because their Social Security would replace a higher proportion of their preretirement income. This would be even more of a problem if, in a period of low interest rates, savers received relatively little retirement income from their savings.

Marketplace Models

A marketplace is a state-sponsored website that enables small businesses to find prescreened retirement saving or pension plans. The marketplace can include a diverse array of plans, including payroll deduction IRAs, SIMPLE IRA plans, MEPs, the then available federal myRA, and perhaps even 401(k) plans and DB plans. Listed options must meet certain requirements, such as low fees. Providers can pay a fee to be listed that covers the cost of the site.

The marketplace model does not require the state to have any involvement with ERISA because a marketplace just connects employers and providers. The website itself is not covered by ERISA, and each type of account retains its current ERISA status. Employers are able to choose for themselves whether to adopt an ERISA plan or another option.

A marketplace does nothing to simplify retirement saving or reduce regulatory burdens or fiduciary responsibilities of smaller employers. By itself, it does little to raise coverage. Pairing a marketplace with a requirement that small businesses provide retirement plans, however, would violate ERISA, which forbids states from imposing such rules.

Other Policy Issues

Several policy design issues are common to all of the models described here. The first is whether coverage should be mandatory. Mandating that employers above a certain size offer coverage would boost the number of workers with retirement plans. If a state requires coverage, it is likely to reduce the number of future retirees with little retirement income other than Social Security benefits. This, in turn, will lower the future demand for taxpayer-financed state services and improve the state's long-term fiscal outlook. In addition, required coverage will increase the number of savers using the state-sponsored plan, thus allowing it to charge lower fees.

Employers who are required to offer coverage would know that their competitors are offering the same benefits to their employees. Further, as knowledge of this employee benefit becomes known, higher-quality job applicants who might have otherwise gone to larger competitors may be more willing to work in smaller businesses. Similarly, employees will benefit from a required offering, both because they will have the opportunity to save and because the accounts would be portable when they change employers. Finally, retirement service providers and the financial services sector will benefit from a required offering because they will have a guaranteed set of customers.

About 97 percent of employers with ten or more employees use an outside payroll processor or payroll processing software (Schmitt and Xanthopoulos 2007). Using either service sharply reduces the burden of complying with a required offering. A plan that exempts smaller firms from the coverage requirement would likely impose small administrative burdens.

Nevertheless, in some states, business associations have remained neutral toward a voluntary system but have indicated strong opposition to any required coverage. Opposition also comes from groups and legislators opposed to placing government requirements on businesses. Limiting the requirement to employers above a certain size has not significantly reduced the opposition.

A second issue is consumer protection. Explicit consumer protections will help to build confidence in the state-sponsored plan and to encourage participation, especially for non-ERISA plans since the protections provided by that law would not be present. Appropriately structured state consumer protections could provide the same or greater protection as ERISA. Friedman and Stein

(2014a) propose six consumer protections that parallel those in ERISA. These include creating a board of trustees charged with protecting the interests of savers and retirees, with representation from savers, retirees, employers, and others, but not from providers or the financial industry. The board would work with the state entity that oversees or operates the state-sponsored plan to annually review its investment choices and other aspects of the plan to ensure that savers receive the best service at the lowest cost.

State-sponsored plans should provide clear disclosures to employees and retirees and specify standards of conduct for outside providers. Similar to the disclosures required under ERISA, these should include clear and simple explanations of the plan itself, investment choices, consumer and employer rights and responsibilities, and other aspects of the plan. Starting with the notices provided through employers to employees when they are first enrolled, clear disclosures are essential to help employees understand how the plan operates, their rights under the plan, and how to proceed if they feel that their rights have been breached.

A state-sponsored plan's primary contact with its participants will be through regular statements of account balances. Plan statements should be more than just investment reports; they need to provide information on retirement readiness by focusing on investment performance. A state-sponsored plan's statement should focus on the amount saved and how much income can be expected if the recipient continues to save at the current rate until retirement (John 2015).

Other consumer protections should include a dispute resolution process with an independent ombudsman to resolve problems between savers and their employers or other aspects of the plan. Finally, a state-sponsored plan should have clear and explicit spousal protections. These should include having spouses as default beneficiaries if savers die before retirement and an effective administrative process to divide plan assets in the event of a divorce or legal separation. If the plan includes an annuity-like guaranteed lifetime income option, it should require married savers to choose a joint and survivors option unless the other spouse agrees to a different payout scenario.

A related issue is the link between the state-sponsored plan and ERISA. ERISA includes many important consumer protections, but also places regulatory burdens on the employer. These requirements are often cited as reasons that small businesses do not offer retirement plans to their employees.

ERISA and the extent to which it applies to state-sponsored plans is one of the most contentious issues facing these plans. ERISA does not cover a payroll deduction IRA if all contributions come from the employee, and participation is voluntary. The effect of adding automatic enrollment is a gray area, though. Toth (2014b) and Morse (2014) argue that automatic enrollment would not trigger ERISA, but other legal opinions differ. The question revolves around whether automatic enrollment meets the requirement that employee participation is completely voluntary. The Department of Labor ruled in 2006 that automatic enrollment in a Health Savings Account (HSA) meets that standard (Employee Benefits Security Administration 2006), but it has not yet done so in the case of a payroll deduction IRA. In response to a direct request from President Obama, the Department of Labor stated that it would issue clarifying rules on this issue by the end of 2015 (Perez 2015).

MANAGEMENT ISSUES

When considering the structure of state-sponsored plans, there is more to the picture than just a strategic vision. There are many implementation and management issues that must be addressed by the government, by employers, and by employees.

Government Responsibilities

The government must address a number of practical considerations in order to ensure state-sponsored plans are managed effectively.

OPERATION

An important but understudied decision is where in the state government to place the responsible agency. Ideally, the agency would have prior experience in finance and investing but would avoid conflicts of interest with the financial industry.

A related issue is the extent to which services are performed in-house or contracted out. With Section 529 college saving plans, states have had overall control but contracted specific functions to private sector providers. Thus the state might use one or more providers to handle investments, another to handle collecting and crediting contributions, and perhaps another to handle marketing. This structure uses the minimum number of state employees to operate the plan while utilizing the expertise and participation of private sector providers. Combining contracts that last for only a certain period of time with a regular cycle of rebidding allows the state-sponsored plan to control costs and benefit from the latest innovations.

Contracting out specific services increases the responsibilities of the state entity using it. State employees must understand how the different pieces fit together and structure the contracts so that different providers can mesh to create the whole. They must also have enough expertise in the functions to create contract specifications that state which services are needed and set clear expectations about performance standards. The contracts need a well-defined set of deliverables that can be regularly monitored by state employees and a set of penalties or other measures if the provider fails to meet its responsibilities.

Private operation differs from contracting out specific services in that the entire state-sponsored plan is handled by a private entity—either one company or a consortium of providers—with all decisions made by them. The state entity's function would be limited to oversight and branding. This structure is attractive to some because private professionals who know the industry handle the details of the plan, rather than state employees who may not understand all the implications of a decision. By using the existing structure, it becomes clear that the state is not directly competing with the private sector. However, private operation under state oversight also carries potential risks. First, the process of selecting a single entity or consortium must be completely open to avoid indications of favoritism. And because the state is at arm's length from the day-to-day operations of the entire plan, oversight responsibilities may be more difficult. Decisions about the plan will be folded into the provider's overall corporate culture, strategy, and managerial style. States will need to take special care to ensure that there is no appearance of the operator favoring its own investment products over others, structuring aspects of the plan to meet its existing corporate practices, or having an inappropriate fee structure.

Another option is to allow a state entity, such as that which makes investment decisions for the state or operates the state employee retirement plan, to operate the state-sponsored plan. Under this structure, the state might use existing tax collection or pension contribution structures to gather contributions, existing state or pension plan investment mechanisms to structure and handle plan investments, or existing state financial literacy experts to handle educating participants. The use of existing state competencies for an expanded purpose would be cost effective and expedient. However, if this structure is chosen, the state must be careful to avoid conflict-of-interest problems or the appearance that the plan is being used to benefit some other program or group. The state must also ensure that direct operation is compatible with federal laws and regulations. Another factor is that while the existing state functions may appear to be similar to those needed for the state-sponsored plan, the two may require different skills. For instance, investing excess state funds or trust funds may in practice be very different from investing for a retirement plan.

Special care should be taken if a state uses a state employee pension plan to administer the state-sponsored plan. In such a situation, the pension plan should consider whether to set up a legally separate subsidiary or entity to handle the state-sponsored plan. Such a step would help to avoid the appearance of using assets from small-business employees to prop up an underfunded state employee plan or using fees collected from private sector employees to pay the costs of the state employee plan. Also, investment decisions for a state employee defined benefit plan may be different from those needed for a defined contribution plan that serves a different workforce.

STARTUP COSTS

Even if a state-sponsored plan is to be self-supporting from fees paid by savers or participating service providers, there will be some advance expenses to set up the program. This may include the cost of a feasibility study, legal fees, seeking providers, publicity, and the time of some state employees. The actual costs would not necessarily be very high. The costs described are essentially the same as those that would have been necessary to set up a state's Section 529 college saving program or a state employee retirement saving program, and in many cases, knowledge gained from setting up and managing those programs will be directly transferable to the state-sponsored retirement saving plan. There are a number of ways to raise the money. In some states, most notably California and Connecticut, funds for feasibility studies and legal fees came from outside contributions by nongovernmental sources. Depending on the state's ethics laws and practices, nonprofits or private sector providers, or both, could make these contributions. In no case has one entity funded the entire share of startup costs or even provided funds to pay for a large proportion of them. It is preferable to have a wide number of groups participating in the funding because it demonstrates support and discourages questions about conflicts of interest.

The state or state entities are a second source of funding. Depending on its preferences, money could come from a direct appropriation, a direction to a state official such as the treasurer to build such costs into the budget, or an allocation from a fund such as the state's unclaimed property fund or a similar entity. The startup costs could be regarded as a direct expense to the state or as a loan to be repaid over time from the plan's revenues. If it is a loan, it would be best to spread the repayment over a period long enough so that the fees needed to cover it are not so high that they discourage participation or make the plan uncompetitive.

REGULAR REVIEW

Retirement plans, fee structures, and the workforce are constantly evolving, and a regular review of the state-sponsored plan and all of its elements are important to ensure that it continues to meet the needs of the state's small-business employers and their employees. As part of the review, the state can consider innovations and ensure that the plan's costs and fees are as low as possible and that it complies with any new federal laws and regulations. It also ensures that the state is meeting its fiduciary duties and protects it from unnecessary controversy.

If possible, enacting legislation should provide for a full study of the state-sponsored plan at regular intervals of at least every five years. In addition, the legislation should require an annual review of investment and other fees charged to savers. Both reviews can be handled by benefit consultants or other experienced financial professionals, and their results should be made public as quickly as possible.

In addition to the reviews by financial professionals, states should consider establishing a review commission composed of representatives of employers, employees, financial professionals, and others that meet every two years or so. A commission can help to ensure that the plan continues to meet the needs of its savers and review the plan's progress in increasing coverage among small-business employees. In addition, the commission could propose changes to help the plan better accomplish its mission. However, such a commission should not replace the review by financial professionals. Rather, it should use that report as the basis for its considerations and supplement it with testimony and other resources.

In the case of a marketplace plan, the regular review should evaluate the products that it offers to ensure that they continue to meet its standards and the standards themselves. As with other models, it would also be useful to review the progress toward increasing coverage; if progress were less than satisfactory, it could recommend changes to the model and its standards.

The Role of the Employee

Participation in a state-sponsored plan should be as simple and easy as possible. In states with automatic enrollment, employees do not need to take action in order to participate. They are automatically enrolled in the plan and will save a recommended amount in an appropriate investment unless they make a different decision.

Employees always have complete control over their participation and saving choices, including whether to stop. When state-sponsored plans do not offer automatic enrollment, employees need to choose whether to participate, how much to contribute, how to invest the funds, and how to withdraw the funds. Inevitably, those who participate or are thinking about participating will have questions about participation, investments, and other issues both before they start to save and during their participation. As a result, plans should provide a website or a call center that savers can consult for information.

The Role of the Employer

Employers' responsibilities depend on the structure of the state-sponsored plan and whether participation is required or just encouraged. In either case, states can keep the employer's duties at a minimum by keeping the plan as simple as possible. If the state chooses an Automatic IRA, employers are required to perform four simple functions: enrolling employees or handling their paperwork to opt out; setting up the payroll deduction; forwarding contributions to the plan; and dealing with an annual open enrollment period (Cowan 2015). Not all plans have open seasons. Most employers use either an outside payroll provider or payroll processing software, so the cost and burden of setting up the deduction and forwarding contributions are minimal. Changing the contribution amount is no more difficult than adding or subtracting the number of tax deductions when an employee has a child, or gets married or divorced. The Illinois plan uses automatic enrollment, which may require the employer to distribute state-provided notices that explain the implications of the process before it begins. The enrollment process and open season in an automatic enrollment plan simply requires the employer to distribute materials, collect and return forms, and forward them to the plan provider. Some employees may have questions, but if the plan has a website or call center, the employer can refer employees there. This would be the same process for enrollment and open season (if there is one) in a nonautomatic enrollment plan.

If the state chooses a marketplace model, the employer's responsibilities will depend on which option the employer chooses. Those could be minimal if the employer chooses the myRA, or more complex if it chooses a SIMPLE IRA or even a 401k. Under this model, since the state's role is limited to prescreening the different providers, it does not take on any of the employer's functions or legal responsibilities. They remain the same as those associated with the retirement savings option, had it not been selected through the marketplace.

Other than arranging for a payroll deduction, the employer's most important duty is to ensure that an employee's contributions reach the plan in a timely manner. Employers with outside payroll processors need only to notify the processor of the deduction and provide routing information for the payment. Once this is done, the processor handles the retirement contributions just like it handles FICA contributions, federal income tax withholding, and any other deductions by forwarding the money to the plan manager for each pay period. Employers using payroll processing software would handle retirement plan contributions in much the same way. Once the deduction is set up, contributions are routinely forwarded for each pay period.

Companies doing their own payrolls without payroll processing software may find the process slightly more complex, but once the deduction is arranged, payment becomes a routine part of the process. In no case is forwarding payments any more difficult than handling income tax withholding.

States that use an Automatic IRA or similar model can simplify the employers' contribution process by establishing a single routing address that receives all payments to the plan. If the state-sponsored plan has several investment options or even several different investment managers, the central receiving location can allocate payments to the different final locations as well as record that the money was received and when. In addition, states can simplify the contributions process for very small employers that are more likely to do payroll by hand by allowing them to send payments using the same schedule that the state uses to collect state income tax withholding. This ensures that small employers do not have to set up a different schedule just for retirement plan payments. States without an income tax can allow employers to use the schedule for federal income tax withholding payments.

Employer contributions depend on the structure of the state-sponsored plan or the specific choices allowed under the marketplace model. It would be very difficult for a state to require an employer to contribute. If the state-sponsored plan's underlying account is a traditional or Roth IRA, employer contributions are prohibited. Both the SIMPLE IRA and the Simplified Employee Pension (SEP) IRA can receive contributions from the employer, and a SIMPLE IRA requires one. However, because ERISA prohibits states from requiring employers to offer an ERISA-covered plan, employers would have to choose to offer such an account. Under the SIMPLE IRA, the employer can choose matching employee contributions of up to 3 percent of pay or a flat contribution of 2 percent of pay. In addition, employers who chose a 401(k) through a marketplace would be permitted to match contributions at their discretion. Employer contributions are not required for 401(k)s except in certain types of safe harbor plans.

States can reduce the potential liability of employers by adopting a simple plan design and by assuming responsibilities that would otherwise fall to the employer (Toth 2014a). By doing so, liability can be placed where the responsibility for a decision lies and with those who are best able to handle it. In the case of a state-sponsored plan where the plan itself sets contribution amounts, chooses the fund manager, and makes other decisions about the plan structure (and the role of the employer is limited to collecting employee contributions and forwarding them), the enacting law should clearly place all liability for plan structure and similar decisions with the state entity. Employer liability should be limited to their primary roles. In marketplace plans, where the employer selects an option from a prescreened list of providers, liability for selecting an appropriate provider should also rest with the state entity or the contractor that administers it, if there is one. However, to the extent that the employer makes decisions on investments or other aspects of the chosen plan, it should be responsible for the consequences of its decisions. Ideally, liability issues should be directly addressed in legislation and regulation to avoid mistaken assumptions and misunderstandings.

In addition, employers need clear disclosures stating what their responsibilities are and what standards they are expected to meet. Inevitably, employers and payroll providers working on their behalf will make a mistake, such as using a wrong number or missing a deadline. Fear that such an innocent error would result in a stiff penalty or other punishment has been raised in several states as a reason for small-business opposition to a state-sponsored plan. For this reason, states would be best served by making it clear that they will treat innocent and occasional errors leniently as long as a correction is made quickly after the mistake is identified. This could include working with the employer or provider to develop ways to prevent future problems, having low penalties that could be waived in many cases, and encouraging employers to self-report errors. Treating unintentional errors lightly does not mean that intentional or habitual failures should receive the same treatment. Penalties should match the seriousness of the infraction. Willful failure to forward employees' contributions promptly or at all is essentially stealing from employees and should result in strong penalties. It is important, however, for the state to determine if the failure is the fault of the employer or the payroll provider if there is one, and to penalize only the guilty party.

A CONSIDERED INVESTMENT IN RETIREMENT SECURITY

State-sponsored retirement saving plans for private sector small-business employees have a real potential to improve the retirement security of their participants and improve the state's fiscal outlook. By increasing the number of people with access to a payroll deduction plan, states can reduce the number of retirees with few financial resources other than Social Security benefits. Equally as important, a state-sponsored plan can reduce the number of future retirees who would need to depend on taxpayer-financed services. State-sponsored retirement saving plans offer the best chance in the near term to increase the number of Americans with access to payroll deduction retirement saving plans. In the absence of a comprehensive federal program, they could provide the most significant improvement in coverage for many decades. But there is still a great deal of work to be done before the plans reach their full potential. In order to make a difference, these plans must be carefully structured and implemented. The success of the plans in achieving their goals requires addressing the host of issues related to plan design and plan management outlined in this chapter.

NOTES

We thank the Laura and John Arnold Foundation for funding this work. The findings and conclusions contained within are solely the responsibility of the authors and do not necessarily reflect positions or policies of the Retirement Security Project, the Brookings Institution, or their funders.

1. John and Koenig (2014) estimate that 55 million US wage and salary workers between the ages of 18 and 64 lack the ability to save for retirement through an employer-sponsored payroll deduction plan.

2. Among such workers with wages between $30,000 and $50,000, only about one out of twenty contributes regularly to an IRA (Employee Benefit Research Institute 2006).

3. These are 2015 income levels. The IRS adjusts the amount annually for inflation.

4. Roth IRAs may roll into another Roth IRA, and a Roth 401(k) can roll into another Roth 401(k) or a Roth IRA, but Roth IRAs are currently not allowed to roll into a Roth 401(k). SIMPLE IRA plans cannot accept Roth contributions.

5. In one poll, over 98 percent of savers who were automatically enrolled were glad that their employer used this mechanism, as were over 80 percent of those who chose not to participate (Retirement Made Simpler 2007).

6. Schmitt and Xanthopoulos (2007) found that 97 percent of employers with ten or more employees used either an outside payroll processor or payroll processing software. Using either service sharply reduces the burden of complying with a required offering. Thus a plan that restricted the coverage requirement to those firms would likely impose small administrative burdens.

7. VanDerhei (2015) shows the effect of increasing the default contribution rate from 3 percent of earnings to 6 percent. In his simulations, an Automatic IRA resulted in a 10.6 percent reduction in retirement savings shortfalls for savers aged between 35 and 39 with a 3 percent contribution rate, growing to a 17.9 percent reduction if the contribution rate increased to 6 percent.

8. Also known as a cash balance plan, a hybrid plan accepts contributions from the employee and employer if allowed and credits them with a predetermined amount of investment earnings each year. If the plan earns more in a year, it could pay special higher dividends or retain that money to make up the difference in years when it earns less than the promised return.

REFERENCES

Beshears, John, James J. Choi, David Laibson, and Brigitte C. Madrian. 2013. "Financial Inertia among Low-Income Individuals—Plan Carefully When Setting 401(k) Defaults." Cambridge, MA: National Bureau of Economic Research.

Carroll, Gabriel D., James J. Choi, David Laibson, Brigitte C. Madrian, and Andrew Metrick. 2009. "Optimal Defaults and Active Decisions." *Quarterly Journal of Economics* 124 (4): 1639–74.

Chalmers, John, and Jonathan Reuter. 2012. "How Do Retirees Value Life Annuities? Evidence from Public Employees." *Review of Financial Studies* 25 (8): 2601–34.

Chandler, Peter, and Gary Mottola. 2014. "Five Tips for Successful Default Contribution Rates in Automatic Retirement Savings Plans." Spotlight 6. Washington, DC: AARP Public Policy Institute.

Cowan, Spencer. 2015. "What Types of Costs Would a State-Sponsored Retirement Savings Plan Impose on Employers: A Case Study Using the Illinois Secure Choice Savings Program." Washington, DC: AARP Public Policy Institute.

Employee Benefit Research Institute. 2006. Unpublished estimates of the 2004 Survey of Income and Program Participation Wave 7 Topical Module (2006 data).

———. 2014. "2014 RCS Fact Sheet #6 Preparing for Retirement in America." https://www.ebri.org/docs/default-source/rcs/6_rcs14-fs-6-prep-ret-final.pdf?sfvrsn=c1ea302f_2.

Employee Benefits Security Administration. 2006. "Field Assistance Bulletin 2006-2." www.dol.gov/ebsa/regs/fab_2006-2.html.

Friedman, Karen, and Norman Stein. 2014a. "Consumer Protections in State-Sponsored Retirement Plans for Private Sector Workers." Spotlight 7. Washington, DC: AARP Public Policy Institute.

———. 2014b. "Investment Platform: The Advantages of Placing Retirement Savings Assets in Pooled Accounts." Spotlight 10. Washington, DC: AARP Public Policy Institute.

Gale, William G., David C. John, and Bryan Kim. 2015. "You Get What You Pay For: Guaranteed Returns in Retirement Saving Accounts." Working Paper. Brookings.

Government Accountability Office (GAO). 2013. "Retirement Security: Challenges and Prospects for Employees of Small Businesses." Statement of Charles A. Jeszeck, Director, Education, Workforce, and Income Security. GAO-13-748T. July 16.

Iwry, J. Mark, and David C. John. 2009. "Pursuing Universal Retirement Security through Automatic IRAs." Brookings.

Iyengar, Sheena S., Wei Jiang, and Gur Huberman. 2003. "How Much Choice Is Too Much? Determinants of Individual Contributions in 401(k) Retirement Plans." Working paper presented at the Wharton Pension Research Council, April.

John, David C. 2015. "Model Notices and Plan Sponsor Education on Lifetime Plan Participation." Testimony before the US Department of Labor Advisory Council on Employee Welfare and Pension Benefit Plans, May 28.

John, David C., and Gary Koenig. 2014. "Workplace Retirement Plans Will Help Workers Build Economic Security." Factsheet 317. Washington, DC: AARP Public Policy Institute.

Kahn, Melissa, and Jodie Strakosch. 2015. "Making State Retirement Plans Work for Private Employers: Including Lifetime Income Options." Washington, DC: AARP Public Policy Institute.

Kim, Hank H. 2011. "The Secure Choice Pension: A Way Forward for Retirement Security in the Private Sector." Washington, DC: National Conference on Public Employee Retirement Systems.

Madrian, Brigitte C. 2014. "That Was Easy: The Importance of Auto Features in Promoting Retirement Savings." Spotlight 12. Washington, DC: AARP Public Policy Institute.

Madrian, Brigitte C., and Dennis F. Shea. 2001. "The Power of Suggestion: Inertia in 401(k) Participation and Savings Behavior." *Quarterly Journal of Economics* 116 (4): 1149–87.

Morse, David E. 2014. "State Initiatives to Expand the Availability and Effectiveness of Private Sector Retirement Plans: How Federal Laws Apply to Plan Design Options." Center for Retirement Initiatives, Georgetown University.

Pension Rights Center. 2015. "State-Based Retirement Plans for the Private Sector." www.pensionrights.org/issues/legislation/state-based-retirement-plans-private-sector.

Perez, Tom. 2015. "Clearing a Path for State-based Retirement Plans." *US DOL Blog*, July 13. https://blog.dol.gov/2015/07/13/clearing-a-path-for-state-based-retirement-plans.

Retirement Made Simpler. 2007. "Poll by Harris Interactive of Employees Who Had Been Automatically Enrolled." www.retirementmadesimpler.org/Library/FINAL%20RMS%20Topline%20Report%2011-5-07.pdf.

Schmitt, Mary M., and Judy Xanthopoulos. 2007. "Automatic IRAs: Are They Administratively Feasible, What Are the Costs to Employers and the Federal Government, and Will They Increase Retirement Savings?" Optimal Benefit Strategies, LLC. https://www.aarp.org/work/retirement-planning/info-2007/auto_ira.html.

Thaler, Richard H., and Shlomo Benartzi. 2004. "Save More Tomorrow: Using Behavioral Economics to Increase Employee Saving." *Journal of Political Economy* 112 (1): 164–87.

Toth, Robert J. Jr. 2014a. "Employer Liability under a State-Sponsored Retirement Program." Spotlight 8. Washington, DC: AARP Public Policy Institute.

———. 2014b. "The Impact of ERISA on State-Sponsored Retirement Plan Designs." Spotlight 9. Washington, DC: AARP Public Policy Institute.

VanDerhei, Jack. 2015. "Auto-IRAs: How Much Would They Increase the Probability of 'Successful' Retirements and Decrease Retirement Deficits? Preliminary Evidence from EBRI's Retirement Security Projection Model® (June 1, 2015)." *EBRI Notes* 36 (6): 11–29.

Wu, April Yanyuan, and Matthew S. Rutledge. 2014. "Lower-Income Individuals without Pensions: Who Misses Out and Why." CRR WP 2014–2. Center for Retirement Research, Boston College.

NINE

Public Pensions in Flux

HOW THE FEDERAL GOVERNMENT'S EXPERIENCE CAN INFORM STATE RESPONSES

William G. Gale, Sarah Holmes Berk, and David C. John

In many policy-related situations, the states can be useful laboratories for determining the most appropriate federal actions. Differences among states in health care programs, earned-income credit rules, minimum wages, and other policies have helped inform debates about federal interventions.

In this chapter, we reverse that approach. Many state and local governments face difficulties financing future pension obligations for their workers. The federal government, however, faced similar circumstances in the 1980s and successfully implemented a substantial reform. We examine the situation the federal government faced and how it responded to the funding challenge. We present key aspects of the situation state governments are confronting, and draw comparisons between them and the federal situation in the 1980s. Our overarching conclusion is that states experiencing distress today over the cost and funding of their pension plans could benefit from following an approach similar to the federal government's resolution of its pension problems in the 1980s.

The federal government retained the existing Civil Service Retirement System (CSRS) for existing employees and created a new Federal Employees' Retirement System (FERS) for new employees. FERS combined a less generous defined benefit (DB) plan than CSRS, mandatory enrollment in Social Security, and a new defined contribution (DC) plan with extensive employer matching. Although we do not wish to imply that a "one size fits all" solution applies to the very diverse situations that different states face, we nonetheless conclude that the elements of durable, effective, and just reforms for state pension plans will likely include the major elements of the federal reform listed above.

The chapter begins by discussing the federal experience with pension reform, and then follows with a discussion of the status and recent developments regarding state and local pensions. Finally, the chapter discusses the similarities in the two situations and how policy changes structured along the lines of the federal reform could help state and local governments and their employees.

THE FEDERAL PENSION TRANSITION

The history of federal pensions, especially the federal government's experience with pension reform, provides a number of key insights relevant to state government.

The Creation and Evolution of CSRS

The modern US Civil Service was created in 1883, marking the end of the "spoils era" of American politics, in which most public sector employees were replaced at the end of each election cycle with workers who were sympathetic to the newly elected officials. The Civil Service initiated a merit-based public employment system and protected public workers from having their employment terminated for arbitrary reasons, including old age (OPM 2015b, 2015d). As a result, over time, the federal workforce became older and longer tenured. In addition, the overall federal workforce was growing, both in absolute terms and as a share of the total workforce (Fabricant 1949). By 1920, there were many federal employees age 70 or older who, because of the rules protecting workers' employment, could not be separated from service (Hustead and Hustead 2001). There were no provisions for retirement from public service, pensions for federal workers, or other public retirement programs such as Social Security. These factors led to the creation of the Civil Service Retirement System (CSRS) in 1920.

CSRS created a defined benefit plan for government workers. Covered workers were required to contribute between 7 and 8 percent of pay, with their employing agency matching these contributions. CSRS-covered employees were generally eligible to retire at age 55 (with thirty-plus years of service),

60 (with twenty-plus years of service), or 62 (with five-plus years of service). The CSRS annuity was determined by calculating a worker's "high-3" salary, "the highest average basic pay [an employee] earned during any 3 consecutive years of service" (OPM 2015b). Retirees received 1.5 percent of their high-3 pay for the first five years of service; 1.75 percent of their high-3 pay for the second five years of service; and 2 percent of their high-3 pay for any years of service beyond ten, with an overall limit of 80 percent of high-3 pay (which would be reached with just over forty-two years of service) (OPM 2015b). Automatic cost-of-living adjustments (COLAs) began in 1962 and were linked to the consumer price index (CPI) (CRS 2013a).

Once it was enacted, CSRS quickly became an appealing benefit of working for the federal government. Several factors, however, led to stress in the system in the late 1970s and early 1980s. First, current and projected costs in CSRS increased significantly as the government workforce expanded and aged. The number of executive branch civilian employees rose from 1.4 million in 1950 to 2.3 million in 1985 (OPM 2015c). Between 1967 and 1979, the number of primary CSRS annuitants more than doubled, and the median CSRS annuity rose by about 50 percent (adjusted for inflation). By the end of the 1970s, about one in three CSRS annuitants was under the age of 62, implying that costs would persist for a long time (Dalrymple, Grad, and Wilson 1983). In addition to these trends, high inflation in the 1970s drove up salaries and, in turn, the cost of future retirement benefits.

Second, the budget crunches of the early 1980s put pressure on CSRS. Spurred by recession, tax cuts, and defense buildups, federal deficits in the early 1980s rose to their highest level as a share of the economy since World War II, and the debt-to-GDP ratio rose from about 25 percent in 1979 to about 40 percent in 1985 (OMB 2010). Under pressure to curb spending, Congress enacted the Omnibus Budget Reconciliation Act of 1981, which included provisions for significant federal spending cuts. The 1981 act reduced the frequency of CSRS COLAs from semi-annual to annual. The annual COLAs were calculated based on December-to-December CPI changes and took effect the following March. The Omnibus Budget Reconciliation Act of 1982 delayed the annual COLA implementation by one added month in 1983, 1984, and 1985. The same act restricted COLAs in some circumstances. Further acts reduced or delayed COLAs again and converted the COLA calculation to the one used by the Social Security Administration, in which COLAs are based on the percentage change in the price index over the preceding year (CRS 2013a).

A third factor was Social Security reform. As of the early 1980s, federal employees had always been exempt from Social Security. In January 1983, the National Commission on Social Security Reform, chaired by Alan Greenspan, recommended that all newly hired federal employees be covered under Social Security, partly in order to help that system address both short- and long-term funding problems. By March, that recommendation was made law with the Social Security Amendments of 1983, which called for all federal employees hired on or after January 1, 1984, to be covered under Social Security (H.R. 1900). In response, as a stopgap measure, Congress reduced the contributions that federal employees were required to make to CSRS (Cowen 2011). This gave Congress time to tackle the bigger question of reform without over-burdening federal employees in the meantime with full contributions to both the old CSRS system and Social Security.

Collectively, these and other factors led to reform of the pension system for federal workers, but the road was not easy. Earlier, in 1981, the Senate Subcommittee on Civil Service asked the Congressional Research Service (CRS) to report on options for government employee pension reform; each of the CRS recommendations included Social Security as part of a larger retirement plan. The following year, Senator Ted Stevens (R-AK) introduced the Civil Service Reform Act of 1982, which also featured a Social Security component and called for a new, defined contribution plan structure and private investment component (S. 2905). Most federal employees opposed the bill. They did not want to make the switch from the guaranteed benefits of a DB plan to the potential rate-of-return risk of a DC plan, and they did not like the private investment of retirement funds proposed by Stevens's bill. The employees also saw Social Security as a struggling system and worried that by the time they retired it would not be able to pay promised benefits. At a time when the generous retirement plan offered through CSRS was seen as one of the few financial perks of federal employment, the proposed changes added too much uncertainty and perceived unreliability (Cowen 2011). Stevens's bill did not pass, but it was a major step toward reform. And by 1984, the question of whether to incorporate Social Security into the federal retirement package had become moot.

Disagreements on these issues reflected broader philosophical differences, and compromises were hammered out by a bipartisan congressional working group and conference sessions between the House and Senate. However, two more complicated issues presented challenges: how to handle workers in specialized occupations and how to manage the risks associated with investing government money in the private sector.

CSRS covered a remarkably diverse set of workers and jobs. There were concerns about the treatment of certain groups of employees in specialized occupations such as public safety and law enforcement, the military, and the intelligence arena. Under CSRS, many workers in those groups enjoyed valued benefits that took their unique or special career characteristics into consideration, and of course, those groups wanted to ensure that they received similar treatment in the future. The concerns included earlier retirement for those who worked in hazardous conditions (such as firefighters and police officers) and proper security protocols for those who supported covert missions (such as CIA operatives). Ultimately, it was decided that when the next reform bill was introduced on the Senate floor, it would not address these specific issues. Instead, federal agencies with such concerns would offer amendments to the reform bill via the appropriate congressional committee. In addition, there were trepidations about Stevens's proposal to create a Civil Service Pension Fund that would be invested in both government bonds and private assets. Some worried that investing large amounts of federal funds in the private sector could create a "federal monster" that exercised too much influence over the market (Cowen 2011).

The Creation and Implementation of FERS

Senators Stevens and William Roth (R-DE) introduced S. 1527 in July 1985. Congress enacted the bill in June 1986 and President Ronald Reagan signed it into law the same month. The new law, which took effect on January 1, 1987, created the Federal Employees' Retirement System (FERS), a new system that includes all federal employees hired on or after January 1, 1984, and federal workers who were hired before that date and chose to voluntarily switch over from CSRS. Unlike CSRS, which consisted of only a defined benefit plan, FERS offered a three-pronged approach to retirement: Social Security benefits, a smaller defined benefit plan than the one offered through CSRS, and the Thrift Savings Plan (TSP), a defined contribution platform. The legislation also included special provisions for people with careers in law enforcement, firefighting, air traffic control, and other specialized fields (OPM 1998).

Two of the three FERS components (Social Security and the TSP) are portable and move with the employee as he or she changes jobs either within or outside of the federal government (table 9-1). Two components (Social Security and the DB plan) require employees to contribute part of their pay to the system. TSP is voluntary, but it depends heavily on employee contributions.

Participants accrue benefits in the defined benefit plan at slower rates than in CSRS. After the most recent FERS reforms, workers accrue a benefit equal

Table 9-1. *States with the Largest Unfunded Liabilities, Lowest Funding Ratios, and Lowest Percentage of ARC Paid in 2012*

Largest unfunded liabilities (millions of $)		*Lowest funding ratios (percent)*		*Lowest ARC paid (percent)*	
California	131,318	Illinois	40	New Jersey	39
Illinois	94,582	Kentucky	47	Pennsylvania	43
Ohio	63,143	Connecticut	49	North Dakota	53
Pennsylvania	47,286	Alaska	55	Ohio	57
New Jersey	47,209	New Hampshire	56	Virginia	59
Texas	31,670	Kansas	56	Florida	59
Michigan	31,159	Louisiana	56	Kentucky	65
Florida	28,956	Rhode Island	58	Kansas	67
Virginia	28,138	Mississippi	58	Montana	69
Massachusetts	28,104	Hawaii	59	Texas	69

Source: Pew Charitable Trusts (2014a).
ARC = Actuarial Required Contribution.

to 1 percent per year of service, or 1.1 percent for workers who retire at age 62 or later with twenty or more years of service.

The TSP operates like a private sector 401(k). Initially, participants could only make contributions using the traditional tax treatment where contributions and investment gains were tax free and taxes are paid on withdrawal. More recently, TSP has added a Roth option where contributions are after tax, with gains and withdrawals being tax exempt. Starting in August 2010, all newly hired or rehired federal employees are automatically enrolled in TSP and contribute 3 percent of their pay to the system.

The government makes an unconditional contribution of 1 percent of salary for each employee and then matches the first 3 percent of salary in an employee's contribution on a 1-to-1 basis and the next 2 percent of salary on a .5-to-1 basis. Employees can contribute up to $17,500 per year (plus an extra $5,500 for those over the age of 50). Voluntary participation in the TSP among FERS beneficiaries approaches 90 percent and as of October 2014, the TSP included about 4.7 million active and retired participants (CRS 2015a). When TSP began operations in April 1987, it only offered investment in the G Fund (government securities). In January 1988, TSP began to offer both the F Fund (fixed income securities), and the C Fund (common stocks) (Schreitmueller 1988). At first, participants were limited to placing only a portion of their savings in these two funds, but all such restrictions ended in January 1991. Starting in May 2001, TSP added both the S Fund (a stock index fund of small and medium-sized businesses), and the I Fund (a stock index fund that replicates the Morgan Stanley Capital International EAFE Index). Several L Funds (life-cycle) that offer various combinations of investment in the G, C, F, S, and I Funds that change as the investor ages were added in 2005 (CRS 2015a).

While it was originally viewed as a step down from the rich benefits offered through CSRS, FERS in many ways offers better benefits for many workers, including those who spend only a portion of their career with the federal government, those who are not with the federal government at the time of their retirement, those who work beyond the standard retirement age, and those who are savvy investors (Flanagan 2015). Under CSRS, annual benefits for a regular federal worker with thirty years of service equal 56.25 percent of a retiree's high-3 average pay (CRS 2014a). Under FERS, benefits accrue in all three components of the program. A worker with thirty years of service retiring at age 62 or later would receive 33 percent of high-3 average pay from the defined benefit plan. In addition, if the worker contributed 10 percent of wages to TSP and earned a 6 percent (nominal) return, benefits from the defined contribution account would equal about another 32 percent of high-3 average pay. And, of course, the worker would receive Social Security benefits as well.

Some FERS retirees receive annual benefits equal to as much as 128.2 percent of high-3 average pay (CRS 2013b; SSA 2014). FERS also tends to be more generous than private sector plans. "Most people in the United States, if they understood what was going on, would be extremely jealous of the benefits that FERS employees have" (Stein 2012). Brown, Clark, and Rauh (2011) note that career employees in the public sector tend to receive retirement benefits that are "substantially higher" than those their private sector counterparts receive.

Figures 9-1a, 9-1b, and 9-1c illustrate the difference in FERS and CSRS costs to employers and employees. Overall, FERS costs are very close to CSRS costs. CSRS costs 29.3 percent of payroll, of which 22.3 percent comes from the employer and 7 percent from the employee. The DB portion of FERS costs 14 percent of pay for employees hired before 2013, and 14.2 percent of pay for employees hired in 2013 or later.[1] The government also pays the 6.2 percent of taxable payroll that all employers contribute toward Social Security and a maximum of 5 percent of salary in TSP contributions (1 percent in unconditional contributions and up to 4 percent in matching contributions). All told, FERS costs between 27.6 percent and 31.6 percent, depending on the extent to which employees take advantage of TSP matching contributions.

FERS costs the government as the employer less than CSRS. CSRS costs the government 22.3 percent of payroll, while FERS costs the government

Figure 9-1a. **Comparison of Employer and Employee Contributions in CSRS and FERS**

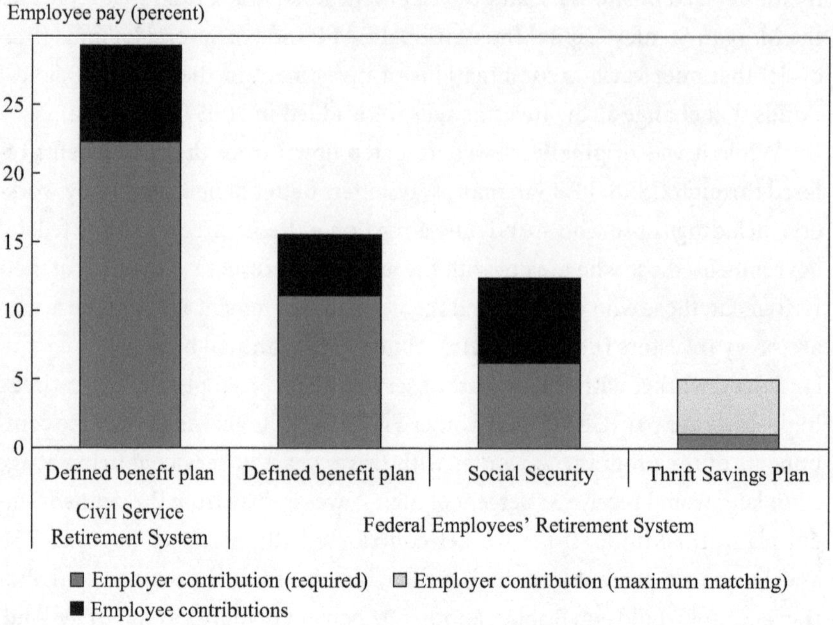

Source: Congressional Research Service (2015b).

Figure 9-1b. **Comparison of Employer Costs in CSRS and FERS**

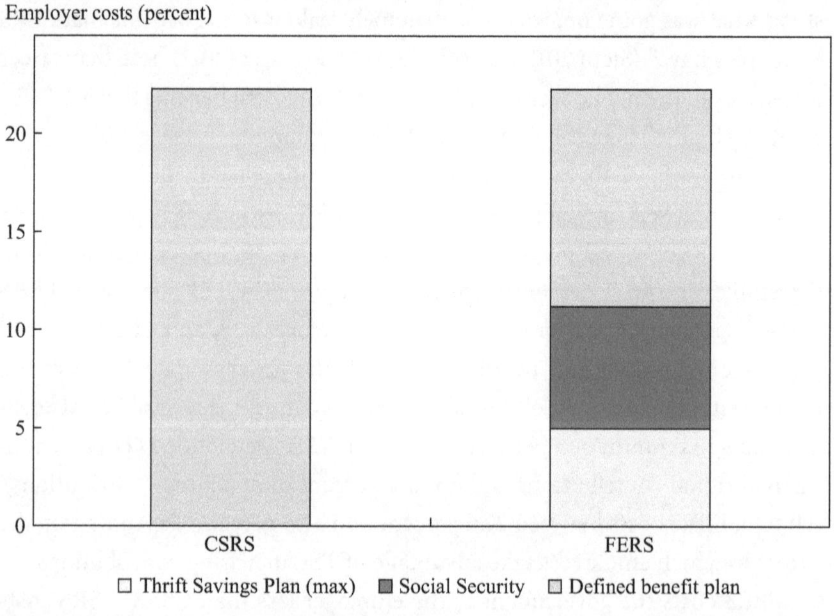

Source: Congressional Research Service (2015b).

Figure 9-1c. **Comparison of Employee Costs in CSRS and FERS**

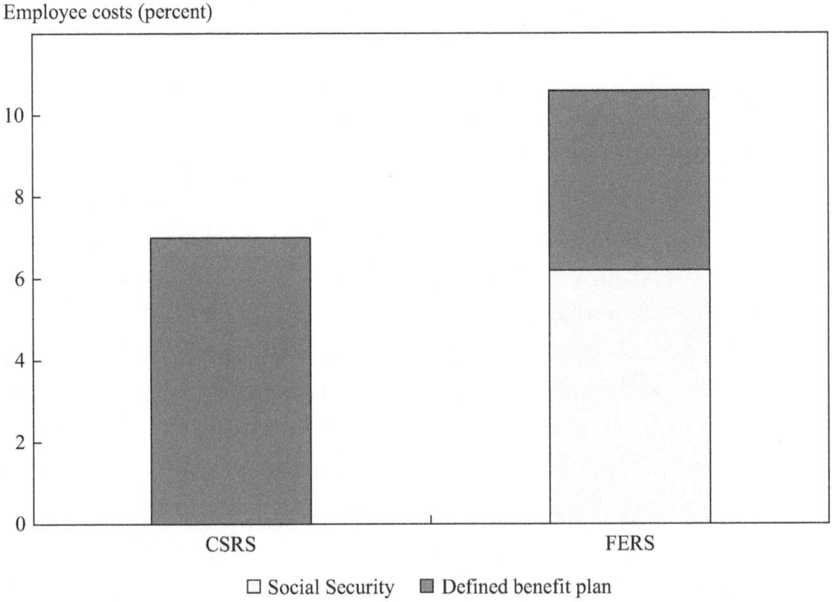

Source: Congressional Research Service (2015b).

between 21.2 and 25.4 percent of payroll (depending, again, on the extent to which employees take advantage of TSP matching contributions).[2] On the other hand, FERS costs *employees* more than CSRS does. Employees contribute 7 percent of pay under CSRS, and a total of 10.6 percent of pay (4.4 for the DB plan and 6.2 for Social Security) under FERS, excluding optional contributions to the TSP. The cost of these combined retirement benefits has caused some in Congress to propose either further reduction in the FERS defined benefit or its elimination. While no action has been taken on this, the cost remains a concern to some legislators.

Surveys indicate that current FERS participants strongly support the plan. In an OPM (2013b) survey, 85 percent of federal employees described the TSP as "extremely important" and 76 percent felt the same way about the FERS defined benefit plan. In the same survey, over two-thirds of respondents said that the TSP met their needs "to a great extent," while just under half said the same of the defined benefit plan. Almost 79 percent of respondents described the TSP as a good or excellent value for the money, and almost 57 percent described the DB plan in those terms. The TSP is consistently the most popular federal employee benefit program, and the FERS DB plan is among the top three most popular (OPM 2013b). This seems to point to a major increase in support for FERS over the past three decades, even though when the FERS legislation gave existing federal employees the opportunity to switch from CSRS to the new program, only 4 percent of eligible employees voluntarily made the transition (Cowen 2011).

The creation of FERS did not do away with, or even change, CSRS. Employees who were in that plan could stay in it. As of 2013, about 90 percent of federal civilian and Postal Service employees (2.5 million) participated in FERS, with the remaining 10 percent in CSRS. CSRS will continue to exist until its beneficiaries pass away.

Several other issues with regard to FERS are worth noting. First, FERS benefits are prefunded through contributions from the government and the employees. When FERS was created, prefunding was required to force agencies to recognize these costs in their budgets. CSRS benefits are partially prefunded, but the cost of benefits exceeds employer and employee contributions plus earnings on assets in the trust fund.

In FY2014, the Civil Service Retirement and Disability Fund (CSRDF) reported an unfunded liability of $785 billion, of which the overwhelming majority is for CSRS. Annuities for both CSRS and FERS are financed through the CSRDF. Despite this major unfunded liability, however, OPM reports that the CSRDF is not at risk of insolvency (CRS 2015a). The trust fund is expected to grow for at least sixty-five more years, "at which point it will hold assets equal to more than 5.3 times total payroll and about 20 times total annual benefit payments" (CRS 2014a). However, the CSRDF is invested solely in government bonds, so like the Social Security trust funds, its earnings come from other federal revenues.

Second, the transition from CSRS to FERS has been successful, but it encountered some administrative hurdles along the way. The most serious challenge was the fact that even after January 1, 1987, some new federal hires were mistakenly placed in CSRS by their agency HR offices. The problem was ultimately resolved with the Federal Erroneous Retirement Coverage Corrections Act (FERCCA), which President Clinton signed in late 2000. FERCCA gives those employees who were wrongly entered into CSRS—and who spent at least three years in federal employment in 1987 or later—the option to either remain in CSRS or switch into FERS. FERCCA also provides some additional benefits that are meant to offset the costs associated with the mistaken retirement plan assignment (OPM 2015a).

Third, a more recent issue with both CSRS and FERS is the introduction of phased retirement. OPM started accepting applications for the new program in November 2014; approved workers could then switch to half-time employment and receive a proportionate salary and half of their DB benefits. CSRS retirees are positioned to benefit from this more than FERS retirees because the Social Security component of FERS does not accommodate early or phased retirement. For CSRS retirees, the entire retirement package is available for phased retirement; for FERS retirees, only a portion is (Yoder 2014).

In general, the CSRS-to-FERS transition has been smooth. Even though we are decades away from the complete phase-out of CSRS, the most challenging parts of the transition are likely in the past.

PENSIONS FOR STATE AND LOCAL GOVERNMENT WORKERS

Understanding the history and status of state and local government pensions is essential to considering possible federal government–guided reforms.

Historical Development

The earliest public pensions for state and local government workers (SLGWs) predate the creation of CSRS in 1920. Several large cities started offering retirement and disability benefits to public safety officers, teachers, and other workers in the mid-1800s (Clark, Craig, and Wilson 2003). In 1857, police officers in New York City became the first group of civilian employees to participate in a public retirement plan for local government employees (Rajnes 2001). In 1911, Massachusetts created the first pension plan for state employees.

Even so, it took some time for public pensions to become de rigueur among the states. By 1930, only six states had created public pension systems for their civilian employees, and it took until 1947 for all states to offer plans (Rajnes 2001). As of March 2014, the take-up rate of retirement benefits among state and local government workers was 91 percent (BLS 2014).[3] This slow path toward nationwide retirement coverage for employees of state and local governments, lagging well behind the federal government's creation of CSRS, may not be surprising, considering the diverse situations across states as well as the piecemeal nature (state by state, locality by locality) of these policy changes.

Despite its gradual enactment, the pension system for SLGWs has grown steadily and dramatically over the past fifty years. The number of state and

Figure 9-2. **Number of State and Local Retirement System Participants, Selected Years 1962–2013**

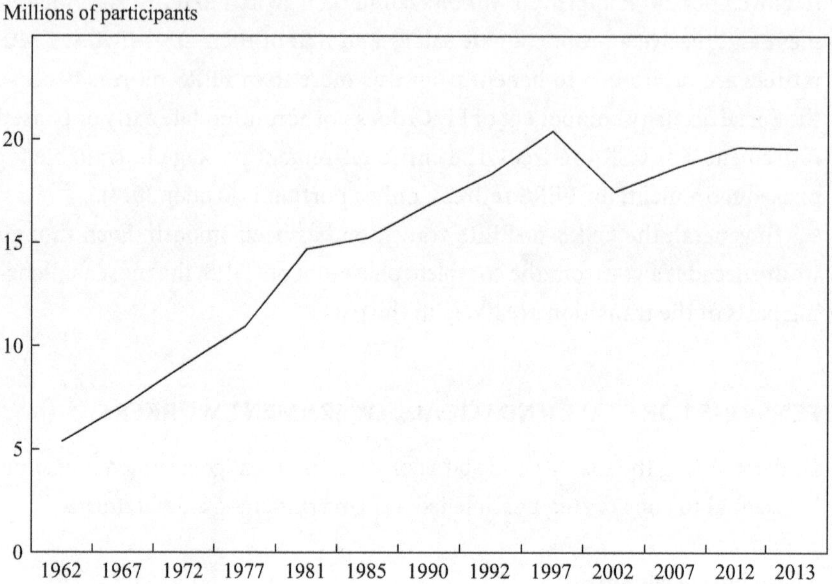

Source: Rajnes (2001); US Census Bureau (1993–2013b).

local pension plans rose from less than 2,400 in 1962 to almost 4,000 in 2013 (Rajnes 2001; US Census Bureau 1993–2013b).

The number of workers participating in state and local government pension plans has grown even more dramatically. In 1962, there were just over 5 million participants. The number of participants rose steeply and steadily between 1962 and 1997, approximately doubling between 1962 and 1977, and again between 1977 and 1999, to exceed 20 million participants. However, between 1999 and 2002 the number of participants dropped by about 20 percent (Rajnes 2001). Since the early 2000s, though, the number of participants has trended upward again, though less steeply than in the decades before the dot-com bubble (US Census Bureau 1993–2013b, data for 2002, 2007, 2013). As of 2013, there were about 19.5 million participants. Figure 9-2 shows these trends.

However, while *overall* participation in state and local pension plans has been rising steadily for decades, *active* participation saw only modest gains between 1997 and 2009, and in the postcrisis years has been slowly declining.[4] Over the same period, the number of beneficiaries rose steadily (US Census

Figure 9-3. **Active Participants, Inactive Participants, and Beneficiaries of State and Local Pension Systems, 1993–2013**

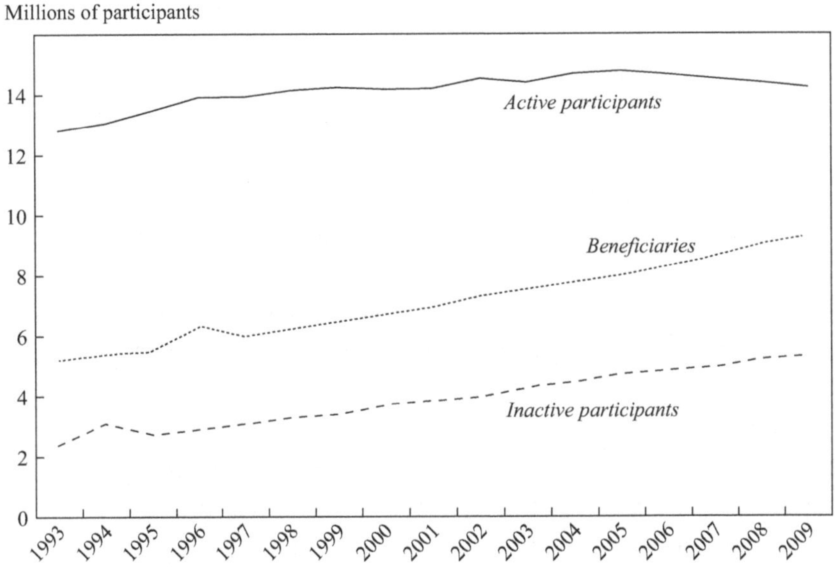

Source: US Census Bureau (1993–2013b).

Bureau 1993–2013b). Figure 9-3 shows that the gap between active participants and beneficiaries has been steadily narrowing, and in 2013 was less than 68 percent the size of the gap in 1993. As this trend continues and the number of retirees approaches the number of active participants, underfunded state and local governments will face even greater difficulties in meeting benefit payments.

Funding levels of state and local pension plans have also fluctuated over the years. The first comprehensive review of state and local pension plans was conducted in 1978 and revealed an average funding ratio of 50 percent (Peng 2008). During the 1980s and 1990s, funding ratios improved gradually, peaking in excess of 100 percent in 2001 after several years of rapid economic expansion and strong stock market growth (Peng 2008; CBO 2011; US GAO 2012). Funding ratios fell in the early 2000s following the collapse of the dot-com bubble and hovered in the mid-80s until the 2007–2009 financial crisis (CBO 2011; US GAO 2012). During that crisis, funding ratios declined significantly. Brown, Clark, and Rauh (2011) describe the 2007–2009 financial crisis as "the proximate cause of the current funding problems facing many state and local pensions."

In addition, however, longer-standing dysfunctional policies have played an important role in current funding problems. For example, Schieber (2011) reports that during fiscal year 2009, the states on average contributed 10.7 percent of payroll to their pension plans, about 15 percent less than the average actuarially required contribution of 12.6 percent of payroll.[5] This type of chronic underfunding occurs in both good times and bad, creating a financial hole that becomes almost impossible for a state or local government to fill without severely reducing other services. Elliott (2010) points to short-term political horizons and public apathy as important factors in the failure to provide adequate funding for pensions.

State and local governments have often raised retirement benefits when they are flush with cash—such as during economic booms; but they are generally loath to decrease them when their budgets are tight, such as during recessions, or unable to do so because the pension benefits are legally protected (Schieber 2011). This problem is mainly a political one and is affected by the presence of strong unions and politicians' irresponsible spending habits: "As it turns out, many lawmakers found that increasing pensions was very good politics. They placated unions with future pension commitments, and then turned around, borrowed the money appropriated for the pensions, and spent it paying for public services in the here and now." Also, because many states' pension obligations are constitutionally or otherwise guaranteed, reforms passed at the eleventh hour to resolve serious fiscal distress are unlikely to succeed (Disalvo 2010).

Pew (2014b) reports that the structure of public pension investments is also changing. Between 1952 and 2012, allocations to fixed income and cash fell while allocations to equities and alternative investments rose. Since 2002, the share of allocations to equities and alternative investments has exceeded 60 percent. Fixed income investments are generally low-risk and low-reward; equities offer more risk and more opportunity for reward; and alternative investments tend to be high-risk and high-reward. Any shift toward riskier investments puts some pension plans in an even more precarious position and makes the need for reform more urgent. Economic downturns tend to bring with them a variety of fiscal problems for state and local governments; adding potentially serious losses to their pension plans due to high-risk investments only fuels the fire. It is easy to justify increased allocations to equities and alternative investments when the economy is performing well and these allocations are generating high rewards. However, state and local governments normally would benefit from taking a longer view on pension investments to avoid compounding future budgetary issues.

Recent Policy Changes and Current Status

Motivated primarily by fiscal distress, more than thirty-five states and many local governments have made some reforms to their pension programs in recent years (US GAO 2012). Munnell, Aubry, and Sanzenbacher (2014) distinguish recent pension changes by the underlying goals: (1) to reduce existing defined benefit plan costs or (2) to shift all or part of a given pension program into a defined contribution format. The first type of reform often requires higher employee contributions, fewer benefits for new hires, suspended or lower cost-of-living adjustments, or increased age and tenure requirements (Bradford 2014). The second type of reform has shifted in scope and intent in recent years. Munnell, Aubry, and Sanzenbacher (2014) note that before the 2007–2009 financial crisis, states were introducing optional DC plans. But after the crisis, many states have focused primarily on proposing mandatory DC plans that affect or would affect only new hires. The precrisis proposals were designed to give employees more retirement planning choices; the postcrisis proposals, on the other hand, have been designed almost exclusively to reduce costs. Even though these defined contribution proposals have generated significant press attention, overall activity to date is described as "modest." Most states that introduced pension changes have focused on new mixed plans including both DC and DB components, and on cash balance plans rather than on a full-on transition from DB to DC.

McGuinn (2014) reviews recent public pension reforms in four states, ranging from major changes in Rhode Island and Utah to less significant moves in New Jersey and Illinois. Rhode Island made the most radical reforms despite the fact that it is both heavily Democratic and has some of the strongest public employee unions in the country. The state ended up creating a new DC plan to work in conjunction with a reduced DB plan, suspended DB COLAs until the plan reached at least 80 percent funding (although that decision will be reviewed every five years), reduced the vesting period to qualify for a pension from ten years to five, and increased retirement ages for existing employees.

Utah, a heavily Republican state, closed its DB plan to new hires and replaced it for new employees with either a DC plan or a mixed plan that incorporated both DB and DC elements. Workers who failed to choose would be placed in the mixed system. Because reform proponents recognized that both plans would produce less generous retirement benefits, the state also offers a supplemental saving plan with no employer match. Clark, Hanson, and Mitchell (2015) report that employees of Utah hired after the reform were less likely to stay in public employment for the long term, and they suggest that the reform may have made public employment in Utah less attractive.

Both Illinois and New Jersey made much less ambitious piecemeal reforms focusing on contributions from employees and COLAs, for example. However, as of 2016 both states' reforms are at risk. In New Jersey, Governor Chris Christie refused to make the full state contribution to the plan, and in June 2015 the state's Supreme Court ruled that he could legally skip these contributions (Zernike 2015). At the same time, New Jersey had the least-funded public pension system in the country and endured nine credit downgrades after Governor Christie's tenure began in January 2010 (NASRA 2015; Zernike 2015). In Illinois, state courts have ruled that even the partial reforms violate the state constitution, regardless of the fact that public pensions there were in some of the worst shape in the nation. Brown and Dye (2015) find that the problems facing Illinois were primarily the result of inadequate contributions, and they note that the state's public pensions were used almost as a loan so that the state could maintain lower taxes and higher spending. They conclude that even if Illinois had successfully reformed its pension system in 2013, the outcome would have been the same: over time more and more of Illinois's budget will need to go toward its pension problems at the expense of other state spending programs.

Despite these recent changes, many states continue to face serious pension underfunding. Novy-Marx and Rauh (2011) estimated that, as of June 2009, the shortfall was between $1.2 trillion and $2.5 trillion, depending on the discount method. They later estimated that in order to achieve full funding over thirty years, taxes would need to increase by $1,385 per household per year (Novy-Marx and Rauh 2014). Pew (2014a) calculated a total shortfall of $915 billion and an average funding ratio of 72 percent, meaning that the assets that state pension funds have set aside are sufficient to cover only 72 percent of their liabilities. State Budget Solutions (2014b) reported a shortfall of $4.7 trillion and a funding ratio of just 36 percent. The difference in findings is due largely to different ways of discounting future liabilities. State Budget Solutions uses a rate based on the long-term (fifteen-year) Treasury yield, implicitly assuming that state pension benefits are riskless. In contrast, Pew uses the figures for public plans that discount their liabilities according to their assumed investment return, which is typically between 7 and 8 percent. The difference in calculations is substantial, but even the more modest numbers reported by Pew reveal a serious problem for states with extremely poor funding ratios. For example, Pew (2014a) reports that Illinois, Kentucky, and Connecticut have the lowest funding ratios: 40, 47, and 49 percent, respectively. Not every state is in a dire situation—but those with a big underfunding problem are likely to need pension reform sooner than later. Table 9-1 shows which states have the largest unfunded liabilities, lowest funding ratios, and lowest percentage paid of the Actuarial Required Contribution (ARC)—the contribution required annually to fully fund promised pension benefits.

There are a very limited number of ways in which these underfunding problems can truly be resolved, and the most reliable options—cutting benefits and raising employee contributions—are the most unpleasant from the perspective of workers. States will naturally look for clever ways to avoid such painful changes. For example, they might hope for a federal bailout of pension liabilities. This option seems inappropriate, however. States as employers make their wage and pension agreements with their employees. Having the federal government step in ex post does not seem advisable, and it would set a very difficult precedent for the federal government: If the federal government helped one state in this regard, it would soon find forty-nine more states and a large number of municipalities and counties asking for the same assistance. And then states would find that the federal government would use the bailout as a reason to micromanage first state pension plans and agreements with their employees, and then other aspects of state financial and policy decisions.

A second way states might try to avoid such difficult choices is to take on even more investment risk in their pension funds in hopes of seeing higher average returns on their assets. In general, this move would not be well advised, for two main reasons. First, the share of state pension assets allocated to riskier investments is already substantial: in 2012, 50 percent of public pension fund portfolios were allocated to equities and 23 percent were allocated to alternative investments (Pew 2014b). Second, the liabilities that states face share many characteristics with bonds rather than equities or alternative investments. Liabilities may be rising over time, but they are not especially volatile on an annual basis. Therefore financing liabilities with investments that could fluctuate dramatically with changing market conditions adds unwanted risk to the equation. Biggs (2014b) notes that in many states—regardless of political party—treasurers and other senior officials are resistant to proposals to increase contributions and decrease risk. Others echo this sentiment, suggesting that investment decisions made today skew future outcomes. Even though chances of a positive outcome persist, they are dramatically outweighed by chances of a negative outcome (Novy-Marx and Rauh 2009).

Of course, there is a fairly extensive debate on ideal investment choices for state and local pension plans, and not all experts agree that states should avoid making high-risk investments. For example, Dean Baker (2013) of the Center for Economic and Policy Research argues that state and local governments should be primarily concerned with average returns in the long run rather than short-term market fluctuations.

Lucas and Zeldes (2009) provide an excellent overview of both sides of the debate and conclude with arguments "for holding a portion of pension assets in higher returning [and higher risk] equities."

COMPARING THE FEDERAL AND STATE SITUATIONS

In many ways, the situation in states with underfunding problems today closely resembles the one faced by the federal government in the early 1980s. Besides the most obvious consideration—the presence of sizable pension shortfalls—both the states now and the federal government then face the problem of ensuring appropriate and adequate retirement for an extremely diverse workforce. They also both face the need to attract and retain high-quality employees. Government workers perform a wide variety of jobs. Some work in highly specialized occupations—such as law enforcement and firefighting—and have unique retirement needs.

Second, within states, there are fundamental political disagreements about how generous and costly a pension plan should be, just as there were within the federal government during the 1980s. Many state and local government workers strongly oppose pension reform, as did all but the most senior federal employees when changes to CSRS were first considered. Many workers worry that they will lose out in pension reform and that, despite the increased portability and diversification offered through some reforms, their retirement benefits could be less generous. The resulting political obstacle to reform among many workers is a characteristic of the environment the states face currently, as the federal government did in the 1980s.

A third issue for certain state and local government workers is that they are not covered by Social Security. At the time of the federal pension reform, all federal workers had just been covered. Indeed, as noted earlier, coverage of federal workers brought about a reduction in employee contributions to CSRS as a short-term fix to avoid overburdening workers. This development sped up the clock for pension reform and helped generate passage of the legislation authorizing FERS shortly thereafter. Currently, about a quarter of the 24 million state and local government workers are not covered by Social Security (CRS 2011).

Fourth, a number of existing state DB plans, like the federal CSRS system, tend to be more generous than their private sector counterparts. Biggs (2014a) reports that, "for employees who spend a career in state government, generous pensions put retired public workers among the highest earners in their state." Schieber (2011) discusses the theory and evidence supporting the idea that states may compensate for a lack of Social Security coverage by offering correspondingly better pension benefits. States where lower percentages of SLGWs participate in Social Security tend to offer higher overall pension benefits (Gale, Holmes, and John 2015). Due to the costly nature of the state DB plans, some states are now considering pension reform that would ease their budgetary issues and bring state and local government workers into closer alignment with their federal government and private sector counterparts. Costliness made CSRS difficult for policymakers to justify, and it makes many state pension programs hard for state legislators to defend. Even though private sector retirement plans have been trending away from defined benefit and toward defined contribution, most public sector pension plans remain defined benefit (Butrica and others 2009; National Institute on Retirement Security 2010). Of course, policy changes that decrease the overall generosity of a state or local pension package will have other implications, some of which are undesirable. For example, as Clark, Hanson, and Mitchell (2015) suggest, these changes could make government employment less attractive to job seekers and could make workers more likely to exit public sector work altogether.[6]

Fifth, after the financial crisis ended, many states continued to face serious overall budgetary pressures, just as the federal government did in the early 1980s. The National Association of State Budget Officers (NASBO) (2014) reported that although the states' fiscal situation had become relatively stable, a combination of slow revenue growth and increasing spending persisted. NASBO (2015) reported that "budgets have been constrained by factors such as the decline in the price of oil, lower than anticipated revenue growth, federal uncertainty, and continued pressures from long-term obligations." States had already been forced to make difficult budget cuts and consider tax increases. Bosman (2015) noted that although the economy was in its sixth year of recovery since the 2007–2009 financial crisis, many states were still struggling. "In some states, lawmakers have gone into overtime with unresolved budgets, special sessions and threats of widespread government layoffs. Only 25 states have passed budgets, according to [NASBO].” She also writes that far more Republican-led states (twenty-three) than Democrat-led states (seven) were facing serious budget pressures.

The similarity between the states’ situations now and the federal government’s in the 1980s suggests that a reform along the same lines as those introduced in FERS could provide a suitable model for states to follow. The key elements of such a reform are clear. It must leave existing workers in the unchanged defined benefit system, create a new defined benefit system that is somewhat less generous and less costly, enroll all workers in Social Security who are not already in the program, and create a defined contribution plan with generous matching contributions. We take these points in turn.

First, maintaining CSRS contributed to the success of FERS. By ensuring that current employees and retirees already drawing a pension could continue to participate in CSRS without major changes to that program, Congress removed a source of potential opposition to reform and ensured that the reforms were fair to existing workers, who had paid into and participated in the CSRS. In 1986, many federal employees were still skeptical about the new system—as evidenced by the fact that only 4 percent voluntarily transferred into FERS—and a forced transition would likely have created significant political resistance. State legislators can use the federal government’s experience as an example of how to orchestrate a successful, albeit slow, phasing out of their existing DB system.

The three-part combination of a DB pension, Social Security, and a DC plan has much to offer. Policy changes that only reduce DB plan costs or eliminate those plans altogether will help rein in state budgets, but they will leave workers poorly prepared for retirement. This may render such reforms politically infeasible and therefore unlikely to survive in the long term. It is important for legislators to look beyond just costs, and to ensure that the remaining type and size of DB benefit provides significant retirement benefits when combined with the other elements of the reform. Reforms that omit universal Social Security coverage will fail to provide an important element of retirement security, disability, and survivors’ insurance to workers (see Gale, Holmes, and John 2015 for further discussion). The increased portability offered through Social Security may also make employment with state and local governments more palatable for workers (particularly mid-career workers) and improve governments’ ability to hire and retain qualified, expert employees. Reforms that omit DC coverage will be passing up what has turned out to be an extremely popular element of the federal program, and would make state government retirement arrangements quite different from the typical private sector retirement plan. Moreover, the investments risks associated with DC plans are reduced considerably when a worker can also expect to receive both a DB pension and Social Security benefits upon retirement. Inclusion of a DC plan will also provide an important framing device; as with the federal government's transition from CSRS to FERS, the TSP was popular, presumably at least in part because it allowed public sector workers to enjoy the same potential rewards as their private sector counterparts. A key element in this popularity is TSP's very low administrative fees and the presence of only carefully selected investment options that are suitable for retirement saving. The autonomy offered by a plan like the TSP could help make pension reform more palatable for many. States that encourage workers to choose from a variety of benefit options may enjoy more success than those that simply default employees into a program (Choi and others 2002; Beshears and others 2011).

Diversifying SLGWs' retirement portfolio into three components also helps insulate them from risk in the marketplace and the political arena. This was the logic behind the FERS approach that relies on Social Security, a DB plan, and the TSP (Cowen 2011). A more diversified retirement package would also better protect workers and retirees from a temporary or permanent loss of benefits and would help states balance their budgets by reducing DB benefits.[7] State and local pensions are often treated as a political "third rail" because workers fear the loss or reduction of their promised benefits. However, if state and local governments could offer their employees better retirement packages that also happen to be more cost-effective, they would likely see less opposition to reform.

McGuinn (2014) notes that pension changes should be framed as ultimately in the best interests of pension participants. He suggests avoiding making state and local pension reform an ideological issue, focusing on factual financial information instead to justify changes. State legislators could make pension reform more acceptable by emphasizing that changes along the lines of the federal reform would be advantageous to SLGWs. In order to avoid an exodus of key employees from the public sector into the private sector, state legislators should take care to ensure that SLGWs feel included in the process and that they are likely to benefit rather than suffer from reform. As DC retirement plans become the accepted standard across all sectors of the economy, both the relatively generous DB plans that most states offer and the absence of DC plans will become more challenging to justify. State and local governments can use that momentum to their advantage in order to craft reform policies that appeal to many stakeholders.

There is no single strategy for pension reform that will work for every state and municipal government. Each state faces a different pension, political, and economic situation and has its own traditions and norms. The results of any reforms must be monitored to ensure that they adequately address a state's fiscal issues and that any negative effects are quickly identified and appropriately handled. States that find themselves in difficult situations today might learn valuable lessons from the federal government's CSRS-to-FERS transition. States in relatively comfortable situations today may be better prepared for the future if they keep the federal government's transition in mind as they move forward. Even allowing for variation in program design, the basic building blocks for effective reform that the federal government adopted in the 1980s should also be considered by states.

NOTES

We thank the Laura and John Arnold Foundation for funding this work. The findings and conclusions contained within are solely the responsibility of the authors and do not necessarily reflect positions or policies of the Retirement Security Project, the Brookings Institution, their funders, or any other organization.

1. For FERS employees hired before 2013, the government contributes 13.2 percent of pay and employees contribute the remaining 0.8 percent. For FERS employees hired in 2013, the government contributes 11.1 percent of pay and employees contribute the remaining 3.1 percent. For FERS employees hired after 2013, the government contributes 11.1 percent of pay and employees contribute 4.4 percent. The "extra" 1.3 percent of pay (11.1 + 4.4 – 14.2) goes toward the CSRS unfunded liability (CRS 2015b).

2. According to a 2013 survey, 91 percent of FERS employees actively participating in the TSP contribute 5 percent or more of their pay and max out their matching contributions (Aon Hewitt 2013).

3. This figure includes both DB pension plans and DC retirement plans. The take-up rate of DB plans and DC plans was 89 and 48 percent, respectively, in March 2014 (BLS 2014).

4. Active participants are current workers and/or contributors to a pension system. Inactive workers are former contributors who have left the system but have not yet started receiving retirement benefits. Overall participation includes active participants, inactive participants, and beneficiaries.

5. During the same time period, the states on average contributed 3.5 percent of payroll to retiree health insurance plans, about one-third of the average actuarially required contribution of 10.5 percent of payroll (Schieber 2011).

6. For a review of the role pensions play in recruiting and retaining workers, see Munnell, Aubry, and Sanzenbacher (2014).

7. In 2009, the pension fund in Prichard, Alabama, ran out of money. For over a year it was unable to make benefit payments to its retirees. Eventually payments were reinstated, but they were much smaller than they had been before (Cooper and Walsh 2010; State Budget Solutions 2013).

REFERENCES

Aon Hewitt. 2013. "2013 Thrift Savings Plan Survey Results." Federal Retirement Thrift Investment Board. www.frtib.gov/ReadingRoom/SurveysPart/TSP-Survey-Results-2013.pdf.

Arnett, Sarah. 2014. "State Fiscal Condition: Ranking the 50 States." Mercatus Center, George Mason University, January 14.

Auxier, Richard C. 2010. "Reagan's Recession." Washington, DC: Pew Research Center, December 14.

Baker, Dean. 2013. "The Financial Health of Public Pensions." www.cepr.net/blogs/cepr-blog/today-the-financial-health-of-public-pensions.

Beshears, John, James J. Choi, David Laibson, and Brigitte C. Madrian. 2011. "Behavioral Economics Perspectives on Public Sector Pension Plans." *Journal of Pension Economics and Finance* 10 (2): 315–36.

Biggs, Andrew. 2014a. "How to Become a (Public Pension) Millionaire." *Wall Street Journal*, March 14.

———. 2014b. "Public Pensions Need Gamblers Anonymous." *Wall Street Journal*, December 2.

Bosman, Julie. 2015. "States Confront Wide Budget Gaps Even after Years of Recovery." *New York Times*, June 7.

Bradford, Hazel. 2014. "Pace of Pension Reform Ebbs after 49 States Change Laws." *Pensions & Investments*, April 14.

Brown, Jeffrey R., and Richard F. Dye. 2015. "Illinois Pensions in a Fiscal Context: A (Basket) Case Study." NBER Working Paper 21293. Cambridge, MA: National Bureau of Economic Research.

Brown, Jeffrey R., Robert Clark, and Joshua Rauh. 2011. "The Economics of State and Local Public Pensions." NBER Working Paper 16792. Cambridge, MA: National Bureau of Economic Research.

Bureau of Labor Statistics (BLS). 2014. "Employee Benefit Survey—Retirement Benefits: Access, Participation, and Take-up Rates." www.bls.gov/ncs/ebs/benefits/2014/ownership/govt/table02a.htm.

———. 2015. "Consumer Price Index—All Urban Consumers." www.bls.gov/data/.

Burtless, Gary. 2013. "The Impact of Population Aging and Delayed Retirement on Workforce Productivity." Center for Retirement Research, Boston University.

Butrica, Barbara A., Howard M. Iams, Karen E. Smith, and Eric J. Toder. 2009. "The Disappearing Defined Benefit Pension and Its Potential Impact on the Retirement Incomes of Baby Boomers." *Social Security Bulletin* 69 (3). https://www.ssa.gov/policy/docs/ssb/v69n3/v69n3p1.html.

Centers for Disease Control and Prevention. 2014. Table 18 in "Health, United States, 2013." www.cdc.gov/nchs/data/hus/hus13.pdf.

Choi, James J., David Laibson, Brigitte C. Madrian, and Andrew Metrick. 2002. "Defined Contribution Pensions: Plan Rules, Participant Choices, and the Path of Least Resistance." In *Tax Policy and the Economy*, edited by James M. Poterba. MIT Press.

Clark, Robert L., Lee A. Craig, and Jack W. Wilson. 2003. *A History of Public Sector Pensions in the United States*. University of Pennsylvania Press.

Clark, Robert L., Emma Hanson, and Olivia S. Mitchell. 2015. "Lessons for Public Pensions from Utah's Move to Pension Choice." Pension Research Council Working Paper 2015-05. Philadelphia: The Wharton School, University of Pennsylvania.

Congressional Budget Office (CBO). 2011. "The Underfunding of State and Local Pension Plans." Washington, DC, May.

Congressional Research Service (CRS). 1984. "Designing a Retirement System for Federal Workers Covered by Social Security." Prepared for the House Committee on Post Office and Civil Service. Washington, DC, December.

———. 2011. "Social Security: Mandatory Coverage of New State and Local Government Employees," by Dawn Nuschler, Alison M. Shelton, and John J. Topoleski. Washington, DC, July 25.

———. 2013a. "Cost-of-Living Adjustments for Federal Civil Service Annuities," by Katelin P. Isaacs. Washington, DC, November 1.

———. 2013b. "Federal Employees' Retirement System: The Role of the Thrift Savings Plan," by Katelin P. Isaacs. Washington, DC, March 8.

———. 2014a. "Federal Employees' Retirement System: Benefits and Financing," by Katelin P. Isaacs. Washington, DC, January 30.

———. 2014b. "Federal Employees' Retirement System: Budget and Trust Fund Issues," by Katelin P. Isaacs. Washington, DC, March 24.

———. 2015a. "Federal Employees' Retirement System: Benefits and Financing," by Katelin P. Isaacs. Washington, DC, July 15.

———. 2015b. "Federal Employees' Retirement System: The Role of the Thrift Savings Plan," by Katelin P. Isaacs. Washington, DC, March 10.

Cooper, Michael, and Mary Williams Walsh. 2010. "Alabama Town's Failed Pension Is a Warning." *New York Times*, December 22.

Cowen, Jamie. 2011. "Twenty-Five Years after Federal Pension Reform." Issue Brief 359. Washington, DC: Employee Benefit Research Institute.

Curry, Timothy, and Lynn Shibut. 2000. "The Cost of the Savings and Loan Crisis: Truth and Consequences." *FDIC Banking Review* 13 (2): 26–35.

Dalrymple, Robert, Susan Grad, and Duke Wilson. 1983. "Civil Service Retirement System Annuitants and Social Security." *Social Security Bulletin* 46 (2): 39–59.

Disalvo, Daniel. 2010. "The Trouble with Public Sector Unions." *National Affairs* 5 (Fall). www.nationalaffairs.com/publications/detail/the-trouble-with-public-sector-unions.

Elliott, Douglas J. 2010. "State and Local Pension Funding Deficits: A Primer." Brookings, December 6.

Fabricant, Solomon. 1949. "The Rising Trend of Government Employment." Occasional Paper 29. Cambridge, MA: National Bureau of Economic Research.

Flanagan, Tammy. 2015. "Unlocking the Secrets of FERS." *Government Executive*. www.govexec.com/pay-benefits/retirement-planning/2015/01/unlocking-secrets-fers/103548/.

Gale, William G., Sarah E. Holmes, and David John. 2015. "Social Security Coverage for State and Local Government Workers: A Reconsideration." Brookings, March 31.

Gotbaum, Joshua. 2014. "Why Detroit's Bankruptcy Spared Retirees." *Fortune*, December 4.

Hustead, Edwin C., and Toni Hustead. 2001. "Federal Civilian and Military Retirement Systems." In *Pensions in the Public Sector*, edited by Olivia S. Mitchell and Edwin C. Hustead. University of Pennsylvania Press.

Kaiser Family Foundation. 2012. "State Budget Shortfalls, SFY2013." http://kff.org/other/state-indicator/state-budget-shortfalls-sfy13/.

Lewis, Gregory B., and Yoon Jik Cho. 2011. "The Aging of the State Government Workforce: Trends and Implications" *American Review of Public Administration* 41 (1): 48–60.

Lucas, Deborah J., and Stephen P. Zeldes. 2009. "How Should Public Pension Plans Invest?" *American Economic Review* 99 (2): 527–32.

Masters, Jonathan. 2012. "U.S. Deficits and the National Debt." Council on Foreign Relations. www.cfr.org/united-states/us-deficits-national-debt/p27400.

McGuinn, Patrick. 2014. "Pension Politics: Public Employee Retirement System Reform in Four States." Brown Center on Education Policy. Brookings, February 2014.

Munnell, Alicia, Jean-Pierre Aubry, and Mark Cafarelli. 2014. "Defined Contribution Plans in the Public Sector: An Update." Center for Retirement Research, Boston College, April.

Munnell, Alicia, Jean-Pierre Aubry, and Geoffrey Sanzenbacher. 2014. "Do Public Pensions Help Recruit and Retain High-Quality Workers?" Center for Retirement Research, Boston College, October.

National Association of State Budget Officers (NASBO). 2014. "Summary: Fall 2014 Fiscal Survey of States." December 9. www.nasbo.org/sites/default/files/Fall%20 2014%20Fiscal%20Survey %20of%20States%20Summary.pdf.

———. 2015. "Summaries of Fiscal Year 2016 Proposed Executive Budgets." April 8. www.nasbo.org/sites/default/files/pdf/FY16%20Proposed%20Budget-Summary.pdf.

National Association of State Retirement Administrators (NASRA). 2015. "The Annual Required Contribution Experience of State Retirement Plans, FY01 to FY13," by Keith Brainard and Alex Brown. Washington, DC, March.

National Institute on Retirement Security. 2010. "Strong Public Pensions for Today and Tomorrow." Washington, DC, January.

Novy-Marx, Robert, and Joshua D. Rauh. 2009. "The Liabilities and Risks of State-Sponsored Pension Plans." *Journal of Economic Perspectives* 23 (4): 191–210.

———. 2011. "Public Pension Promises: How Big Are They and What Are They Worth?" *Journal of Finance* 66 (4): 1211–49.

———. 2014. "The Revenue Demands of Public Employee Pension Promises." *American Economic Journal: Economic Policy 2014* 6 (1): 193–229.

Office of Management and Budget (OMB). 2010. Budget of the U.S. Government, FY2011, Historical Tables, Table 7.1. www.whitehouse.gov/omb/budget/Historicals.

Office of Personnel Management (OPM). 1998. "Special Retirement Provisions for Law Enforcement Officers, Fire Fighters, Air Traffic Controllers, and Military Reserve

Technicians (Chapter 46)." www.opm.gov/retirement-services/publications-forms/csrsfers-handbook/c046.pdf.

———. 2013a. "Executive Branch Retirement Statistics: FY2003–2012," by Stanislas Ezoua. April.

———. 2013b. "Federal Employee Benefit Programs: Results from the 2013 Federal Employee Benefits Survey." www.opm.gov/policy-data-oversight/data-analysis-documentation/employee-surveys/2013-program-ratings.pdf.

———. 2015a. "Benefits Officers Center: FERCCA." www.opm.gov/retirement-services/benefits-officers-center/aids/#url=FERCCA.

———. 2015b. "CSRS Information." www.opm.gov/retirement-services/csrs-information/computation/.

———. 2015c. "Historical Federal Workforce Tables." www.opm.gov/policy-data-oversight/data-analysis-documentation/federal-employment-reports/historical-tables/total-government-employment-since-1962/.

———. 2015d. "Our Mission, Role & History: Theodore Roosevelt." www.opm.gov/about-us/our-mission-role-history/theodore-roosevelt/.

Peng, Jun. 2008. *State and Local Pension Fund Management.* Boca Raton, FL: CRC Press.

Pew Charitable Trusts. 2014a. "The Fiscal Health of State Pension Plans: Funding Gap Continues to Grow." April 8.

———. 2014b. "State Public Pension Investment Shift over Past 30 Years." June.

Rajnes, David. 2001. "State and Local Retirement Plans: Innovation and Renovation." Washington, DC: Employee Benefit Research Institute, July.

Schieber, Sylvester J. 2011. "Political Economy of Public Sector Retirement Plans." *Journal of Pension Economics and Finance* 10 (2): 269–90.

Schreitmueller, Richard G. 1988. "The Federal Employees' Retirement System Act of 1986." *Transactions of Society of Actuaries* 40 (1): 543–602.

Social Security Administration (SSA). 2014. "Replacement Rates for Hypothetical Retired Workers." Actuarial Note 2014.9, by Michael Clingman, Kyle Burkhalter, and Chris Chaplain. July.

"Social Security Amendments of 1983." P.L. 98–21, April 20, 1983. Social Security Administration. www.ssa.gov/history/1983amend2.html.

State Budget Solutions. 2013. "Cincinnati Can Learn from Prichard, Alabama on Pension Crisis." www.statebudgetsolutions.org/about_us/newsroom/cincinnati-can-learn-from-prichard-alabama-on-pension-crisis.

———. 2014a. "Pew's Latest Pension Report Understates Unfunded Liabilities, but Still Shows Growing Pension Problem," by Cory Eucalitto. April 4.

———. 2014b. "Promises Made, Promises Broken 2014: Unfunded Liabilities Hit $4.7 Trillion," by Joe Luppino-Esposito. November 12.

Stein, Arthur. 2012. "25 Years Later, FERS Still 'Excellent' Plan for Feds." Interview by Michael O'Connell, Federal News Radio. www.federalnewsradio.com/1084/ 3153999/25-years-later-FERS-still-excellent-plan-for-feds.

University of Michigan. 2015. "Surveys of Consumers." Table 1: The Index of Consumer Sentiment. http://data.sca.isr.umich.edu/data-archive/mine.php.

US Census Bureau. 1993. Historical Data. www2.census.gov /govs/apes/93stlus.txt.

———. 1993–2013a. Annual Survey of Public Employment and Payroll. https://www.census.gov/programs-surveys/apes/data/datasetstables.html.

———. 1993–2013b. Survey of Public Pensions: State & Local Data. https://www.census.gov/programs-surveys/aspp/data.html.

US Government Accountability Office (US GAO). 2012. "State and Local Government Pension Plans: Economic Downturn Spurs Efforts to Address Costs and Sustainability." March.

US House of Representatives. 1983. H.R.1900, Social Security Amendments.

US Senate. 1982. S.2905, Civil Service Pension Reform Act.

"Voluntary Agreements for Coverage of State and Local Employees." 42 U.S.C. § 418, 2010. GPO FDsys. http://www.gpo.gov/fdsys/search/home.action.

Yoder, Eric. 2014. "Phased Retirement to Be Worth More to Some Than Others." *Washington Post*, September 8.

Zernike, Kate. 2015. "New Jersey's Top Court Rules Christie Can Skip Pension Payments." *New York Times*, June 9.

Zorn, Paul. 1999. "Mandatory Social Security Coverage of State and Local Government Employees." Gabriel, Roeder, Smith & Company Research Memorandum, Feb. 5.

TEN

You Get What You Pay For

GUARANTEED RETURNS IN RETIREMENT SAVING ACCOUNTS

William G. Gale, David C. John, and Bryan Kim

The sharp downturn in the value of financial assets resulting from the financial crisis of 2007–2009 serves as a pointed example of how risky assets can quickly lose significant value. This experience, coupled with continuing concerns about retirement security, has generated new interest in the idea of having the government provide minimum rate-of-return guarantees for retirement savings accounts.

Guaranteed returns are not a new concept. Defined contribution plans in several countries provide minimum rate-of-return guarantees, as do some defined contribution plans in the United States. TIAA-CREF's Traditional Annuity is a prominent example of an account with a guaranteed minimum return. Cash balance plans offer savers a fixed rate of return—thus the guaranteed minimum return is equal to the ceiling on returns that the saver can receive. Many 401(k)s and mutual funds offer "stable value" options that guarantee return of the principal.

A variety of proposals would offer guarantees for new types of saving plans, including some state-sponsored retirement saving plans for small businesses. In 2016, state governments in California and Connecticut were actively researching the possibility of offering state-level guarantee programs.

The key economic issues are the level of costs and benefits associated with a government-provided guarantee and who would bear the costs. Guarantees are a classic example of the economics dictum that it is impossible to get something for nothing. In principle, rate-of-return guarantees are simple: they could protect savers from losses and ensure that they receive at least a minimum return on their investments. In practice, they raise a variety of complex issues and are more costly than meets the eye. First, someone—the saver, the plan sponsor, or the taxpayers—has to pay for the guarantee. When the government pays the costs, budget documents tend to severely underreport the economic costs associated with the guarantees. Those costs are resources that have to be forgone in order to finance the promises. When private insurers offer guarantees, the costs reflect the true economic costs more accurately and are often quite high. Second, the net benefits may not be as obvious as they seem, since markets often respond quickly and since for most people Social Security, Medicare, and housing provide the vast bulk of their retirement resources.

Discussion of government provision of guarantees has often been confused by the comingling of different measures of costs. The expected, budgetary cost of a guarantee is simply the discounted value of revenues and payments under the program, where discounting occurs at the government's risk-free rate. This measure describes the impact on the government's budget but it is not sufficient to understand the economic costs and value associated with the program.

The economic costs are a measure of the value of the forgone resources used to implement the guarantee. This measure is the same regardless of whether the government or the private sector provides the guarantee. Ultimately, the level of economic costs and value associated with a guarantee depend on how high the guaranteed rate of return is and what time period is covered. The allocation of those costs—to savers, plan sponsors, and taxpayers—depends on how the guarantee is financed. The financing could be done explicitly through general revenues or premiums paid by workers. It could also be done implicitly via controls over the saver's portfolio choices or a cap on the maximum amount that the saver can earn (or both), with profits above that level going to the government or insurer.

The rest of the chapter is organized as follows. The next section discusses basic design elements, followed by a section that discusses guarantees existing in other countries and in certain US plans, as well as policy proposals. We then discuss the determinants of the level and allocation of economic costs of the guarantees, followed by a review of estimates of those costs.

GUARANTEE DESIGN

A rate-of-return guarantee is essentially an insurance policy that ensures that a saver receives a certain return on her investments. When those investments earn less than the guarantee over a set time period, the saver receives the difference between the actual earnings and the promised amount from the guarantor. If the investments earn more than the guarantee, the investor receives the investment earnings; the insurer (government or private) does not make a payment.[1]

While all minimum rate-of-return guarantees share these basic features, they can differ in a variety of ways. The guarantee can apply to investment returns in a particular year or to cumulative returns over a specified longer period. The promised rate of return can be constant over time or it can vary year by year in response to factors such as economic conditions. For example, an insurer might guarantee a minimum 3 percent return on contributions made in all years, or it might guarantee at least 3 percent on contributions made in the first year but apply some other minimum, say 2.5 percent, on contributions made in following years. Also, the minimum guaranteed return might be enforced at the end of each specified time period or only when the employee changes jobs or retires.

Common rate-of-return guarantees include principal protection only (a guaranteed minimum nominal return of zero), a guarantee that the principal is returned with an adjustment for inflation (a guaranteed minimum real return of zero), or a guarantee based on the rate of return on a specific type of government bond or government bond portfolio. Other guarantees might be based on the rate of return on a specific market portfolio, sometimes expressed as a "reference portfolio" (Consiglio, Tumminello, and Zenios 2015). Alternatively, a guarantee might just promise a nominal return of a set level. Most nominal rate-of-return guarantees are in the 2–4 percent range. Some proposals also include protection against catastrophic market events by limiting losses to a set percentage of the initial investment.[2]

Guarantees are not free. They might be paid for explicitly, via insurance premiums that savers or plan sponsors pay. Alternatively, the costs may be implicit. For example, savers can pay for a guarantee by accepting restrictions on their investment portfolio or allowing the insurer to manage the fund and pay a minimum return plus any additional amount that trustees deem appropriate. In both of these cases with implicit payments, the costs take the form of the savers forgoing potentially higher returns on their investments.

Another way the saver could pay for a minimum guarantee is by selling some of the upside potential returns (Feldstein and Ranguelova 2001a; Smetters 2002). In such a situation, the saver would be guaranteed a minimum rate of return, but there would be a ceiling on the maximum return he could keep from his investments, with any actual return above the ceiling going to the insurer. This combination is usually known as a "collar."[3] For example, the saver might be guaranteed that his investments would earn no less than 3 percent annually. In exchange, the saver would forfeit any upside beyond a specific ceiling (e.g., 6 percent annually) to the insurer. In this scenario, the saver's portfolio is "collared" to generate only a 3–6 percent annual rate of return.

An appropriately designed collar allows the saver to receive a rate-of-return guarantee within a specified band and the insurer to be compensated at market rates for the risk it is underwriting. Note that if the floor and the ceiling are the same rate of return, then the account simply has a guaranteed return, not a guaranteed minimum return.

Figure 10-1 demonstrates the returns to buyers and sellers under minimum return guarantees and collars. With no guarantees or ceilings, the relationship between the rate of return earned on investments and the rate of return received by the saver/employee is given by the 45 degree line *OBCD*. The saver simply receives the actual return. If a guaranteed minimum return is put in place at level *A*, the returns to the saver as a function of actual returns are represented by *ABCD* (not including premium costs). This provides downside protection, as the saver is guaranteed a return of at least *A*. If there is a collar imposed at the actual rate of return given by point *C*, then the saver's returns, as a function of actual returns, are shown by *ABCE*. (If the minimum guaranteed return and the maximum allowed return are the same—as, for example, in a cash balance plan—*B* and *C* would be at the same point and the line *ABCE* would be flat.)

Figure 10-1 also shows the net costs to the insurer as a function of actual returns received. In the graph, a positive number for the insurer reflects a positive cost, and a negative number represents a negative cost (i.e., a positive return). With a minimum guarantee, the returns to the insurer are provided by the line *AFGH*. When the asset generates actual rates of return below *A*, the insurer pays the difference between the actual return and the return given by *A*. When the asset generates actual returns at *A* or above, the insurer pays nothing. If a collar is in place at point *C*, the insurer's costs are given by the line *AFGI*. For returns above C, the cost is negative; that is, the insurer receives the difference between the actual asset return and the ceiling on returns.

Figure 10-1. **Returns to Savers and Insurers under Various Guarantees**

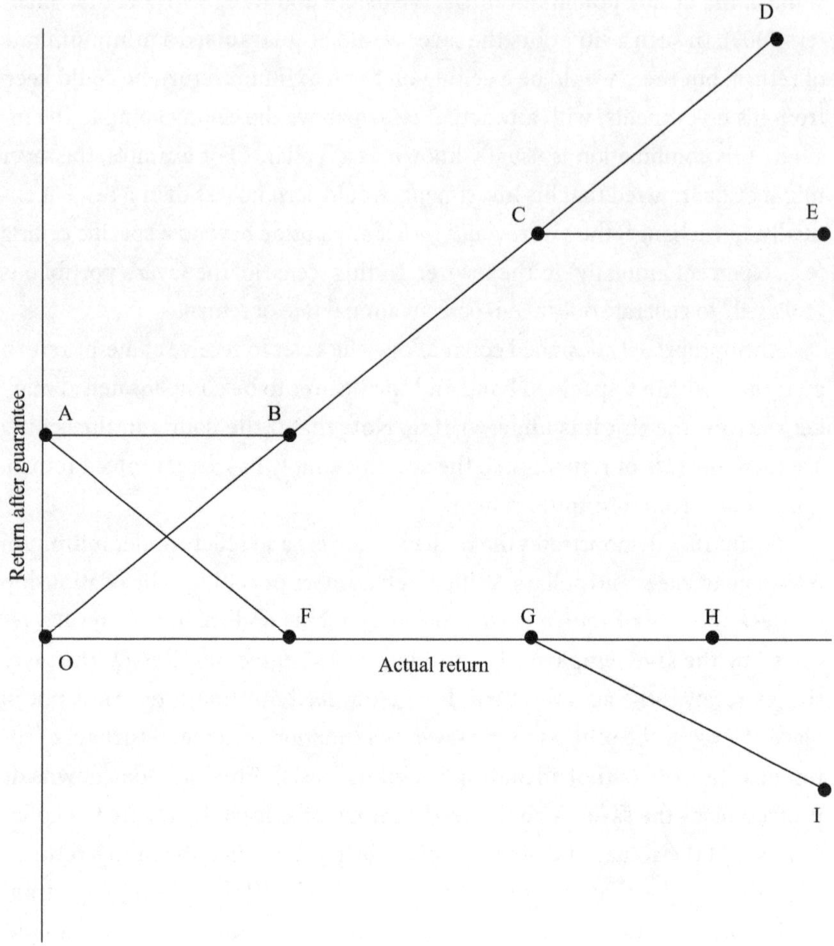

Source: Authors' calculations.

Note: See text for discussion.

EXISTING AND PROPOSED GUARANTEES

Minimum rate-of-return guarantees are offered in a number of existing and proposed plans in both the United States and some other countries around the world (Lachance, Mitchell, and Smetters 2003; Turner and Rajnes 2003, 2009). As an example, several Latin American countries have instituted guarantees, often in conjunction with social security reforms. In Chile, the required return is defined in relation to returns in other plans. Uruguay offers a minimum guarantee that is the lesser of 2 percent real or average returns in the retirement system less 2 percent (Turner 2006).

In Japan, defined contribution plans must offer at least one principal-guaranteed account. In Germany, Reister (defined contribution) plans provide principal guarantees (Lachance and Mitchell 2003). Belgium provides a minimum return of 3.75 percent for employee contributions and 3.25 percent for employer contributions. In Switzerland, pension funds must meet a minimum threshold return that the government sets and periodically adjusts. Denmark has a nationwide, mandatory defined contribution plan that is required to provide a minimum return tied to current long-term interest rates (Muir and Turner 2011). Several other OECD countries have less extensive guarantee programs. The European Union's Third Directive on Life Assurances stipulates that a rate-of-return guarantee cannot exceed 60 percent of the rate of return on government bonds denominated in the relevant currency, gross of taxes (European Commission 2002). The National Provident Fund in New Zealand offers a guaranteed nominal return of 4 percent (National Provident 2014).

In the United States, defined contribution accounts with guaranteed minimum rates of return are rare. The federal Employee Retirement Income Security Act (ERISA) requires that all investment returns be used solely for the benefit of pension participants, with reasonable allowances to defray administrative costs. This makes it very difficult to develop reserve funds that could be used to smooth out actual returns and help meet a guaranteed return target. As a result, US plans that offer guaranteed minimum returns typically exist outside the reach of ERISA. They include plans for state government employees in Ohio and Indiana, as well as plans for public employees in the three Texas counties that seceded from Social Security in the early 1980s.

The TIAA Traditional Annuity offers a guaranteed minimum rate of return. The guarantee is set annually at the time of the contribution and is valid on contributions made in that year until retirement. The rate for new contributions is adjusted each year in conjunction with economic conditions and typically varies between 1 and 3 percent. The TIAA Board of Trustees may also declare, on a year-to-year basis, higher rates of return for a specific year only, but they are not guaranteed for future years. TIAA has credited such additional amounts every year since 1948. The rate of return (the sum of the guaranteed minimum and the credited rate) averaged 8.16 percent per year between 1980 and 2007 (Biggs 2010).[4] In comparison, the S&P 500 averaged a return of

12.86 percent, the Lehman Brothers United States Aggregate Bond Index returned 9.01 percent, and the ten-year Treasury bond yielded an average return of 8.88 percent (Bloomberg 2015; Damodaran 2015).[5]

Cash balance plans are a hybrid form of pension. From the saver's perspective, they closely resemble retirement saving plans, but in legal terms, they are defined benefit plans and are regulated as such. Cash balance plans provide notional accounts for their participants and annually credit a return to each participant's notional account. The plans essentially have a guaranteed return, with both a minimum and maximum set at the same level. As defined benefit plans, cash balance plans are backed by pooled assets that are managed by trustees and can be allocated in part to a reserve fund in years with high returns to help cover the implicit guarantee in low-return years.

The important point is not just that TIAA's Traditional Annuity and cash balance plans provide guaranteed minimum rates of return, but that they finance this guarantee by imposing a fairly low ceiling on returns. This strategy compensates the plan sponsor for risk and controls costs. Savers in these plans receive guaranteed minimum returns and thus avoid the downside possibilities, but they pay for this guarantee by giving up the upside potential for higher returns.

There have been numerous proposals for minimum guaranteed rates of return in the United States. Feldstein and Samwick (2001) propose private accounts in Social Security with a real principal guarantee (an inflation-adjusted minimum return of zero). Feldstein and Ranguelova (2001a) propose what they call "accumulated pension collars" on private retirement accounts as a way of ensuring that partial privatization of Social Security would not reduce benefits relative to current law.

Ghilarducci (2007) proposes a new system of retirement savings accounts managed by a government entity with a minimum guaranteed real return of 3 percent. Importantly, this proposal would set up a system like TIAA's, in which trustees would build and manage a reserve fund and could, but would not have to, allocate additional rates of return to savers (see also Ghilarducci, Hiltonsmith, and Schmitz 2012).

COSTS AND BENEFITS OF GUARANTEES

The benefits of guarantees depend on their effects on the expected level and variability of savers' retirement wealth balances, savers' risk aversion, and the share of retirement wealth that is expected to come from the guaranteed account. The value of a guarantee will also depend on a host of psychological factors, including loss aversion on the downside and regret aversion on the upside. Moreover, guarantees may exploit money illusions on a real basis.

Expected Costs versus Economic Costs

Analyses of the costs of guarantees have often proven to be confusing because they fail to distinguish between the different methods of measuring costs. In particular, adding up the budgetary costs and receipts that were recorded or would be recorded by a government entity that is running a guarantee program reflects the *expected costs* to the government. This is not equivalent to the *economic cost* of providing a guarantee. The economic cost is the value—to the saver and the insurer—of the resources devoted to providing the guarantee. It includes both the actual costs paid out and any investment gains that might have been lost if the saver did not have that guarantee or had a different type of guarantee. Insurers also face economic costs that represent the risk of having underfunded liabilities. The determinants of economic costs are discussed further in the next section.

Feldstein and Ranguelova (2001b) explain how to distinguish between expected cost and economic cost. In their example, a 45-year-old worker contributes $1,000 to an account and allocates 60 percent to the S&P 500 index and 40 percent to corporate bonds. The account makes a single payout at age 65. Assuming that the account earns the historical rates of return for this portfolio, the expected value of the payout would be $3,510.[6] However, the payout amount is subject to uncertainty and the actual return could be higher or lower. Assuming perfect markets, perfect deployment of options pricing techniques, and certain market parameters, the authors show that the saver could buy, at no explicit cost, a collar that provided a minimum guaranteed payout of at least $2,000 and a maximum of $2,610.

Clearly there is an enormous difference between the expected and economic costs of a minimum guaranteed return for this saver's portfolio. The economic cost to the saver of having such a guarantee would be substantial. The saver has an expected payout of $3,510 but can only insure (at no explicit cost) a payout in the range of $2,000 to $2,610. That is, the saver would have to give up about 26 percent of the expected final payout in order to be guaranteed that she will receive at least 57 percent of the expected final payment but no more than about 74 percent of that amount. To be clear, the saver might value the reduced range of uncertainty in returns more than the costs and so might choose to buy the collar in question. However, the saver is not getting something for nothing; she is forgoing considerable, yet uncertain upside benefits in exchange for a less substantial, but certain range of benefits.

This distinction between expected and economic costs explains much of the divergence in the literature, which seems to reach two broad, seemingly contradictory conclusions. One conclusion is that it would not have cost the government (or another insurer) much, if anything, to guarantee reasonably high minimum returns in the past based on ex post returns (Munnell and others 2009; Stubbs and Rhee 2012). The other conclusion is that providing guarantees can result in substantial costs for both an insurer and a saver. These findings may seem even more contradictory when it is noted that the prospective studies base their analysis on asset returns patterns and economic conditions that are taken from historical data. But the discrepancy between these findings is in fact easy to explain. The retrospective analysis focuses on *expected (average) costs* to the insurers of providing guarantees (which, in the cited studies, is reported as the budgetary costs to the government), whereas the prospective analysis examines the *economic costs* to generate cost estimates of guarantee provision.

Determinants of the Level of Economic Costs

The level of economic costs of providing a rate-of-return guarantee will depend on several factors and can vary enormously across different types of guarantees. The first factor is simply the level of the guarantee that is provided. Other things equal, the costs of providing principal guarantees (i.e., a zero nominal return) will be less than the cost of providing any level of positive nominal return. Likewise, as long as inflation is positive, ensuring a real return of *X* percent will cost more than ensuring a nominal return of *X* percent.

A second factor is the time horizon of the guarantee. This can work either way—a longer time horizon can increase or reduce the cost of guarantees depending on the interplay between the guarantee, the saver's portfolio, and the pattern of asset returns (Lachance and Mitchell 2002, 2003). Guarantees that are "tested" more often (e.g., a guarantee that is applied annually, rather than only at retirement or when a saver changes jobs) will be more expensive.

Lachance and Mitchell (2002) argue that the determination of the economic cost should not depend on whether the government or a private insurer provides the guarantee. As they write: "While alternative approaches might be valid depending on the use to which they are put, here we propose to define guarantee cost such that the values generated indicate *true economic resource costs*. If the guarantee commitment were made to the capital market investors, the value of the guarantee could be determined by using option pricing techniques, and a 'market value' approach for the guarantee could be derived. Since the nature of the counterparty should not influence the economic value of the liability, the approach used with capital market investors should also be valid" with government provision of insurance (Lachance and Mitchell 2002, 7).

This suggests that, to a first-order approximation, the *economic* costs would be the same if the insurance were provided by the government or by the private sector. There would be differences in actual pricing, of course. A guarantee set by the government might be priced with political economy factors in mind. On economic grounds, however, a guarantee set by the government should factor in the economy-wide marginal costs of funds. A guarantee set by the private sector would need to account for return on capital, profits, administrative and regulatory costs, and risk management, as well as any market imperfections.

In addition, the government may be able to handle certain long-lived risks better than the private sector, even abstracting from political economy considerations and the day-to-day costs of running a firm. As Smetters (2002) points out, the proposed guarantees that would cover very long time periods can be better handled by government, as the private market does not typically provide such lengthy guarantees. Savers need to know that the insurer will be able to stay in the market long enough to fulfill its contractual obligations. In the presence of nondiversifiable financial risk or intergenerational risk, government is probably better suited than the market to smooth the associated risks.

The private sector would likely either charge very high fees to compensate for taking on such risks, because otherwise it would be unable to provide insurance against massive investment risks, or charge a lower rate and create the potential risk of needing to be bailed out.

Informal evidence suggests that quotes offered by financial institutions for various guarantees are typically higher and often much higher than would be suggested by theoretical calculations using perfect markets.

Determinants of the Allocation of Costs

As noted earlier, someone has to pay for the economic costs of the guarantee. One option is for taxpayers to bear the burdens through general revenues. Another way to cover the costs would be for workers to pay premiums. A third approach would impose the costs on savers by turning the unencumbered offer of a minimum guarantee into an offer that provides the minimum guarantee but also gives the insurer a portion of the upside returns. The most obvious option in this regard is a collar. The cost to the insurer of providing a collar is lower than the cost of providing the same minimum guarantee without a ceiling. The saver would pay for this feature by forgoing returns above a certain level.

Likewise, allowing the insurer to use some of the actual returns from the saver's portfolio in excess of the guaranteed rate to create a reserve fund that can be used to supplement actual returns in years when returns are lower than the guaranteed rates would shift costs to the saver. Both the TIAA Traditional Annuity and cash balance plans are examples of this mechanism, and Ghilarducci (2007) includes this feature as a central part of her proposal for guaranteed returns. To be clear, this approach does not reduce the overall economic costs of the guarantee: it just provides a way for the saver to compensate the guarantor for taking on risk.

More generally, restrictions on the saver's portfolio composition impose costs on savers. Actual portfolio composition is determined by the restrictions placed on portfolio contents by the insurer and the saver's subsequent portfolio construction given those restrictions. It is well understood that, with a minimum rate-of-return guarantee, a saver has an incentive to pursue more risky returns, since the guarantee protects the saver from downside risk. What attracts less attention, however, is the notion that portfolio restrictions can materially affect the risk associated with minimum guarantees. As an extreme example, a guarantee of principal repayment can be honored at zero risk to the insurer by requiring that the saver invest his entire portfolio in FDIC-insured bank accounts. As long as each bank account holds less than the maximum FDIC guarantee, there is no risk of loss. Likewise, a minimum guarantee of the return on Treasury bonds or a broad stock index can be provided by an insurer at no cost if the saver is required to invest his entire portfolio in Treasury bonds or the broad stock index in question. These portfolio restrictions act by exactly matching the risks associated with the guarantee and the risks associated with the assets backing the guarantee. By doing so, they eliminate the risk of insuring the restricted portfolio, and of course, at the same time, they eliminate any benefit of insuring the restricted portfolio. As with collars, tight portfolio restrictions do not eliminate or even affect the total economic costs. They just provide a way for savers to bear the costs.

The minimum guarantee imposes economic costs on the insurer only when there are different risks embodied in the minimum guarantee and in the saver's portfolio. For example, a guaranteed minimum that is tied to inflation or interest rates creates risk for the insurer to the extent that the saver's portfolio contains investments like stocks.

These conclusions imply that any guaranteed return below the risk-free rate of return can be provided at zero risk to the insurer *if suitable portfolio restrictions are placed on the saver.*[7] Likewise, even returns that are *expected* to be above the risk-free rate—such as that on a broad portfolio of stocks—can be insured at no or little cost of loss if the saver's portfolio is required to match the nature of the guarantee.[8] But "bond-style" guarantees (that insure something akin to an interest rate) are risky to the insurer and are of benefit to the saver if they underwrite portfolios that contain riskier assets like stocks; as expected, the risk to insurers and benefits to the saver grow with the equity share of the portfolio.

PREVIOUS ESTIMATES

In this section, we review several studies that estimate the costs of rate-of-return guarantees under different economic conditions and assumptions. Cost estimates differ widely depending on the assumptions used. Earlier work on the cost of pension guarantees was conducted by Pesando (1982), Marcus (1985, 1987), Bodie and Merton (1993), Bodie (2001b), Smetters (2001, 2002), and Feldstein and Ranguelova (2001a, 2001b).

Munnell and others (2009) provide both retrospective and prospective estimates of the costs of guarantees. Retrospectively, they find that, under certain circumstances and assumptions, including the use of ex post returns, the *budgetary (expected)* cost to the government of having provided even a fairly high minimum rate-of-return guarantee would have been quite small. Prospectively, they find that the *economic* costs of providing guarantees going forward could be expensive under a number of conditions, even under assumptions that would generate the same low budgetary costs that they obtained using historical data. But they also show that, under a variety of conditions, the economic costs of providing certain guarantees would be small or vanishing.

Their retrospective calculations are based on a model in which workers enter the workforce at age 22, work for forty-three years with real annual wage growth of 2 percent, and then retire at age 65. Workers contribute 4 percent of their wages to a retirement account and invest the funds entirely in equities. The calculations cover eighty-four cohorts, beginning with the cohort of 24-year-olds in 1883 who reached age 65 in 1925, and ending with the cohort that was 65 years old in 2008. During that period, real stock market returns averaged 7.6 percent per year, with a standard deviation of 19.5 percent.

The authors examine the frequency and size of payments that a guarantor would have had to make in order to provide workers when they reached age 65 with real returns ranging from 2 percent to 6 percent on their lifetime contributions. Remarkably, they show that guaranteeing a real return of 3 percent on lifetime contributions would never have required the insurer to make a payment. Moving to a real return of 4 percent would have triggered payments only three times, twice at the onset of the Depression—in 1931 and 1932—at 0.06 percent and 0.17 percent of GDP, and once in 1941, at just 0.01 percent of GDP.[9] Even a real required 5 percent rate of return would have required payment in only eight years, all between 1931 and 1948, averaging 0.35 percent of GDP in those years (and averaging just 0.13 percent except in 1931 and 1932). However, guaranteeing a real return of 6 percent would have cost substantially more—payments would have been triggered in twenty-seven of the eighty-four years and would have averaged 0.57 percent of GDP in those years.

These calculations assume that the insurer only provides a floor on returns. The net cost of guarantees to the insurer, however, depends on whether there is a ceiling as well. If there were a guaranteed real annual return (i.e., both a floor and a ceiling) of 6 percent on lifetime contributions, with the insurer being able to keep the upside returns as reserves to be used when needed, the collar would have had *negative* net costs of 0.8 percent of GDP over the entire time period. It is crucial to note this retrospective analysis looks at the insurer's (presumably the government's) budget costs—the expected values of payments and receipts; it does not calculate the economic cost of providing the insurance. Nevertheless, the analysis shows that the expected budgetary costs could have been negative over the 1925–2008 period even under a very generous guarantee program.

Moving to analysis of the prospective *economic* costs to the insurer, the authors use finance theory to calculate the market price of future guarantees. Their estimates of the prospective economic costs are based on several key assumptions: the insurers' aversion to risk matches that of the market; the saver is invested in an all-equity portfolio; future equity returns follow a random

Table 10-1. *Cost Estimates of Alternative Minimum Guarantees as a Percentage of Contributions*[a]

	Insurers are as risk averse as the market			*Insurers are half as risk averse as the market*		
Rate of return	*Price of floor*	*Price of ceiling*	*Price of collar*[b]	*Price of floor*	*Price of ceiling*	*Price of collar*[b]
2	29	29	0	13	97	−84
3	46	22	24	23	83	−60
4	71	16	55	40	68	−28
5	107	11	97	66	53	13
6	157	7	150	106	40	66
7	224	4	220	163	28	135

Source: Munnell and others (2009).
[a] Saver's portfolio is assumed to be all equity.
[b] Price of collar = price of floor less price of ceiling.

walk with the same mean and standard deviation as the historical data; and there is a 2 percent real risk-free rate of return.

Table 10-1 shows their estimates. The price of a floor at 2 percent (the risk-free rate) is 29 percent of contributions. That is, for every dollar contributed to the plan, an additional 29 cents would have to be paid just for the guarantee. Thus a saver would have to contribute $1.29 to make a $1 contribution with a guaranteed return. Another way to think of this is that, for every dollar the saver contributes, 22.5 cents goes to a guarantee, and only the remaining 77.5 percent is invested. This estimate depends critically on the saver's portfolio. If the saver were required to invest in the risk-free asset, the costs would be much lower. Any other administrative costs for the plan would be on top of the cost for the guarantee.

As the floor rises, the required fee rises more than proportionately. A 3 percent real floor would cost 46 percent of contributions, a 4 percent real floor would cost 71 percent of contributions, and a 6 percent real floor would cost 157 percent of contributions. Obviously, such premiums would make it virtually impossible for any saver to achieve any rate of return in excess of the guaranteed rate even with a portfolio of 100 percent equities.

As before, if there is a ceiling as well as a floor, the economic costs to the insurer and the saver fall. Guaranteeing a fixed—minimum and maximum—return of 2 percent would be costless to the insurer under the stated assumptions (since it is the risk-free rate). Guaranteeing 4 percent would require a payment of 55 percent of contributions. More interesting results appear if one allows the floor and the ceiling to diverge. For example, a 2 percent floor with a 6 percent ceiling would cost 22 percent of contributions.

If the insurer is only half as risk averse as the market, these figures change substantially and the economic costs fall dramatically. Under these assumptions, the price of a 2 percent floor is only 13 percent. It can even be coupled with a 7 percent ceiling and still have a negative economic cost to the insurer. Indeed, a floor/ceiling combination of 3 percent and 7 percent or 4 percent and 6 percent could be handled at no economic cost to the insurer. Interpolating from the table results, a guaranteed real return of about 4.6 percent should be possible to achieve at no net economic cost to the insurer under these assumptions. Companies offering such a guarantee would still need to charge for administrative costs associated with the guarantee and would include an amount for profit.

Lachance and Mitchell (2002, 2003) estimate the costs of minimum guarantees for principal repayment (i.e., a guaranteed minimum nominal return of zero) and one equal to the Treasury ten-year bond rates. They define the cost as the price that would be charged by market participants to provide the guarantee, using option pricing techniques, and obtain several major results.

First, as expected, the more stringent the minimum guarantee, the more expensive it is to finance. If backed by a saver portfolio that is split evenly between stocks and bonds, nominal and principal guarantees have almost no cost—less than 0.5 percent of contributions over forty years. With the same portfolio, bond return guarantees, which are significantly more stringent than the other principal guarantees, cost more—16.1 percent of contributions.

Second, the costs of insurance depend dramatically on the saver's portfolio. A higher equity share in the saver's portfolio raises the cost. This occurs because the higher expected return of equities becomes more volatile over the long term as the equity share rises (Bodie 2001a). In contrast, if the saver can be restricted to holding an all-bond portfolio, or chooses to do so voluntarily, there is no cost to any of the guarantees examined.

Third, the results vary in a nonmonotonic way with respect to the duration of the guarantee. The longer time duration raises the costs of the bond return guarantee but reduces the cost of the nominal principal guarantee. For example, for an all-stock portfolio, the cost of a nominal principal guarantee falls from 3.6 percent of lifetime contributions over ten years to just 0.8 percent over forty years. In contrast, for the same all-stock portfolio, the cost of a bond return rises from 16.1 percent of contributions over ten years to

31.3 percent over forty years. In both cases the value of the underlying stock portfolio becomes more volatile over time, which should raise guarantee costs (Bodie 2001a). But in the case of the principal guarantee, the real value of the guarantee decays over time, assuming inflation is positive, which offsets the volatility effect.

Lachance and Mitchell (2002) also report data on required fees as a share of net asset value, shown in the right half of table 10-2. Two of the three main results above continue to hold. More stringent guarantees generate higher costs, controlling for the saver's portfolio. Higher equity shares raise costs as well. What is different is that longer duration uniformly reduces costs *as a share of net asset value*, including for the all-equity proposal, whereas costs rise with the duration for the all-equity portfolio *as a share of lifetime contributions*. This difference occurs because expected net asset value is higher when savers have an all-equity portfolio than when they have a portfolio evenly split between stocks and bonds, but lifetime contributions are the same in the two cases.[10]

Grande and Visco (2010) examine the potential economic costs of insuring minimum rate-of-return guarantees in the European market. They examine three minimum guarantees: a nominal principal guarantee (a zero nominal rate of return), a 2.5 percent nominal return (which they take as approximately a real principal guarantee—that is, a minimum real return of zero), and a return equal to the annual nominal GDP growth rate. Table 10-3 shows that their estimates of the economic costs of guarantees share several features with those of Lachance and Mitchell (2002, 2003) but differ in an important way as well. Grande and Visco (2010) obtain three results very similar to Lachance and Mitchell's: (1) costs relative to lifetime contributions are higher for more stringent guarantees; (2) the costs rise with the equity share of the saver's portfolio and are zero for the nominal and real principal guarantee if the saver invests the portfolio entirely in bonds; and (3) the costs of the most stringent portfolio option rise over time with the all-equity proposal. As in Lachance and Mitchell's (2002) estimate, the costs of the most stringent guarantee fall over time as a share of net asset value, even if the saver holds all equities in his portfolio. Again, this is due to the expected growth over time of the assets in the portfolio.

Grande and Visco (2010) have significantly higher cost estimates for rate of return guarantees than Lachance and Mitchell (2002). Grande and Visco (2010) estimate the cost of a nominal principal guarantee as 11.4 percent of contributions over ten years and 6.39 percent of contributions over forty years when the saver has an all-equity portfolio. Lachance and Mitchell (2002, 2003)

Table 10-2. *Cost Estimates of Alternative Minimum Guarantees*

		Guarantee cost as a percentage of lifetime contributions			*Guarantee cost as a percentage of net asset value*		
Saver's portfolio	*Investment horizon*	*Principal (zero nominal return)*	*Real principal (zero real return)*	*Treasury ten-year bond rate*	*Principal (zero nominal return)*	*Real principal (zero real return)*	*Treasury ten-year bond rate*
100% Equity	10 years	3.6	8.2	16.1	0.60	1.36	2.67
	40 years	0.8	5.9	31.3	0.03	0.24	1.27
50% Equity/	10 years	0.2	2.0	8.1	0.04	0.33	1.35
50% Bonds	40 years	0.0	0.5	16.1	0.00	0.02	0.65
100% Bonds	10 years	0.0	0.0	0.0	0.00	0.00	0.00
	40 years	0.0	0.0	0.0	0.00	0.00	0.00

Source: Lachance and Mitchell (2002, 2003).

Table 10-3. *Cost Estimates of Alternative Minimum Guarantees*

		Guarantee cost as a percentage of lifetime contributions			*Guarantee cost as a percentage of total asset value*		
Saver's portfolio	*Investment horizon*	*Principal (zero nominal return)*	*Nominal 2.5 percent*	*Yearly nominal GDP growth rate*	*Principal (zero nominal return)*	*Nominal 2.5 percent*	*Yearly nominal GDP growth rate*
100% Equity	10 years	11.40	18.48	23.49	1.47	2.39	3.04
	40 years	6.39	20.05	37.17	0.26	0.83	1.54
50% Equity/	10 years	2.68	7.42	11.81	0.35	0.97	1.54
50% Bonds	40 years	0.48	6.22	19.27	0.02	0.26	0.81
100% Bonds	10 years	0.00	0.00	3.33	0	0	0.44
	40 years	0.00	0.00	5.53	0	0	0.23
Lifecycle[a]	10 years	1.89	12.37	28.71	0.08	0.52	0.93
	40 years	0.22	2.65	7.16	0.03	0.34	1.20

Source: Grande and Visco (2010).

[a] Lifecycle = initial investment in equities, which is converted into bonds ten years before retirement date.

estimate these costs at 3.6 percent and 0.8 percent, respectively. Similar differences persist across different savers' portfolios and different types of guarantees. These differences stem from the fact that the two sets of authors use different assumptions about risk-free interest rates, stock volatility, and the source of the error terms used to simulate randomized stock market time-series patterns.[11] A key factor in the higher cost estimates by Grande and Visco (2010) is their assumption that stocks will be much more volatile, which increases the possibility that the guarantor will suffer losses.

Interestingly, Grande and Visco (2010) also provide estimates of the costs of guarantees assuming that savers use a lifecycle investment strategy in which they hold all of their portfolio in equities until age 55 and then shift the percentage linearly to zero by age 65. The benefits of the lifecycle portfolio strategy are clear. The forty-year costs of guaranteeing a fund are lower for all three guarantee options under the lifecycle investment strategy than they are under either the all-equity portfolio or the 50-50 split portfolio.

Scheuenstuhl and others (2011) examine several different guarantees, including a nominal return of zero, a real return of zero, nominal returns of 2 and 4 percent, and a floating guarantee of a return that equals current government bond interest rates plus one percentage point. For their calculations, the authors assume investors use a lifecycle investment strategy over forty years using an approach similar to Grande and Visco's (2010). The saver's portfolio is 80 percent invested in equities and 20 percent in government bonds until age 55. At that point, the equity allocation is linearly reduced to 20 percent by age 65. The authors then specify how much money would be needed to finance a given guarantee in the private market; that is, they calculate the fair value of a guarantee based on a risk-neutral pricing framework. However, they also note that guarantee prices in the real world might deviate from their estimates because of transaction costs, liquidity premiums, and solvency and capital requirements, and thus could be higher than those they estimate.

In general, Scheuenstuhl and others (2011) reach similar results as the other researchers. They find that costs rise with the stringency of the guarantee. They also find that costs of providing a guarantee fall as the duration of the guarantee period increases. Given that Scheuenstuhl and colleagues assume that savers follow a lifecycle investment strategy, their results are most comparable to, and are consistent with, those in Grande and Visco (2010), which also assumes that savers are lifecycle investors. Their cost estimates differ from those of other studies that use different portfolio assumptions. This highlights the importance of the saver's portfolio (either through the saver's choice or through restrictions placed by the insurer) in determining the costs of a guarantee.

The importance of how the portfolio is structured is emphasized by additional lifecycle investment strategies that start with lower initial allocations to equity (50 percent and 20 percent, rather than the 80 percent in the base case) and have lower costs. This is consistent with the general point that, other things equal (where other things might include the final allocation to equity and the date at which a saver starts shifting to bonds), a higher equity share in the saver's portfolio raises the costs of providing a minimum guarantee.

Finally, although the cost estimates are not quite comparable to other research because they use different saver portfolio assumptions, the estimates by Scheuenstuhl and others (2011) appear to be between those of Lachance and Mitchell (2002, 2003) and Grande and Visco (2010). For example, they estimate that guaranteeing a nominal return of zero over forty years in their lifestyle portfolio would require premiums of 1.244 percent of contributions (table 10-4). Grande and Visco (2010) find that the same guarantee would vary in cost depending on whether savers' portfolios were all equity (6.39 percent), all bonds (0.48 percent), or invested in a lifecycle portfolio (0.22 percent). Lachance and Mitchell (2002, 2003) find that the same guarantee would cost 0.8 percent of contributions if savers held an all-equity portfolio and nothing if savers held evenly split portfolios.[12]

COSTS ULTIMATELY EXCEED BENEFITS

The steep losses suffered by savers close to retirement during the financial crisis of 2007–2009 motivated an increase in attention to rate-of-return guarantees for retirement saving plans. Although guarantees in various forms clearly offer some benefits to savers, the benefits come at a cost. The costs can be paid in many different ways, including insurance premiums, caps on the maximum returns that savers can receive on their investments, or portfolio restrictions. The last option may also serve to cap returns and limit the risks that savers can take. In any of those cases, the true economic costs of providing a guarantee will substantially exceed the expected budgetary costs to the government of offering the guarantee. A private insurer would likely charge the economic cost to offer a guarantee. The government might not, for political reasons, but that does not make the economic costs disappear.

Table 10-4. *Cost Estimates of Alternative Minimum Guarantees*

Saver's portfolio	*Investment horizon*	*Guarantee cost as a percentage of lifetime contributions*					*Guarantee cost as a percentage of net asset value*				
		Principal (zero return)	*Real inflation*	*Nominal 2%*	*Nominal 4%*	*Floating*[a]	*Principal (zero return)*	*Real inflation*	*Nominal 2%*	*Nominal 4%*	*Floating*[a]
Lifecycle	20 years	. . .[b]	. . .	. . .	. . .	. . .	0.24	0.843	0.886	4.036	3.321
(80% equity, 20% bonds)	40 years	1.244	5.583	4.936	18.709	26.088	0.055	0.241	0.218	0.887	1.224
Lifecycle	20 years	. . .	. . .	. . .	. . .	. . .	. . .	. . .	. . .	. . .	. . .
(50% equity, 50% bonds)	40 years	–	. . .	. . .	. . .	. . .	0.027	0.154	0.138	0.705	0.900
Lifecycle	20 years	–	. . .	. . .	. . .	. . .	. . .	. . .	. . .	. . .	. . .
(20% equity, 80% bonds)	40 years	–	. . .	. . .	. . .	. . .	0.007	0.071	0.062	0.490	0.441

Source: Scheuenstuhl and others (2011).

[a] Floating = current interest rate + 1 percent.

[b] . . . = not applicable.

NOTES

We gratefully acknowledge helpful comments from Jeffrey Brown, Hilary Gelfond, Ted Gayer, Joshua Gotbaum, Richard Kopcke, Aaron Krupkin, Olivia Mitchell, Kent Smetters, and Anthony Webb. We thank the Laura and John Arnold Foundation for funding this work. The findings and conclusions contained within are solely the responsibility of the authors and do not necessarily reflect positions or policies of any organization with which they are associated or their funders.

1. For those familiar with investing, the creation of a minimum rate-of-return guarantee is the equivalent of the saver/employee buying a put option from the insurer. A put option gives the saver the opportunity to sell an asset to the counterparty (the insurer), who is required to buy it if it is offered for sale by a given date for a given price. For example, if the saver contributes $100 and the annual rate-of-return guarantee is 3 percent, the insurer commits to make up any shortfall between the actual account value at the end of the year and $103.

2. All of the options mentioned in the text guarantee rates of return on contributions. Rather than ensuring a minimum rate of return, guarantees could instead be provided for a minimum level of wealth at retirement, regardless of contribution levels. Neither rate-of-return guarantees nor minimum wealth guarantees, however, ensure a particular level of retirement income, since the rate that can be earned on an annuity varies over time. Thus a third type of guarantee would ensure a minimum level of retirement income or minimum rate at which assets could be annuitized. In this chapter we focus on rate-of-return guarantees during the buildup stage.

3. The creation of a maximum rate of return allowed for the saver is the equivalent of the saver/employee selling a call option to the insurer. A call option gives the owner (the insurer, in this case) the opportunity to sell an asset to the counterparty (in this case, the saver/employee), who is required to buy it if it is offered for sale by a given date for a given price. For example, if the saver contributes $100 and the annual rate-of-return maximum is 6 percent, the saver commits to give up any excess of the actual account value at the end of the year over $106.

4. The Traditional Annuity is a guaranteed benefit policy. The assets backing guaranteed benefit policies are not plan assets subject to ERISA and thus not subject to ERISA requirements regarding asset management.

5. Average returns/yields calculated as compound annual averages over the period 1986–2007.

6. In this case, the historical rates of return have a mean of 5.5 percent and standard deviation of 12.5 percent.

7. The saver might still be required to pay fees that cover administrative or regulatory costs.

8. There is little or no risk of loss, but the firm still has to cover cost of capital and profit margin as compared to other uses of the resources.

9. While a cost as a percentage of GDP might be sustainable for a government, it would be far higher than any private insurer could bear.

10. Even though equities are assumed to be more volatile, they are assumed to have a greater average return than bonds.

11. First, Grande and Visco use a higher risk-free interest rate. Second, they assume that stock market prices follow a stochastic process with jumps. With no jumps, the underlying process has annual volatility of 16 percent. The process has an expected 1.8 jumps per year, with an average jump size of –12.8 percent (i.e., the stock market declines). In contrast, Lachance and Mitchell assume volatility of 20 percent with no jumps. Third, Grande and Visco generate the distribution of shocks to stock returns using data from 2000–2002. Lachance and Mitchell use stock data from 1926–2000. The first difference should reduce Grande and Visco's estimates relative to Lachance and Mitchell's, while the second should have the opposite effect. The impact of the third difference is unclear a priori.

12. Scheuenstuhl and others (2011) also utilize risk-neutral valuation techniques to derive their cost estimates. However, they conceptualize bond returns using a Hull-White process rather than the Vasicek process that Lachance and Mitchell (2002, 2003) and Grande and Visco (2010) employ. The primary difference between the Vasicek and Hull-White processes is that the Hull-White model allows for time dependency in some of the coefficients.

REFERENCES

Aresimowicz, Joe, and Martin Looney. 2014. S.B. No. 249. *An Act Promoting Retirement Savings.*

Biggs, John. 2010. "How TIAA-CREF Funded Plans Differ from a Typical 401(k) Plan." *Trends and Issues* (February). TIAA-CREF Institute.

Bloomberg LP. 2015. Total Return Analysis Graph for Barclays Aggregate US Bond Index. New York.

Bodie, Zvi. 2001a. "On the Risk of Stocks in the Long Run." *SSRN Electronic Journal.* doi:10.2139/ssrn.5771.

———. 2001b. "Retirement Investing: A New Approach." *SSRN Electronic Journal.* doi:10.2139/ssrn.260628.

Bodie, Zvi, and Robert C. Merton. 1993. "Pension Benefit Guarantees in the United States: A Functional Analysis." In *The Future of Pensions in the United States.* University of Pennsylvania Press.

Consiglio, Andrea, Michele Tumminello, and Stavros A. Zenios. 2015. "Designing Guarantee Options in Defined Contribution Pension Plans." *SSRN Electronic Journal.* doi:10.2139/ssrn.2563087.

Damodaran, Aswath. 2015. "Annual Returns on Stock, T.Bonds and T.Bills: 1928—Current." Stern School of Business, New York University.

De León, Kevin. 2012. S.B. No. 1234. *California Secure Choice Retirement Savings Trust Act.*

European Commission. 2002. *Directive 2002/83/EC Concerning Life Assurance.* https://eur-lex.europa.eu/legal-content/EN/ALL/?uri=CELEX%3A32002L0083.

Feldstein, Martin, and Elena Ranguelova. 2001a. "Accumulated Pension Collars: A Market Approach to Reducing the Risk of Investment-Based Social Security Reform." In *Tax Policy and the Economy*, vol. 15, edited by James M. Poterba. MIT Press.

Feldstein, Martin, and Elena Ranguelova. (2001b). "Individual Risk in an Investment-Based Social Security System." NBER Working Paper 8074. Cambridge, MA: National Bureau of Economic Research.

Feldstein, Martin, and Andrew Samwick. 2001. "Potential Paths of Social Security Reform." NBER Working Paper 8592. Cambridge, MA: National Bureau of Economic Research.

Ghilarducci, Teresa. 2007. "Guaranteed Retirement Accounts: Toward Retirement Income Security." EPI Briefing Paper 204. Washington, DC: Economic Policy Institute.

Ghilarducci, Teresa, Robert Hiltonsmith, and Lauren Schmitz. 2012. "State Guaranteed Retirement Accounts: A Low-Cost, Secure Solution to America's Retirement Crisis." Schwartz Center for Economic Policy Analysis, The New School.

Grande, Giuseppe, and Ignazio Visco. 2010. "A Public Guarantee of a Minimum Return to Defined Contribution Pension Scheme Members." Working Paper 742. Rome: Banca D'Italia.

Lachance, Marie-Eve, and Olivia Mitchell. 2002. "Understanding Individual Account Guarantees." NBER Working Paper 9195. Cambridge, MA: National Bureau of Economic Research.

———. 2003. "Guaranteeing Individual Accounts." *American Economic Review* 93 (2): 257–60.

Lachance, Marie-Eve, Olivia S. Mitchell, and Kent Smetters. 2003. "Guaranteeing Defined Contribution Pensions: The Option to Buy Back a Defined Benefit Promise." *Journal of Risk & Insurance* 70 (1): 1–16. doi:10.1111/1539-6975.00044.

Marcus, Alan. 1987. "Corporate Pension Policy and the Value of PBGC Insurance." In *Issues in Pension Economics*, edited by Zvi Bodie, John B. Shoven, and David A. Wise. University of Chicago Press.

Marcus, Alan J. 1985. "Spinoff/Terminations and the Value of Pension Insurance." *Journal of Finance* 40 (3): 911–24. doi:10.1111/j.1540-6261.1985.tb05018.x.

Muir, Dana M., and John A. Turner. 2011. *Imagining the Ideal Pension System: International Perspectives.* W. E. Upjohn Institute for Employment Research. Kalamazoo, MI: Upjohn Institute Press.

Munnell, Alicia H., Alex Golub-Sass, Richard W. Kopcke, and Anthony Webb. 2009. *What Does It Cost to Guarantee Returns?* 9–4. Center for Retirement Research, Boston College.

National Provident. 2014. *National Provident Pension Scheme: Summarized Annual Report.* Peterborough, UK.

Pesando, James. 1982. "Valuing Pensions (Annuities) with Different Types of Inflation Protection in Total Compensation Comparisons." NBER Working Paper 956. Cambridge, MA: National Bureau of Economic Research.

Scheuenstuhl, Gerhard, Sandra Blome, David Karim, Matthias Moch, and Stefanie Brandt. 2011. "Assessing the Nature of Investment Guarantees in Defined Contribution Pension Plans." Financial Study. Zurich: RiskLab.

Smetters, Kent. 2001. "The Equivalence of the Social Security's Trust Fund Portfolio Allocation and Capital Income Tax Policy." NBER Working Paper 8259. Cambridge, MA: National Bureau of Economic Research.

———. 2002. "Controlling the Cost of Minimum Benefit Guarantees in Public Pension Conversions." *Journal of Pension Economics and Finance* 1 (01). doi:10.1017/S1474747202001014.

Stubbs, David M., and Nari Rhee. 2012. "Can a Publicly Sponsored Retirement Plan for Private Sector Workers Guarantee Benefits at No Risk to the State?" Policy Brief. Center for Labor Research and Education, UC Berkeley.

Turner, John A. 2006. *Individual Accounts for Social Security Reform: International Perspectives on the U.S. Debate*. W. E. Upjohn Institute for Employment Research. Kalamazoo, MI: Upjohn Institute Press.

Turner, John A., and David Rajnes. 2003. "Retirement Guarantees in Voluntary Defined Contribution Systems." In *The Pension Challenge*, edited by Olivia S. Mitchell and Kent Smetters. Oxford University Press.

———. 2009. "Guarantee Durability: Pension Rate of Return Guarantees in a Market Meltdown." Turin, Italy: Center for Research on Pensions and Welfare Policy, Collegio Carlo Alberto.

ELEVEN

From Saving to Spending

A PROPOSAL TO CONVERT RETIREMENT ACCOUNT BALANCES INTO AUTOMATIC AND FLEXIBLE INCOME

David C. John, William G. Gale, J. Mark Iwry, and Aaron Krupkin

In response to a nationwide poll in 2019, 73 percent of Americans said they do not have the financial skills to manage their money in retirement.[1] Converting retirement savings balances into a stream of retirement income requires making difficult choices. The necessary decisions—made in the presence of uncertainty about investment returns, future health care expenses, lifespan, and other factors—must balance the twin goals to maintain one's current living standards and avoid outliving one's assets.

For many people, the solution will involve some form of guaranteed lifetime income—benefits that will be paid regularly as long as the individual survives. Social Security benefits, for example, provide lifetime income, as do payments from defined benefit (DB) pension plans. However, Social Security provides only a modest income for most people, and DB pensions are disappearing in the private sector. The only other way to generate a guaranteed lifetime income stream is through a commercial income annuity, but very few people purchase these contracts.

New and innovative financial products, however, are disrupting traditional markets by offering alternative ways to receive retirement income. New approaches combine existing products in different ways. Although they do not always provide guaranteed lifetime income, the innovations nevertheless can give savers options and features that annuities do not provide.

In this chapter we explore these nonannuity options and propose a default decumulation solution that could be added to retirement plans in much the same way that automatic choices have simplified enrollment, contribution, and investment allocation decisions for millions of savers.[2] Our proposal centers on pooled investment accounts known as managed payout funds that deliver monthly income that is likely, though not guaranteed, to last a lifetime. Coupled with longevity annuities that begin to make payments when the owner reaches an advanced age, managed payout funds could help protect retirees from longevity risk without unduly reducing their current living standards. Unlike many annuities, these managed payout funds allow retirees to revise their decisions as circumstances change.

Retirement systems across the world are dealing with the same issues and considering many of the same solutions. While still in its early stages, this growing international consensus is similar to the one that has prompted the adoption of automatic enrollment and similar features in many countries.

We first provide background information on the need for guaranteed retirement income and the role of annuities. We then discuss managed payout funds in the United States and in other countries. We follow with a proposal for an automatic and flexible retirement income solution for American savers. In the appendix we review current retirement income discussions and evolving proposals in the United Kingdom, Australia, New Zealand, and Canada.

ANNUITIES AND THE NEED FOR GUARANTEED INCOME

Social Security is the primary source of retirement income in the United States. The program provides at least half of income during retirement for more than three-fifths of beneficiaries and at least 90 percent of income during retirement to more than one-third of beneficiaries.[3] Yet it is widely agreed that most US households need additional income to maintain their preretirement living standards.

Individual savings have always played a role in providing retirement income. Until relatively recently, many retirees also received income from employer-sponsored defined benefit pension plans. These plans typically pay regular monthly benefits or, in many cases, an optional lump sum, based on a formula that usually accounts for the recipient's highest earnings, length of tenure with the employer, and other factors. However, DB plans cover fewer workers in the private sector than they used to, for a variety of reasons. Many private sector employers have replaced DB plans with other retirement saving plans—predominantly the 401(k) plan for employer-sponsored retirement benefits and the Individual Retirement Account (IRA) for individual savers.[4]

The strengths and weaknesses of those plans during the saving phase have been extensively discussed elsewhere and are beyond the scope of this chapter. Retirement saving plans place the burden of funding retirement benefits on the worker, although many employers provide matching contributions. The amount of retirement income from those plans is limited to either the contributions plus any investment returns or the level of benefits those assets can buy. This system exposes the saver to the risks associated with poor investment returns, as well as the possibility of running out of money in old age. According to one survey, about two-thirds of adults believe there is a chance they will outlive their retirement savings.[5] Simply withdrawing savings without guidance can lead to problems. Poterba, Venti, and Wise (2011) found that wealthier retirees tend to be conservative about withdrawing their retirement assets, possibly because they want to leave a bequest, while those who are poorer tend to withdraw assets more rapidly.

Some retirees are willing simply to draw down their savings, exposing themselves to investment and longevity risks; others choose the more stable and certain income streams that annuities provide. The traditional form of annuity—an income annuity—is a contract with an insurance company in which an individual purchases a guaranteed income stream in return for a set premium. An immediate annuity, the most well-known type, pays purchasers a lump sum in advance for the right to a regular, scheduled amount of income for the rest of their life. Payments start either immediately or shortly after purchase. Many such contracts allow savers to choose from a range of additional features in return for a smaller monthly benefit. These include joint and survivor benefits for the lives of two married annuitants, a guarantee that payments will be made for a fixed period to the owner or a designated beneficiary, or a lump-sum death benefit.

A deferred-income annuity is similar, but it delays the start date of payments, usually by several years. In return for the delay, the annuitant receives a higher monthly payment. In theory, if the purchaser dies before benefits begin, she forfeits the purchase price to the insurance carrier. However, as with

Figure 11-1. **Preference for Retirement Products among NEST Customers**

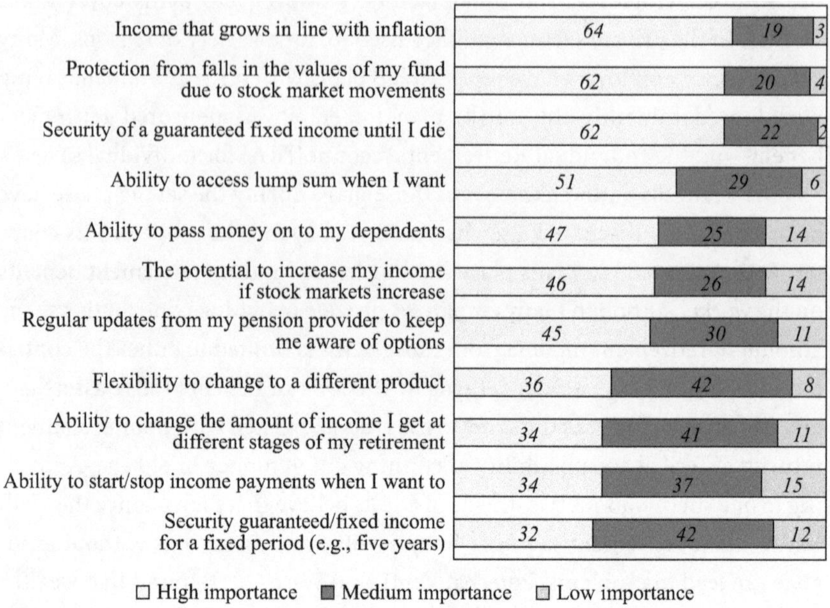

Source: National Employment Savings Trust (2015, figure 3.1).

immediate annuities, most companies offer various types of guarantees, such as a lump-sum death benefit or a guarantee that payments will be made for at least a set number of years in return for a reduced monthly payment.[6]

In principle, the guaranteed income stream provided by annuities offers fairly obvious value for many retirees. Retirees face competing risks in deciding how much to spend each year. The more they spend, the greater the risk of outliving their assets—especially given the sequence-of-returns risk of having to fund monthly income payments by selling assets while their value is at a temporary low point in a falling market, so that later market rebounds will be operating with a diminished capital base. On the other hand, if they spend too little, they unnecessarily sacrifice their living standards. An income annuity provides a powerful means of resolving this tradeoff. Guaranteeing a fixed level of income for life eliminates uncertainty by protecting retirees from depleting their savings too soon while giving them guidance as to how much they can safely spend without concern.

Surveys show that retirement savers value guaranteed lifetime income (figure 11-1). Benartzi, Previtero, and Thaler (2011) show that many savers are interested in and value annuities. Yaari (1965), Mitchell and others (1999), and others demonstrate the value of annuities to retirees under a variety of assumptions. In practice, however, annuity reserves account for about 8 percent of US retirement market assets—a share that has been fairly constant since the mid-1980s, fluctuating between 7.3 and 10.0 percent.[7]

Those figures, however, overstate the amount of retirement-income-related annuity assets because much of the "annuity" market consists of products that are not expected to provide a stream of guaranteed lifetime income. Instead, these products—variable, indexed, and other types—are designed to function as equity-based investment products with accumulation features that benefit from the tax-deferred treatment originally intended for life insurance or life annuities. At the beginning of 2018, $453.7 billion was held in fixed annuity assets—15 percent of the total assets held by forms of deferred annuities and less than 2 percent of overall retirement assets.[8]

Relatively few people purchase annuities to provide retirement income. The major industry trade group reports that only about 100 immediate annuities, the one most commonly used for retirement income, are sold per day in the United States. That number is about 1 percent of the more than 10,000 baby boomers who retire every day.[9]

Many factors combine to limit utilization of annuities. The presence of Social Security significantly reduces the demand for private annuities, and the remaining demand for this product is very price sensitive.[10] Most annuities are expensive, and individuals who desire to leave bequests will have little demand for annuities.[11]

Consumers' perceptions also play an important role. Consumers often are affected by the "wealth illusion" of perceiving their 401(k) balance as far more valuable than its income (or annuity) equivalent. They also may perceive annuities to be unfair. In one study, people who believed that it was unfair for insurance companies to keep any remaining assets after an annuitant's death were unwilling to consider annuities even after being shown that the value of the product to the purchaser could far exceed the cost.[12]

For competitive reasons, many investment firms and advisers have long refrained from selling annuities because they would reduce the advisers' assets under management. In many instances, their criticisms and unfair or debatable attacks have stuck (such as comparing income annuities unfavorably with diversified investments based on return-on-investment projections without regard to the value of the guarantees). For their part, annuity companies and distributors seeking to compete with the investment industry have designed relatively complex and nontransparent accumulation products. Some have also engaged in aggressive sales tactics and charged high commissions and surrender charges. Certain providers and advisers have presented annuities as investment opportunities rather than as guaranteed income, thus deemphasizing less profitable simple income annuities, even though Brown and others (2008) show that people respond more favorably to annuities that are presented as consumption insurance than those presented as investments. The large number of features and products for annuities may also scare off investors. Brown and others (2019) find that complexity reduces investors' ability to value annuities and hence makes them reluctant to purchase them.

Plan sponsors generally have hesitated to include annuity contracts in their 401(k) plans, largely because they believe doing so might expose them to liability if the annuity carrier were later unable to meet its obligations; they are also concerned about annuity portability from plan to plan and do not perceive much participant demand. While some regulatory changes have lessened these concerns, much more remains to be done before annuities are likely to be considered by a high percentage of plan sponsors.[13]

Given all the obstacles to expanding annuity participation, including the ultimate difficulty of persuading large numbers of individuals to overcome their own behavioral inhibitions and convert even a portion of their account balance to an income annuity, nonannuity products merit attention as a vehicle for providing retirement security.

A full guarantee against any investment risk may not be essential for all retirees. Some would be comfortable with an investment that offers a high probability of receiving a somewhat higher target level of income for life and a small probability of receiving less. Others will want the security provided by an annuity or a combination of equally safe nonannuity financial products, such as a series or "ladder" of very low risk bonds, to replicate a similar outcome. The annuity might be more costly, for example, because of commissions, fees, or other investment expenses, or less costly because of its ability to pool longevity risk to generate mortality credits.

To help determine which approach best meets a retiree's needs, Pfau and Cooper (2014) describe two fundamentally different approaches to thinking about retirement income that might be viewed as defining the opposite ends of the spectrum of preferences (table 11-1). What they call the "probability-based" school has goals similar to those of the accumulation phase in seeking to maximize risk-adjusted returns from the total portfolio in accordance with

Table 11-1. *Retirement Income Philosophies*

Issue	*Probability based*	*Safety first*
How are goals prioritized?	Retirees have lifestyle goals in mind; not meeting these goals indicates failure. Essential and discretionary spending are given equal weight.	Goals are prioritized. For instance, the need hierarchy could be: (1) basic needs, (2) contingency funds, (3) discretionary expenses, (4) legacy goals.
What is the investment approach?	Most commonly, a total returns perspective framed in the same terms as preretirement accumulation using techniques such as portfolio diversification. The focus is wealth management for the financial portfolio.	Asset-liability matching. Assets are matched to goals so that risk levels are comparable. Lifetime spending potential with an uncertain horizon is the focus, not maximizing wealth. There is a wider role for products to hedge interest rate risk and provide longevity insurance.
What is the role of an account-based pension?	The account-based pension is all that is needed for an outcome that will probably work. It is flexible enough to make whatever adjustments are required.	The account-based pension can be utilized after the safety requirements have been met. It can then deliver aspirational or discretionary spending.

Source: Pfau and Cooper (2014).

modern portfolio theory. Probability-based retirees tend not to base their retirement planning on a distinction between essential needs and discretionary wants, but instead look at ways to meet their total budget. Their investment portfolio during retirement balances market risk against the probability that the money will run out prematurely. This approach usually requires a high concentration of equities.

By contrast, Pfau and Cooper's "safety-first" approach engages in asset-liability matching, or financing different income uses with different assets. For example, consumption of necessities would be financed from an annuity or largely riskless portfolio, while less essential goals could be financed with higher-risk investments. This school tends to believe that retirees must develop a strategy that will at least meet their essential needs (as opposed to desires and preferences), no matter how long they live or how their investments perform.

This discussion is useful in thinking about default mechanisms that would convert retirement savings into income. While the safety-first school appears to prefer an annuity of some size, its adherents are also most likely to be actively involved in structuring a retirement income solution that meets its more specific set of priorities. Thus it appears that this group would be more likely to move beyond a default solution, probably by moving either some or all of its savings out of the default and into a different arrangement.

In contrast, the probability-based school, which focuses mainly on aggregate retirement income and is more flexible, would be better served by a default that provides some level of immediate retirement income while still allowing retirees to make other arrangements if their circumstances change. As long as there is an appropriate level of disclosure, an automatic retirement income solution that is flexible and focuses on overall income levels would meet the needs of the probability-based approach, while still allowing the safety-first school the ability to opt for other alternatives (perhaps, for example, an annuity covering essential expenses plus other investments to finance other expenses or goals).

MANAGED PAYOUT FUNDS

A major alternative to an annuity is a managed payout fund, a diversified pool of investments that is designed to produce a relatively consistent level of annual income but that does not guarantee that outcome.

Managed payout funds are similar in some respects to target-date funds (TDFs) but have a different objective. TDFs typically invest in a mix of asset classes, including diversified equities and bonds, designed to build retirement assets. Although some TDFs are actively managed, TDFs increasingly use some level of passive index funds to reduce costs. As the investor ages, the fund continues to seek maximum growth, but the proportion of the balance held in risky assets falls. Distributing income is not necessarily an objective.[14]

In contrast, managed payout funds serve as decumulation vehicles, paying monthly or quarterly cash distributions to retirees. Their investment strategy is to generate regular investment earnings and gains for income with carefully managed risk to reduce losses. The goal is stable income payouts stemming from consistent investment returns, and possibly growth, over time rather than maximum gains. The annual income amounts are calculated using both investment performance and, in the case of many managed payout funds, a gradual distribution of the principal amount invested in the fund. Other managed payout funds seek to preserve capital (though they have authority to distribute it if needed to maintain targeted payments) and therefore try to fund their targeted payments solely with investment returns.

Typically, managed payout funds are actively managed investment vehicles with at least initially a fairly high allocation to equities combined with countercyclical alternative investments or strategies intended to reduce losses when the markets are down.[15] Although the investments are actively traded, the size of the pool and a legal structure that imposes a fiduciary requirement on management help keep administrative costs low. The funds could also use other investment strategies to achieve these goals, including gradually derisking the portfolio and combining the phased withdrawal fund with other types of retirement income products.

These funds are designed to produce level monthly income throughout a given year, although income is likely to vary somewhat from year to year, increasing when markets rise and dropping when they decline. To limit variation in income amounts, managed payout funds can use smoothing mechanisms such as reserve funds that spread investment gains and losses over several years.

In proposing such a pooled investment for Canadians, Ryerson University professor Bonnie-Jeanne MacDonald noted that:

> Not only do pension plans offer a safer way to turn retirement savings into lifetime pensions, but they also have greater investment power—meaning the amount of money you get is much higher than you could likely achieve on your own. Pension plan members pay significantly reduced fees for asset management and administration compared with what is available on the retail market, and they generally achieve higher investments returns (owing to economies of scale, better asset purchasing power and better capacity to diversify investments, across asset classes and over time). Left to their own devices, people tend to be overly conservative or aggressive in their investment choices, without the added investment return for taking that risk.[16]

The largest managed payout fund in the United States, the Vanguard Managed Payout Fund, accounted for almost half of the \$3.5 billion in pooled managed payout investment funds held in the country in 2017. All of those funds were retail offerings; most managed payout funds that are part of an employer-sponsored retirement plan would be much larger.

The Vanguard fund holds a portfolio that is about 55 percent stocks, 6 percent bonds, 21 percent commodities, and 18 percent alternatives such as hedge funds, private equity, and others. Over time, the fund expects to pay investors an annual amount equal to about 4 percent of their assets, but this may vary depending on the returns on its investments. The fund sets a target level of income every year and then pays that amount in twelve equal monthly payments, while charging a fee of 34 basis points on a minimum investment of $25,000.[17]

Other similar funds exist in the United States, although they are very small.[18] Some are extensions of TDFs where the investment strategy shifts from accumulation to income. Various funds have differing target annual income amounts, such as 4 percent of invested assets over the life of the investment for some or 5.4 percent over twenty years for Fidelity. A similar product using exchange-traded funds (ETFs) is being developed to allow investors to benefit from market increases while limiting potential losses.[19]

Shell Netherlands uses a managed payout fund for employees hired after July 1, 2013.[20] While participants have individual accumulation accounts during their working lives, starting about ten years before retirement, their investments gradually transfer to the managed payout fund until retirement. At retirement, the employee can choose variable benefits or use the money to purchase a fixed annuity in the private market. Almost all choose the variable benefit. The Shell pool has about 35 percent of its assets in equities, and it smooths both investment and longevity risks over a five-year period.

Pooled investment trusts are under consideration in several other countries as well under a variety of names. The details vary, but the basic structure is the same.

The United Kingdom's National Employment Savings Trust (NEST) has a proposal for its members that would combine (1) a managed payout pool, (2) the ability to take partial lump-sum payouts, and (3) protection against longevity risk. Under the NEST proposal, initially 90 percent of a saver's retirement assets would go into a managed payout pool and 10 percent would be available for lump-sum payouts to help with financial emergencies or other purposes.[21] The pool would make monthly income payouts roughly from age 65 to 85. During those years, portfolio investments would be designed to produce income and protect against both investment and inflation risk. NEST proposes to sell futures contracts when market volatility is high and to seek to balance fund payouts with income from property investments and dividends. Inflation risk would largely be handled by inflation adjustments to retirees' state pension payments as well as higher returns from property and equities.

During the managed payout years, 1.5 to 2 percent of assets would be transferred each year to a separate fund designed to provide income after age 85. NEST considers US QLAC-style longevity annuities to be a promising way to provide stable cash payments for life.[22] Regardless of what form of deferred annuity is used, the actual purchase would not be made until (and unless) the retiree has reached age 75.

Australia is actively developing a retirement income framework called Comprehensive Income Products for Retirees (CIPR) that must be offered as an option, although not necessarily a default option, to all retirees starting in 2022. CIPRs would use the same basic three parts contained in the NEST proposal. Legislation creating the regulatory structure for the pools is expected to be considered during 2019, and the government proposes to allow Super fund trustees to design specific products that meet this regulatory framework.

Collective defined contribution plans (CDCs) (also known as defined ambition plans) offer another promising way to employ a pooled managed payout approach. CDCs, which exist in the Netherlands, Denmark, and Canada, are being considered in the United Kingdom in the form of multiple employer plans, and they use a single large, pooled fund for both the accumulation of balances and the payment of retirement benefits.[23] Benefits are paid in the form of regular pension income. Specific benefit levels are targeted, but they are not guaranteed because benefits are based on the fund's performance and the individual's income and contributions. Thus both contribution rates and retirement income payments could vary depending on how actual investment returns affect the ability to pay promised benefits.[24] The fund would invest in a broadly diversified pool, similar to the pools discussed earlier, except that retirement payments would provide roughly the same replacement rate of preretirement income for all participants rather than being calculated individually. Investing is done collectively and professionally, not self-directed by each individual participant as in 401(k) plans. The multigenerational investment pool seeks to smooth variable investment returns over several years, thus reducing at least some of the potential volatility.

A variation on this plan design would guarantee a minimum pension benefit, as a DB plan does, but would target higher, nonguaranteed benefits. A key challenge facing CDC plans of all types is how to ensure that participants understand that the targeted benefits are not guaranteed and accept the risk of permanent shortfalls without seeking to hold the plan accountable for inherent volatility and uncertainty in market performance.

AUTOMATIC RETIREMENT INCOME FOR AMERICAN SAVERS

Defined contribution (DC) plans will not fulfill their potential to deliver retirement security until they include an automatic mechanism that efficiently helps participants convert retirement savings into income. Experience has demonstrated that most new retirees who are handed a lump sum are ill-equipped to understand and successfully navigate the many complex risks, tradeoffs, and necessary decisions.

Automatic features can have a dramatic effect on participants' ability to best use their retirement assets. As first shown in research by Madrian and Shea (2001) and Thaler and Benartzi (2004), automatic enrollment and automatic escalation in 401(k) plans is an effective and popular way to guide people to appropriate retirement saving decisions. The same kind of automatic guidance that has helped millions to build retirement assets could similarly help them use those savings effectively.

Because it is not mandatory, an automatic income mechanism does not need to—and could not—provide a perfect solution for every retiree. It should, however, provide significant value to the largest number of retirees possible. To meet this goal, we believe that the mechanism should meet several standards.

First, it should be simple, transparent, and inexpensive. Second, it should protect against the risk of outliving one's savings and provide regular lifetime income that is reasonably stable over time.[25] Third, it should be reasonably protected against sequence-of-returns, market, and inflation risks. Fourth, it should be flexible, allowing the retiree to change course and pursue a different income strategy without causing undue adverse selection. And finally, it should include a separate fund from which retirees could make lump-sum withdrawals for emergencies or other purposes without unduly disrupting their regular retirement income.

Several strategies could meet one or more but not all of these standards. For example, purchasing an annuity would provide stable lifetime income but would be inflexible, and could also generate high and obscure fees.[26] Similarly, leaving the retirement savings in an employer plan and withdrawing a fixed amount at regular intervals would be simple but would fail to manage the longevity risk, the sequence-of-returns risk, the market risk, and the risk of paying higher fees than necessary. These alternatives could be the best choice for some retirees, but they would not work as default income mechanisms.

We propose that the automatic retirement income mechanism have three features: a pooled managed payout fund; a fund from which retirees could withdraw partial lump sums for emergencies or other special purposes; and a QLAC-type longevity annuity.[27] In addition, we strongly urge employers to assist participants with the timing of their Social Security benefits. This element would not be part of a default income strategy, but the two together would enable participants to optimize their total retirement income.

This structure is similar to proposals in the UK and Australia described in the appendix. At the time of the transition from savings to income, retirement assets would be divided into the three components. Most of the money would go into a managed payout fund. Approximately 10 percent would be set aside for emergencies or other lump-sum withdrawals and placed in a liquid investment or even a bank account. The remainder would be earmarked for the purchase of a QLAC-style longevity annuity that would begin payments at about age 85.

Since most individuals will not have all of their retirement savings in one account, the managed payout fund would be designed also to accept money from the plans of past employers, rollover IRAs, and IRAs started by individuals on their own. Ideally, an individual's assets from all these sources would be combined and managed as a whole in a managed payout fund, QLAC, and emergency fund. These packages would also be established as multiple-employer plans, with the fund making transfers, rollovers, and consolidations as simple and easy as possible. In addition, the fund would be structured to provide income from both Roth and traditional accounts through internal subdivisions.

The managed payout fund could be structured with a similar asset mixture and income goals as existing retail funds and the Shell Netherlands fund. It would be designed to produce a regular stream of retirement income roughly equal to a set percentage of the individual retiree's fund balance based on both investment performance and a gradual distribution of the initial investment, although this amount would not be guaranteed. Because the fund would include significant investments in equities and other growth investments, it should be able to pay out more on average than if it were invested solely in bonds or safer assets.

The actual payment amount would be set annually based on the performance of the investments in a preceding period or periods. To reduce fluctuations in payment levels, the fund would include countercyclical investments intended to hold down losses during market declines. In addition, income could be smoothed by multiyear averaging or by using a reserve account to retain some investment income during high-return years that could be used to offset lean years.

Once payments begin, the retiree would receive a regular monthly check, a service that could easily be provided by most existing record-keepers.[28] Payments would be designed to also satisfy any federal required minimum distributions (RMDs) that apply to the retiree.

The separate emergency fund is an essential part of the package. Studies by the JP Morgan Chase Institute show that older households are more likely to have extraordinary expenditures for health care, auto repair, and taxes than younger families.[29] Having a separate fund for these emergencies and other occasional necessary withdrawals will make it easier to meet these eventualities without depleting the retirement fund.

The QLAC (which could be a joint and survivor annuity for the retiree and a spouse or other beneficiary, or a single life annuity) would continue payments for life and would serve as a safety net to ensure that retirees cannot outlive their savings. As such, it would be packaged with the overall mechanism. The QLAC's guarantee of lifetime income starting at age 85 (or at an earlier age if the participant so chooses) would enable the managed payout fund to be managed to produce regular income across a finite time horizon instead of trying to plan drawdowns over an uncertain lifespan. It is not essential, however, that the actual purchase of the QLAC be made upon retirement. Retirees could request a delay of up to several years in order to decide whether a different retirement income option better suits their needs.[30]

In addition, we recommend that retirement saving plans offer lifetime annuities as an option—including annuities that are limited to a portion of the account balance intended to fund essential expenses—as well as other retirement income options that participants could use instead.

This structure meets all of the standards proposed above. It is simple to explain. Appropriately managed and regulated, the plan would not be expensive to administer. The proposal is structured to provide income for life through the longevity annuity, as well as predictable, regular income and money for emergencies. Investments through the managed payout fund would also help to protect retirees against inflation, and the separate fund could be drawn upon to help protect against sequence-of-returns risk. It would also allow for both different circumstances and different retirement income choices. If some participants wished to use a different retirement income strategy, they would only need to opt out of the default, in much the same way that someone whose savings are automatically enrolled in a TDF can opt out and choose another investment.

At least initially, this automatic retirement income solution would be provided through employer-sponsored and similar plans.[31] Thus the transfer into a managed payout fund and the other elements of the mechanism would be handled by the plan, not outside of it. In time, however, financial institutions and plan service providers might be expected to relieve plan sponsors of many of these responsibilities.[32]

As part of an employer plan, the managed payout funds do not need to be part of a TDF or other type of accumulation vehicle, although they could be structured to grow organically out of a TDF at retirement, with a shift in objectives to include the regular payouts. They would be a separate fund in which an individual saver is automatically enrolled on a certain date, with the transfer either spread out over a number of years or all at once. The transfer would not be irreversible. If the employee changes jobs during the transition, the money could be rolled into the new employer's plan. Similarly, the participant could choose a different retirement income strategy either before retirement or even after payments begin.

Ideally, rather than being limited to one employer, the funds could serve many different employers to achieve economies of scale. Just as employer plans typically use preexisting investment options such as mutual funds during the saving phase, the payout funds could manage the retirement assets from many retirement plans. Since the funds are designed to provide retirement income for roughly twenty years and plan sponsors would be reluctant to have a fiduciary responsibility for a period that long, we propose that Congress and the regulators take appropriate steps to address the concerns of plan sponsors while still protecting participants. There are a number of ways those goals could be accomplished, but the discussion is beyond the scope of this chapter.

The proposal focuses on participants in employer-sponsored retirement saving plans. A similar design could be used for IRAs in the retail market, which, through rollovers, continue to accumulate an increasing share of retirement assets. The retail solutions would contain the same three elements and options, and they could even use the same managed payout funds that the employer plans do. To increase the availability and potential use of these options in the retail market, it would be helpful to consider ways to make them more attractive to financial advisers. If feasible, advisers could receive appropriate, unconflicted, and reasonable compensation in the form of a commission financed by a portion of fees charged during the payout phase. Over time, this retirement income mechanism could become an integral feature of individual savings products such as IRAs.

However, before some plans can offer an automatic retirement income option, they need to take other preliminary steps. Unfortunately, many 401(k) plans do not provide for payouts other than RMDs and lump-sum distributions—sometimes only allowing a single lump-sum distribution of the entire balance. This restriction unnecessarily hinders participants' ability to craft an effective retirement income strategy and to draw benefits in a manner that suits their needs, including the ability to meet emergencies or for other purposes. We recommend that all 401(k) and other DC plan sponsors review and amend their plans as needed to enable participants to receive their benefits through periodic or other withdrawals—including annuities, installment or other managed payouts, other systematic and regular income, or ad hoc withdrawals made from time to time.

In addition, the regulatory situation needs to be clarified. Currently, the applicable Department of Labor regulations do not classify most lifetime income vehicles, including annuities and managed payout funds, as "qualified default investment alternatives (QDIAs) that DC plans can offer on an automatic or default basis without concern about losing safe harbor protection from potential liability under ERISA.[33] Certain annuity contracts and related features and certain managed payout funds would or might also qualify as QDIAs. However, many would not, and in other cases regulatory or legislative clarification will be necessary. We therefore urge the Department of Labor to amend its regulations so that plans could confidently offer appropriate income annuity contracts, managed payout funds, and certain other retirement income investment vehicles automatically. This action would mirror the way that plan fiduciaries were earlier given a measure of protection, so they could confidently offer target-date funds and certain other investments as default investments.

In addition to the automatic retirement income mechanism, we propose that plan sponsors and others take a fundamental prior step in promoting retirement income.[34] Employees approaching age 60 should receive information and counseling on the related set of basic choices for future work options, when to start Social Security benefits, and when to start drawing retirement plan or IRA benefits. Among other things, plans could connect participants to video and written explanations prepared by the Social Security Administration and other appropriate sources regarding the potential advantages to many individuals of, in effect, "buying" a meaningful additional amount of secure, guaranteed, inflation-indexed, lifetime Social Security income by delaying the start of their Social Security benefits. Doing so might involve working longer or drawing on plan or IRA savings in order to postpone Social Security commencement and increase the monthly benefit.

A NEW TOOL FOR RETIREES

Choosing the best way to convert retirement savings into a stream of income is one of the most complex financial decisions individuals have to make. Most retirees will have difficulty making informed decisions about these choices without guidance. As the UK's NEST pointed out, "Research has shown that even the most financially capable individuals can make irrational and suboptimal choices when it comes to financial matters, or defer making those choices out of regret aversion."[35]

Ideally, individuals would choose a retirement income program based on timely preretirement education, appropriate robo-advice, and individual counseling, although there are not enough unbiased and qualified financial planners available to meet the need. Inevitably, therefore, guidance in the form of behaviorally informed choice architecture will play a key role.

Any effort to develop default options, though, must recognize that optimal retirement choices are heterogeneous. Individual circumstances vary, and a one-size-fits-all solution will not work. Similarly, retirement income options will undoubtedly continue to evolve and improve over time. For these reasons, any automatic or other retirement income strategy should be reexamined regularly to ensure that savers have the best available solutions.

Gale and others (2008) proposed an automatic trial annuity that would place an individual's retirement assets in the annuity for two years, after which the individual could either leave it there or take the balance and use it differently.[36] The goal would be to help new retirees see and experience their savings as a lifetime income stream rather than a lump sum. In certain circumstances, the trial annuity would still be an appropriate, and even optimal, solution, but as explained here, there are other valid ways to convert savings into income. Some of them also feature an annuity, but in the form of a deferred longevity annuity rather than an immediate lifetime annuity. Retirees will be best served by income choices that are not limited to the same approaches and products that have been tried in the past.

In our view, retirement saving plans should offer automatic mechanisms that make it easy for participants to convert savings balances into income. Properly structured and regulated, automatic retirement income structures could help new retirees in much the same way that automatic enrollment and escalation help savers.

As noted, we recommend that plans offer an automatic mechanism that combines a pooled managed payout fund, a QLAC longevity annuity, and an amount for emergencies and special expenditures. This flexible structure would allow participants to make changes during retirement as their circumstances evolve. In addition, we recommend that plans offer lifetime income annuities as an option. For many people, acquiring an appropriately consumer protective and reasonably priced income annuity with at least a portion of their savings will still be the best choice for retirement income, and for many others it will play a key role in a broader postretirement financial strategy.

Retirees need innovative solutions that help them make the best use of their savings as they transition to a new phase of life. Guidance in the form of an automatic choice is needed to help them make appropriate decisions. There are many specifics to work out, but we believe that the combination of features discussed here offers a sensible and sound approach to providing income security in retirement.

APPENDIX. THE INTERNATIONAL DEBATE ABOUT RETIREMENT INCOME

This appendix briefly reviews policy discussions and proposals in Australia, the United Kingdom, New Zealand, and Canada.

Australia

Australia's retirement income debate is one of the more sophisticated. The country's retirement system combines a means-tested government pension and a defined contribution Superannuation (retirement) account to which employers are required to contribute 9.5 percent of wages for their employees.[37] The Superannuation system provides retirement income for a growing number of Australians, but there are increasing problems with asset decumulation. Most Australians withdraw their retirement assets either in a lump sum or by taking out regular streams of income. Although the account owners must make required annual minimum withdrawals, there is no protection against longevity risk.

Recognizing this growing problem, the 2014 Financial System Inquiry (known as the Murray Inquiry after its chairman, David Murray) called for the creation of Comprehensive Income Products for Retirement (CIPR), which would be offered to all retirees.[38] A CIPR would be a composite retirement income product with several elements that the inquiry estimated could provide a retiree with an income that could be 15 to 30 percent higher than would be available otherwise.[39] However, the inquiry did not define what a CIPR would look like, recognizing that there could be a number of combinations that could achieve these goals.

In 2016, the government published a proposed framework for the CIPR, explaining how the trustees of Superannuation funds should offer the program to savers and how the CIPR should be regulated.[40] The framework proposed that a CIPR provide at least a minimum level of income that would exceed the amount that would be available using just a drawdown of saving, a roughly stable lifetime income level, and access to part of the savings in a lump sum if desired. It asked for comments on how to accomplish these goals. The framework is open about what mechanism would best achieve the goals, and it noted that the proposal was not intended to promote annuities over other types of products, impose a choice on savers, or replace the need for financial advice.

A further position paper in May 2018 requested comments about the government's proposed retirement income covenant that would specify how fund trustees should structure a CIPR, present it to its members, and remove regulatory barriers.[41] It noted that while there is broad agreement about the need for a CIPR, there is a great deal of disagreement about how it should be structured. The paper called for reporting Superannuation balances as retirement income rather than as lump sums (somewhat similar to legislative proposals in the United States; see Iwry and others 2019). It also noted that a CIPR should "incorporate any one (or more) of a range of pooled lifetime income products (either immediate or deferred), such as a group self-annuitization products or a guaranteed lifetime annuity."

This occurs against a backdrop of a limited Australian annuity market. The regulatory system in Australia prohibits deferred and variable annuities since annuity vehicles are required to provide fixed payments. This restriction has created political pressure to expand access to annuities in order to make the annuity market more competitive, and to explore alternatives. As a result, there have been proposals for longevity insurance programs that provide an account-based option to increase flexibility.[42] Some variation of these proposals is expected to be adopted.

A key question is how an annuity feature in a CIPR would be counted for Australia's means-tested government-paid pension. Under government legislation that may be approved in the near future, "a fixed 60 percent of all lifetime product payments will be assessed as income for age pension eligibility, and 60 percent of the purchase price will be assessed as assets, reducing to 30 percent from the later of age 84 or five years after purchase."[43] The government proposes to legislate the CIPR covenant by July 1, 2019, to go into effect a year later. However, Superannuation funds will not be required to offer a CIPR until July 1, 2022.[44]

United Kingdom

The retirement income debate in the United Kingdom for retirement saving plans has moved from favoring a mandatory annuity purchase to recognizing that some default strategy to convert savings into income is needed. Before April 2015, most UK retirement savers were required to convert 75 percent of their savings into an annuity. Although several tools were available that allowed savers to compare the income they would receive from various providers, most simply purchased an annuity from the same entity that had handled their account before they retired. If the amount of savings was fairly small, the regular annuity income was tiny, a problem that became even more acute when interest rates declined after the 2007–2009 financial crisis and stayed low.[45] However, as a result of the 2012 automatic enrollment reforms that created a universal retirement saving system (including mandatory employer contributions) that would cover almost all workers in the United Kingdom, future retirees were expected to have significant amounts of savings that could supplement their state pensions.

In April 2015, the UK Treasury announced a new policy that would allow anyone over the age of 55 to access any or all of their retirement savings.[46] At the same time, it abolished the mandatory annuity purchase requirement. Those who chose to withdraw retirement assets could take 25 percent of the total tax-free and pay tax on the remainder at their normal income tax rates. After the removal of the annuity requirement, the Work and Pensions Committee in the House of Commons found that only 5 percent of new retirees at one major provider bought an annuity, while 53 percent chose to draw down their savings.[47]

A regulator found that 94 percent of those who withdrew retirement savings also had other income such as defined benefit pensions and that many people were simply not spending the money.[48] There is growing concern about the future, however. The Work and Pensions Committee noted that the automatic enrollment feature increased retirement saving through consumer inertia, but the withdrawal options enabled by the pension freedoms required savers to make active, informed choices. Most savers took withdrawals without receiving any professional guidance. As more people come to depend on a combination of the state pension and savings for retirement income, uninformed decisions could cause retirees to run out of money.

As a result, the committee suggested that the government require plan sponsors to provide account holders with a default drawdown strategy beginning in April 2019 that could allow annuities as part of the overall program. This would protect retirees' savings and encourage plan sponsors to aid with decumulation.[49] The government has yet to act on the recommendation.

One approach was suggested by the National Employment Savings Trust (NEST).[50] As NEST serves many lower-income savers, its proposal is considered suitable for a general population. It recognizes that needs change as retirees age, and therefore combines a drawdown from an actively managed account with a cash account for unforeseen needs and the possibility of a longevity annuity that starts at about age 85.[51] NEST stresses that, unlike automatic default options during the accumulation process, this mechanism may not be appropriate for decumulation. As a result, the NEST proposal is a recommendation and would not necessarily become a default option. The NEST proposal is discussed in more detail in the body of this chapter.

New Zealand

New Zealand has a unique retirement system that includes a residency-based pension paid by the government and a universal, automatically enrolled retirement saving system designed to supplement the government-paid income. New Zealand superannuation pays a flat-rate amount to individuals who have lived in the country for a specified length of time regardless of need or any alternative source of income.[52] KiwiSaver, an automatic enrollment retirement saving plan, is intended to provide retirement income above that amount. Unfortunately, KiwiSaver balances are far too low, and enrollees may also use their savings to make a down payment on housing, which further depletes potential retirement assets.

Financed in part by KiwiSaver, many New Zealanders invest in real estate, with the idea that the equity released from the sale of the house upon retirement will finance the gap between the government benefit and their current standard of living. Unfortunately, this money tends to last only a few years.[53] While many of the problems could be mitigated by increasing the amount saved in KiwiSaver and improving investment outcomes, the system still leaves retirees exposed to longevity risk.

For the most part, annuities do not exist in New Zealand. In 2009, the only remaining annuity provider in the country sold a grand total of seventeen contracts.[54] However, there is increasing attention to the need for better retirement income outcomes.

In a report submitted to the government, Susan St. John, director of the Retirement Policy and Research Centre at the University of Auckland, recommended creating a "limited-value generic annuity with generic branding, with oversight by FMA (the regulator), and default provisions."[55] She believes that KiwiSaver should default savers into an annuity and provide an opt-out option. The annuity should be gender-neutral, have low administrative costs, and protect retirees from inflation. Benefits could be linked to average wages or average investment returns, and there could be an option for long-term care insurance. In lieu of tax incentives, the annuity program could include decumulation subsidies that would be limited by an overall annuity size cap.

At this writing in 2019, the government has not acted, but as KiwiSaver balances grow, the need for stable retirement income is causing a revival of interest in retirement income strategies in New Zealand.[56]

Canada

The Canadian government's 2019 budget proposed to create both longevity annuities and tontines[57] (though under different names). An advanced life deferred annuity (ALDA) would have to start making payments at age 85. Savers could use up to 25 percent of the assets in a plan to purchase an ALDA; the purchase price would be subtracted from mandatory withdrawal calculations.[58]

The budget also proposed the creation of a variable payment life annuity (VPLA), which would be offered through a retirement plan with a minimum of ten participants. A VPLA would provide payments determined by both the performance of investments in the pool and the participants' mortality.[59]

The Canadian budget provisions followed a 2017 Association of Canadian Pension Management study on asset decumulation, which suggested that the country develop multi-employer retirement plans that are risk-pooled and provide default investment options. This scheme would encourage the development of solutions to draw down assets that are part of the plan rather than requiring employees to sell them in the open market. The report concluded that related proposals or programs in other countries "often feature managed withdrawals, provide limited access to lump sums, and permit longevity pooling through deferred annuities."[60]

In October 2018, seven major pension stakeholders in Canada called on government leaders in Ottawa to remove barriers to longevity risk pooling.[61] According to the group, risk pooling "is the logical solution" to hedge against seniors outliving their retirement savings.[62] They argued that the changes would benefit the Canadian economy, including government budgets, since resources are increasingly being used for retirement programs such as the Canada Pension Plan. The risk-pooling strategy could mirror approaches found in existing programs in Canada, including the Canada Pension Plan and the Quebec Pension Plan. The group recommended that the strategy focus on two key goals: withdrawal flexibility early in retirement and guaranteed payments later in life. For example, the group suggested, "a retiree should be able to purchase an insurance contract through a registered retirement income fund that would begin a payout at age 85 and continue until death.[63] These arrangements would be available through DC plans, as well as group registered retirement saving plans and tax-free savings accounts."[64] Implementing this strategy would require legislative changes, however, since existing pension and tax rules do not allow longevity risk pooling.

NOTES

The authors thank the Laura and John Arnold Foundation for research support. For helpful comments, the authors thank Fredrick Axsater, Michael Davis, Josh Gotbaum, Melissa Kahn, Elizabeth Kelly, Anne Lester, Emily Merola, Moshe Milevsky, David Morse, Bob Toth, Bruce Wolfe, and participants at a breakout session at the Aspen Leadership Forum on Retirement Savings.

Disclosure: Iwry provides, through J. Mark Iwry, PLLC, policy and legal advice to plan sponsors and other corporations, private equity, fintech, and other investment firms, trade associations, and nonprofit organizations regarding retirement and savings policy, pension and retirement plans, and related issues. Iwry is a member of the American Benefits Institute Board of Advisors, the Board of Advisors of the Pension Research Council at the Wharton School, the Council of Scholar Advisors of the Georgetown University Center for Retirement Initiatives, the Panel of Outside Scholars of the Boston College Center for Retirement Research, the CUNA Mutual Safety Net Independent Advisory Board, and the Aspen Leadership Forum Advisory Board. He also is currently serving as an expert witness in federal court litigation relating to retirement plans. The authors did not receive any financial support from any firm or person for any views or positions expressed or advocated in this chapter. None of them is currently an officer, director, or board member of any organization that has compensated or otherwise influenced them to write this chapter or to express or advocate any views or positions. Accordingly, the views and positions expressed here are solely those of the authors and should not be attributed to any other person or organization.

1. Oakley and Kenneally (2019). In the same poll, 79 percent said that retirees do not have the investment skills to ensure that their retirement savings last throughout retirement.

2. For ways to change annuity regulation to encourage more annuity options to be offered and selected in defined contribution plans, see Iwry and others (2019).

3. Social Security Administration (2017).

4. Employees in the nonprofit and public education sectors are eligible for 403(b) plans; federal employees and certain state and local government employees are eligible for 457(b) plans. Some employers may offer more than one type of account. These plans are similar in structure to 401(k) plans. DB plan coverage in the public sector has not declined as severely as it has in the private sector.

5. Northwestern Mutual (2018).

6. Other types of annuities exist, but they are not widely used or recommended as vehicles for retirement income. Instead, they are often complex and high-cost tax-favored investment products seeking accumulation of value. In variable annuities, the purchase price is invested in various assets (often mutual funds), and growth (or future income payments, if any) is determined by the performance of the underlying investments. Indexed annuities track a market index (or an index developed by the annuity company) and provide a portion of the growth in the index in exchange for downside protection if investments do not perform as expected (for example, through minimum payment guarantees), all at an additional cost. While variable and indexed annuities can benefit from strong market growth, the investment risk is similar to that of traditional investments. Thus the payments from these contracts may end up being significantly lower if investments do poorly, and the fees and commissions are often significantly higher than for many other investment choices. Other types of annuities, such as those that guarantee a stream of payments for a set period, are often used for income smoothing or tax shelter purposes and are beyond the scope of this chapter.

7. Investment Company Institute (2019).

8. LIMRA (2018).

9. Benartzi and Shu (2019).

10. Illanes and Padi (2019).

11. Friedman and Warshawsky (1990); Lockwood (2012).

12. Shu, Zeithammer, and Payne (2018).

13. For a discussion of these barriers and possible ways to reduce them, see Iwry and others (2019).

14. Certain TDFs could be structured to both provide maximum returns before retirement and a relatively stable amount of income during retirement. However, this is not the primary objective of most TDFs, and to avoid confusion, we use the term "managed payout funds" when discussing funds that provide retirement income.

15. These countercyclical strategies could include investments in real estate, commodities, the use of derivatives, de-risking the portfolio over time through bond investments, and others. The choice will depend on the strategy of the managed payout fund and conditions in the financial markets.

16. MacDonald (2019).

17. Vanguard (2019).

18. Pechter (2017).

19. Pechter (2018).

20. Preesman (2019).

21. National Employment Savings Trust (2015).

22. To help encourage DC plans and IRAs to provide lifetime income, the US Treasury Department and IRS in 2014 authorized "qualifying longevity annuity contracts" (QLACs). QLACs are longevity income annuities for DC plans and IRAs that may begin payments as late as age 85 and are subject to other conditions designed to promote simplicity and transparency and to facilitate product and price comparisons (US Department of the Treasury 2014; Internal Revenue Service 2014).

23. Department for Work and Pensions (2019). A handful of such plans exist in the United States as well.

24. Wilkinson (2018).

25. Another goal of the default would be to include spousal protections.

26. However, negotiation of a group purchase by plan officials on behalf of participants might achieve institutional pricing and address this problem.

27. The QLAC's deferral of required minimum distribution (RMD) liability would be an additional advantage but would not apply if the longevity annuity exceeded the applicable QLAC dollar and percentage limits. If a larger amount was desired, the annuity would be treated as a non-QLAC longevity annuity, which would not enjoy the special RMD treatment.

28. Some managed payout funds might be structured so that a participant's entire savings are consumed by the time that the QLAC starts to make payments. Others might allow retirees to have an amount remaining at that time to use for bequests or to transfer into the emergency fund.

29. Farrell and Greig (2017).

30. Because rates for a longevity annuity depend on the age at which the contract is bought, a delay is likely to increase the price of the annuity. In addition, if a significant number of people delay or fail to purchase a longevity annuity, adverse selection would likely result in higher prices for this product.

31. For instance, state-facilitated retirement saving programs might eventually use the retirement income mechanism once account balances reach a size that would make this efficient. New types of plans designed to meet the needs of contingent workers could also possibly use it.

32. In addition, we encourage financial institutions and plan service providers to facilitate the offering of in-plan or out-of-plan annuity bidding platforms or another type of platform presenting a menu of lifetime income options.

33. ERISA section 404(c)(5). But see Borzi (2014). QDIA protection is not the only path, however. Plan fiduciaries can make their own judgments that such default options would satisfy their ERISA duties of prudence and loyalty. See, e.g., Campagna (2016). Alternatively, plan fiduciaries can prudently engage and monitor an investment manager or other independent fiduciary to assume fiduciary responsibility for such a retirement income arrangement. Ultimately, if responsible financial providers have sufficient interest and capacity, and if appropriate regulation can be achieved, this may hold the most promise, especially for mid-market and smaller DC plans.

34. The Department of Labor should facilitate this type of guidance by issuing regulations enabling employers to offer this service without fearing that it will be considered investment advice or expose them to liability.

35. National Employment Savings Trust (2015).

36. Gale and others (2008).

37. Starting in 2021, the amount employers are required to contribute to the account will gradually rise until it reaches 12 percent of wages in 2025.

38. Murray and others (2014).

39. In 2017, the government decided to call a CIPR "MyRetirement products," but later consultation papers continue to use the term CIPR (Australian Treasury 2017).

40. Australian Treasury (2016).

41. Australian Treasury (2018).

42. Lee (2017).

43. Mather and Cleveland (2018).

44. Fry (2019).

45. Work and Pensions Committee (2018).

46. The UK allows people to access their savings before the age of 55 only in exceptional circumstances.

47. Work and Pensions Committee (2018).

48. Financial Conduct Authority (2017).

49. Pielichata (2018).

50. NEST is a trust-based DC pension provider that UK employers can use to meet the new workplace pension duties set out in the Pensions Act 2008. NEST is designed to be an easy-to-use, low-charge scheme. It was set up by government and must accept all employers that want to use it to comply with their duties.

51. National Employment Savings Trust (2015).

52. New Zealand annual Superannuation payments are about US$13,000 for a single person and US$20,000 for a couple. For details, see Ministry of Social Development (2019).

53. Financial Services Council (2018).

54. St. John (2009).

55. St. John (2018, p. 2).

56. Good Returns TV (2018).

57. A tontine is an asset pool that pays its investors a regular income. When investors in the tontine die, the survivors' income rises as the pool's earnings are divided among them, along with a share of the deceased members' assets.

58. Burgess (2019).

59. Ernst & Young (2019).

60. Melnitzer (2018).

61. The stakeholders include the Association of Canadian Pension Management, the Canadian Life and Health Insurance Association, the Canadian Institute of Actuaries, the Canadian Association of Retired Persons, Common Wealth, the National Institute of Aging, and the Pension Investment Association of Canada.

62. Benefits Canada Staff (2018).

63. These would be longevity annuities that are generally similar to the QLAC longevity annuities that the US Treasury Department authorized the insurance industry to create in US 401(k) and IRA markets beginning in 2014.

64. Benefits Canada Staff (2018).

REFERENCES

Australian Treasury. 2016. "Development of the Framework for Comprehensive Income Products for Retirement." Australian Government Discussion Paper. Sydney.

———. 2017. "Developing a Framework for the Retirement Phase of Superannuation." Australian Government Fact Sheet. Sydney.

———. 2018. "Retirement Income Covenant Position Paper: Stage One of the Retirement Income Framework." Australian Government Position Paper. Sydney.

Benartzi, Shlomo, Alessandro Previtero, and Richard H. Thaler. 2011. "Annuitization Puzzles." *Journal of Economic Perspectives* 25 (4): 143–64.

Benartzi, Shlomo, and Suzanne Shu. 2019. "Why Retirees Are Wary of Annuities." *Wall Street Journal*, February 10.

Benefits Canada Staff. 2018. "Pension Stakeholders Call on Feds to Remove Barriers to Longevity Risk Pooling." *Benefits Canada*, October 15.

Borzi, Phyllis C. 2014. "Letter to J. Mark Iwry." US Department of Labor, Employee Benefits Security Administration, October 23. https://www.dol.gov/sites/default/files/ebsa/ employers-and-advisers/guidance/information-letters/10-23-2014.pdf.

Brown, Jeffrey R., Jeffrey R. Kling, Sendhil Mullainathan, and Marian V. Wrobel. 2008. "Why Don't People Insure Late Life Consumption: A Framing Explanation of the Under-Annuitization Puzzle." NBER Working Paper 13748. Cambridge, MA: National Bureau of Economic Research.

———. 2019. "Behavioral Impediments to Valuing Annotates: Evidence on the Effects of Complexity and Choice Bracketing." NBER Working Paper 24101. Cambridge, MA: National Bureau of Economic Research.

Burgess, Mark. 2019. "Federal Budget Introduces Annuities Deferred to Age 85." *Advisor's Edge*, March 19.

Campagna, Louis J. 2016. "Letter to Christopher Spence." US Department of Labor, Employee Benefits Security Administration, December 22. https://www.dol.gov/agencies/ebsa/ employers-and-advisers/guidance/information-letters/12-22-2016.

Department for Work and Pensions. 2019. "Delivering Collective Defined Contribution Pension Schemes." Government Response to the Consultation. Department for Work and Pensions. London.

Ernst & Young. 2019. "Federal Budget 2019–20: Investing in the Middle Class." *Tax Alert Canada* (9).

Farrell, Diana, and Fiona Greig. 2017. "Coping with Costs: Big Data on Expense Volatility and Medical Payments." Washington, DC: JPMorgan Case Institute.

Financial Conduct Authority. 2017. "Retirement Outcomes Review Interim Report." MS16/1.2. London.

Financial Services Council. 2018. "Shaping Futures: Closing the KiwiSaver Gap." Auckland: Financial Service Council of New Zealand.

Friedman, Benjamin M., and Mark J. Warshawsky. 1990. "The Cost of Annuities: Implications for Saving Behavior and Bequests." *Quarterly Journal of Economics* 105 (1): 135–54.

Fry, Elizabeth. 2019. "A Kickstart for CIPRs: New Rules for Annuities." *Investment Magazine*, February 12.

Gale, William G., J. Mark Iwry, David C. John, and Lina Walker. 2008. "Increasing Annuitization in 401(k) Plans with Automatic Trial Income." Retirement Security Project. Brookings.

Good Returns TV. 2018. "NZ Annuities Market Will Grow: Challenger." Good Returns TV, March 21. https://www.goodreturns.co.nz/article/976506364/nz-annuities-market-will-grow-challenger.html.

Illanes, Gaston, and Manisha Padi. 2019. "Competition, Asymmetric Information, and the Annuity Puzzle: Evidence from a Government-Run Exchange in Chile." WP 2019-2. Center for Retirement Research, Boston College.

Internal Revenue Service. 2014. "T.D. 9673." *Internal Revenue Bulletin* 2014-30. Washington, DC.

Investment Company Institute. 2019. "Report: The U.S. Retirement Market, Fourth Quarter 2018." Washington, DC.

Iwry, J. Mark, William Gale, David John, and Victoria Johnson. 2019. "When Income Is the Outcome: Reducing Regulatory Obstacles to Annuities in 401(k) Plans." Retirement Security Project. Brookings.

Lee, Jann. 2017. "How Are Different Countries Tackling Decumulation?" *Benefits Canada*, April 11.

LIMRA. 2018. "U.S. Individual Annuities, 1st Quarter 2018." Windsor, CT: LIMRA Secure Retirement Institute.

Lockwood, Lee. 2012. "Bequest Motives and the Annuity Puzzle." *Review of Economic Dynamics* 15 (2): 226–43.

MacDonald, Bonnie-Jeanne. 2019. "Here's a Way DC Pension Plans Could Give Canadians a More Secure Retirement." *Globe and Mail*, January 14.

Madrian, Brigitte, and Dennis F. Shea. 2001. "The Power of Suggestion: Inertia in 401(k) Participation and Savings Behavior." *Quarterly Journal of Economics* 116 (4): 1149–87.

Mather, Joanna, and Debra Cleveland. 2018. "Federal Budget 2018: Super Tweaks You Need to Know About." *Financial Review*, May 11.

Melnitzer, Julius. 2018. "DC Plan Sponsors' Wish List for Legal Protections Supporting Decumulation Offerings." *Benefits Canada*, August 10.

Ministry of Social Development. 2019. "New Zealand Superannuation (NZ Super) Overview." Wellington: New Zealand Government. https://www.workandincome.govt.nz/eligibility/seniors/superannuation/superannuation-overview.html.

Mitchell, Olivia S., James M. Poterba, Mark J. Warshawsky, and Jeffrey R. Brown. 1999. "New Evidence on the Money's Worth of Individual Annuities." *American Economic Review* 89 (5): 1299–318.

Murray, David, Kevin Davis, Craig Dunn, Carolyn Hewson, and Brian McNamee. 2014. "Financial System Inquiry Final Report." Sydney: Australian Government.

National Employment Savings Trust. 2015. "The Future of Retirement: A Retirement Income Blueprint for NEST's Members." London: NEST Corporation.

Northwestern Mutual. 2018. "Living Long and Working Longer." *2018 Planning and Progress Study*. Milwaukee, WI: Northwestern Mutual Life Insurance Company.

Oakley, Diane, and Kelly Kenneally. 2019. "Retirement Insecurity 2019: Americans' Views of the Retirement Crisis." Washington, DC: National Institute on Retirement Security.

Pechter, Kerry. 2017. "T. Rowe Price Reopens the Market for Payout Funds." *Retirement Income Journal*, June 29.

———. 2018. "Meet the First 'Structured Outcome' ETF." *Retirement Income Journal*, August 30.

Pfau, Wade, and Jeremy Cooper. 2014. "The Yin and Yang of Retirement Income Philosophies." *Challenger*. http://www.republicast.com/publications/ 6a490775ca994e50a54ca9ac68b550c3/ #p=1&c=0&v=1.

Pielichata, Paulina. 2018. "Drawdown Strategies on Retirement Income Gain Attention in U.K." *Pensions and Investments*, April 30.

Poterba, James, Steven Venti, and David Wise. 2011. "The Composition and Drawdown of Wealth in Retirement." *Journal of Economic Perspectives* 25 (4): 95–118.

Preesman, Leen. 2019. "Netherlands: A New Dutch Blueprint." *IPE Magazine*, January.

Shu, Suzanne B., Robert Zeithammer, and John W. Payne. 2018. "The Pivotal Role of Fairness: Which Consumers Like Annuities?" NBER Working Paper 25067. Cambridge, MA: National Bureau of Economic Research.

Social Security Administration. 2017. "Fast Facts and Figures about Social Security, 2017." SSA Publication 13-11785. Washington, DC: Office of Retirement and Disability Policy, Office of Research, Evaluation, and Statistics.

St. John, Susan. 2009. "The Annuities Market in New Zealand." Retirement Policy and Research Centre, University of Auckland.

———. 2018. "Divestment and Decumulation—Planning for Post-Retirement." Retirement Policy and Research Centre, University of Auckland.

Thaler, Richard H., and Shlomo Benartzi. 2004. "Save More Tomorrow: Using Behavioral Economics to Increase Employee Saving." *Journal of Political Economy* 112 (1): 164–87.

US Department of the Treasury. 2014. "Treasury Issues Final Rules Regarding Longevity Annuities." Washington, DC.

Vanguard. 2019. "Vanguard Managed Payout Fund." https://investor.vanguard.com/mutual-funds/managed-payout/#/mini/fees/1498.

Wilkinson, Lauren. 2018. "What Is CDC and How Might It Work in the U.S.?" London: Pensions Policy Institute.

Work and Pensions Committee. 2018. "Pension Freedoms: Ninth Report of Session 2017–19." London: United Kingdom House of Commons.

Yaari, Menahem E. 1965. "Uncertain Lifetime, Life Insurance, and the Theory of the Consumer." *Review of Economic Studies* 32 (2): 137–50.

TWELVE

When Income Is the Outcome

REDUCING REGULATORY OBSTACLES TO ANNUITIES IN 401(K) PLANS

J. Mark Iwry, William G. Gale, David C. John, and Victoria Johnson

From 1980 to 2010, the share of all workers participating in defined contribution (DC) plans, including retirement savings accounts such as 401(k)s, rose from 17 percent to 42 percent, while the share participating in defined benefit (DB) pension plans fell from 39 percent to 14 percent.[1] Over the same period, participation and balances in Individual Retirement Accounts (IRAs) grew substantially.[2]

The shift from DB plans to retirement savings accounts like 401(k)s and IRAs creates different and greater risks and more retirement planning tasks for workers. Unlike in DB plans, workers who participate in 401(k)s and IRAs are responsible for making choices during the accumulation stage (including whether to participate, how much to contribute, and how to allocate their balances across assets), as well as during the decumulation stage (choosing when and in what form to withdraw accumulated balances). The rise in automatic features has mitigated these concerns for many workers during accumulation, but not during decumulation.

Retirees face a key dilemma as they consume their retirement resources: how to manage the risk of outliving their savings without sacrificing their standard of living. Social Security and DB plans, which pay regular, guaranteed benefits for the lifetime of the worker (and often the worker's spouse), provide one solution. Commercial income annuities sold by insurance companies provide another key source of lifetime income. Even though income annuities appear to have significant potential to improve retirees' well-being, the market for such products has proven small to date.

In this chapter we explore legislative and regulatory changes that could encourage workers to annuitize more of their 401(k) and other DC plan retirement assets.[3] Though not traditionally or frequently used to provide lifetime income, 401(k) and other DC plans have become a natural focal point for efforts to expand the use of annuities.

Providing income annuities through DC plans has many advantages. First, they offer economies of scale, giving employers that make group purchases bargaining power with insurers. Second, institutional pricing for groups and direct purchasing from insurers can reduce customer acquisition costs by circumventing the labor-intensive, costly distribution channels that use agents, brokers, and advisers. Third, because they have fiduciary responsibilities, plan sponsors are more likely to protect participants' interests when selecting and negotiating the type, terms, and price of contracts. Fourth, earlier and group purchasing decisions have the potential to reduce adverse selection by employees and as a result lower their costs. And finally, DC plans, facilitated by the workplace, payroll system, and plan structure, can support behaviorally effective strategies for overcoming participants' reservations about annuities.[4]

We propose policy reforms that would create an appropriately protective fiduciary safe harbor for plans' selection of annuity providers, increase the portability of annuities offered in plans, and reform the required minimum distribution (RMD) rules related to retirement income.

The chapter first provides background information on annuities and then outlines the three areas for reform and our proposals. The appendix provides further discussion of fiduciary safe harbor issues.

BACKGROUND

A life annuity is a financial product or contract (a) offered by an insurance company and issued to an owner, in which (b) the owner makes one or more payments to the company (like insurance premiums) and (c) at a specified later date, the company initiates regular (typically, monthly) payments to the owner that last for the duration of the owner's life.[5]

Annuities vary in many ways around this basic structure. Payments to the owner can begin soon after the annuity is purchased (an "immediate annuity" or "single premium immediate annuity") or years later (a "deferred annuity" or "deferred income annuity"). "Longevity annuity" sometimes refers to any deferred annuity but often refers specifically to a deferred annuity that begins payment only when its owner reaches an advanced age such as 80 or 85.[6]

Fixed income annuities typically provide regular payments (usually monthly) that are guaranteed to be a set nominal amount; they either continue for a specified number of years (a fixed term or installment distribution) or are guaranteed to last for the lifetime of the owner (and, often, a spouse or other designated beneficiary). An annuity that is "principal protected" or provides a "return of premium" death benefit pays the designated beneficiary the remaining value of the annuity principal if the annuity purchaser dies before receiving it in the form of payments. Some annuities offer partial or full protection against inflation.

Fixed income annuities, which convert a sum of money into a predictable income stream for life, tend to be relatively straightforward. Insurers back up the promised payouts by maintaining capital reserves largely invested in bonds (and other assets) of appropriate quality and duration pursuant to state regulatory requirements. In addition, insurers can manage their longevity risk by pooling customers with a range of lifespans (premiums from those who die earlier subsidize continued payments for those who live longer); and insurers can hedge the longevity risk they assume when issuing annuities with their mortality risk from selling life insurance.

Insurers also compete with market-based investment products outside the insurance industry using annuities designed as tax-favored investment products, such as variable annuities. These provide payments that vary depending on the performance of the product's underlying investments (mutual funds, equity-indexed investments, and the like) and therefore entail higher risk and potentially provide higher returns.[7] Their emphasis on asset accumulation departs from annuities' original and distinctive role: to protect against longevity risk by pooling mortality credits and providing guaranteed lifetime income in retirement.

However, the variable annuities are often sold together with a "guaranteed lifetime withdrawal benefit" rider that provides a form of longevity risk protection by guaranteeing a specified lifetime benefit under certain circumstances.

The fastest-growing investment-oriented annuity type is the equity indexed or fixed indexed annuity. Indexed annuities are hybrids that combine elements of variable and fixed income annuities, offering guaranteed minimum returns while also allowing higher returns linked to a market index (such as the S&P 500).[8]

Accumulation products such as indexed and variable annuities also tend to be more complex and opaque because they pursue a variety of objectives: for the consumer, the upside potential for tax-deferred investment growth, often combined with some form of guarantee against losses; for annuity providers and distributors, higher profit margins, commissions, and fees, with the ability to compete against mutual funds and brokerage firms. As a result, consumers who purchase (tax-deferred) variable annuities within a tax-qualified plan or IRA also may be paying for redundant tax advantages. In addition, when offering investment growth with guarantees against market risk, insurers may find it more difficult to hedge their risks because market risk, unlike longevity risk, is not managed through diversification of insured lifespans or hedged through life insurance in which insurers take on countervailing mortality risk.

The Benefits of Lifetime Annuities

Economic theory shows that life annuities can increase individual welfare by balancing the risk associated with lifespan uncertainty against the risk associated with unnecessary reduction in living standards. Under certain conditions, risk-averse individuals with uncertain lifespans will choose to annuitize all their wealth. These conditions are restrictive and include the presence of complete markets, the availability of actuarially fair annuities (with zero transaction costs), and the absence of bequest motives.[9]

But even in more realistic models, individuals are still predicted to have welfare gains from partial annuitization of their wealth.[10] Mitchell and others (1999) find that in a simplified stochastic life-cycle model, without bequest motives, individuals would prefer certain annuities over an optimal consumption strategy without annuities. Horneff and others (2006) find that the optimal age to purchase an annuity varies; younger individuals and those with lower levels of risk aversion would likely choose to keep assets out of annuities, but older individuals and those with high risk aversion would derive benefit from annuitization.

The Market for Income Annuities

Despite the theoretical advantages of annuities, the market for private annuities in the United States appears to be small relative to total retirement assets. As of the last quarter of 2018, US retirement assets amounted to $27.1 trillion, of which $2.1 trillion was held in annuity reserves.[11] As a share of total retirement assets, annuity reserves have remained relatively constant—ranging between roughly 8 percent and 10 percent—since the mid-1980s.

These figures, however, overstate the amount of retirement-income-related annuity assets because much of the "annuity" market consists of products that are not expected to provide a stream of guaranteed lifetime income. Instead, as noted, these products—variable, indexed, and other types—are designed to function as equity-based investment products with accumulation features that benefit from the tax-deferred treatment originally intended for life insurance or life annuities. At the beginning of 2018, $453.7 billion was held in fixed annuity assets, comprising 15 percent of the total assets held by forms of deferred annuities or less than 2 percent of all retirement assets.[12]

Why Is the Income Annuity Market So Small?

Why the retirement income annuity market is not larger, even though it seems as if many individuals could benefit from additional annuitization, is a key question (sometimes referred to in the literature as the "annuity puzzle") for policymakers and researchers.[13]

In fact, numerous factors limit annuity participation.[14] First, Americans already own annuitized wealth through Social Security and (effectively) Medicare. Many may view these programs as sufficient security against the risk of outliving assets and thus prefer to keep the rest of their wealth in more liquid and flexible forms, to be used to fund uncertain health care expenses, bequests, and other necessary and discretionary spending.[15] Second, for some retirees, traditional risk sharing within families can further reduce the need to buy a commercial annuity.[16] Third, annuities can be expensive (or are perceived as such) relative to actuarially fair instruments. Adverse selection, high fees, and other issues drive up costs.[17] Fourth, income annuities need to be illiquid to limit adverse selection and to support the guaranteed income level. Typically, purchasers are contractually locked in to annuity contracts once income begins and face substantial surrender charges if they exit early. Fifth, the many financial advisers who charge clients a percentage of the assets they manage have a financial incentive to avoid recommending investments (such as annuities) that reduce their assets under management. Sixth, since the Great Recession, interest rates have been low by historical standards, while stock market returns over the past decade have been high. Low interest rates reduce the income that investors can obtain from an annuity purchase of a given size.[18]

Behavioral research has identified additional factors that plausibly limit consumers' interest in annuities. Many feel uncomfortable spending a large sum to guarantee what seem like comparatively small monthly payments or have little experience trading off resources over long periods of time. Thus, even when offered an actuarially fair annuity, they may prefer a lump-sum payment.[19] Another common concern is financial loss in the event of death soon after purchasing the annuity ("What if I get hit by a bus tomorrow?"). This concern may be allayed by joint and survivor annuities or a lump-sum "return of premium" death benefit. More fundamentally, however, this worry reflects the view of annuities as a gamble, rather than as insurance against outliving one's resources—in essence, the perception that if the purchaser dies too soon after purchasing the annuity, the annuity will be lost and the money wasted.[20]

Negative press coverage, reputational issues, and related factors have also affected consumers' perceptions and demand. Indexed and variable annuities and related products are often criticized for presenting a confusing array of nonstandard features, terminology, and branding, with high fees, commissions, and surrender charges. Complexity and lack of transparency can raise costs to consumers by impeding price and product comparisons, dampening competition, and possibly depressing even the sales of simpler, lower-margin products such as fixed income annuities.[21] Also, some annuity providers retain the ability to unilaterally modify contract terms years after the customer entered into and paid for the contract. This possibility presumably reduces consumers' trust of annuities and those who sell them, especially given press reports that insurers have resisted disclosure to prospective customers (or the public) of their past pattern of unilateral modifications to similar contracts.

The distribution of annuities by insurance agents, brokers, "insurance marketing organizations," and other intermediaries has also been widely criticized on the ground that conflicts of interest, complexity, and lack of transparency—as well as legislation blocking efforts by the Securities and Exchange Commission (SEC) to regulate indexed annuities[22]—reportedly have protected and promoted higher commissions, fees, and other charges.[23]

Problematic product designs and sales practices for some types of annuity products should not obscure the fact that straightforward and competitively priced commercial income annuities can play an important, pro-consumer role in retirement planning, especially as one portion of a broader portfolio.[24] Moreover, in our view, variable and indexed annuities are not inherently problematic; appropriately designed, regulated, and sold, competitively priced, and free of the troubling issues that have arisen too often in the market, some of those products can be consumer protective and help savers convert their balances into valuable retirement income with longevity risk protection.[25]

FIDUCIARY LIABILITY

Perhaps the most salient regulatory impediment to utilizing annuities to provide retirement income from employer-sponsored plans is plan sponsors' fear of long-term fiduciary liability for selecting an insurer that fails to meet its obligations. We recommend mitigating the risk of liability by enacting an appropriate statutory fiduciary safe harbor for DC plan fiduciaries that select annuity providers that are highly qualified (i.e., highly rated for financial strength). We also recommend exploring the need for a "universal" independent fiduciary.

Background

The Employee Retirement Income Security Act of 1974 (ERISA) obligates plan sponsors and plan officials to comply with fiduciary requirements that they act prudently, in the interests of participants, and with a high degree of care and expertise in selecting, monitoring, and deciding whether to retain investment and service providers. Plan sponsors fear potential long-term fiduciary liability for violating ERISA's high standard of prudence when selecting and retaining an annuity provider. The concern does not stop with actual liability: employers that sponsor 401(k)s commonly worry about class actions aimed at pressuring them into an expensive settlement as an alternative to an even more expensive verdict. Plan sponsors often express concern that, if they offer an annuity option (instead of a cash lump sum), their legal exposure could easily stretch three or four decades into the future, until the last retired annuitant dies. They fear that, even if fiduciaries selected an annuity provider that gave every indication of being fully capable of meeting its annuity obligations, if decades later it became unable to pay, the plan sponsor could face ERISA fiduciary liability for having imprudently retained that provider. In view of the long-term commitment (including high surrender charges that make it costly to get out of an annuity), a fiduciary's selection of an annuity option is commonly seen as entailing greater risk and lock-in for consumers than more common liquid plan investments such as mutual funds. These considerations have discouraged many 401(k) plan sponsors from offering annuities.

Department of Labor regulations provide guidelines for DC plan fiduciaries selecting annuity providers for "benefit distributions." The regulations describe a series of analytical steps fiduciaries must take to satisfy ERISA's prudence requirement when selecting an annuity provider.[26] The regulations appear to require employers to make assessments and determinations of insurance companies' long-term financial strength that are beyond most employers' reasonable capacity, although they call on employers to consider retaining an independent expert to advise them. They also require fiduciaries to "appropriately consider" insurers' financial capability and costs, and "appropriately conclude" that the insurer is financially capable and that costs are reasonable. Although use of the term "appropriately" helps ensure that the fiduciaries' analyses are not cursory or otherwise inadequate, it also leaves fiduciaries uncertain whether they have complied. Despite being labeled "safe harbor" regulations, they are not sufficiently objective to satisfy plan sponsors' desire for a safe harbor in the traditional sense—that is, a simplifying decision rule or process specifying definitive, objective, and readily ascertainable steps fiduciaries can follow to be sure they have "checked the box" and will be deemed to have acted prudently in selecting an annuity provider. [27]

As an alternative to DoL regulations, the insurance industry for some years has proposed a simple, straightforward, and objective statutory safe harbor that is one of many provisions included in a legislative package approved unanimously by the Senate Finance Committee in 2016 and a generally similar package passed by the House of Representatives in 2018 and 2019.[28] However, it has not been widely recognized—by policy analysts, interest groups, lawyers, actuaries and other industry experts who have not been involved in developing or lobbying for the provision, and probably members of Congress—that this legislative version of the long-awaited (and much-needed) safe harbor has no financial strength standard.[29] Under the safe harbor, if a fiduciary receives certain factual representations from the insurer (and meets several other procedural requirements), it would be protected from liability for any losses to participants resulting from an insurer's inability to meet its financial obligations under an annuity contract. Likewise, the fiduciary would be excused from considering the insurer's financial capability to meet those obligations and from concluding that it is capable of meeting those obligations. The representations are quite basic. They could be readily provided by any state-licensed annuity provider that is in good standing and not currently (or in the past seven years) officially in trouble with its state insurance department.[30]

As drafted in 2019, therefore, the safe harbor reads much like a lowest-common-denominator industry-wide trade association consensus among competing insurers. Neither limited to, nor even favoring, financially stronger providers, it grants the same stamp of approval to virtually any annuity provider that has been licensed to do business for seven years—even insurers with below-investment-grade ratings—regardless of relative claims-paying ability. (The bill does not clearly require that any portion of that experience be specific to the offering of annuities.) While providing fiduciaries sufficient clarity and certainty, the safe harbor falls short in protecting retirees, protecting fiduciaries, and remaining true to the policy underlying ERISA's high fiduciary standards.

The statutory safe harbor appears to exceed the scope of the DoL "safe harbor" regulation in another way as well: by expanding to encompass accumulation-type annuities designed mainly or largely to serve as tax-favored investments, not merely fixed income annuities that simply pay a regular stream of retirement income. This issue is discussed further in the appendix.

Proposed Fiduciary Safe Harbor

To address these concerns, the following describes our recommended statutory fiduciary safe harbor for selection of annuity carriers. Where necessary, DoL regulations would then flesh out specific terms of the safe harbor in accordance with the statutory guidelines.

APPROPRIATE SCOPE OF SAFE HARBOR

The safe harbor would be unambiguously limited to selection of the annuity carrier based on its financial strength and stability; it would not apply to fiduciaries' decisions regarding the type, price, or other terms of annuity contracts.[31] Those decisions would continue to be subject to ERISA's regular fiduciary standards, but the safe harbor would streamline the full fiduciary analysis normally required to prudently select an insurer. It would enable plan fiduciaries to rely on appropriate third-party factual information (though often transmitted through insurer representations) instead of making a full independent analysis of the insurer's financial capability to meet its annuity contract obligations.

A MEANINGFUL QUALITY STANDARD

A fiduciary safe harbor should include a meaningful quality standard—expressed through simple, objective indicators—relating to insurers' financial strength.[32] A safe harbor that appears to include substantially all providers (that have been licensed for seven years) without regard to their financial strength or creditworthiness would be politically expedient—a quick fix facilitating consensus within insurance industry trade associations. But it might not serve participants, plan sponsors, or even insurers collectively. It is less likely to maximize protection of employees and retirees, deter litigation, protect fiduciaries from liability or large settlements, or impress plan sponsors as credible and sustainable. A safe harbor without a meaningful financial strength standard means that plan sponsors could feel compelled to incur the cost of engaging an independent expert consultant to do almost as much as is required today to narrow the field of hundreds of insurers that would qualify under such a safe harbor.[33]

In our view, regulatory safe harbors are not and should not be designed to lower basic statutory or statutorily derived standards (such as financial strength, in this case). They are designed instead to simplify the process of applying standards, making the process less costly, faster, more objective, and therefore more certain.[34]

The commercial annuity market—even where ERISA does not apply—ordinarily gives careful attention to insurers' relative financial strength, as we explain in the next section. To cite just one example, the Alliance for Lifetime Income provides the following question-and-answer on its website: "How do I know that my protected income is safe?" "All insurance companies have a rating for financial strength provided by rating agencies like AM Best, Standard & Poor's, Moody's, and Fitch. Ask your financial advisor about the financial ratings of the insurance company you are considering"[35] But where ERISA's exacting fiduciary standards apply, it is all the more important to focus on financial strength. Since the market and ERISA fiduciary analysis cannot and do not turn a blind eye to relative claims-paying ability (see appendix), neither should an ERISA safe harbor.

SIMPLIFIED INDICATORS OF FINANCIAL STRENGTH

A meaningful standard of quality would maximize the likelihood that benefit promises will be backed by insurers that are experienced in providing annuities and are among those with the greatest claims-paying capacity. Accordingly, our proposed safe harbor would be limited to insurers that are very strong financially. While their products need not be "the safest available" annuities in the market (which is how DoL has described the DB plan standard), they should be at least among the safest. To be workable, the safe harbor would streamline the process of distinguishing among annuity providers based on financial strength (or claims-paying ability) with reference to the financial strength ratings assigned by the leading Nationally Recognized Statistical Rating Organizations (NRSROs), which are registered with the SEC and which it oversees and examines.[36]

Our proposed inclusion of a high financial strength standard is in no way limited to a plan's selection of a single annuity provider. It is equally applicable when a plan selects multiple providers, such as multiple highly rated insurers to diversify any solvency risk, or gives participants access to an annuity quotation and purchase platform to collect real-time quotes and promote ongoing competition among multiple highly rated insurers to provide the best value.

Whatever the format, the annuity market does not stop with the basic question of whether an insurer is licensed; it does not treat all licensed life insurers as having the same financial strength. Rather the market has shown considerable demand for insurer financial strength and credit ratings as determined by NRSROs that for decades have been in the business of researching and providing such carefully differentiated assessments (see appendix). To be sure, certain NRSROs have come in for sharp criticism and distrust based on their role in, and lack of independence before and during, the Great Recession.[37] Their high ratings of collateralized debt obligations proved to be disastrously unreliable, and Congress recognized that most existing rating services are conflicted because they are paid by the companies they rate (or in some cases by owners of the investments being rated).[38] In fact, Congress responded in the Dodd-Frank legislation by requiring each federal agency, "to the extent applicable," to review and modify its regulations "to remove any reference to or requirement of reliance on credit ratings" and replace it with some other appropriate "standard of credit-worthiness."[39] But during the ensuing years, at least some lessons have been learned. Efforts have been made (largely pursuant to Dodd-Frank) to improve rating agency practices, including the development and prevalence of risk-based capital standards and the establishment of an Office of Credit Ratings within the SEC to provide oversight of NRSROs.

Accordingly, it is unclear that the problems affecting the pre-2009 credit ratings of mortgage-backed securities are likely to apply equally to financial strength ratings of insurance companies in future years. Therefore, in a world with few benchmarks or comparable centers of expertise regarding financial strength and creditworthiness, we question the justification for dismissing the work of all of the NRSROs.[40]

Put simply, the issue is not whether financial strength ratings are fallible—of course they are (as are the state insurance departments and everything else in the regulatory process)—but whether on net they would add value to a safe harbor. Recognizing the rating services as a potentially useful resource, an annuity provider in good standing with state regulators would qualify under the safe harbor only if it had high financial strength ratings from the major national NRSROs and sufficient experience in providing annuities.[41] For example, the "highly qualified" standard could require the insurer to have

(1) current and recent financial strength ratings, provided by at least two of the four major NRSROs, that are in the NRSROs' top few ratings categories,[42] and (2) no lower financial strength rating from any NRSRO. Because each NRSRO has its own scale of rating categories and letter ratings, without any alignment or correspondence among them, Congress could direct DoL, in consultation with the Treasury Department (which houses the Federal Insurance Office), the SEC (which includes the Office of Credit Ratings), and perhaps other neutral experts, to specify, to the extent necessary, roughly comparable thresholds for each NRSRO, and otherwise fine-tune the financial strength ratings standards. To support this, insurers' representations would include (1) all NRSRO financial strength and credit ratings the insurer has requested and received going back a specified number of years, and (2) disclosure of which affiliated entities are and are not liable (and how that relates to the ratings).

One existing model for the use of multiple ratings can be found in the COMDEX composite index. For more than 500 insurers, COMDEX reports the rating provided by each of the four major NRSROs, determines each insurer's relative ranking by each NRSRO, and then combines those relative rankings into a single composite ranking calculated similarly for each insurer on a scale of 1 to 100.[43] Accordingly, an alternative approach might limit the safe harbor to insurers whose most recent COMDEX rating is above a specified threshold or might direct DoL to apply its own similar method of combining the NRSRO ratings.

It would be fair to ask why a safe harbor needs to include a standard higher than the level of adequacy state regulators normally require to license an insurer and permit it to continue in business. The answer is that, to protect retirees,[44] ERISA requires DC plan fiduciaries to select annuity providers in accordance with ERISA's prudent expert fiduciary standard—which the courts have characterized as "the highest known to the law."[45] As noted, a new fiduciary safe harbor automatically approving virtually any insurer that has been in business for seven years (except the few that are not in good standing with their state regulators) would amend ERISA to effectively confer automatic approval on hundreds of insurers that have not achieved "superior," "excellent," or "very strong" financial strength ratings. It would even sweep in many insurers with speculative-grade (equivalent to "junk bond") ratings, as well as others that are only marginally investment grade.[46]

Unless limited in some way to highly rated insurers, a safe harbor based merely on insurers' representations that they are in good standing with their state insurance department would be inconsistent with a "best-in-class" approach reflecting ERISA's high fiduciary standards. In the long term, it may not be wise or sustainable to allow such representations to substitute for an objectively ascertainable, expert, and independent third-party rating of each insurer's financial capability. Although most NRSROs are not or might not be sufficiently independent, they are experienced and expert, and for now they are all we have. Moreover, as described in the appendix, steps have been taken, and further steps might be taken, to improve, for this purpose, the rating agencies' independence and procedures or to provide additional oversight.[47]

Requiring high ratings in addition to other safe harbor conditions would hardly be a novel or untried approach. Previous DoL rulemakings on selection of annuity providers[48] and prohibited transaction exemptions have also relied on ratings, as described in the appendix.

A UNIVERSAL INDEPENDENT FIDUCIARY?

As currently interpreted by DoL, ERISA's fiduciary standards look to each plan sponsor to engage its own expert consultant or independent fiduciary to assess and advise on an identical factual issue—the long-term financial strength of each interested insurance company. (In-house fiduciaries who have the requisite expertise may make these assessments on their own.) Because this issue is relevant to all plans, it is unnecessary and inefficient to expect each plan to pay for its own independent expert to perform the identical analysis based on the same public information. As suggested, for purposes of a fiduciary safe harbor, NRSRO financial strength ratings (though imperfect) are the best available simple stand-in for a full fiduciary analysis of claims-paying ability. However, as a possible eventual replacement or alternative to such ratings as a key element of a safe harbor, a strictly independent, expert, nonprofit entity might perform this analysis for all plans. For example, the Labor Department's safe harbor guidance could refer to, evaluate, or assist in establishing or certifying such an expert panel or entity to serve as a kind of universal independent fiduciary to advise solely on the financial strength of annuity providers.

Instead of establishing a new entity, the role of universal independent fiduciary for insurer financial strength could conceivably be delegated to DoL (the Employee Benefits Security Administration), the Treasury Department (Federal Insurance Office), the Consumer Financial Protection Bureau, the SEC (Office of Credit Ratings), or the Federal Trade Commission. That said, each of these options—and for that matter any governmental agency—has substantive or political drawbacks. Alternatively, one or more existing professional organizations or other nonprofit entities might conceivably set up a panel of independent experts with a dedicated staff that includes detailees from NRSROs. Staffing and other costs could be limited because the mission would be far narrower than that of the NRSROs: simply assessing which insurers, among those that meet the basic licensing requirements imposed by state insurance departments, have sufficient financial strength to be selected under an ERISA fiduciary safe harbor.

The independent entity or panel would not need to "reinvent the wheel" in rating the claims-paying ability of annuity providers; it could take note of or in some measure rely on (though not uncritically) NRSRO ratings in arriving at its own, independent conclusions. It could determine how to take into account the different NRSRO rating scales or perhaps devise its own rating scale to assess financial strength for DC plan annuity purposes. Ratings would not be funded or controlled by insurance companies. Instead, the independent board, which might be publicly funded, would determine which annuity providers it rates, taking into account interest or requests from plan sponsors. It would not be a guarantor. Its ratings or other determinations would not be binding on plan fiduciaries (but would carry considerable weight and might even be determinative in a safe harbor context), and its personnel would be protected from liability.

Alternatively, the independent entity might contract with NRSROs to have them perform annuity provider financial strength rating assessments expressly for DC plan ERISA fiduciary purposes. The assessments would be performed in accordance with appropriately rigorous guidelines and procedures, prescribed by the independent fiduciary entity, designed to preclude "rating shopping" and undue control or influence by insurers. Each insurer wishing to offer annuities to ERISA-governed DC plans might, for example, be required to be evaluated and rated in this manner by at least two contracting NRSROs. Alternatively, short of contracting for ratings, the independent entity could condition the use of ratings for these purposes on NRSRO agreement to comply with specified procedural requirements.

Precedents for such independent expert advisory entities exist in other regulatory spheres.[49] Support for such an approach, based on applicable metrics, can be found in a Treasury Department report issued during the first year of the Trump administration and in a 2016 Report of the Bipartisan Policy Center's Commission on Retirement Security and Personal Savings.[50]

ANNUITY PORTABILITY

The limited portability of annuities is a second key regulatory concern. A plan sponsor that discontinues offering an in-plan annuity in which employee or employer contributions have been invested interrupts the steady accumulation of annuity benefits. No further contributions would go to the annuity, and in many instances employees would be subjected to nontrivial annuity liquidation or surrender fees unless they moved the annuity to another plan or an IRA. However, current law generally would prohibit such a distribution from a 401(k) plan.

We recommend a statutory exception to the 401(k) withdrawal restrictions that would permit direct rollover of the annuity contract to another plan or an IRA to increase portability and make annuities more attractive.

Current Limited Portability

While some annuities are offered as distribution options at the time a plan participant retires, others are offered as both an investment and distribution option. Sometimes referred to as "in-plan" or "accumulation" annuities, these products increase in value over time as contributions are invested in the deferred annuity (or deferred annuity "units").

A portability challenge arises if a plan offers annuities and then stops doing so. For example, the plan's record-keeper might stop maintaining the deferred annuity option on its platform, or the plan might replace its record-keeper with one that does not offer the annuity product. Alternatively, the plan's fiduciaries might decide that the annuity no longer is a prudent or desirable investment option (for example, if the plan's annuity provider unfavorably changes the financial terms of its annuities).[51]

If a plan stops offering in-plan accumulation annuities, participants might feel that their future annuity has not accumulated sufficiently to have made the investment worthwhile. A participant might then want to cash out the annuity or be effectively forced to do so by the action of the plan and the terms of the annuity contract. In either case, the participant could face significant surrender or liquidation charges or other fees.[52] Others might want the option of continuing to add to their previous contributions even if the plan stopped offering the annuity. But if the plan's annuity option were discontinued, contributions generally could not continue to be invested in the product on a stand-alone and similarly tax-favored basis unless the annuity contract was distributed from the plan and the annuity provider was willing to continue receiving contributions. However, current law restricts most 401(k) and similar plans' ability to distribute benefits resulting from pretax contributions of a participant who is still employed by the plan sponsor and is under age 59½. (This restriction applies even if the distribution is rolled over to an IRA or another plan.) Many such plans permit hardship withdrawals to active employees, but these circumstances probably would not ordinarily qualify as a financial hardship; and even if they did, hardship withdrawals cannot be rolled over.

Proposed Legislative Exception

To address this portability problem, we propose legislation that carves out an exception to the 401(k) plan withdrawal restrictions to allow a participating employee, absent any other distributable event, to withdraw and directly roll over an in-plan annuity to an IRA or another employer plan that would accept the annuity.[53] The legislation would also exempt the withdrawal from the 10 percent additional tax on early withdrawals.

Participants could then continue holding the annuity and adding to it (accumulating additional deferred income units, for example). Plans would not be permitted to make such a special withdrawal election available, however, unless the annuity was no longer authorized to be held as an investment option under the plan or participants' ability to invest in it was suspended indefinitely. To prevent the special exception from being used solely to benefit one or a few individuals, the withdrawal event should be limited to cases in which a lifetime income investment is no longer available to all or a broad class of participants.

REQUIRED MINIMUM DISTRIBUTION RULES

The required minimum distribution (RMD) rules applicable to tax-favored DC plans and IRAs create additional obstacles. While they are used by some as a rough-and-ready, de facto decumulation strategy, the RMD rules are complex, not designed to optimize decumulation, poorly targeted, and enforced by a whopping 50 percent tax penalty if the saver fails to take the required distribution.

We propose a comprehensive package of provisions to bring the RMD rules into closer alignment with their purposes: exempting those to whom the rules need not apply, closing a key loophole, and simplifying and reforming the rules in a progressive way.

Current RMD Rules

RMD rules as of this writing require participants in most tax-qualified retirement plans and IRAs to begin removing assets from the plan beginning soon after they reach age 70½. The benefits are required to be distributed, in accordance with regulations, over the participant's life or life expectancy (or joint lives or life expectancies of the participant and participant's spouse or other beneficiary), or more rapidly.[54] Savers need to take only a small share of their assets each year in order to comply (generally a fraction of the account balance each year that is calculated to distribute the entire account ratably over the individual's or married couple's remaining life expectancy). For example, the 2019 RMD rules require married retirees turning age 70½ to distribute only 3.65 percent of their retirement savings in the first year (and less if the spouse is more than ten years younger than the retiree). The percentages increase gradually as retirees age.[55] The rules do not actually require participants to stop saving and begin consuming amounts required to be distributed, only to remove them from the tax-deferred plan or IRA so that they will be taxed currently and will no longer benefit from tax-deferred accumulation.

DC plans and IRAs are subject to RMD rules that differ from those applicable to DB plans and qualified plan annuities. Roth IRAs are exempt from lifetime but not postdeath RMDs; Roth 401(k) accounts are not exempt from RMDs at all. Related to the age 70½ RMD commencement deadline, traditional IRAs may not accept new contributions after that age, but qualified plans and Roth IRAs are not subject to that restriction.[56] Special and complicated RMD rules apply after the account owner's death, varying based on whether the account holder died before RMDs began, the type of beneficiary (or beneficiaries), and other factors.

Since they are not designed to serve as guidelines for optimal asset decumulation, the RMD rules can restrict planning and impede the optimal use of savings. While the one-divided-by-life-expectancy (annually recalculated) approach prescribed by the RMD rules is far from the worst rough rule of thumb for decumulation that might be devised, it also is not good enough. In practice, many retirees might misinterpret the taxation pattern prescribed by the RMD rules as officially endorsing an optimal consumption pattern (minimum and maximum), and this is one reason why apparently the rules often affect the pace at which balances are withdrawn.[57] Yet the regular RMD pattern does not match most retirees' needs or desires—which of course are neither uniform nor consistent from year to year—and does not lend itself to dynamic drawdown planning based on periodic reassessments reflecting changes in circumstances. Social Security already provides a relatively inflexible income stream; private sector retirement savings need not follow suit. In addition, because the RMD rules apply a fraction each year to the current account balance (one divided by the annually recalculated life expectancy, in years), they automatically translate annual market losses or gains into proportional annual retirement pay cuts or raises, which can be disruptively volatile.

The RMD rules also are poorly targeted. They are intended chiefly to help ensure that tax-advantaged retirement benefits are used for their intended purpose—increasing financial security in retirement—rather than for estate planning purposes, such as transferring wealth tax-free across generations. Wealthy individuals already disproportionately benefit from tax-advantaged retirement accounts, and, with more savings than they need to maintain their standard of living, can benefit from letting their tax-favored retirement plan balances continue accumulating untaxed returns for as long as the law permits. In fact, affluent retirees and their advisers have long been exploiting weaknesses in the RMD regime to achieve substantial cross-generational tax deferral. In addition, the 50 percent excise tax on noncompliance ultimately threatens mainly retirees with modest resources who misinterpret or fail to understand the rules and who cannot afford to delegate compliance to personal financial advisers or CPAs.

A one-year RMD holiday in 2009 served as a natural experiment showing that retirees with greater assets—as well as the typically wealthier retirees who choose to take their RMDs annually instead of monthly—were more likely to take advantage of the holiday by suspending distributions.[58] This provides further evidence that retirees with less accumulated wealth tend to depend on ongoing plan distributions for financial support; ordinary retirees commonly are neither interested in nor in a position to adhere to a strategy that maximizes tax deferral.[59]

For these reasons, the legitimate policy goal of preventing the misuse of retirement tax preferences for estate planning is not efficiently advanced by taxing a prescribed portion of ordinary retirees' savings annually pursuant to inflexible rules that can be complex, confusing, and costly to comply with.[60]

Proposed RMD Reforms

To address these concerns, a comprehensive package of provisions could bring the RMD rules into closer alignment with their purposes by exempting those to whom the rules need not apply, closing a key loophole, and otherwise reforming the rules in a progressive manner. We propose the following steps to reform the existing rules to reduce their burden, reduce noncompliance, and reduce the number of individuals affected or threatened by the stiff enforcement penalty.

EXEMPT ORDINARY RETIREES FROM RMDS

Accordingly, we propose to better target the RMD rules by totally and permanently exempting from RMDs those retirees with average or below-average assets.[61] As noted, those retirees are likely to be relying on their savings to finance current or upcoming consumption, to be making relatively consistent withdrawals without regard to the RMD rules, and to exhaust their account balances over the course of their lifetime. Therefore exempting them would reduce their compliance burden and lose less revenue than relief for the affluent.[62] We recommend that the specific maximum aggregate balance (qualified plans and IRAs) needed to qualify for the exemption be set at $100,000 as of age 70 (phasing out ratably over the next $10,000) with a view to exempting at least a majority of retirees, but the amount should be adjusted upward (not to exceed $250,000) or downward depending on the affordability of the estimated revenue cost.

CLOSE THE STRETCH IRA LOOPHOLE

We propose to offset the revenue cost of this proposed exemption (at least in large part) by closing a sizable gap in the RMD regime: the extended period permitted for postdeath distributions to many heirs (as of 2019). This enables wealthy retirees to pass their retirement savings down to later generations at a reduced tax rate. In many cases, for example, young grandchildren inherit the plan account or IRA from a wealthy deceased grandparent and stretch the RMDs out over their entire lifetime (hence known as a "stretch IRA"). We propose to require distribution of retirement account assets upon the owner's death or within five years thereafter.[63]

We also recommend the following additional statutory changes to simplify and otherwise improve the RMD rules and reduce taxpayer burdens.

REGULARLY UPDATE LIFE EXPECTANCY TABLES

Another useful, but much smaller, change to the RMD rules would update the RMD life expectancy tables. While Congress has the authority to change the statute (i.e., change the fundamental structure of RMDs or exempt certain savers from the rules), Treasury has the authority to adjust the life expectancy tables in the RMD regulations. In 1987 and 2002, the Treasury Department used its authority to update and simplify the life expectancy tables to reflect the increase in life expectancies in the United States. The tables have not been similarly updated since then,[64] but a 2018 Trump administration Executive Order directed Treasury to determine whether the life expectancies used in the RMD regulations are requiring unduly large withdrawals and should be updated, and whether updates should be made annually or on some other periodic basis.[65] Given net gains in life expectancy since 2002, updated tables would afford retirees slightly more flexibility in drawing down their savings, although the impact would be small.[66] That said, we propose that Congress direct the Treasury Department to update the RMD life expectancy tables at least every five years to reflect any changes in life expectancy. While this likely would have only a small impact, it is sound policy because tax parameters should be updated to reflect changes in the economy.

IRA TRUSTEES SHOULD AUTOMATICALLY CALCULATE RMDS

Qualified plan administrators are responsible for calculating RMDs for their retirees who still have benefits in the plan when they reach age 70. However, retirement funds have continued increasingly to roll over from plans to IRAs, whose trustees and custodians are not required to do so. IRA trustees are required only to notify the retiree that the RMD rules apply and offer to perform the calculations if requested. Not surprisingly, many IRA owners in their seventies or older fail to read these notices and are unaware of this offer or, in many cases, are unaware of the RMD rules. We propose, therefore, that IRA trustees and custodians be required not only to inform retirees of their RMD responsibilities but also to automatically calculate and distribute the RMDs for their customers. IRA owners who wish to use some of their IRAs to satisfy the RMDs for their other IRAs can so inform the IRA trustees and specify the amounts they want distributed. IRA trustees would be protected from any responsibility that depends on knowing about any other IRAs or IRA balances owned by the same individual.

SIMPLIFY AND HARMONIZE ROTH AND TRADITIONAL IRA RULES

As noted earlier, the RMD rules apply to qualified plan accounts, including Roth 401(k) accounts, as well as traditional IRAs, but Roth IRAs are exempt from the lifetime RMD rules. Though not compelled by sound retirement or tax policy, this gives Roth 401(k) participants an incentive to roll over plan benefits to a Roth IRA (or save in a Roth IRA instead of a plan) to avoid RMDs (even though ERISA-governed qualified plans more often offer participants lower fees, carefully curated investment options, and professional fiduciary oversight). Accordingly, we propose to harmonize the RMD rules to apply in the same way to all IRAs and qualified plans by eliminating the special Roth IRA RMD exemption.[67] Existing Roth IRA balances would be grandfathered for those who rely on the current exemption.

At the same time, we would harmonize the different treatment (as of 2019) of contributions to traditional IRAs (prohibited after age 70½), Roth IRAs, and qualified plans (no such prohibition) by permitting post-age-70½ contributions to traditional IRAs. The rationale for prohibiting contributions after 70½ simply because RMDs are required to begin is not compelling: the prohibition does not apply to other types of plans, most of which are also subject to RMDs, and the choice to continue saving may be increasingly meaningful as people work and live longer.

CLARIFY THAT PLANS CANNOT BUY BACK ONGOING LIFE ANNUITIES

An additional RMD reform would direct Treasury and IRS to amend the RMD regulations to make clear that DB plan sponsors generally are not permitted to offer to buy back from retirees ongoing DB plan life annuities in exchange for lump-sum payments.

A number of the DB plan sponsors that have been seeking to "de-risk" their balance sheets by cutting back on existing DB plan liabilities have been advised by consultants that they might reduce DB liabilities and participants by offering to buy back lifetime annuities from retirees who have been receiving them (in some cases for many years). A retiree who accepts the offer to cash out his or her DB lifetime retirement income might find that, upon seeking advice from a financial adviser regarding the optimal investment of the resulting lump-sum payment, some advisers recommend using at least a portion of the lump sum to purchase a commercial annuity (at a retail premium cost that did not apply to the DB plan annuity). For many years, it was widely believed that such buybacks were not permitted, but employer requests several years ago resulted in a number of IRS private letter rulings addressed to specific employers indicating that the buybacks were not prohibited.[68]

ENACT OTHER RMD IMPROVEMENTS

Our comprehensive package of RMD reforms would also include improvements (statutory or regulatory) to the regulatory RMD exemption for QLACs.[69] We would also recommend specific limited relaxations of existing RMD regulations that prohibit certain modest increases in annuities. However, since these proposals are beyond the scope of this chapter, we leave them to be addressed at another time.

FIRST STEPS TO DEPENDABLE LIFETIME INCOME

Promoting appropriate annuity options in 401(k) and other DC plans is a challenge worth taking on. Greater use of income annuities—by more participants for some portion of their benefits—promises to increase retirement security and provide meaningful help in addressing retirees' decumulation dilemma. DC plans could begin to offer lifetime income to tens of millions of participants, with group purchasing, institutional pricing, economies of scale, and behavioral strategies. To that end, we propose policy reforms to establish an appropriately worker-protective fiduciary safe harbor for the selection of annuity providers, increase annuity portability, and reform the RMD regime. These changes could begin to restore the pension to our private pension system. However, they would constitute only the first step toward broader reform in this area: in addition to reducing the complexity, opacity, and cost in the annuity market, much more remains to be done to help savers take a thoughtful approach to retirement planning.

APPENDIX

This appendix provides additional context for our fiduciary safe harbor proposal, further detailing its rationale and adding several more detailed recommendations. The following sections: provide further background and discussion of the use of financial strength ratings, followed by pertinent private and public sector examples. They address the scope of the safe harbor including potentially limiting safe harbor coverage to fixed income annuities rather than including variable and indexed annuities, as well as potentially requiring that insurers have experience providing annuities. Finally, it considers whether risk-based capital ratios should be an element of the safe harbor.

Use of Financial Strength Ratings: Further Background and Discussion

Going back at least to 1995, the Department of Labor has provided guidance to plan fiduciaries on their selection of annuity providers to make benefit payments to plan participants.[70] The guidance has been focused on the insurers' claims-paying ability and creditworthiness, and the ratings have played a leading role. In fact, the centrality of ratings among the factors to consider in the ERISA fiduciary analysis was so obvious to DoL in 1995 that, before even referring to other factors (such as the level of the insurer's capital and surplus or the quality of its underlying investment portfolio), DoL took pains to make clear that ratings were *not the only* factor to take into account.[71] Since the 1990s, however, private sector stakeholders have complained that DoL guidance requiring plan fiduciaries to select "the safest available annuity" on the market ("unless, under the circumstances, it would be in the interest of participants and beneficiaries to do otherwise") was unduly strict and impractical (at least as applied to DC plans)[72] and could expose them to litigation for arguably failing to select, in general, the "safest available" annuity (although DoL made clear that multiple annuities might qualify under this standard).

In reaction, the Pension Protection Act of 2006 directed DoL to exempt annuities offered as optional forms of benefit in DC plans from the "safest available" standard. DoL complied, and in 2007 proposed a new regulation, which it termed a "safe harbor," expressly for DC plan annuities. As noted, the regulation, finalized in 2008, requires plan fiduciaries to take certain steps (summarized in endnote 26) which, however, are not sufficiently objective and automatic to give plan sponsors the certainty needed in a safe harbor. The insurance industry then developed and discussed with DoL its proposals, substantially similar to the statutory fiduciary safe harbor. DoL strongly opposed that approach but announced that it was seeking to develop a regulatory safe harbor that would seek to provide the requisite certainty for plan sponsors while including standards that would adequately protect participants and their retirement security.[73] However, DoL's work and discussions with the insurance industry and other stakeholders, including the National Association of Insurance Commissioners (NAIC), were ultimately unavailing.

One key obstacle was Dodd-Frank's prohibition on regulatory reliance on credit ratings. In view of inaccurate credit ratings' contribution to the Great Recession, the Dodd-Frank legislation required federal agencies to minimize their reliance on credit ratings and substitute other standards of creditworthiness. Accordingly, DoL proposed in 2013 to revise a number of its prohibited transaction exemptions (which relied on the use of credit ratings in various instances) by following the SEC's lead in replacing previous references to high credit ratings with at least one NRSRO with qualitative descriptions.[74]

Meanwhile, however, Dodd-Frank was depriving DoL of a critical tool in formulating a workable annuity safe harbor: protecting plan sponsors from liability if, among other conditions, they limited their selections to insurers highly rated for financial strength. While at an impasse with DoL, the insurance industry eventually negotiated a successful compromise among disparate interests within the industry (such as highly rated, higher-cost insurers versus lower-rated, lower-cost insurers) and then won bipartisan support for its proposal as part of a multifaceted legislative package in the Senate Finance Committee. Ironically, Dodd-Frank's ban on the use of credit ratings by federal regulatory and administrative agencies would not have prevented Congress from including a highly rated financial strength standard as a key element of a legislative safe harbor. However, the legislative process moved quickly in the late summer and fall of 2016 without serious engagement on the financial strength ratings possibility, and the industry's proposal was adopted by the Senate Finance Committee in 2016 and later passed by the House of Representatives (in 2018 and 2019).[75]

As noted, in our view a safe harbor could improve on the legislative proposal by adding an objective quality standard based on insurers' financial strength and claims-paying capacity. It would specify a high ratings level and direct DoL to issue more detailed administrative guidance on the financial strength ratings and any other metrics to flesh out and apply a statutory safe harbor standard limited to annuity providers financially strong enough to be considered "highly qualified." For example, the legislation could direct DoL (in consultation with Treasury, and after considering any advice from the SEC's Office of Credit Ratings and the American Academy of Actuaries) to determine the combination of financial strength ratings (and possibly credit ratings) that should be required to satisfy such a high financial strength safe harbor standard. In addition, DoL should obtain from insurers specific disclosures of how their corporate structure relates to the insurer's liability to pay claims (e.g., whether the obligated entity is a subsidiary only or includes the parent company or affiliates, and how the ratings apply to these entities).

In addition, it would be worth exploring whether (and if so, how) a safe harbor with an appropriate financial strength condition could take into account the applicable guarantees put in place by state guaranty associations as a backup in the event of insurer insolvency, up to the applicable state guarantee limits (often $250,000, but often higher or lower, depending on the state). The limits mean participants' annuities might not be fully covered and make the insurer's claims-paying ability even more important, as does the fact that the state guaranty association system—while a significant factor—is unfunded, relies on payment by insurance companies rather than the state or federal government, and has yet to be fully put to the test of major or multiple insolvencies (as opposed to smaller and relatively isolated ones).[76]

Our proposed safe harbor's partial reliance on third-party financial strength ratings has also been advocated by the Bipartisan Policy Center's June 2016 Report of the Commission on Retirement Security and Personal Savings. That report recommended that a "more objective approach to assessing carrier solvency" might consider not only the basic license, accreditation, and good standing factors included in the current proposed statutory fiduciary safe harbor but also "*insurer-financial-strength ratings from third-party analysts* (emphasis added).[77]

Moreover, both our recommendation that the safe harbor direct fiduciaries to rely in part on third-party financial strength ratings and our suggestion to explore the possibility of using a universal independent fiduciary approach find support in a 2017 Treasury Department report. The report notes that, "Despite the benefits that annuities can provide, they are not widely offered in defined contribution plans" and observes that the fear of liability under ERISA is "the principal deterrent to offering an in-plan annuity option." It recommends that Treasury and DoL "develop proposals on how to establish or certify one or more expert, independent fiduciary entities to assess the long-term financial strength of annuity providers." Such assessments "could be in the form of ratings or other specific metrics" and "could assist ERISA-governed plan sponsors in complying with their fiduciary duty obligations in selecting annuity providers for plans and enable fiduciaries to rely on such assessments as a safe harbor." The report made clear that this "independent fiduciary function would not otherwise affect the fiduciaries' ERISA responsibilities to evaluate all other aspects of the annuity purchase decision" such as the price and other terms of the annuity contract.[78]

Use of Financial Strength Ratings: Private and Public Sector Examples

Imperfect as they are, NRSRO financial strength ratings of insurers have long been and continue to be commonly relied on in various contexts as a leading measure of claims-paying ability. By way of illustration, the following are examples—from the private and public sectors, including annuity quotation platforms, marketing materials, regulations, policy recommendations, and other sources—of how annuity providers' NRSRO ratings are used for this purpose.[79]

FIDELITY INVESTMENTS

Fidelity Investments offers annuities provided by various insurers and by its own insurance subsidiary. When offering deferred income annuities provided by other insurance companies, Fidelity shows the financial strength ratings of each insurer from two different rating agencies—AM Best and S&P—and shows, as of this writing, that each such insurer is rated Superior (A++ or A+) by AM Best and Very Strong or Strong (AA+, AA–, or A+) by S&P.

ANNUITIES.COM

Annuities.com advertises that it provides quotes "from A+ rated companies."

IMMEDIATEANNUITIES.COM

Immediateannuities.com encourages customers to "maximize the safety of your annuity by learning which companies have the highest ratings."[80]

HUELER INCOME SOLUTIONS

Hueler Income Solutions' annuity purchase and quotation platform is "a web-based lifetime income annuity purchase system" with an online platform stating that "multiple highly rated insurance companies compete on each quote" and showing customers each annuity provider's current financial strength ratings from three different rating agencies. As of this original publication in 2019, all but one of the providers on the platform are rated A+ by AM Best, and the other one is rated A.

ERISA COUNSEL

Experienced, respected ERISA counsel have recommended that ERISA plan fiduciaries selecting insurers to provide annuities consider the insurers' financial strength ratings.[81] Moreover, in testimony before DoL's 2018 ERISA Advisory Council, ERISA counsel had this to say about the legislative safe harbor for selection of annuity providers that was then pending in Congress:

> We are concerned, though, about a safe harbor that has, as its foundational basis, a certificate of authority from the insurance commissioner of its domiciliary state. Unfortunately, the quality of State regulation and oversight varies. As a result, it is possible that an insurer could be domiciled in a state that does not have robust requirements and supervision of its insurance companies. That deficiency [could] be offset in a number of ways. For example, we list a number of factors in our white paper on evaluating in-plan guarantees. . . . However, if a safe harbor is created via legislation, information provided by rating agencies could be used. . . . In that case, one of the standards could be that the insurance company be rated by at least one of the major agencies as being financially strong and that none of the

> rating agencies have a financial strength rating below their designation of good financial health. . . . The ratings should be viewed for both the most recent completed year and for the preceding five or 10 years. In other words, the safe harbor should require that the financial strength be maintained for over a full economic cycle. To meet the needs of plan sponsors, the criteria would need to be objective.[82]

Outside the context of a safe harbor, addressing the "four main areas that fiduciaries should consider when evaluating an insurance company," the first two specified by these ERISA counsel are "financial strength of the company" and "evaluation by the rating agencies." Stressing the important role that ratings play, they advise that, "Since the capital adequacy, balance sheet strength, claims paying ability, and financial strength of an insurer are all analyzed and incorporated into the rating agencies' assessment, one of the most important steps a plan sponsor can take is to understand the current ratings and ratings over recent past and to ensure the insurance company offering the retirement income product fully cooperates with the information requested by the rating agencies."[83]

Counsel's discussion proceeds to describe and explain the separate rating categories and scales used by each of "the four major" ratings services, stating that "acceptable ratings for financially strong companies are considered" to be A or higher from AM Best, A– or higher from Fitch Ratings, A3 or higher from Moody's, and A– or higher from S&P. The discussion also summarizes approvingly and elaborates on DoL's statements (in its 2007 proposed regulations and preamble to its final 2008 regulations) regarding the importance of the rating agencies' insurer financial strength ratings, including the importance of taking into account any adverse comments or negative information the rating agencies might provide.

MICHIGAN PERS INVESTMENT LEGISLATION

Michigan's statutory guidelines for fiduciaries investing pension funds for plans covering state and local government employees have long authorized investment in annuity contracts if the annuity provider has "a claims-paying ability rating" of at least A from AM Best or AA– from Duff & Phelps (now Fitch) and an overall company financial strength rating of at least Aa3 from Moody's or AA– from S&P. (The law also requires insurers to have been in operation for at least five years and to have specified minimum assets under management.)[84]

Scope of Insurer Selection Safe Harbor

The determination that a selected annuity provider is sufficiently strong financially to be a prudent choice is an issue that generally does not vary from plan to plan and accordingly is suitable for safe harbor treatment. By contrast, prudent ERISA fiduciaries should carefully examine and compare the costs and other specific terms of annuity contracts; and in many, if not most, cases they should negotiate those terms. Therefore a safe harbor from liability should not cover contract terms.[85]

Earlier drafts of proposed regulatory and legislative fiduciary safe harbors did extend beyond the selection of the insurer(s), but more recent versions were for the most part limited to the financial strength of the insurance company. In some cases, however, the more recent safe harbors might have been read as also extending safe harbor treatment to the terms of the annuity contracts. After one of the authors of this chapter raised this concern in the legislative process in 2018, ambiguous legislative language was partially revised to make clear that the safe harbor applies to the selection of the annuity provider, not selection or negotiation of the annuity contract terms.[86] The remaining ambiguous language should be clarified to confirm the limited scope, consistent with the relevant House Ways and Means Committee Report.[87]

Coverage of Variable and Indexed in Addition to Fixed Income Annuities

The legislative safe harbor provision pending in Congress departs significantly from the scope of the DoL safe harbor regulation and other DoL guidance. The regulation refers to contracts for "benefit distributions," which could be read to be limited to income annuities—that is, annuity contracts designed simply to distribute benefits in the form of a regular, predictable stream of income in retirement. This differs from accumulation-type annuities designed largely to serve as tax-favored investments, such as indexed or variable annuities (often supplemented by "guaranteed lifetime withdrawal benefits"). DoL's 2015 bulletin on annuities in ERISA plans also focused on "benefit distributions," and its examples were limited to fixed income annuities.[88] Essentially the same is true of Treasury's 2014 guidance on QLACs and its guidance on annuities embedded in target-date funds.[89] By contrast, the term used in the 2019 proposed legislative safe harbor ("guaranteed retirement income contract") would broaden the scope to cover the selection of providers of variable and indexed annuities.

As noted, variable and indexed annuity products and associated sales practices have for years been criticized for undue complexity and lack of transparency that confuse and mislead consumers and make comparing products and prices difficult. Relatedly, these products have long been taken to task for excessive fees and commissions that can bias brokers in favor of the highest-commission products and that are hard for consumers to identify and evaluate.[90] Consumer advocates also maintain that most state insurance departments have effectively addressed these well-publicized problems, and that, for all of these reasons, a safe harbor for selection of annuity providers should be limited to providers that offer fixed income annuities.[91] Meanwhile, mutual funds and other financial services industries have complained that the insurance industry would be unfairly advantaged by a fiduciary safe harbor that covers the selection of insurers providing products that are called annuities but are overwhelmingly used to provide tax-deferred investment accumulation rather than guaranteed retirement income for life. A strong case can be made, therefore, for limiting the ERISA fiduciary safe harbor to insurers providing types of annuities that are designed mainly to provide guaranteed income in retirement (while continuing to permit plans to offer variable, indexed, or other accumulation-oriented types of annuities outside of the safe harbor if prudent and in participants' interests under normal ERISA fiduciary standards).

There are several policy arguments against limiting the safe harbor to fixed income annuities. First, variable and indexed annuities are not necessarily or invariably complex, nontransparent, or high-priced. Such products could be made far more understandable, transparent, comparable to competing products, and therefore more reasonably priced, although much in their history and reports of current practices give grounds for concern.[92] A fiduciary safe harbor that is justified based on annuities' distinctive capacity to protect retirees from longevity and market risk could still apply to the selection of insurers providing variable annuities that are designed to be consumer protective and mainly to provide guaranteed retirement income.[93]

Second, the industry would point out that excluding these products from the safe harbor would constrain market creativity in designing products that are responsive to consumers' needs (while consumer advocates would reply that the prevalent forms of creativity in the annuity market have too often involved complexity and obfuscation, maximizing adviser compensation at consumers' expense). A third argument would contend that, because the scope of the safe harbor is limited to selection of the insurer, the design and terms of the annuity contracts would remain outside the safe harbor and hence subject to ERISA's full fiduciary analysis. Accordingly, plan sponsors' concerns about the risk of litigation and liability might also help make them sufficiently wary of complex, high-priced products.

In addition, while concerns about risks to consumers from variable annuities have focused on the retail market, the offering of annuities, including variable annuities, in ERISA plans might be expected to involve less inequality of bargaining power between the insurance industry and consumers and therefore more institutional rather than retail pricing. ERISA requires fees to be reasonable, and its duties of prudence and loyalty obligate plan officials to represent participants' interests by competently seeking the best deal possible for them.

That said, even though ERISA's normal fiduciary duties (not the safe harbor) apply in determining the terms of the contract, this might matter less to medium-sized and smaller plans that, as a practical matter, are less likely to benefit from expert, specialized advice or representation than larger plans. There may still be a risk that the legal distinction—that the safe harbor applies to the selection of insurers offering variable and indexed annuities but not the selection of the terms of those annuities—will be blurred for smaller plans. The practical result might be that the fiduciary analysis of the type of contract and its terms would be colored by an overall sense that Congress, in the safe harbor, has in effect approved the use of variable and indexed annuities in ERISA-governed plans.

This is another reason some consumer advocates argue that the safe harbor for selection of insurers should be limited so as to apply only when insurers are offering fixed income annuities. The Consumer Federation of America has opined that "there are two characteristics of [variable and indexed] market-guaranty annuity products that require exclusion from the RESA safe harbor—an untested and evolving state regulatory framework and the consumer protection problems of high fees and misleading products."[94] A related argument for limiting the safe harbor is that the statutory exemption for indexed annuities precludes the SEC from regulating those products and protecting consumers from what many describe as inappropriate and misleading marketing practices facilitated by complicated indexed annuity product designs (see endnote 21). Consumer advocates contend that "the new market-guaranty annuity products have posed a challenge for [state] insurance regulators, and the regulatory framework for such products is a work-in-progress"—including an ongoing multiyear NAIC project "to establish a capital and reserving framework for variable annuities." Implicit in this is the possibility of limiting a current fiduciary safe harbor to the selection of insurers providing fixed income annuities but amending it later to include insurers providing indexed and variable products once an appropriate regulatory framework is in place and working adequately.

Finally, consumer advocates have maintained that state insurance departments have less experience regulating these evolving and rapidly expanding indexed and variable annuity products even from a solvency (not only a consumer protection) standpoint.[95] In the case of a fiduciary safe harbor that does apply to the selection of insurers providing indexed and variable annuities, this would be another reason to include a ratings-based financial strength standard as part of the safe harbor.[96]

Requiring Insurer Experience Providing Annuities

Annuity providers included in the safe harbor should be sufficiently experienced in providing annuities. The pending legislative safe harbor provision requires insurers to represent that they are licensed to provide annuities and have operated in accordance with a valid certificate of authority for at least seven years. We would make clear that this seven-year experience requirement means that the insurer or its organizational unit that provides annuities has been in the business of providing annuities for that period. (The pending legislative language is ambiguous on this point.)[97]

Should Risk-Based Capital Ratios Be an Element of the Safe Harbor?

Another potential metric would be the risk-based capital (RBC) ratios that state insurance departments approve or determine and take into account.[98] Insurers file annual statements reporting on their capital reserves, which are compared with a minimum RBC requirement that varies depending on the type of insurance and the kinds of risks to which an insurer is exposed. Those whose capital falls short of the minimum required amount must take or be subjected to certain preventive or remedial actions. RBC formulas and ratios were designed to provide early warning of problems, helping state regulators keep watch over particular companies' financial situations and identify any solvency issues or financial distress situations that call for regulatory intervention.

RBC ratios are intended primarily to help identify troubled insurers rather than to serve as a basis for comparing insurance companies based on their financial strength. That said, in a proposed safe harbor designed to rely on state regulators to determine insurance companies' financial strength and claims-paying ability, representations that merely address whether the insurer is the subject of unusual and dire regulatory intervention such as an order of supervision, rehabilitation, or liquidation is of limited utility to fiduciaries, especially in view of ERISA's exacting fiduciary standards. Disclosure, as part of the insurer's representations to plan fiduciaries, of the insurer's state-approved RBC ratios (and related data) might be more helpful. State regulators and rating agencies rely on RBC ratios (which are normally kept confidential) as one major factor in assessing financial strength and stability. However, before any such RBC ratio disclosure is required, we recommend that DoL (in consultation with Treasury, NAIC, the actuaries, insurance industry representatives, and other expert organizations) determine and advise on whether disclosure of state-approved RBC ratios could add value to a safe harbor (and if so, how), even if the safe harbor criteria were based on financial strength ratings and not also on RBC ratios. Pending the results of such an analysis, we would not recommend that RBC ratios be included in the safe harbor criteria because they already are taken into account by the NRSROs, together with other information, in formulating financial strength ratings, and because reportedly the ratios can be somewhat readily manipulated.[99] However, RBC ratios might, for example, inform analyses by plan sponsors that decide not to rely on a new fiduciary safe harbor but instead to select an annuity provider pursuant to ERISA's normal fiduciary standards, using financial strength determinations such as those prescribed by DoL's annuity selection regulations (as is generally done when selecting annuity providers for DB plans, where no safe harbor applies).

NOTES

The authors thank the Laura and John Arnold Foundation for research support. For helpful comments, we thank the participants in an April 18, 2019, conference at Brookings (including Phyllis Borzi, Michael Davis, Kelli Hueler, Moshe Milevsky, and Richard Thaler) as well as Josh Gotbaum, Aaron Krupkin, and Emily Merola.

Disclosure: Iwry provides, through J. Mark Iwry, PLLC, policy and legal advice to plan sponsors and other corporations, private equity, fintech, and other investment firms, trade associations, and nonprofit organizations regarding retirement and savings policy, pension and retirement plans, and related issues. Iwry is a member of the American Benefits Institute Board of Advisors, the Board of Advisors of the Pension Research Council at the Wharton School, the Council of Scholar Advisors of the Georgetown University Center for Retirement Initiatives, the Panel of Outside Scholars of the Boston College Center for Retirement Research, the CUNA Mutual Safety Net Independent Advisory Board, and the Aspen Leadership Forum Advisory Board. He also is currently serving as an expert witness in federal court litigation relating to retirement plans. The authors did not receive any financial support from any firm or person for any views or positions expressed or advocated in this paper. They are currently not an officer, director, or board member of any organization that has compensated or otherwise influenced them to write this paper or to express or advocate any views or positions in this paper. Accordingly, the views and positions expressed in this paper are solely those of the authors and should not be attributed to any other person or organization.

1. Employee Benefit Research Institute (2012).

2. Investment Company Institute (2018); Government Accountability Office (2017).

3. For ways to provide retirement income for DC plan participants that involve nonannuity vehicles, see John and others (2019).

4. These strategies include choice architecture using default options, framing the annuity purchase decision in terms of guarantees, risk-shifting insurance, and consumption rather than in investment terms that emphasize return on investment, and other techniques to encourage take-up; employer-provided financial education and expert counseling; incremental participant decision making; gradual acquisition of deferred annuities that includes dollar-cost-averaging of interest rate risk; group arrangements with annuity quotation and purchase platforms; and other plan- or workplace-based approaches.

5. "Life annuities" are also sometimes called "income annuities" to distinguish them from "deferred fixed annuities," which provide a fixed, guaranteed rate of return for a specified period of years, and from other annuity contracts that are generally designed as tax-favored investment vehicles with accumulation features that could, but usually are not expected to, provide a stream of income.

6. To help encourage DC plans and IRAs to provide lifetime income, the US Treasury Department and IRS in 2014 authorized "qualifying longevity annuity contracts" (QLACs). QLACs are longevity income annuities for DC plans and IRAs that may begin payments as late as age 85 and are subject to other conditions designed to promote simplicity and transparency and to facilitate product and price comparisons (US Department of the Treasury 2014; Internal Revenue Service 2014b).

7. Unless these annuities are included in tax-qualified plans, they are not subject to nondiscrimination standards, maximum limits, or most other rules that apply to tax-qualified plans.

8. Numerous other indexes have been developed for these products in recent years, raising concerns about performance illustrations used in marketing to investors. The Financial Industry Regulatory Authority (FINRA) has said that indexed annuities are complex and that investors will find it difficult to compare one indexed annuity with another.

9. Yaari (1965).

10. See, e.g., Davidoff, Brown, and Diamond (2005).

11. Investment Company Institute (2019).

12. LIMRA (2018).

13. Benartzi, Previtero, and Thaler (2011) provide a particularly thoughtful discussion, including data suggesting that significant numbers of DB plan participants choose lifetime income streams even when offered a lump-sum alternative.

14. For an overview, see Beshears and others (2018); Abraham and Harris (2015); and Brown (2007).

15. See Dushi and Webb (2004); Lockwood (2012).

16. Brown and Poterba (2000). Reichling and Smetters (2015) show, building on the Yaari (1965) model, that when mortality risk is correlated with shocks to health care status and hence health care spending, demand for annuities falls significantly.

17. When consumers have private information about their health, insurance companies can expect individuals with longer life expectancies to be more likely to buy annuities and those with shorter life expectancies to stay out of the market. The resulting pool of annuity purchasers lives longer than average and therefore raises the costs of providing annuities. High fees also drive up the costs of annuities (Brown 2007).

18. Brown, Poterba, and Richardson (2017).

19. Brown, Casey, and Mitchell (2007). The tendency to undervalue the income equivalent of an account balance, for example, is sometimes characterized as "wealth illusion."

20. Brown and others (2013) find that life annuities are more attractive when presented in a way that emphasizes what the annuity will finance than when presented in a way that highlights the wealth accumulation aspects of annuities. With the investment frame, many people, if willing to purchase an annuity at all, prefer products that offer a principal guarantee (such as the return of unrecovered premium upon death), ensuring that they cannot "lose" their investment. Consumers' tendency to bring an investment rather than an insurance or consumption frame to the purchase decision may be promoted by the industry's pursuit of investment products. In addition, savers' perceptions may be shaped by institutional culture, including longstanding institutional framing, traditions, and norms. These factors might help explain, for example, why, despite the popularity of lump sums in the many DB plans that offer them, many other DB plans have continued to offer only annuities and not lump sums, as well as why annuity take-up among traditional TIAA-CREF customers has historically been higher than among other groups.

21. A FINRA "Investor Alert" (2010) included the following: "Why an Alert on Equity-Indexed Annuities? Sales of equity-indexed annuities (EIAs)—also known as 'fixed indexed insurance products' and 'indexed annuities'—have grown considerably in recent years. . . . EIAs are anything but easy to understand. One of the most confusing features of an EIA is the method used to calculate the gain in the index to which the annuity is linked. To make matters worse, there is not one, but several different indexing methods. Because of the variety and complexity of the methods used to credit interest, investors will find it difficult to compare one EIA to another." Because of concerns such as these, one type of fixed income annuity—the QLAC—is subject to federal regulatory conditions intended to ensure simplicity of product design and promote product and price comparison. Internal Revenue Service (2014b).

According to another FINRA "Investor Alert" (2012), "The marketing efforts used by some variable annuity sellers deserve scrutiny—especially when seniors are the targeted investors. Sales pitches for these products might attempt to scare or confuse investors. . . . Many such claims are not based on facts, but nevertheless help land a sale. While variable annuities can be appropriate as an investment under the right circumstances, as an investor, you should be aware of their restrictive features, understand that substantial taxes and charges may apply if you withdraw your money early, and guard against fear-inducing sales tactics."

22. Section 989J of the Dodd-Frank legislation (known as the Harkin amendment) prohibits SEC regulation of indexed annuities (the fastest-growing type) by treating them as not being securities.

23. Most annuities are sold in a labor-intensive fashion through networks of "producers" working on commission rather than for a flat fee. These competing agents, brokers, wire houses, financial advisers, insurance marketing organizations, and other intermediaries vary widely in their training and standards, and many have been taken to task for their indexed and variable annuity sales practices and sales incentives. See, e.g., Office of Senator Elizabeth Warren (2015). The short-lived Department of Labor (DoL) fiduciary rule had apparently begun to help curb some of the widely reported conflicts and excessive fees and commissions for indexed and variable annuities, but its removal in 2018 may have prompted at least a partial relapse.

24. How best to address these problems in the annuity market is a difficult question. Many would look for the solution in stronger and more broadly applicable fiduciary standards (as in the DoL fiduciary rule), including fee-leveling requirements. Others would argue that the market will inevitably replace commission-based sales models with fee-only compensation, and that this will go far toward curing conflicts of interest and eliminating excessive annuity lock-in and high surrender fees. Still others would advocate repeal of the Harkin amendment, which prevents the SEC from regulating to protect consumers from indexed annuities. In addition, if the kinds of legislative proposals we advocate here would lead to expanded group annuity purchasing by DC plans, including institutional pricing, it could exert positive pressure on the retail market. Finally, at least some industry representatives would maintain that the annuity market is becoming more civilized, leaving behind the occasional abuses of an earlier era, and curing itself without the need for regulatory intervention. Solving these problems in the market is an important challenge, but one that is beyond the scope of this chapter.

25. See, e.g., Milevsky (2018, 2013).

26. To qualify for protection from liability, fiduciaries must engage in an "objective, thorough, and analytical search for" providers, must "appropriately consider information sufficient to assess the ability of the annuity provider to make all future payments under the annuity contract," and "appropriately conclude that, at the time of selection, the annuity provider is financially able to make all future payments under the annuity contract and the cost of the annuity contract is reasonable" and thereafter continually review the appropriateness of that conclusion. See EBSA (2008a, 2008b). See also the preceding DoL (1995) guidance.

27. In our view, a fiduciary safe harbor is not only desired but needed—not as a legal matter but as a practical matter. The existing standards, including DoL's regulations, Field Assistance Bulletin 2015–02, and the application of ERISA's statute of limi-

tations, provide sufficient guidance to enable responsible plan fiduciaries to select annuity carriers without undue fear of liability. Many plan sponsors have unhesitatingly selected highly rated insurers under these traditional fiduciary standards to annuitize their DB pension obligations, driven by incentives to reduce balance sheet pension liabilities and extricate themselves from DB obligations. The DC context, however, is different. Insistent 401(k) sponsor concerns about the risk of ERISA fiduciary liability for selecting an annuity provider that ultimately becomes insolvent have operated much like a self-fulfilling prophecy. Many employers are genuinely concerned; many others find the risk of liability a convenient reason to avoid the cost or trouble of offering annuities. In any event, the industry narrative regarding a need for a safe harbor to limit fiduciary risk has become so entrenched that progress on offering annuities in 401(k) plans will not occur without one.

28. See the Setting Every Community Up for Retirement Enhancement Act of 2019 (SECURE) (2019) and the Retirement Enhancement and Savings Act of 2019 (RESA) (2019) for more recent versions.

29. The authors raised the issue when presenting a summary of the proposals in this chapter at an April 18, 2019, conference at the Brookings Institution. The appendix compares our proposals with pending legislative provisions and makes the case for including a "highly qualified" (financial strength) standard.

30. Specifically, the insurer must represent that it is licensed to offer annuity contracts, has been operating for the past seven years under a current certificate of authority from its state regulator, has filed audited financial statements, has reserves that meet state statutory requirements, undergoes a financial examination by the state every five years (a typical state requirement), and is not operating under an order of supervision, rehabilitation, or liquidation. See RESA section 204; SECURE section 204. To obtain the protection of the safe harbor, fiduciaries also must engage in an "objective, thorough, and analytical search for the purpose of identifying insurers from which to purchase annuity contracts," must consider the contract's cost in relation to its benefits and features, and must conclude that the cost is reasonable.

31. Earlier versions of the pending legislative safe harbor proposal were broader in scope or were ambiguous on this point. At the suggestion of one of the authors of this chapter, the pending legislative language was clarified (though not completely). While a Joint Committee on Taxation (2019) description incorrectly described the scope overbroadly, that document is not part of the official legislative history, and a later House Committee report, Committee on Ways and Means (2019), which is official legislative history, has sought to set the record straight by clearly stating that the scope is specifically limited to selection of the annuity provider.

32. Generally, references here to "financial strength" and "claims-paying" ability are intended to be used interchangeably.

33. For some of these reasons, the 2018 ERISA Advisory Council Report, while supporting the need for a fiduciary safe harbor, refrained from endorsing or supporting the particular approach taken in the RESA fiduciary safe harbor proposal. The council observed that "the bill tries to change ERISA's current safe harbor provision [referring to DoL's 2008 regulation, which is called a safe harbor but, in our view, is not sufficiently clear and objective to provide certainty] to mitigate employer concerns

about adding an annuity option to their retirement plan offerings." Advisory Council on Employee Welfare and Pension Benefit Plans (ERISA Advisory Council or Council) (2018, p. 35). The Council's Report noted that the American Council of Life Insurers (ACLI) supported the RESA safe harbor proposal and that "a few witnesses" (actually two witnesses, both representing insurance companies) also favored such an approach. However, "other witnesses expressed concerns about relying solely on state insurance regulators' certification. Mr. Reish asserted that this approach is not sufficiently protective, noting that oversight quality varies considerably by state. Other witnesses noted that reliance on state insurance guarantee funds could leave participants without adequate coverage if an insurance company defaults. Ms. Dudley of ABC and Ms. Leahy of Siemens suggested that plan sponsors would want more due diligence than simply relying on state certification. Ms. Leahy noted that Siemens would not likely rely on the safe harbor elements of RESA, but rather turn the annuity selection decision over to an independent fiduciary. For smaller plans, this potentially added expense would be a deterrent to using insurance company guaranteed products in LTI [lifetime income] options" (p. 33).

The Council's Report added the following footnote to the sentence quoted in the preceding paragraph that ends with the reference to "simply relying on state certification": "Further, the 2018 Council notes that, in 2012, a representative of the regulators themselves—the National Association of Insurance Commissioners (NAIC)—opined this would not be a good idea—In response to a question from the Council, Ms. McPeak [of NAIC] noted that she did not believe it would be sufficient to establish a safe harbor based solely on the fact that a life insurance company and annuity provider is licensed in a state" (p. 33n33).

34. This commonly means that safe harbors reward, with simplification of process and certainty, decisions that are clearly well within the boundaries of the generally applicable standards. This typically is based on carefully selected, simplified indicators suggesting that, if the generally applicable standards were applied, they would almost certainly be satisfied. Accordingly, consistent with the commonly held "no free lunch" principle, decisionmakers looking to short-cut the generally applicable full-dress fiduciary prudence analysis can reasonably expect to do so only or chiefly by limiting themselves to easier cases designated by the safe harbor. One who instead wants to walk up to the edge of the permissible zone—pushing the envelope to take a position on a close case—can take the additional trouble to engage in the full fiduciary analysis. As experienced ERISA counsel have noted, "'Safe harbors' are ordinarily viewed as creating a higher standard than what the law requires, that is, fiduciaries may satisfy their obligations in ways other than by following the [safe harbor]." Reish and Ashton (2017), Appendix D, p. 33.

35. The Alliance for Lifetime Income is an organization of major insurance companies and investment firms seeking to educate consumers and advisers about the value of commercial annuities for retirement income. See Retirement Checklist Q&A-8 at www.allianceforlifetimeincome.org.

36. Securities and Exchange Commission (2017).

37. White (2018). Some thirty years ago, rating agencies also gave high ratings to the Executive Life Insurance Company before it became insolvent in 1991. Rating agen-

cies seem to have failed to take into account the fact that, while that insurer appeared to be very well capitalized, its own assets were heavily invested in junk bonds. In the ensuing years, the insurance industry has adopted risk-based capital analysis, which is designed to prevent this kind of error in the future.

38. NRSROs are now required to disclose potential conflicts of interest and to address and manage them pursuant to written policies and procedures that they maintain and enforce. Securities and Exchange Commission (2017).

39. Dodd-Frank Wall Street Reform and Consumer Protection Act, sections 939, 939A.

40. Four NRSROs have substantial shares of the market for life insurance company ratings: AM Best Company, Inc., Fitch Ratings (formerly Duff & Phelps), Moody's Investor Services, and Standard & Poor's Insurance Ratings Services. No other NRSROs perform a comparable number of these ratings.

41. The risk of false negatives (erroneously low ratings) is much smaller than the risk of false positives (erroneously high ratings).

42. Example: the top three categories at AM Best and the top four categories at Moody's, Standard & Poor's, and Fitch.

43. See EbixExchange (2007). Each insurer's overall ranking corresponds roughly to a percentile score reflecting a composite of its relative rankings by each NRSRO. Such an approach also would need to give special attention to the appropriate application of financial strength ratings to specific entities as opposed to controlled groups of companies.

44. The American Academy of Actuaries is among those who point out that it is not only the state insurance departments that protect annuitants from the risk of nonpayment. "Insured annuities are issued by insurers and provide guaranteed payments. There is a risk of nonpayment or reduced payment, but that risk is mitigated by the strength of the insurer (its ability to pay claims) as well as requirements from regulators." American Academy of Actuaries (2015, p. 3).

45. *Donovan* v. *Bierwirth*, 680 F.2d 263, 272 (2d Cir. 1982).

46. Debt obligations rated below investment grade have often been colloquially referred to as "junk bonds."

47. Some will object that a quality standard in a safe harbor means the government will be "picking winners and losers." But ERISA's exacting fiduciary standards call for plan fiduciaries (as distinct from the government) to make precisely this kind of discriminating judgment. In fact, DoL regulations continue to require DB plan fiduciaries to choose the "safest annuity available" and make clear that ratings provided by insurance rating services (private sector entities) are a key factor (though by no means the only factor) to consider in determining claims-paying ability. 29 CFR section 2509.95–1(c). Moreover, the approach being explored here for a DC plan annuity provider selection safe harbor would be far less stringent than the "safest available" standard in effect for DB plans.

48. The preamble to DoL's 2007 proposed fiduciary safe harbor regulation explained that, in evaluating an annuity provider's claims-paying ability and creditworthiness, the regulation "requires that the fiduciary consider whether an annuity provider's rating (as determined by an appropriate rating service(s)) demonstrates or

raises questions regarding the provider's ability to make future payments under the annuity contract" and "requires that the fiduciary consider the availability of additional protections [through the state guaranty associations] and the extent of their guarantees." EBSA (2007). In response to insurance industry opposition, the final regulations in 2008 eliminated the requirement to consider ratings, although the preamble stated that, "in many cases, fiduciaries may want to consider them, particularly if the ratings raise questions regarding the provider's ability to make future payments under the annuity contract" and that "information regarding additional protections that may be available through a state guaranty association for an annuity provider also would be useful information to a plan fiduciary." EBSA (2008b).

49. Examples might include, among many others, the National Institute of Standards and Technology or the US Preventive Services Task Force, an independent body of national experts in preventive medicine who make recommendations regarding clinical preventive services that health regulatory agencies rely on in implementing statutory requirements. Another example is the Public Company Accounting Oversight Board, which regulates the auditing of companies and was established after the Enron debacle in the early 2000s.

50. US Department of the Treasury (2017); Commission on Retirement Security and Personal Savings (2016). These are briefly described in the appendix. In addition, for a different approach to policy regarding annuities, Gale, John, and Smith (2012, pp. 28–31) propose federal insurance for life annuities (and similar products) that would replace, supplement, or back up the state guaranty funds insofar as they apply to annuities.

51. A more common portability issue arises when a participating employee leaves the employ of the plan sponsor. Upon termination of employment, the participant would be free to take a distribution of benefits, including the annuity contract, but a new employer, if it has a plan, might not have a similar annuity offering in its plan or might not accept a rollover or transfer of the annuity. In that event, the individual could still roll the annuity contract into an IRA.

52. US Department of the Treasury (2016).

53. Conceivably, such a provision might also allow employees to withdraw the annuity without rolling it over to an IRA or plan and without surrendering or liquidating it. The employee could then continue holding and investing in the annuity even though it would have "leaked" outside of the tax-favored retirement system. However, in the interest of minimizing leakage of retirement benefits, we believe the relief should be conditioned on direct rollover.

54. A single lump-sum distribution also complies.

55. The percentages increase to roughly 4 percent, 5 percent, 6 percent, 7 percent, and 8 percent at ages 73, 79, 83, 86, and 89, respectively, and continue increasing thereafter. See Internal Revenue Service (2018, Appendix B: Table III, Uniform Lifetime Table).

56. See US Department of the Treasury (2013, pp. 215–16).

57. See Forman (2018).

58. Brown, Poterba, and Richardson (2017).

59. There is evidence that most retirement savers who do not take a lump-sum payout take a distribution in a given year equal to their RMD. An Employee Benefit Re-

search Institute study suggests that only 25 percent of retirement savers who did not take lump sums took more than the RMD, indicating that 75 percent either took the exact RMD or failed to comply. See Copeland (2018).

60. Brown and Turner (2018).

61. Most previous proposals to reform RMDs have not focused on progressivity or on encouraging lifetime income. See Brown, Poterba, and Richardson (2017); Brown and Turner (2018); Soled and Wolk (2000). For example, the pending SECURE and RESA bills would postpone the required beginning date from age 70½ to age 72 and, eventually, age 75 to preserve more assets under management for investment firms and financial advisers and extend potential tax deferral for more affluent retirees. Because it would maximize tax-favored assets under management and extend tax deferral, its projected revenue cost was very high and therefore, if paid for, would require painful offsets. The oft-repeated justification is a need to keep up with increases in life expectancy. However, given the purpose of the RMD rules, it is unclear whether there ever was any compelling logic in the first place to postponing RMDs until over half a decade after most people retire. Also, the burden of compliance, weighing more heavily on the less affluent, would not be eliminated but only deferred to age 75.

62. We believe such an exemption was first proposed in 2013 in the Obama administration budget proposals. It would have exempted retirees with aggregate plan and IRA accumulations by age 70½ of less than $75,000 (phasing out between $75,000 and $85,000), later increased to $100,000 (phasing out up to $110,000). At the time, this was estimated to be sufficient to exempt a majority of seniors with retirement savings. The proposal was then introduced by US Representative Richard Neal (D-MA) (with a $250,000 cap) and later was included in the 2018 Republican-proposed Family Savings Act with a $50,000 cap.

63. To the extent this could drive the beneficiary into a higher marginal income tax bracket, Congress might consider allowing use of a five- or ten-year income tax averaging convention.

64. Although the tables have not been updated, Treasury exercised its existing authority in 2014 to issue regulations exempting QLACs from RMDs and thereby making it feasible for them to be offered in the nearly $17 trillion qualified DC plan and IRA market.

65. Executive Order No. 13847 (2018).

66. For example, Gleckman (2018) notes that such updating would reduce the first year's RMD for those age 70½ from 3.65 percent to 3.45 percent of their balances—making only a negligible difference in their retirement finances.

67. See US Department of the Treasury (2016, pp. 145–46). Although qualifying distributions from Roth IRAs are tax-exempt, the requirement to distribute a portion of the Roth IRA balance each year after age 70½ would meaningfully reduce tax benefits by gradually stopping the accumulation of tax-free earnings in the Roth IRA.

68. In 2015, IRS Notice 2015–49, 2015–30 I.R.B. 79 indicated that these buyouts were not permitted but grandfathered all previous ones. The notice provided that the RMD regulations would be amended by proposed amendments making this clear and requesting public comment. However, Treasury and IRS in 2019 issued Notice 2019–18, essentially reversing course and stating that the regulations were no longer intended to

be so amended, that the question is under further study, that pending further guidance the IRS will not assert that such buyouts violate the RMD rules, and that further private letter rulings would not be issued. See Internal Revenue Service (2015, 2019).

69. See note 64, above.

70. The 1995 guidance was prompted largely by the adverse impact on retirement plans of the insolvency of Executive Life Insurance Company.

71. "A fiduciary must evaluate a number of factors relating to a potential annuity provider's claims paying ability and creditworthiness. Reliance solely on ratings provided by insurance rating services would not be sufficient to meet this requirement." U.S. Department of Labor (1995, 29 CFR section 2509.95–1(c)).

72. In 2002, DoL made clear its view that its "safest available annuity" guidance applied to DC as well as DB plans. U.S. Department of Labor (2002).

73. U.S. Department of Labor (2014).

74. In lieu of relying on the rating categories, the SEC characterized the obligation or company as being subject to only "a minimal amount of credit risk" (former top two categories); "minimal or low risk" (former top three categories); or "no greater than moderate credit risk," "at least average creditworthiness," and "investment grade" (former top four categories) and be sufficiently liquid to be sold at or near fair market value within a specified time. An issuer rated in the highest rating category was described by the SEC as having "the highest capacity" or "an exceptionally strong capacity" to meet its financial obligations. Employee Benefits Security Administration (2013). Even in the face of this statutory requirement, DoL evidenced reluctance to forgo use of credit ratings in fiduciary determinations, noting that "credit ratings have been considered useful for fiduciaries of employee benefit plans in evaluating the credit quality of a particular financial instrument or issuer, as plan fiduciaries frequently do not possess the expertise or resources to engage in" such an analysis. Accordingly, DoL said that it recognized that, "while credit ratings may no longer serve as a basis, or threshold, of credit quality, section 939A of Dodd-Frank does not prohibit a fiduciary from using credit ratings as an element, or data point, in that analysis." EBSA (2013), 78 FR 37572, 37577.

75. Plan sponsors' concerns about the risk of selecting an annuity provider for a DC plan without the protection of a safe harbor provision have not prevented DB plan fiduciaries from selecting annuity providers in numerous cases where there was strong motivation to reduce the DB liabilities on the employer's balance sheet.

76. The guarantee limits are stated in terms roughly equivalent to the annuity premium as opposed to the annual annuity payment. Individuals seeking diversification of insurer solvency risk can of course divide their annuity purchase among multiple insurers.

77. Commission on Retirement Security and Personal Savings (2016, p. 66). The report stated that plan sponsors "should be able to look to others for guidance on the financial strength of the carrier."

78. US Department of the Treasury (2017, p. 143). See also BlackRock (2018, 2019); Reish and Ashton (2018).

79. These examples are in addition to DoL regulations and related guidance (including proposed prohibited transaction class exemption amendments) emphasizing

the importance of taking into account NRSRO financial strength ratings in a fiduciary assessment of annuity providers' financial strength and claims-paying ability, as well as the recommendations in the 2017 Treasury Department Report and 2016 Bipartisan Policy Commission Report (all discussed in this chapter's appendix).

80. Similarly, Nerdwallet states that it does not recommend considering insurers unless they are sufficiently highly rated.

81. Reish and Ashton (2017, pp. 35–36); Reish, Ashton, and Faucher (2012, pp. 12–13).

82. Reish and Ashton (2018, pp. 5–6). The ERISA Advisory Council heard generally similar views about the desirability of including financial strength credit ratings in a statutory fiduciary safe harbor from one of the authors in his oral statement to the Council. In addition, BlackRock, Inc., in its written statement to the Council, stated that "plans would benefit from guidance surrounding the steps they need to take to evaluate lifetime income solutions to meet safe harbor requirements. For example, *the safe harbor could look to the credit rating*, licensing, length of operations or size of a particular insurer." BlackRock (2018, p. 3, emphasis added). See also BlackRock (2019, p. 4).

83. Reish and Ashton (2018).

84. See Michigan Compiled Laws (1965).

85. Similarly, the Bipartisan Policy Commission 2016 report took the view that, while insurers' financial strength should be covered by an objective safe harbor because it is difficult for plan sponsors to assess on their own, it is reasonable to require plan sponsors "to carefully evaluate the appropriateness of particular investment and distribution options."

86. Further clarification is important because regulators are conscientious in parsing every word of statutory language to ascertain congressional intent. Indeed, standards of statutory construction presume that there is a reason for all included. Accordingly, in a case such as this, careful clarification can help prevent "safe harbor mission creep" based on post hoc arguments that Congress intended generally to encourage certain activities and therefore the scope of the provision should be "read broadly" to permit related activities even if they do not unambiguously come within the scope of the safe harbor.

The language of the proposed legislative safe harbor suggesting that it covered not only selection of the annuity provider but also selection of the annuity contracts tracked language in the Labor Department DC plan regulation. However, the regulation (unlike the legislative safe harbor proposal) could fairly be said to extend to the selection of the annuity contracts because it expressly required fiduciaries to "appropriately" consider the costs of the contracts in relation to their benefits and "appropriately" conclude that those costs were reasonable. By contrast, nothing in the proposed legislative safe harbor's required representations from insurers regarding their good standing with state authorities bears on the costs or other terms of the annuity contracts. Accordingly, there is no sound basis for extending the proposed legislative safe harbor to the selection of the contracts.

87. A Joint Committee on Taxation summary of the proposed SECURE Act legislation approved by the House Ways and Means Committee incorrectly misstated the scope as including selection of the annuity contract; see Joint Committee on Taxation

(2019, pp. 50–52). The House Ways and Means Committee Report on the SECURE Act, Committee on Ways and Means (2019, pp. 84–87), defines the narrow scope correctly.

Another potential ambiguity in the pending legislative safe harbor language relates to the cost standard. The proposed statutory safe harbor, when largely tracking the language of DoL's DC plan regulation, replaces the regulatory language requiring consideration of annuity contracts' costs "in relation to the benefits" under the contracts with language that refers instead, and more cryptically, to the "relative" costs of the contracts. This unnecessary ambiguity might conceivably be exploited by arguing in the future that, for example, Congress intended to require fiduciaries to consider the costs of a given contract only relative to the (potentially excessive) costs of other contracts in the market.

88. Employee Benefits Security Administration (2015).

89. Internal Revenue Service (2014a, 2014b). See also discussion in Toth and Giller (2013).

90. See, e.g. Backman (2018).

91. Consumer Federation of America (2019).

92. Like the question of whether a statutory ERISA fiduciary safe harbor should be subject to a quality standard based on insurers' financial strength and claims-paying ability, the question of whether the safe harbor should be limited to insurers providing fixed income annuities has not been the subject of much attention in Congress.

93. While a potentially helpful way to introduce annuities to DC plans is to embed them in a 401(k) plan's target-date fund default investment (QDIA) as part of its fixed income asset class, this is different from using variable annuities that attempt to replicate much of the asset diversification of the target-date fund or other QDIAs. Instead, a fixed income annuity could provide both guaranteed retirement income and fixed income asset exposure (which would otherwise commonly be provided by bonds). See, e.g., Internal Revenue Service (2014a) and Internal Revenue Service (2014b).

94. Consumer Federation of America (2019).

95. "While state insurance regulators have a long—and successful—track record regulating the solvency and consumer protection aspects of simple fixed annuities without accumulation features, the same cannot be said for annuities with accumulation features." Consumer Federation of America (2019).

96. Consumer Federation of America (2019). The National Association of Insurance Commissioners (NAIC) has projects under way to develop further regulatory measures.

97. See also Reish and Ashton (2017). Unfortunately, an experience requirement, like most other criteria in this area, is highly imperfect. Given the frequency of corporate transactions and changes in management, a given insurance company's years of experience will not always be meaningful, and it is more challenging and labor-intensive for regulators to assess the experience of smaller business units and individuals. The process of developing financial strength ratings, however, might be better able to verify experience (in much the same way that analysts track management changes in mutual funds).

98. State regulators also rely on NAIC's Insurance Regulatory Information System Ratio Results Reports, which, generally speaking, are intended to be included, to the extent applicable, in the references in the text to RBC ratios.

99. Whether DoL should require annuity providers to disclose their RBC ratios if they wish to be considered for selection by DC or DB plans pursuant to DoL's regulations—without regard to the safe harbor—is a question not addressed here.

For NAIC-aggregated life RBC data, see www.naic.org/documents/research_stats_rbc_results_life.pdf?31. If a fiduciary safe harbor were to specify an RBC ratio threshold that annuity providers had to meet to be treated as highly qualified, insurers seeking that safe harbor designation could voluntarily disclose their RBC ratios (perhaps within appropriate ranges), which NAIC could verify.

REFERENCES

Abraham, Katherine G., and Benjamin H. Harris. 2015. "Better Financial Security in Retirement? Realizing the Promise of Annuities." Brookings.

Advisory Council on Employee Welfare and Pension Benefit Plans. 2018. "Lifetime Income Solutions as a Qualified Default Investment Alternative (QDIA)—Focus on Decumulation and Rollovers." Report to the Honorable R. Alexander Acosta, US Secretary of Labor. Washington, DC.

American Academy of Actuaries. 2015. "Lifetime Income Initiative." Issue Brief. Washington, DC.

Backman, Maurie. 2018. "Why Do Annuities Have Such a Bad Reputation?" CNN Money. https://money.cnn.com/2018/05/25/pf/annuities-bad-reputation/index.html.

Benartzi, Shlomo, Alessandro Previtero, and Richard H. Thaler. 2011. "Annuitization Puzzles." *Journal of Economic Perspectives* 25 (4): 143–64.

Beshears, John, James J. Choi, David Laibson, and Brigitte C. Madrian. 2018. "Behavioral Household Finance." In *Handbook of Behavioral Economics—Foundations and Applications 1*, edited by B. Douglas Bernheim, Stefano DellaVigna, and David Laibson. Amsterdam: Elsevier.

BlackRock, Inc. 2018. "ERISA Advisory Council 2018 Issue Statement on Lifetime Income." www.blackrock.com/publicpolicy.

———. 2019. "Viewpoint: Creating Better Outcomes through Lifetime Income." www.blackrock.com/publicpolicy.

Brown, Jeffrey R. 2007. "Rational and Behavioral Perspectives on the Role of Annuities in Retirement Planning." NBER Working Paper 13537. Cambridge, MA: National Bureau of Economic Research.

Brown, Jeffrey R., and James M. Poterba. 2000. "Joint Life Annuities and the Demand for Annuities by Married Couples." *Journal of Risk and Insurance* 67 (4): 527–53.

Brown, Jeffrey R., Marcus D. Casey, and Olivia S. Mitchell. 2007. "Who Values the Social Security Annuity? New Evidence on the Annuity Puzzle." 2007 NBER Summer Institute, Cambridge, MA.

Brown, Jeffrey R., James Poterba, and David Richardson. 2017. "Do Required Minimum Distributions Matter? The Effect of the 2009 Holiday on Retirement Plan Distributions." *Journal of Public Economics* 151: 96–109.

Brown, Jeffrey R., Jeffrey R. Kling, Sendhil Mullainathan, and Marian V. Wrobel. 2013. "Framing Lifetime Income." *Journal of Retirement* 1 (1): 27–37.

Brown, Jennifer E., and John A. Turner. 2018. "Complex RMD Policy: Behavioral Economics and Principle-Based Public Policy for Older Retiree Participants." Employee Benefits Committee Newsletter. Chicago, IL: American Bar Association.
Commission on Retirement Security and Personal Savings. 2016. "Securing Our Financial Future: Report of the Commission on Retirement Security and Personal Savings." Washington, DC: Bipartisan Policy Center.
Committee on Ways and Means. 2019. "Setting Every Community Up for Retirement Enhancement Act of 2019: Report of the Committee on Ways and Means, House of Representatives, on H.R. 1994." H. Rept. 116–65, Part 1. US House of Representatives.
Consumer Federation of America and Center for Economic Justice. 2019. "CFA and CEJ Call for Essential Consumer Protection Amendment to RESA." Letter to US Senators. https://consumerfed.org/wp-content/uploads/2020/08/cej_cfa_letter_senate_resa_safeharbor_190523.pdf.
Copeland, Craig. 2018. "EBRI IRA Database: IRA Balances, Contributions, Rollovers, Withdrawals, and Asset Allocation, 2016 Update." EBRI Issue Brief. Washington, DC: Employee Benefit Research Institute.
Davidoff, Thomas, Jeffrey R. Brown, and Peter A. Diamond. 2005. "Annuities and Individual Welfare." *American Economic Review* 95 (5): 1573–90.
Dodd-Frank Wall Street Reform and Consumer Protection Act. 2010. Pub. L. No. 111-203, § 929-Z, 124 Stat. 1376, 1871 (codified at 15 U.S.C. § 78o).
Donovan v. *Bierwirth*, 680 F.2d 263, 272 (2d Cir. 1982).
Dushi, Irena, and Anthony Webb. 2004. "Annuitization: Keeping Your Options Open." Working Paper. Center for Retirement Research, Boston College.
EbixExchange. 2007. "What's the Comdex?" VitalSigns Sales Suite. https://www.ebix.com/vitalSales-suite.
Employee Benefit Research Institute. 2012. "About Benefits—Retirement Issues: What Are the Trends in Defined Benefit Pension Plans?" Issue Brief. Washington, DC.
Employee Benefits Security Administration (EBSA). 2007. "Employee Retirement Income Security Act: Individual Account Plans; Annuity Providers Selection." 72 Fed. Reg. 52022. Washington, DC: US Department of Labor.
———. 2008a. "Amendment to Interpretive Bulletin (95–1)." 73 Fed. Reg. 58445. Washington, DC: US Department of Labor.
———. 2008b. "Selection of Annuity Providers—Safe Harbor for Individual Account Plans." 73 Fed. Reg. 58448. Washington, DC: US Department of Labor.
———. 2013. "Proposed Amendments to Class Prohibited Transaction Exemptions to Remove Credit Ratings Pursuant to the Dodd-Frank Wall Street Reform and Consumer Protection Act." 78 Fed. Reg. 37572. Washington, DC: US Department of Labor.
———. 2015. "Selection and Monitoring under the Annuity Selection Safe Harbor Regulation for Defined Contribution Plans." Field Assistance Bulletin 2015-02. Washington, DC: US Department of Labor.
Executive Order No. 13847. 2018. 83 Fed. Reg. 45321.
Financial Industry Regulatory Authority (FINRA). 2010. "Investor Alert: Equity-Indexed Annuities—A Complex Choice." Washington, DC.

———. 2012. "Investor Alert: Variable Annuities: Beyond the Hard Sell." Washington, DC.

Forman, Jonathan Barry. 2018. "Removing the Legal Impediments to Offering Lifetime Annuities in Pension Plans." *Connecticut Insurance Law Journal* 23 (1): 31–141.

Gale, William G., David C. John, and Spencer Smith. 2012. "New Ways to Promote Retirement Saving." Washington, DC: AARP Public Policy Institute.

Gleckman, Howard. 2018. "Treasury Should Review IRA Minimum Distribution Tables but Changes Would Help Few Seniors." *TaxVox Blog*, September 7. Urban-Brookings Tax Policy Center. https://www.taxpolicycenter.org/taxvox/treasury-should-review-ira-minimum-distribution-tables-changes-would-help-few-seniors.

Government Accountability Office. 2017. "The Nation's Retirement System: A Comprehensive Re-evaluation Is Needed to Better Promote Future Retirement Security." GAO-18-111SP. Washington, DC.

Horneff, Wolfram J., Raimond Maurer, Olivia S. Mitchell, and Ivica Dus. 2006. "Optimizing the Retirement Portfolio: Asset Allocation, Annuitization, and Risk Aversion." NBER Working Paper 12392. Cambridge, MA: National Bureau of Economic Research.

Internal Revenue Service. 2014a. "Notice 2014–66." Internal Revenue Bulletin 2014-46. Washington, DC: US Department of the Treasury.

———. 2014b. "T.D. 9673." Internal Revenue Bulletin 2014-30. Washington, DC: US Department of the Treasury.

———. 2015. "Notice 2015–49." Internal Revenue Bulletin 2015-30. Washington, DC: US Department of the Treasury.

———. 2018. "Publication 590-B: Distributions from Individual Retirement Arrangements (IRAs)." Washington, DC: US Department of the Treasury.

———. 2019. "Notice 2019–18." Internal Revenue Bulletin 2019-13. Washington, DC: US Department of the Treasury.

Investment Company Institute. 2018. "The Role of IRAs in U.S. Households' Saving for Retirement, 2018." *ICI Research Perspective* 24 (10). Washington, DC.

———. 2019. "Retirement Assets Total $27.1 Trillion in Fourth Quarter 2018." Washington, DC.

John, David C., William G. Gale, J. Mark Iwry, and Aaron Krupkin. 2019. "From Saving to Spending: Annuities and Nontraditional Retirement Payouts from Retirement Plans." Retirement Security Project. Brookings.

Joint Committee on Taxation. 2019. "Description of H.R. 1994, the 'Setting Every Community Up for Retirement Enhancement' (SECURE) Act of 2019." JCX-11-19.

LIMRA. 2018. "U.S. Individual Annuities, 1st Quarter 2018." Windsor, CT: LIMRA Secure Retirement Institute.

Lockwood, Lee M. 2012. "Bequest Motives and the Annuity Puzzle." *Review of Economic Dynamics* 15 (2): 226–43.

Michigan Compiled Laws. 1965. Public Employee Retirement System Investment Act (Act 314 of 1965), as amended, section 38.1136, 16(3).

Milevsky, Moshe A. 2013. "Life Annuities: An Optimal Product for Retirement Income." CFA Institute Research Foundation Monograph. Charlottesville, VA: CFA Institute.

———. 2018. "Annuity Fables: Some Observations from an Ivory Tower." *Journal of Financial Planning* 31 (12): 46–55.

Mitchell, Olivia S., James Poterba, Mark Warshawsky, and Jeffrey Brown. 1999. "New Evidence on the Money's Worth of Individual Annuities." *American Economic Review* 89 (5): 1299–1318.

Office of Senator Elizabeth Warren. 2015. "Villas, Castles, and Vacations: How Perks and Giveaways Create Conflicts of Interest in the Annuity Industry." Washington, DC: United States Senate.

Reichling, Felix, and Kent Smetters. 2015. "Optimal Annuitization with Stochastic Mortality Probabilities and Medical Expense." *American Economic Review* 105 (11): 3273–320.

Reish, C. Frederick, and Bruce L. Ashton. 2017. "Lincoln *Secured Retirement Income* Solution: Fiduciary Process in Evaluating In-Plan Guarantees." White Paper. Fort Wayne, IN: DrinkerBiddle and Lincoln Financial Group.

———. 2018. Written Statement of Fred Reish and Bruce Ashton to the Employee ERISA Advisory Council, August 15. https://www.dol.gov/sites/dolgov/files/EBSA/about-ebsa/about-us/erisa-advisory-council/2018-lifetime-income-solutions-as-a-qdia-reish-written-statement-08-15.pdf.

Reish, C. Frederick, Bruce L. Ashton, and Joseph C. Faucher. 2012. "Lifetime Income in Defined Contribution Plans: A Fiduciary Approach." White Paper. Philadelphia: Faegre Drinker Biddle and Reath.

Retirement Enhancement and Savings Act of 2019. 2019. H.R. 1007. 116th Congress.

Securities and Exchange Commission. 2017. "Updated Investor Bulletin: The ABCs of Credit Ratings." Washington, DC.

Setting Every Community Up for Retirement Enhancement Act of 2019. 2019. H.R. 1994. 116th Congress.

Soled, Jay, and Bruce A. Wolk. 2000. "The Minimum Distribution Rules and Their Critical Role in Controlling the Floodgates of Qualified Plan Wealth." *Brigham Young University Law Review* 2: 587–625.

Toth, Robert J., and Evan Giller. 2013. "Regulatory and Fiduciary Framework for Providing Lifetime Income from Defined Contribution Plans." In *New York University Review of Employee Benefits and Executive Compensation—2013*. New York: LexisNexis Matthew Bender.

US Department of Labor. 1995. "Interpretive Bulletins Relating to the Employee Retirement Income Security Act of 1974." Interpretive Bulletin 95-1, 60 Fed. Reg. 12329. Washington, DC.

———. 2002. Advisory Opinion 2002-14A. Washington, DC.

———. 2014. "Introduction to the Regulatory Agenda of Federal Regulatory and Deregulatory Actions." 79 Fed. Reg. 895, 1024. Washington, DC.

US Department of the Treasury. 2013. "General Explanations of the Administration's Fiscal Year 2014 Revenue Proposals." Washington, DC.

———. 2014. "Treasury Issues Final Rules Regarding Longevity Annuities." Washington, DC.

———. 2016. "General Explanations of the Administration's Fiscal Year 2017 Revenue Proposals." Washington, DC.

———. 2017. "A Financial System That Creates Economic Opportunities: Asset Management and Insurance." Washington, DC.

White, Lawrence J. 2018. "The Credit Rating Agencies and Their Role in the Financial System." In *The Oxford Handbook of Institutions of International Economic Governance and Market Regulation*, edited by Eric Brousseau, Jean-Michel Glachant, and Jérôme Sgard. Oxford University Press.

Yaari, Menahem E. 1965. "Uncertain Lifetime, Life Insurance, and the Theory of the Consumer." *Review of Economic Studies* 32 (2): 137–50.

THIRTEEN

Retirement Tontines

USING A CLASSICAL FINANCE MECHANISM AS AN ALTERNATIVE SOURCE OF RETIREMENT INCOME

J. Mark Iwry, Claire Haldeman, William G. Gale, and David C. John

Considered as a financial innovation, it [the tontine] was very successful. Considered as insurance, it was actuarially sound. Considered as a gamble, it was a "fair bet." . . . Considered as a life-cycle asset, it proved to be an excellent investment.

—Ransom and Sutch (1987)

Households face two related but distinct financial challenges as they prepare for retirement: first accumulating enough retirement savings during their working years, and then spending down their assets wisely after retiring. A substantial literature has examined the extent to which households are saving adequately for retirement and has reached a wide range of conclusions.[1] But there is more consensus about the challenges households face when deciding how best to spend down their savings. People do not know how long they or their spouses will live (not to mention what their health care costs and investment returns will look like), which makes them prone either to consuming too much too soon, leaving them with insufficient resources as they age, or to consuming too little and thus having a lower standard of living in retirement than they could have afforded.[2]

Managing assets in retirement has become a more widespread problem over time as lifespans have increased and as more retirees depend on defined contribution (DC) retirement savings rather than defined benefit (DB) pensions. DB plans pay benefits at regular intervals, typically monthly, for a retiree's lifetime. This pension annuity ensures that beneficiaries will not run out of income as they age.[3] DC plans rarely provide annuities.

Despite these trends, take-up of private annuities remains low.[4] Other financial products, such as managed payout funds, have certain advantages but are not yet available in most retirement plans.[5] These circumstances leave many households without satisfactory ways to convert their retirement savings into income.

In this chapter we explore the potential for a different financial product—a tontine—to help people manage their assets in retirement. Tontines are investment pools to which members commit funds irrevocably and where the resources and income claims of members who die are given to the members who survive. Tontines can be adapted to a wide variety of financial structures. They have financed everything from European wars to colonial-era capital projects to Americans' retirement. They were quite popular in the United States in the late 1800s and early 1900s until they were effectively (though not literally) outlawed in response to corrupt insurance company management.[6]

The "tontine principle"—that surviving group members benefit financially from the death of other members—can evoke strong reactions and has inspired murder plots in novels, movies, and even a *Simpsons* episode. But the mechanisms involved are not very different from how group annuities operate, and members of modern tontines would be mutually anonymous in any case.

In recent years, analysts have revisited tontines as a theoretical tool, and several countries have created pension plans that incorporate tontine principles. Some current retirement products in the United States have a tontine-style structure as well.

Our central premise is that tontine-style products could play a significantly broader role in financing the retirement of US households, assuming that certain operational questions could be resolved. Such products could provide higher returns than annuities do, but with less security. They would be valuable to those seeking some insurance against their own longevity without requiring a specific, guaranteed level of future income.

We begin by briefly reviewing existing products for managing retirement income, then discuss theoretical and practical considerations regarding tontines as a way to finance retirement income, and finally compare tontines, annuities, and managed payout funds.

CURRENT OPTIONS FOR MANAGING INCOME IN RETIREMENT

Several financial products—chiefly annuities and managed payout funds—can help people manage the assets they have accumulated for retirement. These products differ in how they address longevity risk and investment risk.

Annuities eliminate longevity risk by paying the annuitant guaranteed income for life. Immediate annuities begin payments soon after they are purchased, while deferred annuities begin payments later, usually at a predetermined age. Annuities address investment risk in various ways: some provide a constant nominal payout, some increase the payment regularly over time as a rough hedge against inflation, and others make variable payments based on the returns of the assets underlying the annuity.[7]

In addition to commercial annuities, which are provided by insurance companies, DB plans also pay retirement income in the form of annuities. DC plans—including 401(k)s—do not independently promise their participants income for life, although a small percentage of DC plans provide a lifetime income option by purchasing commercial annuities for participants.[8]

Although annuities provide a way to resolve the competing risks of consuming too little or too much, the private annuity market is small. Only 1 percent of people who reach retirement age choose to annuitize any portion of their private wealth, and only 2 percent of retirement assets are held in lifetime annuities.[9]

The managed payout fund, or retirement income fund, is an alternative way to manage investment and longevity risk in retirement.[10] These funds, which have recently emerged in the United States and other countries, are diversified, professionally managed investment pools designed to provide relatively consistent retirement income. They *manage* but do not eliminate longevity risk and investment risk; thus, unlike annuities, managed payout funds do not guarantee continued payments for life, and they target, but do not guarantee, a specific annual income level. Largely because they lack these guarantees, they are not subject to the capital reserve and other insurance regulatory requirements and costs that apply to annuities. To further address longevity risk, people could combine managed payout funds with a longevity annuity, which provides income continuing for life, starting at age 80 or 85.[11]

Besides annuities and managed payout funds, retirees can follow various "do it yourself" withdrawal strategies. For example, an investor might use simple rules of thumb (the "4 percent rule") or follow the required minimum distribution rules that apply to IRA and DC balances even though the rules were not created to optimize retirement consumption choices. These approaches provide no protection against either market risk or longevity risk. A different strategy is to hold a series of high-quality bonds that reach maturity at times that match the retiree's cash flow needs. This strategy can eliminate market risk but not the risk of outliving one's assets. In addition, holders of an all-bond portfolio would have sacrificed significant rates of return over time relative to holding equities.[12]

All of these products and strategies can play useful roles, but none of them provides a complete solution to households' needs for asset management in retirement. As a result, some attention has turned to another alternative: the tontine.

THEORETICAL CONSIDERATIONS

The idea of a tontine is that a group of people pool their investments and when members of the group die, their share of the pool and its earnings are divided among surviving members. Investing in a tontine, therefore, differs from purchasing an ordinary asset in two ways. While an investor can buy or sell an ordinary asset at any time, the tontine investment is irrevocable. If contributions to the tontine could be revoked, members could withdraw their funds if they received bad news about their lifespan, such as an unexpectedly grim medical diagnosis. Second, while ordinary assets can be bequeathed to heirs, the investment in a tontine, upon the investor's death, does not pass to the investor's heirs or estate but instead is allocated to surviving members of the investment pool.

Some Simple Examples

The simple tontine principle can manifest itself in various ways. Consider one stylized example. Suppose each of ten people who are identical for mortality purposes (same age, race, sex, etc.) irrevocably invests \$100,000 to create a \$1 million investment pool. The pool buys a bond that pays 4 percent interest a year. In this simplest and most extreme form of tontine, no current payouts are made. The interest is reinvested every year. As each participant dies, they forfeit their interests and get nothing. Once there remain only, say, three survivors in the pool, they could divide up the entire balance of the investment, including all accrued interest and the principal, and the arrangement would terminate.

Now suppose that instead of reinvesting the 4 percent bond interest each year, the pool pays it out as an annual dividend.[13] The aggregate annual interest of $40,000 is divided equally among the members of the pool. Each member's annual $4,000 dividend ($40,000/10 = $4,000) could be called their "base return." No principal is paid out until the arrangement terminates.

As shown in figure 13-1A, each member's annual $4,000 income continues until one of them dies. Then the deceased member's annual $4,000 base return is divided equally among the nine surviving members, so that each receives an additional $444 ($4,000/9) per year as a "mortality credit" in addition to the regular $4,000 base return. Thus, for example, after four members have died (forfeiting a total of $16,000 annually), each of the remaining six would receive annual mortality credit payouts of $2,667 (= $16,000/6) in addition to the $4,000 base return.

Over time, the aggregate annual interest payment of $40,000 stays the same but is divided among fewer and fewer survivors. As the number of survivors shrinks, each survivor's annual payout grows. When the group reaches a specified terminal condition, such as only three survivors remaining, the bond is sold, the revenue from the sale is divided equally among the surviving members, and the arrangement terminates.

Although each member receives income for life, like an annuity, this structure would be unsuitable as a retirement income tool because the return to survivors as they age rises sharply as more pool members die. In contrast, most theory and evidence suggest that people prefer age-consumption profiles that are constant or decline in retirement.[14]

The Level-Payout Tontine

To address these retirement income needs, Piggott, Valdez, and Detzel (2005), Sabin (2010), Milevsky and Salisbury (2015), and others have proposed a tontine in which the total return to survivors stays constant over time, which they call a "natural tontine," and which we refer to as a "constant-payout" or "level-payout" tontine.

Their approach is simple and elegant: Invest the tontine in zero-coupon government bonds with maturities and returns that generate cash flows to the pool that decline over time at a rate that matches the expected mortality in

Figure 13-1. **Tontine Income by Pool Mortality**

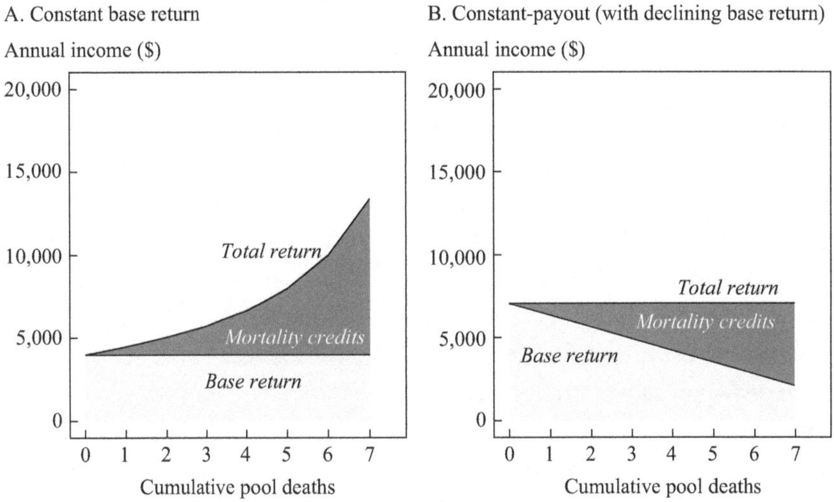

Source: Authors' calculations.

Note: This figure compares the behavior of two stylized tontines with ten participants who have each contributed $40,000 to the pool. In the "constant base return" tontine (A), the fund disburses 4 percent of the overall investment annually, creating a guaranteed 4 percent base return per survivor each year. Over time, as more participants die, their base return is redistributed to the survivors in the form of mortality credits, generating an escalating total return for survivors over time. In the "constant-payout" or "level-payout" tontine (B), the base return is designed to decline over time to offset the increase in mortality credits, so that the total return to a survivor remains constant over time.

the group. The base return will therefore *decline* over time at a rate expected to offset the *increasing* level of mortality credits. As a result, the expected total income each member receives—base returns plus mortality credits—remains roughly constant over time, approximating the constant expected payout of a fixed income life annuity. Forman and Sabin (2015) propose a similar level-payout "tontine annuity," but instead of offsetting the increasing level of mortality credits by structuring declining investment returns over time, they would offset those increases by having the investment pool annually repay members a declining portion of their initial contributions.

Figure 13-1B depicts payouts for a level-payout tontine. The decline in the base return over time offsets the rise in the mortality credit over time, and the fund dissolves at the same terminal condition, when there are three survivors, as in the previous example.[15] This level-payout tontine offers the same expected lifetime payout as the tontine with a constant base return, but it better matches most retirees' needs and preferences by paying retirees more total income in the early years and less in later years than the tontine with a constant base return.

In practice, of course, the pace at which tontine members actually die is uncertain and will differ from expectations, so if the declining base return schedule is set in advance, based on ex ante expected mortality probabilities of the pool, the actual total return payout from the level-payout tontine will vary over time. Figure 13-2 shows this variation in actual total return payouts that would occur in a pool of 1,000 65-year-old men who joined a tontine in 2017 where the rate of decline of the base return is set in advance, based on expected aggregate mortality probabilities.[16]

To generate figure 13-2, we ran 1,000 stochastic scenarios for how actual mortality and investment returns would evolve over time, using published mortality data and historical asset performance; see the appendix for details. The figure reports the median, 10th percentile, and 90th percentile outcomes for the evolution of total return payouts over time. As can be seen, there is little variation, even given stochastic mortality and investment return risk. For example, at age 85, the total payout under the 10th percentile and 90th percentile scenarios is 5.00 percent and 5.48 percent, respectively. At age 100, when only about 7 percent of the original pool would still be alive, the 10th percentile outcome is 4.56 percent, and the 90th percentile outcome is 6.08 percent. Thus, even over long periods of time, setting the declining base return pattern based on ex ante mortality data should not cause major variations in total payouts for a tontine with a large pool of participants who are all of the same age and gender.

When the remaining pool of survivors exceeds 100 years of age, there is more variability in outcomes (not shown), because the sample size is so small that relatively small shocks to mortality translate into relatively large changes in sample size and hence mortality credits. We interpret this as suggesting that, when the surviving pool members reach age 100, the pool should be terminated and the proceeds distributed to survivors.

In figure 13-2, the rate of the decline in the base return is preset for the full multiyear period, based on the pool's *expected* aggregate mortality probabilities. Instead, the base return could be adjusted annually based on the *actual* previous mortality experience. For example, if the tontine began operating in year 0, the rate of decline in the base return between year $t-1$ and

Figure 13-2. **Distribution of Returns on Level-Payout Tontines Using Ex Ante Mortality Rates**

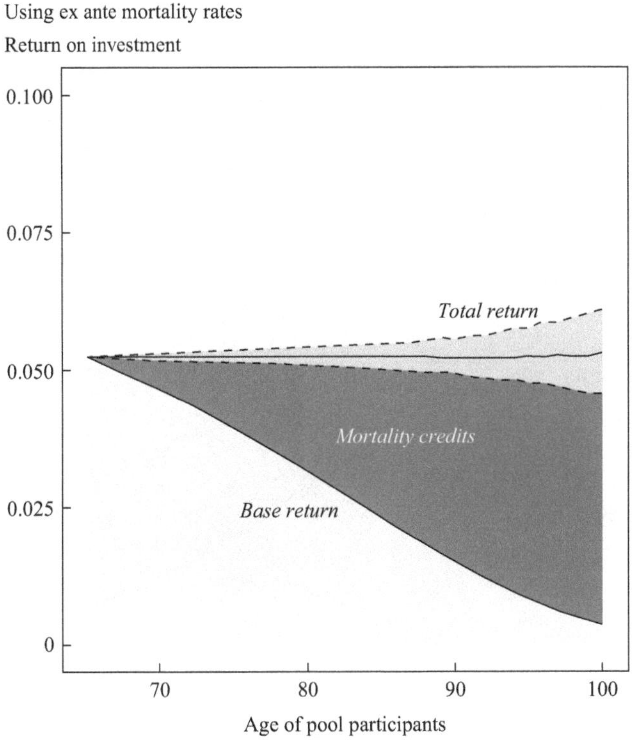

Source: Human Mortality Database (2020) and authors' calculations.

Note: This figure depicts the simulated behavior of a level-payout tontine where the annual disbursement is set in advance to decline inversely proportional to predicted pool mortality. Because actual mortality will differ from predicted mortality, the mortality credits are variable, making the total return variable. The pool is formed by 1,000 men who turned 65 in 2017. The simulation was run 1,000 times. The solid lines indicate the median behavior among the simulations; the dotted lines indicate the bounds of the 10th and 90th percentile total returns.

year t could be based on the observed mortality experience between year 0 and year $t - 1$.[17]

Figure 13-3 shows a tontine pool with characteristics and assumptions identical to those in figure 13-2, except that the rate of decline in the base return is adjusted annually to reflect actual mortality experience to date. These annual adjustments virtually eliminate the variation in total returns over

Figure 13-3. **Distribution of Returns on Level-Payout Tontines Using Realized Mortality Rates**

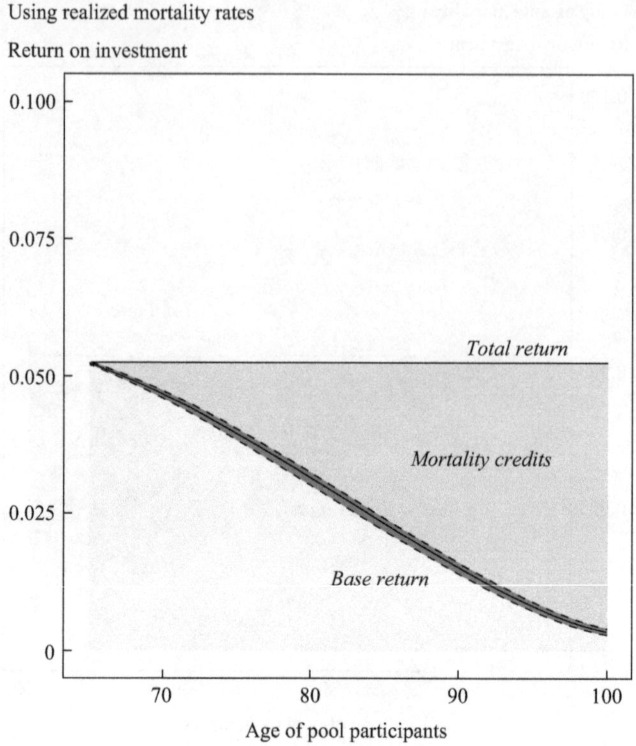

Source: Human Mortality Database (2020) and authors' calculations.

Note: This figure depicts the simulated behavior of a level-payout tontine where the annual disbursement is adjusted to match realized mortality. The pool is formed by 1,000 men who turned 65 in 2017. The simulation was run 1,000 times. The solid lines indicate the median behavior among the simulations; the dotted lines indicate the bounds of the 10th and 90th percentile base returns.

time.[18] For the entire duration of the pool, survivors earn a constant nominal total return of 5.23 percent per year, regardless of whether mortality outperforms or underperforms expectations, and even allowing for variation in the return on underlying assets. Because annual adjustments of base return income offset the variance in mortality credits, total return mirrors the constant total return of the theoretical level-payout tontine in figure 13-1B. Thus a tontine with a declining base return adjusted annually to reflect realized mortality could produce stable retirement income much like an annuity.

Pooling Heterogeneous Participants

In the previous examples, each tontine member is assumed to have identical mortality risk—they are the same age, sex, race, etc. In those circumstances, mortality credits would be actuarially fair if they were divided equally for each dollar invested. But suppose the members face different mortality risks—for example because they differ by age, sex, and race. In that case, allocating mortality credits equally per dollar invested would favor those with low mortality risk and disfavor those with high mortality risk. As a result, how mortality credits are allocated to the survivors is central to whether heterogeneous individuals would want to sign up for a tontine in the first place.

A tontine covering a heterogeneous group of participants can be designed so that the terms of the gamble are a fair bet and avoid favoring one participant over another. Milevsky and Salisbury (2016) show how retirement income tontines can combine heterogeneous cohorts in a single pool in an equitable manner. For example, a tontine-type pool can consist of shares that have equal rights to income but are sold to investors or participants in the pool at different prices designed to adjust for the different life expectancies associated with different ages.

Sabin (2010) and Forman and Sabin (2015) show that in a "fair tontine," for each participant alive at the start of each period, the expected gains of being in the pool should equal the expected losses. Satisfying this "fair tontine" constraint determines the appropriate allocation of mortality credits and allows people with differing life expectancies and initial balances to participate on an equalized or equitable basis.

For example, let $p_i(t)$ be the probability that participant *i* dies in period *t*, so $1 - p(t)$ is the probability that participant *i* survives period *t*. Let $B_i(t)$ be the balance in participant *i*'s tontine account at the beginning of period *t* and let $C_i(t)$ be the mortality credit participant *i* can expect if he survives the period. Therefore, for participant *i* during period *t* (dropping the subscripts), the expected value of the gross loss is $p \times B$, the probability of dying during the period times the loss upon death, and the expected value of the gross gain is $(1 - p) \times C$, the probability of surviving the period times the mortality credit to be gained if they survive. Thus, for any given period, a "fair tontine" requires that $p \times B = (1 - p) \times C$, implying that, in each period, a survivor's *expected* mortality credit, C, is equal to $(p \times B)/(1 - p)$.

Two aspects of a fair tontine are worth emphasizing. First, the expected mortality credit depends *only* on the participant's probability of surviving and an initial balance. Among participants who survive the period, those with higher ex ante probabilities of dying would expect to receive higher credits, as would those with higher initial balances. This makes sense, since they are risking more by participating in the pool in the first place. As a result, in general, surviving members of different ages do not receive equal mortality credits.[19]

Second, both p and B are likely to be readily observable: a simplified version of p could be derived from mortality tables (based on age and gender), and B could be tracked in tontine records. This implies that, *in theory*, requiring a tontine to be fair does not create significant administrative hurdles.[20] We discuss practical concerns below.

Further Applications

The preceding analysis focuses on closed investment pools used to finance retirement.[21] An emerging literature, however, envisions mortality credit pooling in open-ended pools that continue to admit new members and in concert with other financial instruments, while also creating a "fair tontine."

A tontine annuity tool could be molded into a "tontine pension," paying retirement income funded by employer contributions over the participant's career, like DB plans.[22] But since a tontine, unlike a DB plan, would not guarantee a specified monthly payment for life, tontine participants' pension benefits would vary based on the pool's mortality experience and investment experience. Because the other members of the pool could live longer than expected, and because the pool's investments could lose value, a tontine pension would occupy a different place on the risk-return spectrum than a commercial fixed-income annuity or a DB pension plan, both of which generally protect against investment and longevity risks, promising a fixed monthly payment for life.[23]

"Individual tontine accounts" (ITAs) offer another example of the flexibility of fair tontines.[24] While the decision to join an ITA would normally need to be irrevocable, ITAs, like IRAs, would allow participants to select their own contribution level, investments, and payout rate, and to change them, subject to certain constraints. For instance, they could be permitted to reduce, but not increase, their payout rate. The ITA would be attached to a regular investment account that is not governed by tontine principles, that could receive amounts from the ITA and allow them to be withdrawn at any time. When the saver died, ITA assets would be forfeited and reallocated to surviving participants, while the funds in the adjacent regular investment account would remain part of the decedent's estate. Pooled ITA mortality gains would supplement investment returns, thereby accommodating a potentially higher safe rate of withdrawal than could other forms of similarly invested funds, such as managed payout funds.

More generally, survivor income pooling could serve as the centerpiece of a stand-alone fund—a twenty-first-century tontine—or, as one component of a broader retirement strategy, could be combined with or incorporated into a managed payout fund or other investments.[25]

PRACTICAL CONSIDERATIONS

The previous sections argue that, in theory, tontines could be an effective way to finance retirement income. But could they work in practice?

A Brief History

The current status of, and prospects for, tontines—named after seventeenth-century Italian financier Lorenzo de Tonti—are related directly to their long and colorful history.[26] Since their inception four centuries ago, tontine-structured investments have taken a variety of forms, financing capital investments, wars, retirement income, and life insurance.

Capital investment tontines were popular revenue-raising schemes in Europe from the seventeenth to the nineteenth century, helping governments and monarchies raise money for public works and wars.[27] They even made inroads into the United States when, for example, Alexander Hamilton proposed a capital investment tontine to pay off Revolutionary War debt. Although the federal government declined to pursue this option, many communities in the Colonial Era used tontines to finance local investments, and a capital investment tontine financed the construction of the original home of the New York Stock Exchange in the Tontine Coffeehouse.[28] Tontines enabled governments to pay lower interest rates than they had to offer on other types of investment because surviving investors received not only the promised interest rate but also mortality credits, in exchange for giving up the right to pass their investment interest on to their heirs.[29]

The life-insurance-style tontine came to prominence in the United States in the late 1800s. Under these arrangements, policy holders paid premiums during a term (typically twenty years). Beneficiaries of policy holders who died during the term would receive a payout. Policy holders who survived the term were entitled to a life annuity or equivalent lump-sum payout funded by the remaining pooled premiums from their deceased counterparts after insurance payouts to their beneficiaries, as well as premiums from those whose policy had lapsed for failure to make a required premium payment at any point.[30] This product drove the broad uptake of life insurance in the United States in the late 1800s and proved to be an effective vehicle for accumulating retirement savings before the advent of Social Security or private pensions. By 1900, two-thirds of life insurance policies in the United States were tontine-style products, accounting for 7 percent of national wealth.[31]

The popularity of life-insurance-style tontines, which left large amounts of capital in the hands of insurers for decades, combined with a lack of regulation and oversight, made these policies ripe for corruption. The 1905 Armstrong Commission investigation in New York uncovered substantial embezzlement and misuse of funds, as well as unduly draconian triggers for lapse or forfeiture of the policy, leading New York lawmakers to outlaw life insurance tontines as they then existed. The use of tontine-style products effectively ended nationwide, since New York had regulatory authority over 95 percent of the national insurance market.[32] Ransom and Sutch (1987) argue that the policy amounted to "throwing the baby out with the bathwater" and that the better response would have been to allow tontines while overseeing and regulating them more effectively.

Legal Uncertainty

The legal status of tontines remains unclear, though contemporary proposals are fundamentally different from the instruments in use over a century ago. The New York statute, still on the books, prohibits only tontine-style investments that pay out less frequently than once a year, suggesting the possibility that many kinds of tontine-style products might still be lawful.[33] It appears that only a few state statutes explicitly bar tontines.[34] But because of tontines' history and reputation, financial services providers remain wary, consistent with the widespread assumption that tontines are or might be unlawful.[35] Nevertheless, for present purposes, we proceed on the reasonable assumption that applicable US law will not flatly prohibit all financial products that include pooling and allocation of mortality credits.

Current Examples

One reason to be optimistic about the future legal status of tontines is that relevant activity in the United States has long included financial products with tontine-like features. For example, "participating life annuities" pair an income guarantee with a variable surplus distribution depending on realized mortality of the pool of investors.[36] Similarly, some life annuities in the United States, like some offered by TIAA, periodically adjust the value of payouts based on the realized mortality of the pool of annuitants, so the annuitants—not the insurance company—bear the risk of the pool living systematically longer than expected.[37] In addition, an optional variable fund offered by one of the state retirement systems includes tontine-like elements.[38]

Despite these inroads, the United States is lagging the rest of the world in tontine-like arrangements. European Union member states permit tontines, usually as a supplement to government-paid or occupational benefits.[39] The pension for former employees of SwissAir is structured as a tontine.[40] In Sweden, the national pension system redistributes the accrued pension wealth of the deceased among all survivors of the same age cohort.[41] In Japan, some workers pay into a tontine-like annuity from their 50s until retirement, when they begin receiving payouts to supplement their national pensions; when they die most of what they have contributed is reallocated among the other policy holders.[42] Tontine-style funds are explicitly legal in the United Kingdom. Canada paved the way for tontine-style products when its 2019 budget proposed legislation to permit them under the name Variable Payment Life Annuities.[43] In South Africa, a firm offering a tontine-style investment designed to improve retirement security for poor workers was established in 2017.[44]

Operational Complexity and Transparency

In theory at least, most tontine pooling is straightforward, transparent, and fair, especially in comparison with commercial annuities. In practice, of course, complications will arise.

First, specifying mortality risk correctly may be difficult because people who are willing to buy into a tontine pool are likely to have longer-than-average lifespans. However, the extent to which that is the case may not be clear ex ante. Mortality risk, of course, is one of the key determinants of the mortality credit in a "fair tontine." The more diverse the pool's participants, the more difficult this will be. As a result, creating tontines for homogeneous age- and gender-based groups could simplify the actuarial calculations, though it would still be necessary to attract enough investors to reduce the impact of random shocks.[45]

Second, and related, adjusting the base return over time to avoid fluctuations in annual payouts will require additional complex calculations. Third, because a simple bond investment would not be likely to generate the returns necessary to compete with other types of retirement income products, a tontine may require some management of its portfolio, which will further add to both complexity and costs.[46]

As many financial professionals, including variable annuity providers, have discovered, financial plans may work in normal times but not when markets are disrupted. Because tontines will need to provide income over several decades, at some point serious market disruptions or other unexpected developments are almost certain. It remains to be seen whether adjustments made in the interest of actuarial fairness, equitable allocation of mortality credits, and level retirement income would be administratively feasible and practical. The adjustments could also compromise, in the eyes of potential investors, the advantage of tontine structures over commercial annuities in terms of transparency, simplicity, and apparent fairness.[47]

These operational complexities will require some effort to resolve, but they are not fatal problems. Tontines, including level payout tontines, are feasible and could offer a greater variety of retirement income solutions for many future retirees.

Profiting from the Death of Others

The survival-contingent payout that underpins the tontine is both highly controversial and utterly ordinary. The idea of deliberately arranging to profit from other people's death naturally makes people squeamish, and all the more so if members of the pool know one another. As noted, incentives to kill off other members of a tontine pool have inspired novels, television shows, and movies.[48] But a little perspective is warranted. First, the perverse incentive that supplies the necessary element of drama for such fictional accounts is absent when the group participating is sufficiently large or, even if small, when members are mutually anonymous.[49]

Second, other financial products regularly pool mortality credits without controversy. For example, annuitants with shorter lifespans effectively subsidize those who live longer.[50] Conversely, owners of certain types of life insurance policies who live longer effectively subsidize the benefits of those who die sooner. In both cases, the mortality credits are less visible because they go through the insurer, which also takes a portion of the credit as revenue. DB pension plans also pool longevity risk.[51] By contrast, in a tontine, the mortality credits directly benefit the survivors rather than being partially hidden in the role of the financial intermediary. The difference is largely a matter of visibility.

Spousal Protections

Tax-qualified retirement plans provide protection for spouses. DB and certain other pension plans must pay pre- and postretirement survivor annuities to a surviving spouse after a married participant's death unless the participant and the spouse agree to waive that right. In 401(k)s and most other DC plans, a deceased participant's spouse inherits by default the participant's full account balance unless the spouse agrees to the designation of a different beneficiary.[52] In both cases, the spouse's agreement must be written and either notarized or witnessed by a plan official.

Tontines could provide similar protection. Both an unmarried participant and a married participant whose spouse agreed to waive these rights could participate in the tontine as individuals.[53] But a tontine might also allow a married couple that did not waive the spousal protections to participate in a tontine as a single unit, receiving payments and mortality credits until the second spouse's death, at which point the couple's interest in the pool would be reallocated to the surviving participants. For example, the life expectancy of a 65-year-old male is about 84, but if married to a 65-year-old female, the couple's "last survivor life expectancy" is 91.[54] In allocating mortality credits, the couple could be treated as a single participant with a life expectancy of 91.[55]

Equity and Discrimination

An equitable allocation of mortality credits would ensure that tontines do not discriminate against people with shorter life expectancy or favor those with longer life expectancy. Life expectancy varies with age, gender, race, ethnicity, income level, marital status, and other factors. As discussed earlier, if tontines could take all these factors into account, they could generate equitable allocations of mortality credits.

Existing law may forbid some adjustments of this type, even if intended to favor traditionally disadvantaged groups that tend to have shorter life expectancies, such as Black Americans. For example, commercial annuities and other insurance products are generally allowed to engage in price discrimination based on life expectancy differences related to age and gender but not race. In contrast, employer-sponsored pensions are not allowed to discriminate in benefits or contributions based on gender or race and can only discriminate on the basis of life expectancy differences related to age in certain specific ways.

For tontines that are offered neither by insurance companies nor by an employer-sponsored plan, it is unclear how current law would apply to all the possible adjustments for mortality risk. Racial disparities in life expectancy present a particular problem for tontines, as well as for any product that pays benefits until a person dies, including Social Security, commercial annuities, and defined benefit pensions. Because Black Americans, for example, tend to have shorter life expectancies than white Americans, Black participants in a tontine would likely be disadvantaged relative to white participants if no offsetting adjustment were made.

We raise this issue because it must be addressed when implementing tontines, but we do not attempt to resolve it here. Determining how current law should be interpreted, clarified, or changed raises complex and difficult questions that are beyond the scope of this chapter.

COMPARING TONTINES WITH OTHER FINANCIAL PRODUCTS

How useful tontine-style pooling will be in helping people manage assets and income in retirement depends in part on how they compare with existing retirement income options. Table 13-1 provides a detailed summary of the differences between retirement income options.

Tontines vs. Income Annuities

Tontines and income annuities are similar in many respects. Both typically require irrevocable investments to control the risk of adverse selection, and both instruments pool mortality credits. The central difference is that a tontine will not provide the income guarantee that an annuity can, but instead provides a higher average return, greater transparency, less complexity, and lower cost.

A fixed income life annuity guarantees a specified dollar amount per month to last for life. By contrast, while the level-payout tontine can be invested to minimize market risk, and can provide considerable longevity risk protection, it does not guarantee either an exact amount of income or the lifelong duration of income.[56]

Different parties bear the risks if things do not go as predicted. If annuitants, as a group, live longer than expected, the insurer bears the costs through extended payments. If a pool of tontine members, as a group, lives longer than expected, the surviving members bear the costs through lower-than-expected payments. In other words, annuities insure participants against systematic longevity risk, like an unexpected cure for cancer, but tontines do not. Similarly, with its income guarantee, the annuity provider assumes the risk of poor investment performance, while members of the tontine pool bear this risk. The

Table 13-1. *Characteristics of Selected Retirement Income Vehicles from Retiree's Standpoint*

Characteristic	*Level-payout tontine*	*Commercial life annuity*	*Managed payout fund*
Handles retiree's need to convert savings to income	Yes	Yes	Yes
Individual (idiosyncratic) longevity risk (risk that a particular individual will outlive life expectancy)	Individual's risk generally "diversified away"—protected by pooling of mortality credits in a sufficiently large pool	Individual is insured (insurer bears risk)	Individual is exposed, but risk can be mitigated by management over time
Systematic longevity risk (risk that group will in aggregate outlive its life expectancy)	Individual is exposed	Individual is insured (insurer bears risk)	Individual is exposed, but risk can be mitigated by management over time
Risk of adverse selection	Individual is exposed to adverse selection by others, so pool could have above-average life expectancy	Individual is protected (insurer bears risk of adverse selection)	. . . [a]
Guaranteed return	Not guaranteed but targeted	Yes	Not guaranteed but targeted
Investment risk, including sequence-of-returns risk	Depends on how invested; could be exposed but mitigated by mortality credits	Individual is insured (insurer is exposed but invests in bonds, reserves)	Depends on how invested; could usually expect some exposure
Provides mortality pooling gains in addition to investment returns	Yes, and expected return might be further increased if it has equity investments	Yes, lower overall return if fixed income annuity and higher premiums to pay for guarantees	Not usually
Inflation risk	Exposure can be limited by investments	Exposure can be limited by purchasing increasing annuity	Exposure can be limited by investments

(*continued*)

Table 13-1. *(continued)*

Characteristic	*Level-payout tontine*	*Commercial life annuity*	*Managed payout fund*
Counterparty credit/default risk (long-term risk of provider insolvency, underfunding of promised benefits, or breach of contract)	Very limited as participants do not depend on provider for specific promised payments (unlike annuity, like DC plan)	Some. Risk from insurer insolvency is limited by regulation and state guarantees; litigation risk is reduced by fiduciary safe harbor	Some
Illiquidity risk (lack of flexibility to meet shocks)	Exposed because it is irrevocable; for liquidity/flexibility, need to rely on other investments	Exposed because it is irrevocable; for liquidity/flexibility, need to rely on other investments	Investment is quasi-liquid
Health/long-term care shock risk	Exposed because it is an irrevocable investment in regular income; for liquidity/flexibility, need to rely on other investments	Exposed because it is an irrevocable investment in regular income; for liquidity/flexibility, need to rely on other investments	Investment is quasi-liquid
Cognitive decline risk	Risk is limited because investment is irrevocable and on autopilot	Risk is limited because investment is irrevocable and on autopilot	Fairly limited; investment is managed, but individual could exercise some choices

Cost	Probably lowest; assumes fewer risks than annuity, but some oversight will be needed, as well as possible legal advice in early days	Highest, especially because of need for reserves to back up guarantees; may be hard to ascertain because of hidden fees	On the higher side because of generally more discretionary professional investment and payout management
How transparent and how comprehensible to consumers	Basic concept is transparent and easy to grasp, although actuarial adjustments could be complex, less transparent, less understandable	Fixed income product can be straightforward, but typical GLWB,[b] GMWB,[c] and fixed index options can be complicated, confusing, nontransparent, possible hidden fees	Relatively good but would depend on specific arrangements; might attract customers when structured as a familiar, easily accessible mutual fund
Availability to consumers as of 2020	Minimal	Readily available, but choices are complex to navigate	Somewhat limited but rapidly expanding

Source: Authors' summary.

[a] . . . = not applicable.

[b] GLWB = guaranteed lifetime withdrawal benefit.

[c] GMWB = guaranteed minimum withdrawal benefit.

rate of return insurers can provide on annuities is reduced by allowances to cover these risks, to provide reserves, and to comply with other regulatory requirements.

Another distinction is that tontine mortality gains are triggered by actual deaths as they occur and hence are more transparent than annuity mortality gains. In a commercial annuity, pooling takes place "behind the curtain" with the intermediation of an insurance company. It calculates income based on an actuarially expected rate of mortality in the pool, combined with other financial flows, assumptions, and adjustments. The insurance company also adds a series of fees to ensure profitability. It is not annuitants who are seen as profiting from the demise of their fellow annuitants: it is the insurance company.

Of course, real-world annuities should not be compared with an idealized version of tontines. As history illustrates, tontines too would require consumer protections and regulatory safeguards, with attendant costs. These costs can be expected to be lower than the costs of annuity-type guarantees, although complex actuarial fairness adjustments could call for more regulatory oversight.[57]

Tontines vs. Managed Payout Funds

Tontines and managed payout funds allow retirees to convert savings to income but differ in how they address longevity risk and investment risk. By its nature, a tontine reduces longevity risk. The extent to which a managed payout fund would reduce longevity risk depends on how the fund is managed.

Neither instrument provides income guarantees, but the nature of the risks differs in the two instruments. In both, participants face investment return risk and sequence-of-returns risk,[58] as well as a type of risk stemming from participants' mortality experience. Simply put, the longer participants live, the higher the bar for managed payout funds to provide sufficient income as long as it is needed, and the lower the tontine's mortality credits and hence its returns to surviving tontine participants.

Managed payout funds might be more likely to be actively managed and more heavily invested in equities to pay higher levels of income, and therefore more likely to carry some level of market risk. But this is not necessarily the case, as it would depend on how the managed payout fund investment portfolio and the tontine investment portfolio are constructed (and they could be composed identically).

As noted earlier, investment in a tontine generally is irrevocable and leaves nothing for heirs, while managed payout funds allow withdrawals and bequests.

LIFETIME INCOME AT LOWER COST

Everything old is new again, as the adage goes. More than 300 years after being introduced as a way to finance war and capital projects, tontine-inspired structures are now receiving attention around the world as tools to finance retirement income because they are efficient and transparent—with mortality credits accruing to pool members directly and traceably—and outside commercial annuities' insurance system.

While commercial annuities guarantee a specified income for life, tontine pooling offers less but still meaningful protection at what should be a lower cost. Tontines should pay more in expected income for each dollar invested than annuities do. They would not require the charges insurers need to impose or the reserves insurers need to maintain to cover their annuity payment guarantees and insurance against systematic longevity risk. Tontines would also require less and less costly regulation. For many people, the marginal value of *complete* insurance against both investment and longevity risk that a fixed-income annuity provides may not be worth the marginal costs involved, especially as historically low interest rates have depressed annuity returns.[59]

Public policy is only beginning to grapple with the challenges of effectively managing retirement security in a market currently dominated by 401(k) and IRA account structures and lump-sum payouts rather than DB plans. The retirement system stands to benefit from more transparent and effective tools for survivor income pooling. Creative thinking and financial engineering have made a strong case for this.[60]

But the extent to which tontines will penetrate retirement systems or other asset structures in the United States depends not only on the theoretical soundness of the tontine design, but also on the willingness of retirement plans and financial providers to offer such products. In addition to the operational complexity of some tontine types, there is a perception of daunting federal and state regulatory, and perhaps legislative, obstacles, but some of these concerns appear to be unfounded or overblown. Furthermore, any lingering air of disrepute in the United States is attributable to corruption in the age of the robber barons; it should be seen as an artifact of premodern tontine structures rather than anything inherent in tontine principles or in the project of consensual longevity risk pooling.

The fact that several other countries and at least some retirement systems in the United States now use survivor income pooling to augment and allocate pension income suggests that the tontine option can be valuable. Survivor income pooling—as a stand-alone product or as a tool that increases yield in managed payout funds or other retirement income vehicles—could help expand the market for managing longevity risk. Tontine-like structures need not be the entire or main retirement income solution, but can be useful as part of a broader strategy, especially for those who do not have or have otherwise handled any need for spousal protection or other bequests. Accordingly, given the limited diffusion of annuities and managed payout funds, tontines offer an attractive alternative that should have a place among the options households can access to finance retirement income.

APPENDIX: SIMULATION METHODOLOGY

The models used in this chapter are intended to illustrate and compare different types of lifetime income. They are built on mortality patterns and investment patterns, and they assume time is discrete (everything that happens in a particular year happens at exactly the same time).

The mortality mechanism is based on data from the Human Mortality Database, which provides mortality statistics for people of every age from 1933 to 2017, covering people born as early as the 1820s. To extrapolate these insights into the future, we regressed each cohort's life expectancy at age 65 on their mode age of death and then used this relationship to predict the mode age of death of every living cohort older than age 65 in 2017 (birth years 1907–1952). We then used this extrapolated mode age of death as the M parameter in the Gompertz hazard function, where M is the mode age of death, b is the periodic increase in mortality risk, and x is the age of interest:

$$G(x; M, b) = be^{b(x-M)}$$

We then solved this function for the b parameter that would generate a cumulative death rate at age 65 that matched the observed cumulative death rate from the Human Mortality Database data. This provided the foundation for a complete series of lifetime mortality curves where mortality under age 65 is observed, and mortality over age 65 is extrapolated using the Gompertz hazard function. We generated a different set of parameters—and thus a different lifetime mortality curve—for each gender/birth-year cohort. For example, the cohort of men who turned 65 in 2017 used to generate the figures in this chapter were assumed to have a mode age of death, M, of 83.14, and a periodic increase in mortality, b, of .0834.

These lifetime mortality curves were used to generate projected mortality rates and stochastic years of death for members of specific age/gender cohorts. The random generator assigned a "mortality percentile" to each member and then assigned that member a year of death based on the year in which people in that percentile are projected to die. This facilitated the stochastic mortality models used to test the different lifetime income tools. Note that this simple model does not account for the effects of exogenous mortality shifts or correlation between increasing mortality within a cohort, so we may be understating variation in mortality.

The second major mechanism involves investment returns. The values of the S&P 500 index from 1927 to the present were used to derive the mean and standard deviation of stock returns, while the yields on ten-year Treasury bonds were used to derive the mean and standard deviation of bond yields. The models of investment returns assume a 50-50 split between investment in the S&P 500 fund and in the ten-year Treasuries and generate random growth factors for each of these investments over the relevant horizon and combine them to obtain an indexed value of the assets any time during the window. We assume that annual stock and bond performance is independent of previous years' performance and one another's performance, which—though not strictly empirically defensible—provides a straightforward model for projecting the performance of different investment tools.

These simulations were done in R version 3.6.1 and RStudio version 1.2.5001 for Mac. The models used the tidyverse and rootSolve R packages. The underlying data and code are available upon request.

NOTES

The authors thank Jonathan Forman, Moshe Milevsky, and Anna Rappaport for helpful comments. This paper was made possible through generous support from Arnold Ventures. The views expressed here are solely those of the authors and should not be attributed to any other person or to any organization.

Disclosure: Iwry provides, through J. Mark Iwry, PLLC, policy and legal advice to plan sponsors and providers, nonprofit organizations, trade associations, fintechs, private equity firms, other investment firms and financial institutions, regarding retirement and savings policy, pension and retirement plans, and related issues. Iwry is a member of the American Benefits Institute Board of Advisors, the Board of Advisors of the Pension Research Council at the Wharton School, the Council of Scholar Advisors of the Georgetown University Center for Retirement Initiatives, the Panel of Outside Scholars of the Boston College Center for Retirement Research, the CUNA Mutual

Safety Net Independent Advisory Board, and the Aspen Leadership Forum Advisory Board. He also periodically serves as an expert witness in federal court litigation relating to retirement plans. The authors did not receive any financial support from any firm or person for any views expressed or advocated in this paper. They are currently not an officer, director, or board member of any organization that has compensated or otherwise influenced them to write this paper or to express or advocate any views in this paper. Accordingly, the views expressed here are solely those of the authors and should not be attributed to any other person or to any organization.

1. Engen, Gale, and Uccello (1999); Scholz, Seshadri, and Khitatrakun (2006); Munnell, Hou, and Sanzenbacher (2018); Biggs (2020); Bipartisan Policy Center (2016).

2. Of course, many people want to provide bequests to others. With a given level of bequest in mind, those people face the same problem of ensuring that they do not consume their resources too quickly or too slowly.

3. Commercial annuities are rarely indexed for inflation, however, so the inflation-adjusted income flow from most annuities declines over time.

4. Iwry and others (2019).

5. John and others (2019).

6. For an overview, history, and analysis of tontines, see Milevsky (2015).

7. Except where the context indicates otherwise, the term "annuity" here refers to "income" annuities. In contrast, "variable annuities" are typically used to confer tax-favored treatment on otherwise taxable equity investments while seldom providing a stream of income.

8. Iwry and others (2019); Iwry and Turner (2009).

9. Benartzi and Shu (2019). Iwry and others (2019) discuss the "annuity puzzle"—why so few people purchase annuities even when it seems that doing so would benefit them.

10. John and others (2019).

11. The Treasury Department and IRS permit such deeply deferred annuities to be provided in qualified plans and IRAs, where they are known as "qualified longevity annuity contracts" (QLACs). See US Department of the Treasury (2014); US Department of the Treasury, "Treasury Issues Final Rules Regarding Longevity Annuities," July 1, 2014, https://www.treasury.gov/press-center/press-releases/Pages/jl2448.aspx. See also John and others (2019); Horneff, Maurer, and Mitchell (2019); Horneff, Maurer, and Mitchell (2018); and Munnell, Wettstein, and Hou (2019).

12. See "Historical Returns on Stocks, Bonds, and Bills" (2019). Other options for retirement income are in the development phase, including reverse mortgages (Baily, Harris, and Wang 2019) and the "selfie" bond (Merton and Muralidhar 2020).

13. In these examples, we assume that there are no administrative costs or fees.

14. Evidence suggests that consumption tends to decline as retired households age, until there is a sharp increase in medical expenses that might occur at the very end of life. See Butrica, Johnson, and Goldwyn (2005) and Banerjee (2014). In models with stochastic lifespan, the optimal rate of increase in consumption is given by $r - \partial - m$, where r is the rate of return, ∂ is the rate that individuals discount the future, and m

is the current period mortality risk. As people age, m rises, so that optimal consumption growth slows and may go negative. See Hurd (1987).

15. Milevsky and Salisbury (2015) do not specify the terminal condition for their level-payout tontine.

16. Note that the x axis in figure 13-2 shows time, whereas in figures 13-1A and 13-1B the x axis represents the number of deaths.

17. For instance, assume that the initial investment return for a tontine consisting of 100 people was set at 4 percent to keep total annual return at about 4 percent. If, according to actuarial tables, 10 percent of the pool is expected to die in the first year, then the preset annual base return would have been 3.6 percent for the first year, 10 percent lower than the initial base return. But if the base return is determined and adjusted annually based on actual (rather than expected) mortality, and if only 5 percent of the pool dies in the first year, the adjusted base return for the first year would be 3.8 percent, 5 percent lower than the initial base return. The total return of 4 percent would remain unchanged. In contrast, if the base return for each year is preset and not adjusted for actual mortality, and if only 5 percent of members die in the first year, then the total return to survivors would be only 3.79 percent (4 percent × (90 percent /95 percent)).

18. In theory, substantial shocks to the underlying portfolio could result in the insolvency of the tontine, leading to periodic total return income for survivors that rapidly declines to zero. But many of the simulations run experienced periods of negative investment returns and the tontine remained solvent, leaving survivors' income constant. In practice, in most circumstances a tontine experiencing investment losses would be able to avoid exhausting its assets and continue paying income by reducing, to the extent necessary, the amount of income it pays out.

19. In the tontines illustrated in figures 13-1–13-3, the balances of participants who died were split equally among all surviving members. This would be consistent with a fair tontine only if all pool members had the same actuarial probability of death in a given period and the same balance.

20. In addition, as discussed in the examples above, because actual mortality experience (how many die and the size of their balances) will ordinarily differ from actuarially expected mortality experience, actual realized mortality credits will differ accordingly from expected fair mortality credits in a given period.

21. Milevsky and Salisbury (2015).

22. Forman and Sabin (2015).

23. Employer-funded tontine-style survivor income pooling would also raise other issues. One question is whether and how ERISA would apply to such a vehicle. Another issue is portability of benefits. While such a tontine-style vehicle could work for those who spend most of their career at a single employer, it would be harder to implement unless many employers used such an arrangement. If tontine-style pensions became common and were offered in multiple-employer arrangements that any employer could join, portability would be less of a concern. The portability challenge applies also to commercial annuities, although federal legislation has taken some steps to mitigate it in that context.

24. Fullmer and Sabin (2019).

25. John and others (2019) describe a retirement income strategy that, in addition to Social Security benefits, would combine a managed payout fund, an emergency savings account, and a QLAC. A tontine could finance any of these products.

26. It is unclear whether the tontine was named after de Tonti because he actually invented it or was its most prominent early promoter.

27. Examples include King William's tontine; ten French national tontines offered from 1689 to 1759; three Irish tontines offered in 1773, 1775, and 1777; and hundreds of tontines sponsored by Dutch and German city-states in the late seventeenth and early eighteenth centuries. See Milevsky (2015) and McKeever (2009) for specifics.

28. McKeever (2009). Lange, List, and Price (2004) explore the use of tontines as a method of financing public goods.

29. Tontines with a constant base return held out the possibility of astronomical returns, more closely resembling a lottery than a conventional investment. Adam Smith observed that there is a part of human nature that is quite drawn to tontine-style investment and the possibility of winning big. See Smith (1776). While this may help explain the tontine's longtime popularity, it may also help account for its somewhat unwholesome image.

30. Ransom and Sutch (1987).

31. Ransom and Sutch (1987); Christie (1957).

32. McKeever (2009).

33. Wettstein (2018).

34. McKeever (2009).

35. Fullmer (2019).

36. Maurer and others (2016).

37. Forman and Sabin (2015).

38. See Wisconsin Department of Employee Trust Funds (2020, p. 9): "After the year's returns are final, ETF's actuary determines the effective rates to apply to members' account balances. Then they use the effective rates, 5% assumed rate, and actuarial factors (death rates, previous year carryover, etc.) to calculate the annuity adjustments."

39. "Directive 2009/138/EC of the European Parliament" (2009).

40. White (2002).

41. See Milevsky (2015).

42. Hayashi (2020).

43. "Permitting Additional Types of Annuities under Registered Plans" (2019).

44. Nobuntu (2020).

45. The opportunity to participate in an age- or gender-specific tontine might make the mortality pooling and allocation system seem more intuitively fair and appealing.

46. This might take the form of a managed payout fund enhanced by mortality credit pooling, as noted below.

47. Of course, the same concerns about complexity and fairness also apply to annuities and other retirement income products. While it is fairly simple to go on the website of an annuity provider and determine the monthly income that a simple, fixed income annuity would pay, it is virtually impossible to understand exactly how that amount was determined, and challenging to determine its actual cost to the investor, especially for more complex products and features.

48. See e.g., *The Wrong Box*, by Robert Louis Stevenson and Lloyd Osbourne and its film adaptation; *4.50 from Paddington* by Agatha Christie; and *The Simpsons* episode "Raging Abe Simpson and His Grumbling Grandson in 'The Curse of the Flying Hellfish.'"

49. According to *The Economist* (2017), there have been no successfully recorded episodes of actual attempts to kill off other members of a tontine.

50. Fullmer (2019).

51. Although surviving participants do not receive mortality credits that increase their benefit amounts when other participants die, they can benefit indirectly if those deaths result in additional funding becoming available for plan benefits generally. The effect might also be to reduce employers' funding obligations.

52. See ERISA (1974) § 205 (29 USC § 1055); "Qualified Pension, Profit-Sharing, and Stock Bonus Plans" (26 USC § 401(a)(11)); and "Definitions and Special Rules for Purposes of Minimum Survivor Annuity Requirements" (26 USC §417).

53. However, because 401(k) plan rules preclude forfeiture of employees' elective contributions on account of death, the mortality pooling in 401(k)s would be limited to employer matching or nonmatching contributions. Mortality pooling of employer contributions could be pursued in conjunction with a 401(k) plan design providing for employer contributions to be paid out in the form of retirement income, provided that this was not deemed to violate the "definitely determinable benefits" requirements. See "Qualified Pension, Profit-Sharing, and Stock Bonus Plans." 26 CFR § 1.401–1(b)(1)(i). The notion of including tontine-like mortality credits in (or combining them with) a DB plan would raise additional issues under the statutory prohibition on qualified DB plan forfeitures upon a participant's death increasing benefits for other participants. See "Qualified Pension, Profit-Sharing, and Stock Bonus Plans." 26 USC § 401(a)(8). For DC and DB plans, it may be worth exploring whether mortality credits, instead of being viewed as resulting from a forfeiture of the deceased participant's benefits, could be structured as a beneficiary designation whereby participants interested in joining the plan's mortality credit pool could designate the plan's qualified trust as their death beneficiary in accordance with plan provisions for allocation of such mortality credits to surviving participants.

54. See IRS Publication 590-B (2019), Table II (Joint Life and Last Survivor Expectancy). Life expectancies differ slightly depending on which actuarial table is used.

55. The mortality credit allocations would also need to consider the adjusted levels of retirement income payable while both members are alive and then to the surviving spouse. A retiree who is entitled to income of $1,000 per month if payable as a single life annuity (a stream of payments only for that retiree's lifetime) could, if married, receive a joint and survivor annuity payable to the retiree for life and then to the surviving spouse for life. However, the payments made while both spouses are alive would be reduced (for example, to $900 per month) in order to fund the survivor benefit, and the survivor benefit frequently would be a fraction (often 50 percent or 75 percent) of the $900 per month joint benefit. Other aspects of such a spousal protection tontine would also need to be addressed, including how actuarially fair mortality credit allocations should take into account the fact that married individuals tend to have longer life expectancies than those who are unmarried, as well as the

possibilities of divorce, the spouse predeceasing the participant, or the couple's waiver of postdeath spousal protections.

56. Milevsky and others (2018, pp. 33–34) reported, after performing a hypothetical Canadian case study, that the answer to which vehicle would provide the higher payout "isn't quite clear-cut." The result was "neck-and-neck" when both used government bonds as their underlying asset, but retirement income tontines would have yielded higher payouts when using a corporate bond curve. In any event, the authors concluded that their results were uncertain because they could not take regulatory costs, fees, and other institutional factors into account, and that the tontine should not be considered cheaper or more cost effective than a commercial life annuity but instead provided an alternative on the "longevity risk-return spectrum."

57. One other factor could change the comparative analysis: if a QLAC longevity annuity were combined with a tontine-style fund, the QLAC, by guaranteeing a specified payment for life starting at age 85, could fill in much of the missing protection at far lower cost than an immediate annuity. See John and others (2019).

58. Sequence-of-returns risk refers to the risk that even if market downturns are followed, as they usually are, by eventual market recoveries, retirees cannot count on recouping their portfolio losses if the downturns come early in their retirement. This is because, when account owners are steadily spending down their balances, the sequence of down and up markets can make a big difference. If significant losses in market value come first, then—even if the percentage of market gains equals the earlier percentage of market losses—later gains will be insufficient to recoup those losses for investors who have been steadily spending down. (If, instead, market gains precede equal percentage market losses during spenddown, more assets will remain at the end.) Sequence of returns matters more during spenddown because a later percentage increase in market values will be applied to a shrinking account balance (or capital base)—smaller than the account balance (or capital base) to which the earlier losses applied. This risk results from the retiree having no choice but to fund monthly spending by selling market assets while their value is temporarily depressed in a falling market, so that later market recoveries in a similar percentage will be operating on a diminished capital base. However, in a tontine-type mortality credit pool, the inflow of mortality credits would help offset some of the outflow from spending, thereby mitigating any sequence-of-returns loss during spenddown.

59. Friedman and Warshawsky (1990); Mitchell and others (1999).

60. See, for example, Milevsky (2015); Milevsky and Salisbury (2015); Forman (2018); Forman and Sabin (2018); Fullmer and Sabin (2019); Milevsky and others (2018); Fullmer (2019); Fullmer and Forman (2020).

REFERENCES

Baily, Martin, Benjamin Harris, and Ting Wang. 2019. "The Unfulfilled Promise of Reverse Mortgages: Can a Better Market Improve Retirement Security?" Brookings.

Banerjee, Sudipto. 2014. "The Gap between Expected and Actual Retirement: Evidence from Longitudinal Data." EBRI Notes 35 (11). Washington, DC: Employee Benefit Research Institute.

Benartzi, Shlomo, and Suzanne Shu. 2019. "Why Retirees Are Wary of Annuities." *Wall Street Journal*, February 10.

Biggs, Andrew. 2020. "Fact-Check: 41% of Retirees 'Can't Cover Basic Needs' Says the Elder Index." *Forbes* Opinion, February 19.

Bipartisan Policy Center. 2016. *Report of the Commission on Retirement Saving and Personal Savings*. Washington, DC.

Butrica, Barbara A., Richard W. Johnson, and Joshua H. Goldwyn. 2005. "Understanding Expenditure Patterns in Retirement." Working Paper 2005-3. Center for Retirement Research, Boston College.

Christie, Agatha. 1957. *4.50 from Paddington*. London: William Collins, Sons.

"Definitions and Special Rules for Purposes of Minimum Survivor Annuity Requirements." 26 USC §417.

"Directive 2009/138/EC of the European Parliament and of the Council on the Taking-Up and Pursuit of the Business of Insurance and Reinsurance (Solvency II)." 2009. *Official Journal of the European Union* L 335: 1–155.

Employee Retirement Income Security Act (ERISA). 1974. Public Law 93–406.

Enda, Grace, and William G. Gale. 2020. "How Does Gender Equality Affect Women in Retirement?" Brookings Retirement Security Project, July.

Engen, Eric M., William G. Gale, and Cori E. Uccello. 1999. "The Adequacy of Household Saving." *Brookings Papers on Economic Activity* (Fall 1999): 65–187.

Forman, Jonathan Barry. 2018. "Workers and Retirees Could Pool Risk with Tontine Annuities, Tontine Pensions, and Survivor Funds." *Pace Law Review* 37 (1): 204–91.

Forman, Jonathan B., and Michael J. Sabin. 2015. "Tontine Pensions." *University of Pennsylvania Law Review* 163 (3): 755–831.

———. 2018. "Fully Funded Pensions: State and Local Governments Should Immediately Budget for the Pension Costs of Pay Raises." SSRN.

Friedman, Benjamin M., and Mark J. Warshawsky. 1990. "The Cost of Annuities: Implications for Saving Behavior and Bequests." *Quarterly Journal of Economics* 105 (1): 135–54.

Fullmer, Richard K. 2019. "Tontines: A Practitioner's Guide to Mortality-Pooled Investments." Charlottesville, VA: CFA Institute Research Foundation.

Fullmer, Richard K., and Jonathan Barry Forman. 2020. "State-Sponsored Pensions for Private Sector Workers: The Case for Pooled Annuities and Tontines." Wharton Pension Research Council Working Paper 2020-17. University of Pennsylvania.

Fullmer, Richard K., and Michael J. Sabin. 2019. "Individual Tontine Accounts." *Journal of Accounting and Finance* 19 (8): 31–61.

Hayashi, Yuka. 2020. "Japan's Aging Population Breathes New Life into a Centuries-Old Investment Idea." *Wall Street Journal*, February 25.

"Historical Returns on Stocks, Bonds, and Bills—United States." NYU Stern School of Business. http://pages.stern.nyu.edu/~adamodar/New_Home_Page/datafile/histretSP.html.

Horneff, Vanya, Raimond Maurer, and Olivia S. Mitchell. 2018. "Putting the Pension Back in 401(k) Retirement Plans: Optimal versus Default Longevity Income Annuities." *Journal of Banking and Finance* 114 (1): 1–14.

———. 2019. "Automatic Enrollment in 401(k) Annuities: Boosting Retiree Lifetime Income." Brookings Institution.

Human Mortality Database. 2020. University of California, Berkeley (USA), and Max Planck Institute for Demographic Research (Germany). Mortality.org.

Hurd, Michael D. 1987. "Savings of the Elderly and Desired Bequests." *American Economic Review* 77 (3): 298–312.

Internal Revenue Service. 2019. "Distributions from Individual Retirement Arrangements (IRAs)." Publication 590-B. Washington, DC.

Iwry, J. Mark, and John Turner. 2009. "Automatic Annuitization: New Behavioral Strategies for Expanding Lifetime Income in 401(k)s." Retirement Security Project Issue Brief 2009-2. Brookings Institution.

Iwry, J. Mark, William G. Gale, David C. John, and Victoria Johnson. 2019. "Reducing Regulatory Obstacles to Annuities in 401k Plans." Brookings Institution.

John, David C., William G. Gale, J. Mark Iwry, and Aaron Krupkin. 2019. "From Saving to Spending: A Proposal to Convert Retirement Account Balances into Automatic and Flexible Income." Brookings Institution.

Lange, Andreas, John A. List, and Michael K. Price. 2004. "Using Tontines to Finance Public Goods: Back to the Future?" NBER Working Paper 10958. Cambridge, MA: National Bureau of Economic Research.

Matheson, Victor, and Ken Grote. 2006. "In Search of a Fair Bet in the Lottery." *Eastern Economic Journal* 32 (4): 673–84.

Maurer, Raimond, Olivia S. Mitchell, Ralph Rogalla, and Ivonne Siegelin. 2016. "Accounting and Actuarial Smoothing of Retirement Payouts in Participating Life Annuities." NBER Working Paper 20124. Cambridge, MA: National Bureau of Economic Research.

McKeever, Kent. 2009. "A Short History of Tontines." *Fordham Journal of Corporate & Financial Law* 15 (2): 491–521.

Merton, Robert C., and Arun S. Muralidhar. 2020. "SeLFIES: A New Pension Bond and Currency for Retirement." SSRN.

Milevsky, Moshe A. 2015. *King William's Tontine: Why the Retirement Annuity of the Future Should Resemble Its Past.* Cambridge University Press.

Milevsky, Moshe A., and Thomas S. Salisbury. 2015. "Optimal Retirement Income Tontines." *Insurance: Mathematics and Economics* 64: 91–105.

———. 2016. "Equitable Retirement Income Tontines: Mixing Cohorts Without Discriminating." *ASTIN Bulletin: Journal of the International Actuarial Association* 46 (3): 571–604.

Milevsky, Moshe A., Thomas S. Salisbury, Gabriela Gonzalez, and Hanna Jankowski. 2018. "Annuities versus Tontines in the 21st Century: A Canadian Case Study." Schaumburg, IL: Society of Actuaries.

Mitchell, Olivia, S., James M. Poterba, Mark J. Warshawsky, and Jeffrey R. Brown. 1999. "New Evidence on the Money's Worth of Individual Annuities." *American Economic Review* 89 (5): 1299–318.

Munnell, Alicia, Wenliang Hou, and Geoffrey Sanzenbacher. 2018. "National Retirement Risk Index Shows Modest Improvement in 2016." IB-18-1. Center for Retirement Research, Boston College.

Munnell, Alicia, Gal Wettstein, and Wenliang Hou. 2019. "How Best to Annuitize Defined Contribution Assets." WP-19-13. Center for Retirement Research, Boston College.

Nobuntu. 2020. "Nobuntu: A Digital Peer-to-Peer Pension Which Pays People More as They Grow Older." Cape Town, South Africa. https://www.f6s.com/nobuntu.

"Permitting Additional Types of Annuities under Registered Plans." 2019. In *Investing in the Middle Class: Budget 2019*, pp. 358–62. Ottawa: Parliament of Canada.

Piggott, John, Emiliano A. Valdez, and Bettina Detzel. 2005. "The Simple Analytics of a Pooled Annuity Fund." *Journal of Risk and Insurance* 72 (3): 497–520.

"Qualified Pension, Profit-Sharing, and Stock Bonus Plans." 26 CFR § 1.401-1.

"Qualified Pension, Profit-Sharing, and Stock Bonus Plans." 26 USC § 401.

"Raging Abe Simpson and His Grumbling Grandson in 'The Curse of the Flying Hellfish.'" 1996. *The Simpsons* 7 (22). Los Angeles: Fox Broadcasting Company.

Ransom, Roger L., and Richard Sutch. 1987. "Tontine Insurance and the Armstrong Investigation: A Case of Stifled Innovation, 1868–1905." *Journal of Economic History* 47 (2): 379–90.

Sabin, Michael J. 2010. "Fair Tontine Annuity." SSRN.

Sabin, Michael J., and Jonathan B. Forman. 2016. "The Analytics of a Single-Period Tontine." SSRN.

Scholz, John Karl, Ananth Seshadri, and Surachai Khitatrakun. 2006. "Are Americans Saving 'Optimally' for Retirement?" *Journal of Political Economy* 114 (4): 607–43.

Smith, Adam. 1776. *An Inquiry into the Nature and Causes of the Wealth of Nations.* London: Strahan and Cadell.

Stevenson, Robert Louis, and Lloyd Osbourne. 1889. *The Wrong Box.* London: Longmans, Green.

The Economist. 2017. "Death Pools Can Bring Financial Security for the Long-Lived." Finance and Economics, June 7.

US Department of the Treasury. 2014. "Longevity Annuity Contracts: Final Regulations." *Federal Register* 79 (127): 37633–37643.

Wettstein, Gal. 2018. "Could 'Tontines' Expand the Market for Longevity Insurance?" Research Paper 18-7. Center for Retirement Research, Boston College.

White, David. 2002. "The Swiss Do It Differently." *Investments and Pensions Europe*, March 2002. https://www.ipe.com/the-swiss-do-it-differently/14904.article.

Wisconsin Department of Employee Trust Funds. 2020. "Variable Trust Fund." ET-4930. Madison, WI.

CONTRIBUTORS

EDITORS

WILLIAM G. GALE is the Arjay and Frances Miller Chair in Federal Economic Policy in the Economic Studies Program at the Brookings Institution. His research focuses on tax policy, fiscal policy, pensions, and saving behavior. He is director of the Retirement Security Project. He is also codirector of the Tax Policy Center, a joint venture of the Brookings Institution and the Urban Institute. From 2006 to 2009, he served as vice president of Brookings and director of the Economic Studies Program. Gale is the author of *Fiscal Therapy: Curing America's Debt Addiction and Investing in the Future* (Oxford University Press, 2019).

J. MARK IWRY is a nonresident senior fellow at Brookings and a visiting scholar at the Wharton School. Iwry served as senior adviser to the secretary of the Treasury for national retirement and health policy (2009–2017). He previously served as the benefits tax counsel at Treasury, a partner at Covington & Burling, and research professor at Georgetown University. Iwry has worked with members of Congress, their staffs, and numerous other organizations to develop retirement policy initiatives and reforms, including 401(k) automatic enrollment, the nationwide Automatic IRA proposal, the state-based Automatic IRAs, the Saver's Credit, myRA, and the SIMPLE-IRA. His awards for leadership and innovation include recognition in the media as one of the world's "30 top financial players." He graduated from Harvard College, Harvard Law School, and the Harvard Kennedy School of Government.

DAVID C. JOHN is a senior strategic policy adviser at the AARP Public Policy Institute focusing on pension and retirement savings issues. PPI is AARP's internal think tank. John is also a nonresident senior fellow in the Economic Studies Program at the Brookings Institution working with the Retirement Security Project. RSP focuses on improving retirement savings in the United States, especially among moderate and low-income workers. Before joining AARP, John was a senior research fellow at the Heritage Foundation.

CONTRIBUTORS

SARAH HOLMES BERK is a research project director at the National Bureau of Economic Research, where she manages a behavioral economics lab that studies financial well-being. She also serves as associate director of the NIH-funded NBER Roybal Center for Behavior Change in Health, which supports clinical trials that explore the relationship between health outcomes, human behavior, and health dynamics. Previously, she worked at Brookings, managing the *Brookings Papers on Economic Activity* series and supporting a wide range of economic policy research. Her current research interests lie in helping individuals save for emergencies and retirement. Sarah holds an MA in public policy and a BA in philosophy from the George Washington University.

GRACE ENDA is a senior research assistant in the Economic Studies Program at the Brookings Institution, where she has specialized in tax, fiscal, and retirement policy. She received her BA in economics and government with highest honors from the University of Texas, where she was elected to Phi Beta Kappa in 2019.

JASON J. FICHTNER is a senior lecturer in international economics and an associate director of the International Economics and Finance (MIEF) program at the Johns Hopkins University School of Advanced International Studies (SAIS). He teaches courses in behavioral economics, cost-benefit analysis, and public finance. He is also a fellow with the Bipartisan Policy Center. His research focuses on Social Security, federal tax policy, federal budget policy, retirement security, and policy proposals to increase saving and investment. Fichtner earned his BA from the University of Michigan; his MA in public policy from Georgetown University; and his PhD in public administration and policy from Virginia Tech.

HILARY GELFOND is an analyst in the Quantitative Economics and Statistics (QUEST) group at Ernst and Young. She previously worked as a senior research assistant at the Urban-Brookings Tax Policy Center within the Brookings Institution. Gelfond holds a master's in public policy from the Harvard Kennedy School of Government and a bachelor's degree from Cornell University.

CLAIRE HALDEMAN is a senior research assistant in the Economic Studies Program at the Brookings Institution. She received a BA in ethics, politics, and economics from Yale University.

BENJAMIN H. HARRIS is a counselor to the US Treasury secretary. He was formerly an associate research professor at Northwestern University's Kellogg School of Management, chief economist with Results for America, and the chief economist and economic adviser to the vice president of the United States. Earlier in his career, Harris was policy director of the Hamilton Project, a fellow in the Economic Studies Program at Brookings, and deputy director of the Retirement Security Project. He also served as a senior economist with the Council of Economic Advisers and as a senior economist with the Budget Committee in the US House of Representatives. In 2000, Harris was awarded a Fulbright Scholarship to Namibia. He holds a PhD in economics from the George Washington University.

VICTORIA JOHNSON is a regulatory data analyst at the Federal Reserve Bank of San Francisco. After receiving a BA in mathematical economic analysis from Rice University, she worked at the Brookings Institution as a research assistant in the Economic Studies Program with the Urban-Brookings Tax Policy Center. She has also been a research fellow with the Malcolm Wiener Center for Social Policy at the Harvard Kennedy School of Government, where she focused on research in labor and education economics.

BRYAN KIM is currently a research associate with the JPMorgan Chase Institute. His research at the institute focuses on the economic conditions and policy issues facing metropolitan areas and small businesses. Before joining the JPMorgan Chase Institute, Bryan was a research assistant at the Brookings Institution and the Urban-Brookings Tax Policy Center, where his research focused on tax policy, fiscal policy, and retirement security policies. Bryan holds a BA in economics and mathematics from Reed College.

GARY KOENIG is vice president of financial security with the AARP Public Policy Institute, where he leads a team of policy experts working on economic and consumer issues important to people age 50 and older. Since 2016, he has directed the development of AARP's strategy on savings and financial planning and more recently has been leading the development of AARP Money Map™, an online tool to help consumers improve their financial health. Koenig has devoted his career to issues of financial security, focusing on Social Security, retirement savings, the economic well-being of older Americans, and innovative approaches to increasing lifetime income. Before joining AARP in 2008, Koenig was an economist for the Congressional Joint Committee on Taxation, specializing in employer-provided pensions and retirement plans.

AARON KRUPKIN is an associate analyst in the Congressional Budget Office's Budget Analysis Division. From 2014 to 2019, he worked at the Brookings Institution and the Urban Institute & Brookings Tax Policy Center, rising to the position of senior research analyst. His work focused on fiscal policy, federal tax reform, retirement saving policy, and state and local taxation. His work has been published in several outlets, including the *National Tax Journal*, *Tax Notes*, and *Econofact*. He received his BA in economics and political science from the University of Michigan and MA in public policy from the George Washington University.

CHAPTER CREDITS

Chapter 1: "How Will Retirement Saving Change by 2050? Prospects for the Millennial Generation." Originally published by the Peter G. Peterson Foundation, as part of their US 2050 Research Projects, www.pgpf.org/us-2050/research-projects/How-Will-Retirement-Saving-Change-By-2050-Prospects-for-the-Millennial-Generation.

Chapter 2: "Changing Wealth Accumulation Patterns: Evidence and Determinants." Originally published by NBER, as a part of their Conference on Research in Income and Wealth, https://conference.nber.org/conf_papers/f129660.pdf.

Chapter 3: "How Does Gender Equality Affect Women in Retirement?" Originally published by the Brookings Institution, as part of their 19A, the Brookings Gender Equality Series, www.brookings.edu/essay/how-does-gender-equality-affect-women-in-retirement.

Chapter 4: "A Retirement Dashboard for the United States." Originally published by the Brookings Institution, www.brookings.edu/research/a-retirement-dashboard-for-the-united-states.

Chapter 5: "Retirement Plans for Contingent Workers: Issues and Options." Originally published in the *Journal of Pension Economics and Finance*, www.researchgate.net/publication/329716370_Retirement_plans_for_contingent_workers_issues_and_options.

Chapter 6: "Supplemental Transition Accounts for Retirement." Originally published in the *Public Policy and Aging Report*, https://academic.oup.com/ppar/article/28/suppl_1/S22/5069430.

Chapter 7: "State Sponsored Retirement Savings Plans: New Approaches to Boost Retirement Plan Coverage." Originally published in *How Persistent Low Returns Will Shape Saving and Retirement*, Olivia S. Mitchell, Robert Clark, and Raimond Maurer (eds.), Oxford University Press, 2018, pp. 173–93, https://pensionresearchcouncil.wharton.upenn.edu/wp-content/uploads/2017/09/WP-2017-12-John-Gale.pdf.

Chapter 8: "Structuring State Retirement Saving Plans: A Guide to Policy Design and Management Issues." Originally published by the Brookings Institution, www.brookings.edu/research/structuring-state-retirement-saving-plans-a-guide-to-policy-design-and-management-issues.

Chapter 9: "Lessons for the States from the Federal Government's CSRS-to-FERS Transition." Originally published by the Brookings Institution, www.brookings.edu/wp-content/uploads/2016/07/galeholmesjohn_CSRSandFERS_policybrief_03092016_DP_BK.pdf.

Chapter 10: "You Get What You Pay For: Guaranteed Returns in Retirement Saving Accounts." Originally published by the Brookings Institution, www.brookings.edu/research/you-get-what-you-pay-for-guaranteed-returns-in-retirement-saving-accounts.

Chapter 11: "From Saving to Spending: A Proposal to Convert Retirement Account Balances into Automatic and Flexible Income." Originally published by the Brookings Institution, www.brookings.edu/research/from-saving-to-spending-a-proposal-to-convert-retirement-account-balances-into-automatic-and-flexible-income.

Chapter 12: "When Income Is the Outcome: Reducing Regulatory Obstacles to Annuities in 401(k) Plans." Originally published by the Brookings Institution, www.brookings.edu/wp-content/uploads/2019/07/ES_201907_IwryGaleJohnJohnson.pdf.

Chapter 13: "Retirement Tontines: Using a Classical Finance Mechanism as an Alternative Source of Retirement Income." Originally published by the Brookings Institution, www.brookings.edu/research/retirement-tontines-using-a-classical-finance-mechanism-as-an-alternative-source-of-retirement-income.

INDEX

Note: page numbers followed by *f* and *t* refer to figures and tables respectively.